D1263183

An Essay on the Modern State

We live in a world of states. Virtually every landmass of the globe is now the territory of some state. The modern state, considered as the fundamental form of political organization, has swept the world. Yet it was not always so, and it may not always be so.

This important book is the first serious philosophical examination of the modern state. It inquires into the justification of this particular form of political society. It asks whether all states are "nation-states," what are the alternative ways of organizing society, and which conditions make a state legitimate. The author concludes that, while states can be legitimate, they typically fail to have the powers (e.g., sovereignty) they claim.

Many books analyze government and its functions, but none other focuses on the state as a distinctive form of political organization or examines critically the claims states make for themselves. In filling this lacuna, Christopher Morris has written a book that will command the attention of political philosophers, political scientists, legal theorists, and specialists in international relations.

Christopher W. Morris is Professor of Philosophy at Bowling Green State University.

An Essay on the Modern State

CHRISTOPHER W. MORRIS

CAMBRIDGE
UNIVERSITY PRESS

PUBLISHED BY THE PRESS SYNDICATE OF THE UNIVERSITY OF CAMBRIDGE
The Pitt Building, Trumpington Street, Cambridge, CB2 1RP, United Kingdom

CAMBRIDGE UNIVERSITY PRESS
The Edinburgh Building, Cambridge CB2 2RU, United Kingdom
40 West 20th Street, New York, NY 10011-4211, USA
10 Stamford Road, Oakleigh, Melbourne 3166, Australia

First published 1998

Printed in the United States of America

Typeset in Palatino 10/12 pt.

Library of Congress Cataloging-in-Publication Data
Morris, Christopher W.
An essay on the modern state / Christopher W. Morris.
p.   cm.
Includes bibliographical references and index.
ISBN 0-521-49625-X (hardcover)
1. State, The.   I. Title.
JC11.M67   1998
320. 1 – dc21   97-20458

A catalog record for this book is available from
the British Library.

ISBN 0-521-49625-X hardback

Contents

"... that great LEVIATHAN, or rather (to speake more reverently) of that *Mortall God* ..."

Preface

This book has been long in coming to completion, and so perhaps a word of explanation is due. *An Essay* completes or, rather, replaces a project I initiated a decade and a half ago. I had long been perplexed and worried by states, and I had then an idea for "a theory of the state". In outline it was simple and, at the time, quite appealing. States were to serve as supports for markets and, like markets, were to be justified only insofar as they were mutually beneficial. The primary functions of states, on this view, were to guarantee personal and property rights, control fraud and enforce contracts, provide for collective goods, and implement mutually advantageous distributions of resources. The account was to be supported by a contractarian moral theory. Elements for the whole were already to be found in the work of James Buchanan and David Gauthier, and my early formulations of the project borrowed extensively from their writings. I thought that states might be justified in redistributing wealth considerably more than these theorists were likely to find acceptable, and so I conceived of the project as a defense of a kind of "welfare state". In some ways it was to be a corrective to the defense of the "minimal state" Robert Nozick and others defended in the 1970s.

This project failed for a number of reasons, most of them embarrassingly obvious now. Much of the initial inspiration came from welfare economics. Real markets, of any complexity, do not satisfy the conditions for "perfect competition" and leave room for mutually beneficial improvements. That is one of the functions of states. Additionally, they are not entirely self-sustaining – another task of states. Thinking of states as handmaidens to markets is a species of what Jules Coleman has called the "market paradigm". The first set of difficulties with the project had to do with the problems facing this type of approach. It is doubtful that many markets have the sort of

vii

explanatory or normative priority this picture supposes (something Buchanan himself often stresses). In theoretical welfare economics alone, the theory of the second best should have been for me a source of considerable skepticism. I also had a tendency, never clearly articulated, to identify markets with "anarchy". And this betrayed another major difficulty in the original idea. I, like many other theorists, tended to think of anarchy and state as exhaustive alternatives. To justify "the state" was thus to show it superior in relevant ways to anarchy. My project was to investigate its possible superiority as judged according to contractarian criteria. But just as anarchy and market are not the same, so anarchy and state are not exhaustive possibilities. To show one seriously deficient is not to justify the other. It turned out I did not know what I was talking about when I spoke about "the state"; I did not even have a clear idea of the distinction between state and government. Here, it must be said, I was in good company, at least in the English-speaking world, where philosophers are very casual with concepts of the state. Lastly, I have come to have various worries about social contract approaches to politics. For these and some other reasons, the original project fell by the wayside. A few bits and pieces of it may be found in this essay, but for the most part it has gone.

I now think I have a much better understanding of the state (and of government). It is still not adequate, and historical sociologists and historians of political thought are likely to find much that is inadequate. The Eurocentrism of much of my analysis may annoy others, but this is more defensible. The modern state is a European creation, almost French and British, and much of the world today is a variation on a theme. A consequence of an improved understanding of states is that I no longer have a "theory". My subject matter is too complex and my views are too skeptical and piecemeal to merit any such label. I do have an essay, and I reach some conclusions. For the most part, I think states, even legitimate ones, fail to live up to their self-images. Like many things modern, they are pompous and have inflated conceptions of themselves. Aspects of their characteristic ways of arranging things can often be justified, as could many earlier forms of political organization. But other aspects seem, on examination, implausible. My attitudes are mixed. I hope that states will change and that we are able to develop better ways of organizing political life. But many of the alternatives discussed by political philosophers – for instance, anarchy and world government – do not seem very imaginative or promising. Perhaps something interesting (though not a state) will emerge from the European Union and, in the more distant future, from the cities and complex polities of the Pacific. But it is too soon to tell.

I have many debts to record. Some of the most important are to be found in the footnotes. I have borrowed ideas from many sources, given credit whenever memory permitted. For a start, many audiences have been subjected to my reflections, starting with graduate seminars at the University of Ottawa, the Université de Montréal, UCLA, the University of North Carolina at Chapel Hill, and Bowling Green State University. These proved to be very productive fora for me. Versions of the early project were presented to audiences at the University of Waterloo, the meetings of the Société de philosophie du Québec in Montreal, the Canadian Philosophical Association in Saskatoon, and the Ottawa Eis Kreis. Later parts have been discussed with university audiences in Los Angeles, Chapel Hill, Manchester (UK), Davis (California), Bowling Green, New Orleans, Leuven, Prague, Claremont (California), Toledo (Ohio), Gödöllő (Hungary), Vancouver, Leuven, Bologna, Baltimore, and Paris. I am grateful for the assistance these audiences provided. My own department at Bowling Green has been supportive of my work, and equally patient. And the Centre de Recherche en Epistémologie Appliquée (CREA) at the Ecole Polytechnique (Paris) has been my intellectual home abroad for many years. I am grateful as well to the British Museum Reading Room and to university libraries in Chapel Hill, Charlottesville, Princeton, and Paris, as well as Bowling Green.

Many individuals are thanked for specific suggestions in footnotes. Some are not, for instance, when the offending text has been excised – as in the case of an entire chapter that fell victim to brief but skeptical remarks by Richard Arneson, David Gauthier, and John Roemer. I have considerable debts to the writings of many, in addition to those already mentioned – including Leslie Green, Jean Hampton, Gregory Kavka, Joseph Raz. They and others are recognized by the innumerable times their works are cited. Gérard Mairet, writing about sovereignty long before it was the fashion, is to be thanked for leading me to understand much that was missing from the early project and that became the focus of this one. For thoughtful comments on early drafts, I am in the debt of John Gray, Jean Hampton, Mario Pascalev, David Schmidtz, the Press's assiduous reviewers; and to David Copp for several dozen pages of notes on the penultimate draft. Others – G. A. Cohen, Jules Coleman, David

Gauthier, Alon Harel, Thomas May, Pasquale Pasquino, Arthur Ripstein, Sara Shaefer – have been especially helpful with comments on individual chapters, or sometimes merely with suggestions that led me to rethink certain matters.

I have many special debts as well: to my mother and late father, and to my late uncle H. O. H. Frelinghuysen, with whom I first discussed politics and states; to David Gauthier, who first suggested that my views required book-length treatment; to R. G. Frey, who urged me to stop procrastinating and virtually forced me to send a draft to Cambridge University Press for evaluation; to my supportive and patient editor, Terence Moore; to my skilled and assiduous copy editor, Nancy Landau; and lastly to my late friend Jean Hampton, who read more drafts than anyone, who encouraged me at crucial moments, and who exhorted me to finish. She advised me that one never finishes a book; one just stops writing. I have followed her wise counsel, but I remain responsible for the errors that remain (and that might have been cleared up with another decade's work). It is to her memory that I dedicate this essay.

Chapter 1

Introduction

1.1 THE MODERN STATE

As a century of extraordinary turmoil and change comes to an end, it is sobering to take a long look back over the several centuries that have made up modern times. We live in a world of states. Virtually every landmass of the globe is now the territory of some state. The phenomenon is relatively recent, a feature of modern times, and it was initially European. During the last five hundred years, Charles Tilly writes,

three striking things have occurred. First, almost all of Europe has formed into national states with well-defined boundaries and mutual relations. Second, the European system has spread to virtually the entire world. Third, other states, acting in concert, have exerted a growing influence over the organization and territory of new states. The three changes link closely, since Europe's leading states actively spread the system by colonization, conquest, and penetration of non-European states. The creation first of a League of Nations, then of a United Nations, simply ratified and rationalized the organization of all the earth's people into a single state system.[1]

The modern state, considered as the fundamental form of political organization, has swept the world. It was not always so, and it may

---

1. Charles Tilly, *Coercion, Capital, and European States, AD 990–1990* (Oxford: Basil Blackwell, 1990), p. 181. "The European model of the state became the fashionable model. No European state imitated a non-European model, but the non-European states either imitated the European model in order to survive or else went through a colonial experience which introduced large elements of the European system. The modern state, wherever we find it today, is based on the pattern which emerged in Europe in the period 1100 to 1600." Joseph R. Strayer, *On the Medieval Origins of the Modern State* (Princeton: Princeton University Press, 1970), p. 12.

not always be so. This transformation of the globe is a remarkable event, especially as it is now rarely noticed and is taken for granted.

The explanation of the development of "the state system" is a matter of considerable interest and importance. A number of competing accounts are available. Most stress, in one way or another, the competitive advantage of this particular form of political organization in the circumstances that have characterized the last several centuries. Tilly's account stresses the importance of military conflict:

> Why national states? National states won out in the world as a whole because they first won out in Europe whose states then acted to reproduce themselves. They won out in Europe because the most powerful states – France and Spain before all others – adopted forms of warfare that temporarily crushed their neighbors, and [that] generated as by-products centralization, differentiation, and autonomy of the state apparatus. Those states took that step in the late fifteenth century both because they had recently completed the expulsion of rival powers from their territories and because they had access to capitalists who could help them finance wars fought by means of expensive fortifications, artillery and, above all, mercenary soldiers.[2]

Other accounts stress social, institutional, or economic transformations that made possible the impressive war-making capacities and other comparative advantages of modern states.[3]

Understanding these extraordinary changes of political organization is important. There is, as we might expect, considerable controversy about the best ways of characterizing and explaining these developments. My inquiry, however, unlike others, is primarily normative. It takes up where these explanatory accounts leave off. I seek to evaluate the state as a form of political organization – in particular, as *the* characteristic form of the modern polity. I should like to discover the justifications, if any, for these changes in our modes of organizing political life. What exactly is a state, in the sense that will concern us, is discussed in the next chapter. For now, I shall explain my general concerns and the ends of this inquiry.

---

2. Tilly, *Coercion, Capital, and European States*, p. 183.
3. See Hendrik Spruyt, *The Sovereign State and Its Competitors* (Princeton: Princeton University Press, 1994). Strayer argues that European states were able to combine some of the strengths of empires and city-states. The former "were large enough and powerful enough to have excellent chances for survival. . . . At the same time they managed to get a large proportion of their people involved in, or at least concerned with the political process, and they succeeded in creating some sense of common identity among local communities." *On the Medieval Origins of the Modern State*, p. 12.

An appreciation of the history of the modern state is important for an evaluation of it. I shall suggest that lack of attention to this history, as well as fascination with certain individualistic models of explanation, has misdirected the attentions of many Anglo-American political philosophers interested in evaluating the state. Familiarity with the history of modern states will remind us of what we may have forgotten, that our state system has not always existed. Indeed, it is a fairly recent development, at least if one thinks of the four to six centuries of modernity as a relatively short time. In learning about the development of the state system, we learn about earlier forms of political organization – feudalism, empires, Christendom – as well as about the early modern alternatives the state displaced – city-republics and city leagues. We may see in some of these other forms of political organization parallels to alternatives that may in the future alter or displace the state system. At the very least, familiarity with this history may instill open-mindedness about nonstatist alternatives, as well as about the adaptability of states.[4]

Familiarity with history is also important for an appreciation of states. This century has made us painfully aware of the evils committed by, or, if one prefers, made possible by, states. In case memories of the horrors of World War II have receded, revelations about life in the former Soviet Union and in China remind us of the evils unchecked state power can commit. It may be argued that Auschwitz and the gulag would not have been possible in the absence of the concentrated power made possible by states. But even without the horrors of the Holocaust, the awesome destructiveness of the wars of this century may suffice to condemn the state system.

It may be that one of the lessons of these horrors of our century is not the failure of the state per se but the defect of unconstrained state power. The striking fact that democracies do not fight wars with one another may provide additional support for this condemnation of unlimited state power.[5] But there are other sources, more recent perhaps, of the general dissatisfaction with state power. Governments

---

4. This open-mindedness often seems absent, for instance, in recent debates about the development of the European Union. It often seems as if the dominance of the category of the state forces political commentators to understand developing European "federalism" as statist ("the United States of Europe"). We shall see in later chapters how certain understandings of the state's sovereignty may have constrained contemporary debates on transformations of state authority.
5. Immanuel Kant is credited with the conjecture that the establishment of republican government will tend to limit war. See his essay "Perpetual Peace," originally published in 1795. See also Michael W. Doyle, "Kant, Liberal Legacies, and Foreign

everywhere are now criticized for their inability to cope with difficulties facing our societies. It is often suggested that "markets" or the "private sector" offers solutions to these problems that are preferable to government programs or "regulation". Even socialist or social democratic regimes today are reluctant to rely overly on government. Perhaps at no time in the last several centuries has the state been held in such low esteem.

Contemporary skepticism of, and hostility to, government is certainly one of the reasons for this inquiry. Familiarity with the history of states reminds us, I have said, of the evils states can do. But it may also serve to temper this skepticism. For in several respects the development of states has caused significant improvement in the conditions of human life. In many ways the exercise of concentrated power in some parts of the world is less brutal, arbitrary, and exploitative than before. The development of the "rule of law", of democratic forms of government with broad franchises, of constitutional constraints on governments, of divisions of powers and forms of federalisms, and of the institution of norms of tolerance has brought extraordinary improvements in political life. While it is true that many of these improvements have their origins in classical Greece and Rome and the cities of Renaissance Italy, they are largely modern and are inseparable from the modern constitutional state.

To draw attention to the ways in which the development of the state system has improved life is not to deny that many of these changes are partial or fragile, or that many peoples in the world do not benefit from them. Nevertheless, we should not neglect these achievements in our assessment of states. An overall assessment is difficult. The obituary of the state system

will be hard to write. On one side, we see the pacification of European civil life and the fashioning of more or less representative political institutions, both by-products of a state formation driven by the pursuit of military might. On the other side, we notice the rising destructiveness of war, the pervasive intervention of states in individual lives, the creation of incomparable instruments of class control. Destroy the state, and create Lebanon. Fortify it, and create Korea. Until other forms displace the national state, neither alternative will do. The only real answer is to turn the immense power of national

Affairs," *Philosophy and Public Affairs* 12, 3–4 (Summer and Fall 1983), 205–235, 323–353.

states away from war and toward the creation of justice, personal security, and democracy.[6]

What should we think, then, of the state? The purpose of this inquiry is to evaluate the state as a form of political organization. I shall seek to determine in what respects, if any, states can be justified. Although one cannot, without detailed study of the history and circumstances of particular states, make the informed and intelligent assessments of states that we should strive for, one can inquire into general questions about justification. States, or their spokespeople, make many claims, and their credibility can be assessed. Even if we cannot pronounce unambiguously for or against the state, we should be able to sort through many of the difficult normative issues raised by this form of political organization. At the very least, this may help us to determine how we might improve on the manner in which we now organize our polities.

1.2 MODERN POLITICAL PHILOSOPHY

It is characteristic of modern political philosophy to consider the state an *artifice*. While modern philosophers may quarrel about whether humans are by nature social creatures, virtually all agree that states are artificial. As Thomas Hobbes put it, "By Art is created that great Leviathan called a Common-wealth, or State, (in latine Civitas) which is but an Artificiall Man."[7] Some moderns dissent – for instance, Hegel. And we may wonder how much of the thesis will survive a critical analysis of the distinction between nature and artifice. But we need not be detained by such a discussion. For it is the implication of the alleged artificiality of the state that is of interest: this Artificial Man (the state), Hobbes continues, "though of greater stature and strength than the Naturall, for whose protection and defence it was intended . . ." The state, conceived as artificial, is to be understood as created for our ends, our protection and defense. While modern social theorists may quarrel about the explanatory priority of individuals to states, they disagree hardly at all over the

6. Tilly, *Coercion, Capital, and European States*, p. 225.
7. Hobbes, *Leviathan,* ed. Richard Tuck (Cambridge: Cambridge University Press, 1991 [1651]), "Introduction," p. 9.

normative priority of individuals to states. What we are, *contra* Hobbes and many others, may be significantly determined by our forms of social organization. However, the adequacy of these forms of organization – as well as of their corresponding forms of socialization – is to be determined by their success in satisfying our ends. In this sense, modern philosophers tend to have an *instrumental* conception of states.[8]

Certainly this is the general tradition with which I identify in this inquiry. I do not accept many assumptions or doctrines associated with this tradition – much of the individualism, certain simplistic and mistaken accounts of motivation, an instrumentalism about value – but I shall retain this general evaluative perspective. States are to be thought well of to the extent that they satisfy human ends.

This is not yet to say very much. There are many different ways in which ends can be well served. Further, we may wish to give different weight to different ends, to discount others, and so on. We may be unsympathetic, say, to utilitarian evaluations of states in the tradition of Bentham and Mill, or as I mentioned earlier, we may be suspicious of the instrumentalism about value or practical reason that characterizes much of modern political philosophy and political economy. So endorsing a general instrumentalism regarding states does not commit us to very much. It merely signals, first of all, our rejection of classical views according to which then characteristic forms of political organization – the community, the *polis* – need, in themselves, no justification. It also expresses our rejection of premodern assumptions that some forms of subordination – between ruler and subject, noble and lowly born, men and women – are natural and need no further justification.[9]

---

8. "It will follow that whatever activity it is desirable for the State to have, it will only be desirable as a means, and that the activity, and the State itself, can have no value but as a means. . . . Compared with worship of the State, zoolatry is rational and dignified. A bull or a crocodile may not have intrinsic value, but it has some, for it is a conscious being. The State has none. It would be as reasonable to worship a sewage pipe, which also possesses considerable value as a means." John McTaggart Ellis McTaggart, "The Individualism of Value" [1908], in *Philosophical Studies*, ed. S. Keeling (London: Edward Arnold, 1934), p. 109, cited by Leslie Green, *The Authority of the State* (Oxford: Clarendon Press, 1988), pp. 164–165n.

9. Note that we might want to adopt this instrumentalism regarding the evaluation of states while rejecting it for other human institutions. It may also be that while classical theories, according to which humans are by nature political or social animals, imply that the *community* in itself requires no further justification, they do not have this implication for the modern state. In Chapter 2 I discuss the ways in which the state is a different, and modern, form of political organization.

Hobbes, Locke, and Rousseau initiate a modern tradition that evaluates states by reference to the agreement of their members. A state
is justified, we might say, insofar as it is agreeable to its members. We
need to distinguish two different interpretations of this view. One,
which may be associated with Locke, I label the "consensualist"
view.[10] It is the view that *consent* is necessary (and sufficient) for justification. The other view is that states, to be justified, need to be beneficial to all subjects, whether or not they consent. If one understands
the "social contract" of Hobbes and Rousseau and other contractarian thinkers as hypothetical, then the two views may be conflated.
But, as I argue later, hypothetical agreement is not a form of consent.[11] So the two positions should be distinguished. The second
position may be called the "mutual advantage view", after John
Rawls's conception of a society as a "cooperative venture for mutual
advantage".[12] Leaving aside for now misunderstandings that may be
encouraged by the notion of advantage, Rawls's phrase articulates
well the view about states that I wish to distinguish from consensualism. States are to be justified in terms of how they benefit people;
ideally, then, they are to be cooperative ventures for mutual advantage.[13] States stand condemned to the extent that they satisfy the
ends of some at the expense of others. The exploited as well as the
persecuted thus are not bound to their states.

Elements of both views are to be found among the modern social
contract theorists, and the two are commonly conflated. But it is
important to distinguish them as I have. Some of the important questions I wish to raise about modern states may be resolved differently
depending on which view is endorsed. And to the extent that I favor
the mutual advantage account, I will need to address the concerns of
consensualists. The latter tradition is well represented in contemporary political philosophy, especially in the United States, and it is
often developed in forms that are hostile to states. If people have certain rights and "to secure these rights, governments are instituted

---

10. Sometimes such a view is called "voluntarist", but I prefer to retain this label for
    the view in morals and law that the will is the source of normativity. The volun-
    tarist elements in Hobbes's notion of sovereignty are discussed in Chapter 7.
11. Hypothetical agreement requires no act or engagement of the will and so does not
    commit one in the way that consent, express or tacit, does.
12. Rawls, *A Theory of Justice* (Cambridge, Mass.: Harvard University Press, 1971), p. 4.
13. Rawls's characterization is of societies, not states. As I make clear in Chapter 2, I
    do not attribute to societies the unity characteristically implicit in our descriptions.
    The state may be *one*, but societies need not be.

among men, deriving their just powers from the consent of the governed", then justifying states may be very difficult. The assertion of
certain natural rights may, as Bentham thought, threaten the legitimacy of all government.

Consensualism is an implication of most natural rights theories.
The reference to these theories brings to mind another influential
pair of competing views. Natural rights are what I call "prior rights";
they are held to exist prior to, and independently of, states and their
legal systems. Many have denied that there are such rights and have
supposed that all rights are created or "posited" by states – a view
sometimes labeled (misleadingly) "positivist". The facts that natural
rights theories tend to be committed to consensualism and that the
instrumentalist political theories of Hobbes and Bentham denied the
existence of prior claim rights suggest to some that the pairs of views
overlap. But this is mistaken, as I argue later. Mutual advantage theorists can endorse the existence of some prior rights even if they
reject the accounts of certain natural rights theorists. And in any case,
whatever plausibility there was to the view that all rights are created
by states is considerably diminished by an understanding of the
modern states and its alternatives, or so I shall argue. It would be
best, therefore, to keep separate these different pairs of views. The
conflict between the first pair may be of some importance for an evaluation of the modern state. The conflict between the partisans of
prior rights and their critics would be significant were only the position of the latter to have some plausibility.

The mutual advantage view is associated, as I said, with the "social
contract" tradition, in particular the theories of Hobbes and Rousseau.[14] This particular tradition has been revived in recent decades
by Rawls, James Buchanan, David Gauthier, and others. But much of
the tradition of political economy, starting with Adam Smith, up to
welfare economics and "public choice" economics, also endorses this
general view in the form of several "Paretian" principles of efficiency. The mutual advantage view I have sketched is more widely
shared than its identification with contractarian political philosophy
might suggest.

---

14. Hume may be read as endorsing this view. See Rawls, *A Theory of Justice*, pp. 32–33;
David Gauthier, "David Hume, Contractarian," reprinted in *Moral Dealing* (Ithaca,
N.Y.: Cornell University Press, 1990), pp. 45–79; and J. L. Mackie, *Hume's Moral The-
ory* (London: Routledge & Kegan Paul, 1980).

8

These contractarian thinkers and political economists generally share more than a normative position. They also agree on a general account of the ways in which states might be suited to serve the ends of individuals. In the absence of certain cooperative arrangements, individuals acting on their own encounter "collective action problems". The outcome of their individual acts is less good for each than it might otherwise be were they able to coordinate or cooperate in some way. In the absence of some system of cooperation – one capable of establishing mutually beneficial forms of cooperative interaction – individuals, left to their own devices, will be unable to achieve their ends well. Governments, in the view of these theorists, may be understood as providing solutions to many such collective action problems. Individuals, without government, may be unable to provide themselves efficiently with bridges, lighthouses, clean air, or defense (to use the standard examples) or even with social order.[15] Governments, on this view, have

the duty of erecting and maintaining certain publick works and certain publick institutions, which it can never be for the interest of any individual, or small number of individuals, to erect and maintain; because the profit could never repay the expense to any individual or small number of individuals, though it may frequently do much more than repay it to a great society.[16]

While transportation, public health, and the like may pose collective action problems, the most important such problem may be that of social order: how to achieve basic security of person and possessions in the absence of a state. For social order, in this sense, is a good the provision of which poses a collective action problem. States are well suited to provide social order. One might say that it is their main purpose, but we should be cautious with such claims lest they be interpreted as explanatory; many states have provided basic security of person and possessions as a by-product of other, often less admirable activities. There is wide agreement that this is one of the proper functions of states. And there is wide agreement that social order is difficult, if not impractical, to achieve in the absence of states, at least in the conditions of modern life – a claim I critically examined in Chapter 3. The contractarian and political economy traditions

15. Some of the difficulties with these standard examples, as well as a more careful explication of the problems, will be provided in Chapter 3.
16. Adam Smith, *The Wealth of Nations*, 2 vols. (Oxford: Clarendon Press, 1979 [1776]; reprinted by Liberty Classics), Book IV, chap. 9, pp. 687–688.

agree in their understanding of the general problem and the manner in which states may offer a solution.

The contractarian tradition to which I have appealed, as well as the modern natural rights tradition, understands humans to be, by nature, free and equal. Originally these terms merely implied the absence of any nonconventional bonds or forms of political subordination. By proclaiming original freedom and equality, one signaled one's rejection of certain classical views according to which we come into the world with different "stations and duties" assigned us by nature. This claim of original freedom and equality, so interpreted, is relatively uncontroversial today.

The premise that we are by nature free and equal, conjoined with the claim that the state is an artifice, creates a presumption against states. Hobbes and others have attempted to show that at least some states are improvements on the natural condition of freedom and equality and consequently are justified. Where states are not improvements over this condition of nature, they are to be rejected.

The tradition of political economy also maintains a presumption against states. Although the reasoning is similar, it is based on a distinct body of theory, namely, the theory of markets. Since Adam Smith, economists have increasingly distinguished themselves from other social theorists not merely by their approach to social phenomena but also by doctrine. In the absence of government "intervention" and "regulation", it is held, individuals do quite well by themselves in a wide variety of domains. Indeed, it is only with certain goods, those that pose collective action problems, that individual market interaction proves deficient – the case of so-called market failures. I discuss this general theory in greater detail later. For now I shall merely note that it is by reference to this body of theory that political economists join contractarians in accepting a general presumption against states.

The two traditions, then, agree on a criterion for the evaluation of states (mutual benefit), an account of the type of problem states might be better suited to resolve (collective action problems), and a presumption against states, in favor of free interaction among individuals. Although Hobbes valiantly defended absolute states, for the most part the conclusion of these traditions has been limited, rather "minimal" states.[17] In the middle of the twentieth century it was

---

17. Hobbes's own prescriptions for government were rather minimalist. See my "Leviathan and the Minimal State: Hobbes' Theory of Government," in *Early Mod-*

widely thought that the nature of market failures offered considerable scope for government activity. But a body of literature has since grown establishing a variety of "political failures" in government attempts to rectify the apparent deficiencies of markets. This bias against states is reinforced by other theorists, allied with a respected natural rights tradition. The climate of opinion today is distinctively antistatist, especially in the Anglo-American world.

I accept the mutual advantage view and the idea of states as potential solutions to collective action problems. I am, however, uncertain about the presumption against states. How we understand it depends on the alternatives to states and how we think of states themselves. I shall argue that the common distinction between states and anarchy (the "state of nature") is misleading and certainly not exhaustive. Accordingly, it is unclear what the presumption means. This said, I shall critically examine the case for and against states. To some extent, I shall challenge some of the recent skepticism about states. Although recent accounts of political or government failure are to be taken seriously, I shall argue that they do not have the normative implications often inferred. Further, it may be that the demands of justice on states are more redistributive than recent anti-statists have typically recognized.

One of my main claims, however, will be that both critics and defenders of these traditions – contractarianism and political economy – have to some extent misdescribed the dangers and problems individuals face in the absence of states. Certainly, without states or other forms of political organization individuals would have trouble providing themselves with clean air, roads, and the like; the same would be true of defense and protection.[18] However, the nature of the problem is mischaracterized if we imagine, in the customary manner, isolated individuals or small groups seeking to defend themselves against other individuals or groups. The central problem people would face in the absence of states is not so much defending themselves against their neighbors, who may be tempted to steal their possessions while they sleep. Rather, it is to defend themselves against powerful groups, led by ambitious men, intent on conquest and exploitation. While states represent enormous concentrations of

---

ern Philosophy: Epistemology, Metaphysics, and Politics, Essays in Honour of Robert F. MacRae, ed. G. Moyal and S. Tweyman (Delmar, N.Y.: Caravan Books, 1986), pp. 373–395.

18. I consider (in Chapter 3) the critical literature arguing that many of these goods can be provided without government

power, it is not to be expected that in their absence power will be completely decentralized. On the contrary – and it is here that, unlike a number of contemporary political philosophers, I shall appeal to historical evidence – nonstatist power can be more dangerous and exploitative than that of many states. In many respects the anarchy described by Hobbes as the alternative to states is defective; the historical alternative to states is, in many ways, both more orderly and more miserable than he thought. The alternatives to be most feared today may not be chaos and disorder – as in Lebanon – although that is a genuine possibility. Rather, they may be tyranny, exploitation, and barbarism – as in Germany in the 1930s and early 1940s, South Africa under apartheid, the former Soviet Union, the "killing fields" of Kampuchea. Maybe we should understand states as possible means of transforming and taming the concentrations of power that would otherwise rule us. I accept the general view that evaluates states in relation to their alternatives. But the alternatives have been mistakenly characterized, and this general error has affected the conclusions to be drawn.

1.3 THE PROJECT

The main purpose of this inquiry is to determine the justifications for modern states. I seek to determine whether we should have states, and what general forms they should take. One of my conclusions is that answers to these questions depend very much on context. Some forms of states may be justified in some conditions but not others; certainly few forms will be justified for all times. Consequently, without discussion of the particular features of different societies and cultures, my conclusions are somewhat general and abstract. But I do not think they are without interest; for our view of states must be affected by our understanding of them, the nature and extent of their justified claims, and the alternatives available. Our reactions, for instance, to international human rights legislation or to institutional arrangements such as the European Union depend on some of the abstract and general issues I address. And our support for states, or even for "world government", may be in no small part a product of our lack of imagination regarding alternatives.

I first characterize more precisely than I have done the concept of the state as it forms the object of this inquiry (Chapter 2). Anarchy is often considered the main alternative to states, and I examine anarchic social order next (Chapter 3). In the central chapters (4 through 6), I consider the nature of legitimacy and determine the general conditions that states must meet if they are to be justified. The second part of the project will be to determine the implications of my discussions of justification for a number of problematic features of states: sovereignty (Chapter 7), membership and territory (Chapter 8), and the proper functions of governments (Chapter 9).

Chapter 2

The modern state

2.1 PROBLEMS AND WORRIES

Why should we organize our polities in the way we do, as states? The question, as well as the inquiry that follows, is rather abstract. Yet it is motivated, in large part, by a set of particular worries, concerns, and problems. I shall distinguish and clarify these, if only so that the motivation for the inquiry will be clear at the outset.

First and foremost, the *evils of modern states* are striking and appalling. The modern state is the site, if not the agent, of extraordinary evil. Auschwitz, the gulag – these crimes of states need no recounting. To some, however, such a list of evils is too short: Exploitation and other forms of oppression, economic catastrophes (the Great Depression), various social experiments (Mao's "Great Leap Forward" and "Cultural Revolution") should be added. Whatever we think about particular entries in particular lists of *crimes d'Etat*, it should not be unexpected that modern states are capable of enormous wrongs. For modern states are *very* powerful. The modern state is a form of political organization with highly centralized means of administration and control. In theory – and theory is my central concern in this book – states are "sovereign" in their territories, and they claim a monopoly of the use of legitimate force therein. This is held to distinguish states from the Mafia or multinational corporations. Given their power and authority, the institutions of states offer to many the means to realize their greatest ambitions and dreams. No wonder the enormity of the crimes associated with modern states.

The nature and scale of modern wars are made possible by the modern state, and what the future threatens may be worse than what we have already experienced, even – or especially – as the dangers of major nuclear conflict have receded. The relation between war and the development and growth of the modern state is complex. Charles Tilly has argued, "Up to our own time dramatic increases in national budgets, national debts, numbers of governmental employees or any other indicator of governmental scale in European countries have occurred almost exclusively as a consequence of preparations for war. . . . Preparation for war has been the great state-building activity. The process has been going on more or less continuously for at least five hundred years."[1]

Although poverty and misery are not new, the modern state offers new means of systematic exploitation – more neutrally, means of extracting resources from subjects or citizens – that have all too often been put to effective use. Whether one is especially appalled at the systematic exploitation of individuals in capitalist or in socialist states, it would seem that such exploitation has been made possible by the advent of the state. A particularly depressing analysis might link the state's exploitative endeavors to its need for revenue for its own development and growth.[2] My first worry, then, is the evil of modern states.

Reflection on the evils of modern states leads naturally to reflection about the bases for the powers of the state. Presumably, or so we may think at this point, the evils committed by states are wrong and have no justification. But all states require considerable sacrifices from us, burdens most of us do not assume easily. What grounds might there be for such sacrifices? What justifications are there for the obligations we are supposed to have to the state? Why is it that we ought to obey the state and its agents? These questions are familiar – though not transparent – and are addressed in most works of political philosophy.

The distinctiveness of modern states raises a set of particularly perplexing theoretical or philosophical questions. Modern states

---

1. Tilly, "Reflections on the History of European State-Making," in *The Formation of National States in Western Europe*, ed. C. Tilly (Princeton: Princeton University Press, 1975), p. 74. Over the last several hundred years, European wars have become less frequent – but more lethal (Tilly, *Coercion, Capital, and European States*, pp. 70–76). As mentioned in Chapter 1, some think Tilly accords too great an importance to war making in his account of the emergence of states. See especially Spruyt, *The Sovereign State and Its Competitors*, pp. 29–33.
2. See Tilly, "War Making and State Making as Organized Crime," in *Bringing the State Back In*, ed. P. Evans, D. Rueschemeyer, and T. Skopol (Cambridge: Cambridge University Press, 1985), pp. 169–191, and Margaret Levi, *Of Rule and Revenue* (Berkeley and Los Angeles: University of California Press, 1988).

claim a variety of powers for themselves and deny them to nonstates. It is said that states claim a monopoly of the use of legitimate force. Rulers and governments characteristically claim to possess authority. The form this takes in the modern state is sovereignty: a certain exclusive authority over its domain and a certain independence from other states. Only states are held to have such powers. What is the justification for the powers states claim for themselves and deny to others? Questions about the states' powers are not unrelated to our concern with their evils. It is their considerable authority and power that enable states to commit the great evils that concern us. Understanding the bases for these powers may enable us to learn how to constrain states more effectively.

Virtually everyone in the modern world is the subject of a state. Most people are members of a state, and citizenship is the characteristic form full membership now takes. For the most part, membership is not fully optional; it is hard not to be a member of some state. Certainly, one cannot avoid being subject to the authority of some state whenever one finds oneself in that state's territory. Although one can be subject to the authority of several states, membership is typically exclusive; for the most part, states disapprove of their members' allegiance to other states, especially rival ones.

Membership is not always easily abandoned. Some states forbid or limit emigration, and others construe citizenship to be inalienable.[3] We may not break off and form our own society. Even in states with liberal emigration policies, those wishing to leave may not take their land with them, that is, secede.[4] Secession is interesting, as anthropologists note its impermissibility to be a distinguishing feature of states (in their sense of the term): "All political systems except true states break up into similar units as part of their normal process of political activity. . . . The state is a system specifically designed to restrain such tendencies."[5] If a realm is understood as the ruler's property, then one can understand the sort of rationale that might be

---

3. That is, one may not alienate it. Citizenship could be inalienable and still be prescriptible (that is, something that could be taken away).
4. The 1936 and the 1977 constitutions of the Soviet Union were exceptional in according each of the fifteen recognized republics the right to secede (1936, chap. II, article 17; 1977, III, chap. 8, article 72). But these rights were not, of course, upheld.
5. Ronald Cohen, "Introduction," in *Origins of the State: The Anthropology of Political Evolution,* ed. R. Cohen and E. Service (Philadelphia: Institute for the Study of Human Issues, 1978), p. 4. See the discussion of fissioning in Section 2.2.

offered for forbidding secession. But modern states do not so conceive of their territories; their authority is more of a matter of jurisdiction than of ownership.

How can this be? How does the state acquire such normative properties? Modern states claim to possess a remarkable set of powers and rights (as well as immunities). For the most part, these cannot be possessed by mere individuals. If we assume, as virtually every modern political thinker does, that the state is not an entity, much less an organism, with a life and will separate from that of its members, then accounting for the emergent normative properties of the state is problematic. As we shall see, the special nature of the powers of the modern state renders them problematic. It is standard to understand that political authority involves an obligation to obey on the part of those subject to the authority. It is not particularly puzzling to account for obligations of obedience owed to individuals or even to collectivities, even if a plausible account may be difficult in the case of the state. Obligations to obey could, theoretically, be transferred to collectivities or to the state. Accounting for a *new* and *emergent* set of rights and powers attributed to the state is another matter. For these could not have been transferred, as they were never held by individuals before any transfer.[6]

Reflection on the evils of modern states and on the bases of political authority and the nature of their special emergent properties leads naturally to recognition of the modern state's distinctiveness as a form of political organization. Our states are different from earlier forms of political organization. As I have noted, they claim a variety of special powers, and their authority is rather sweeping. Their governance is, as we shall see, territorial in relatively new ways. Government is now more centralized and hierarchical than in earlier, premodern times. In a variety of ways, the sorts of allegiances that are now expected of us and the ways in which our state affects our identities are new. The states that will be the focus of my attention are forms of political organization that are characteristically modern; they emerge in Europe in early modern times and take their now familiar form in the eighteenth and nineteenth centuries. Modern

---

6. G.E.M. Anscombe notes that "civil society is the bearer of rights of coercion not possibly existent among men without government." "On the Source of the Authority of the State," in *Ethics, Religion and Politics, Collected Philosophical Papers*, vol. 3 (Minneapolis: University of Minnesota Press, 1981), p. 147.

states are distinctive forms of political organization. In fact, I should prefer to speak of "states", dropping the qualifier adjective. Gianfranco Poggi rightly notes that "although one often speaks of 'the modern state' . . . strictly speaking the adjective 'modern' is pleonastic. For the set of features [attributed to states] is not found in any large-scale political entities other than those which began to develop in the early-modern phase of European history."[7] It is only the common use of the term to refer to virtually all forms of political organization that requires me to designate the *modern* state as my object of study.

The state's modernity is striking in many ways. There are many aspects of this form of political organization that presuppose features of the modern world. This may be one reason why some who are not entirely comfortable with modernity find the state troubling. The state is, in some respects, an expression of modernity.[8] It is a commonplace that modernity is a time of a sense of alienation and of homelessness. These sentiments may be connected to our new conceptions of nature and possibly the survival of theocentric conceptions of the world (albeit with a distant or absent deity), characteristic of modern thought. Such sentiments of estrangement and homelessness can be as political as they are metaphysical. Even if we take states for granted and pledge allegiance to them without much hesitation, our behavior and attitudes also suggest some distance or alienation from the state. The marked tendency of states to strengthen the support of members by appealing to sentiments of kinship or nationality suggests that identification with the state is difficult if the state is not associated with brethren or nation.[9]

7. Gianfranco Poggi, *The State: Its Nature, Development and Prospects* (Stanford, Calif.: Stanford University Press, 1990), p. 25.
8. "A major theme in continental European theories is that the state is more than simply the system of legal norms, the embodiment of sovereign authority or a collection of public services. It is viewed as a socio-cultural phenomenon, an expression of 'modernity'." Kenneth H. F. Dyson, *The State Tradition in Western Europe* (New York: Oxford University Press, 1980), p. 243.
9. In discussing kinship terms used to describe the Greek *polis*, Michael Mann notes that "the importance of kinship, and its use as a symbolic model for nonkin relations, is virtually universal." Mann, *The Sources of Social Power* (Cambridge: Cambridge University Press, 1986), vol. 1, p. 197. He goes on to remark: "Even in the nineteenth and early twentieth centuries A.D., that large-scale territorial unit the nation-state was conceptualized as being an ethnic, racial unit, which in actuality it was not." See also Anthony D. Smith, *The Ethnic Origins of Nations* (Oxford: Blackwell, 1986).

Estrangement is also the reaction of people who do not easily identify with a state and who do not wish to consider state membership
one of their defining or essential characteristics. Yet the modern state
seems to expect such identification and demands considerable loyalty. It may seem that this estrangement from the modern state is a
condition primarily of itinerant intellectuals and perpetual tourists.
Academics and other intellectuals often feel some distance from their
polities, especially if they think their talents insufficiently appreci-
ated by the forces that be. The predominance of nationalism might
make one hesitant to conclude that such alienation is widespread in
the citizenry of modern states. But note that this would be to identify
state and nation (or country) in ways that are question-begging. I
have been noting phenomena of estrangement from the state, not
from kin or nation. It is interesting that feelings of warmth or pride
are often most forthcoming when a state is able to identify itself with
its country or nation. This may suggest that by itself, apart from these
other communities and identities, the state leaves us cold.

Alienation from the state is not, I think, uncommon. Certainly, as I
have noted, hostility to the state is commonplace. In any case, however prevalent it is, I need perhaps to acknowledge my sense of
estrangement as a motive for this inquiry. Many of us simply would
not devote so much of our time to the problems of the modern state
if we did not find this particular form of political organization problematic and also *strange*. Especially when the state is perceived as
strange and alien does its distinctiveness and modernity become a
concern.

Our worries and concerns, then, may be several. We are troubled
by the evils of the state; we wonder about the grounds for its powers
and may be puzzled about their uniqueness; and we may find the
state a strange form of political organization, one from which we are
to some extent alienated. Addressing these concerns, then, is the
main purpose of my inquiry.

2.2 THE CONCEPT OF THE STATE

The modern state is the object of this inquiry. We need consequently
to be clear about what we are talking about. For reasons related to my
problems and worries, this is no simple matter. There always seems
to be considerable disagreement about how to characterize the

notion. Several decades ago, in the Anglo-American world especially, it was fashionable to decry the concept and to substitute for it
other, less problematic or "metaphysical" notions. Some of this disagreement and skepticism may reflect antagonism to the modern
state. (The American political tradition is rather antistatist, for instance.) And it may also reflect antagonism to antidemocratic conceptions of the state. (This skepticism was especially prevalent after
World War II and the rise of the Iron Curtain.) But the notion of the
state is quite complex, and it turns out to be quite difficult to articulate all of its aspects. Worse, we cannot assume that there is a *single*
notion of the state. Ordinary language, as I shall point out presently,
may suggest several notions.[10] Scholars have argued that the modern
state evolved slowly, emerging from late medieval European forms
of political organization. We may not expect, in such a case, to find a
simple, univocal notion.

So it is not to be expected that 'state' will have a clear, unambiguous meaning, much less one that is easy to discern in common
speech. The term evolved slowly, and there are variations of use in
different countries. I shall try to develop a characterization of the
notion, one that reflects common usage to some extent, but that is
also an attempt to circumscribe the political phenomena that are the
focus of my attention in this inquiry.[11]

In contemporary English, especially in the United States, 'state'
and 'government' are often used somewhat interchangeably. One
can replace one by the other in many works of contemporary American political theory and not substantially affect the meaning of the
theses defended. Part of the explanation for this has to do with the
history of American confederation; the term 'state' was reserved for

---

10. It is not clear, however, that there are several different, perhaps rival, conceptions,
    of the state. Before one infers a multiplicity of competing conceptions, one needs
    criteria of the individuation of concepts.
11. I should mention that neither here nor elsewhere in this volume do I propose a
    "definition" of the state. If a definition of a notion or term must offer necessary and
    sufficient conditions for its use, then it is unclear that there are definitions of many
    words in natural languages. Certainly, the concepts of "state", "people", and
    "nation" examined in this essay will not be susceptible to this sort of treatment. If
    definitions are to characterize the essence of things, then it is not clear that states
    have essences; certainly, they are not natural kinds. In any case, my interests lie in
    the complicated phenomena and not in the regimentation of language. Even
    though I think ordinary usage to be a fount of wisdom, the complexity of modern
    forms of political organization and governance may not be perspicuously ex-
    pressed by our term 'state'.

the independent polities that became the subunits of the federal state.[12] And this usage may also reflect Anglo-American skepticism about states. On the Continent the distinction between state and government is evident. Some remnant of the distinction may be found in British English: the prime minister is head of the *government*, while the monarch is head of the *state*. But in general no great care is taken in the English-speaking worlds to distinguish state and government. As a matter of contemporary usage, this is not possible in other European languages. *'L'Etat'* and *'le gouvernement'*, *'der Staat'* and *'die Regierung'*, *'lo stato'* and *'lo governo'* are not interchangeable. It is true that 'government' in American English has a wider range of meaning than do its European counterparts.[13] But the largely continental concept of the state (as distinct from the government) is in some ways alien to the Anglo-American tradition. Perhaps as a consequence of this the distinction between the two is not easily made in contemporary English.[14]

The distinction between state and government may be indispensable, at least for certain theoretical purposes. A political theory such as Rousseau's, for instance, could not be expressed without the distinction. And the distinction proves essential for a study of the characteristic forms of political organization of the modern world. Consider only the institutions characteristic of our polities. Many "public" institutions are not part of the government yet are part of the state. One can think of the judiciary as one of the branches of government, along with the executive and the legislative branches, although it is not uncommon, especially in parliamentary systems, to identify the government with the latter two alone. The civil service or bureaucracy is often called the fourth branch of government. It is

---

12. Curiously, the American news media will report on events – for instance, severe weather – affecting some part of "the nation" rather than "the country" or simply "the United States". This use of 'nation' as referring to a country or society or territorial unit involves issues to which I return in Chapter 8.

13. This is noted by Dyson, *The State Tradition in Western Europe*, p. 209.

14. This lack of a clear distinction in ordinary English may reflect certain features of Anglo-American history. See ibid., pp. 36–43, for some of the particularities of the British case. As I suggested, the reluctance of Anglophones to distinguish between state and government may reflect not only features of their traditions and forms of social and political organization, but also deep ambivalence about the modern state. As we may share this ambivalence, perhaps we should not hide it from view by resorting to a generic use of 'government'. As a relevant contrast would be with the more statist French tradition, it is interesting to note that in contemporary French, the only words capitalized (aside from proper names) are *'Dieu'* and *'Etat'*.

definitely an institution of the state, and an increasingly important one. One may conjecture that it is the absence of a clear distinction between state and government that forces one to invent a fourth branch of the latter. One should not forget the military (or standing armies) and the various security forces that are now essential institutions of all modern states. Last, public corporations and central banks are institutions of state, as are other public institutions, such as schools and universities. Useful distinctions are collapsed if we attach all of these to government.

Further, it is difficult to talk about continuity and change in modern forms of political organization if no distinction is made between state and government. Consider what happens to a modern state in times of transition between governments, or forms of government, or even in times of revolution. Consider the first: for instance, when a parliamentary government falls with a lost vote of confidence, a new election is called, and a new government is voted in. Or consider the case of a change in the form of government: for instance, the advent of one of the several republics in the last two centuries of French history. In either case there is a change of government, or form of government, but no change in the continuity of state. The latter continues in existence, uninterrupted by the changes in government. Consider the more extreme case of revolution: for instance, that of the French Revolution. The monarchy fell and was replaced by a republican form of government. Yet it is not unnatural to say that the French state continued in existence throughout the whole process; indeed, one might argue that the revolution was one of the main phases of the development of the French state.[15] Certainly the same is true of "the Glorious Revolution"; arguably it is also true of the Soviet and Chinese revolutions.[16] In some instances, it may be said that the government acts as the *agent* or *representative* of the state. In any case, changes of government do not necessarily threaten the existence of the state. Collapsing the distinction between govern-

15. This claim does not, I believe, depend on recent historical work claiming more continuity and less radical change for this period of French history than hitherto acknowledged.
16. But it is difficult to think of the American *state* as existing before the American Revolution or even 1789. The Articles of Confederation (1781), with each state retaining "its sovereignty, freedom, and independence", could not be said to have created a (federal) state. For a suggestive discussion of the evolution of the notion of state in the American context, see J. R. Pole, "The Politics of the Word 'State' and Its Relation to American Sovereignty," *Parliaments, Estates & Representation/Parlements, Etats & Représentations* 8, 1 (June 1988), 1–10.

ment and state limits our powers of expression without any evident gain.

Last, but most important, much of what is distinctive about the modern state as a form of political organization is lost – or, rather, hidden – by the absence of a clear distinction between state and government – certainly much of what should interest political philosophers. Or so I shall claim. Consequently, I shall talk of states in a somewhat continental way.

What, then, is the state (in this sense)? The state is first of all a particular *form of political organization*. This understanding of states is not unusual. It is, for instance, the view of Marx in one of his characterizations of the state: "Through the emancipation of private property from the community, the State has become a separate entity, beside and outside civil society; but it is nothing more than the form of organization which the bourgeois necessarily adopts both for internal and external purposes, for the mutual guarantee of their property and interests."[17] Joseph Raz, who also thinks of states as forms of political organization, usefully distinguishes among states, governments, and the law: "the state, which is the political organization of a society, its government, the agent through which it acts, and the law, the vehicle through which much of its power is exercised."[18] We might think, then, of a state as a distinctive form of political organization of a society.

We need, however, to be careful here lest we transfer to societies some of the features that may be characteristic of modern states. It is interesting that when we talk of "a society", as Raz does, there is implicit individuation in the designation. The United States and Italy, for instance, are societies in this sense, but Europe and North America are not. But what makes a society *one*, a unified social entity?[19] The unity we in effect tend to attribute to societies may be present, but it may be *political* and a consequence and artifact of the political form of organization, namely, its state. (The examples of Italy and the United States, just cited, are cases in point.)

---

17. Karl Marx, "The German Ideology," in *The Marx–Engels Reader*, 2nd ed., ed. R. Tucker (New York and London: Norton, 1978), p. 187.
18. Joseph Raz, *The Morality of Freedom* (Oxford: Clarendon Press, 1986), p. 70.
19. Michael Mann's comparative and historical sociology is based on the assumption that *societies* are not unitary. He urges us to think of them instead "as confederal, overlapping, intersecting networks"; they are "constituted of multiple overlapping and intersecting sociospatial networks of power." Mann, *The Sources of Social Power*, vol. 1, pp. 16, 1 (italics omitted).

Raz elsewhere says, "A state is the political organization of a soci-ety, it is a political system that is a subsystem of a more comprehen-sive social system."[20] Rawls, in *A Theory of Justice*, thinks that "the primary subject of justice is the basic structure of society"; in *Political Liberalism*, he characterizes the basic structure as "a society's main political, social, and economic institutions, and how they fit together into one unified system of social cooperation from one generation to the next."[21] But whence the unity of *society* that seems to be presup-posed by Raz and Rawls and others? What is the cause for attribut-ing unity to sets or networks of people interacting in a geographical space? In most cases, where the geographical setting is not saliently one and distinct – as, for instance, with an island – or where the indi-viduals do not evidently constitute a single "people" or something of the sort, the attribution of unity to "the society" may be question-begging.[22] The unity we implicitly attribute to societies is missing in most of medieval Europe, as I argue shortly. This lack of unity is one reason why understanding the transformation of the Many into One was a theoretical problem for medieval and early modern thinkers. It is not so much that there was constant strife in medieval "society"; it is that there was no single, unitary society, as opposed to complex overlapping networks of individuals.[23]

By characterizing states as forms of *political* organization, I do not mean to deny that they are *social* as well. The distinction between the "social" and "political" is not, of course, very sharp or clear. Some-times the political is limited to concerns about power and rule or gov-ernance. Without distinguishing the two very sharply, I merely want to insist that we not mistakenly attribute to social phenomena (e.g.,

20. Raz, *The Authority of Law* (Oxford: Clarendon Press, 1979), p. 100.
21. Rawls, *A Theory of Justice*, p. 7, and *Political Liberalism* (New York: Columbia Uni-versity Press, 1993), p. 11. In the former work Rawls restricts his attentions to a society "conceived for the time being as a closed system isolated from other soci-eties", and he assumes that "the boundaries of these schemes are given by the notion of a self-contained national community" (pp. 8, 457).
22. But even with islands, attributing unity may not be warranted – for instance, Ire-land or England. And individuating "peoples" turns out to be far from uncontro-versial (see Chapter 8).
23. Hobbes may be forgiven in part for his conflation of state and society if one under-stands him as concerned with this problem of the One and the Many. He needed to account for the unitary nature of polities and could see little unity, much less agency, in early modern societies. His statist account, in terms of artificial person-hood and authorization, is offered in *Leviathan*, chaps. 16–17.

David Copp offers an account of societies that allows them to overlap consider-ably and to be nested within one another. See his *Morality, Normativity, and Society* (New York: Oxford University Press, 1995), chap. 7.

24

societies) unity that derives from forms of political organization (e.g., states). Another mistake, influential in modern political philosophy, is less likely today, especially in the antistatist climate of the end of the century. It is the error of conflating state and society and assuming that in the absence of the first, all social life disappears. In Hobbes, this may be less an assumption than a consequence of his political theory. But there may be a disposition built into "state of nature" approaches to political philosophy to assume that many, if not most, social interactions require something like a state. This view is reflected in the common use of the term 'anarchy' to mean disorder and chaos. But "anarchy" or "states of nature" may not be disorderly.

It is common, as I explain at the end of this chapter, to think of anarchy (and "the state of nature") as *the* alternative to the state. Sometimes it is assumed, in effect, that the two alternatives are exhaustive. (Indeed, as noted in the Preface, I once made this assumption.) When one reflects on the variety of forms of political organization in Western history, of which modern states are only one, it is hard to determine how best to characterize anarchy. Certainly it cannot be understood to be the sole alternative to states. Many anarchists have proposed to do away with all forms of government. Some base their opposition on antipathy to the exercise of power, especially force and coercion; others do not.[24] As will be clear (see Chapters 3, 6, and 10, as well as Section 7.7), there may be many different forms of anarchy that are worth considering. One particular form – that which is often said to exist in the "international relations" between states – in fact presupposes the existence of states.[25]

If the error of some contemporary political philosophers is to understand state and anarchy as exhaustive alternatives and to expand, in effect, the notion of anarchy to cover all nonstatist forms of political organization, anthropologists sometimes take the opposite tack and expand the notion of state to cover virtually all forms of governance. Ronald Cohen notes that in "anthropology 'state' in the broad sense refers to society or polity." While this usage is agreed to be "too general to be useful" ("equating all known political forms by lumping them under one term – 'the state' – does nothing to explain

24. Michael Taylor thinks the *concentration* of force, not its existence, to be crucial. See his *Community, Anarchy and Liberty* (Cambridge: Cambridge University Press, 1982), pp. 7–10.
25. See Spruyt, *The Sovereign State and Its Competitors*, p. 264 n. 30. On the lack of meaning to the notion of "foreign affairs" in the Middle Ages, see Strayer, *On the Medieval Origins of the Modern State*, pp. 27, 83.

the differences among them"), Cohen suggests that this broad usage "makes the worthwhile point that all human beings live out their lives within some form of social order."[26] Even though their objects of study are not mine, anthropologists may be of considerable assistance in characterizing many of the ways states and other formal systems of political organization differ from anarchy. Humans, after all, have lived in anarchic communities for most of their existence, until several thousand years ago.[27] Explaining the development of non-tribal or kinship forms of association may shed some light on modern states. It is especially anthropologists who study the emergence of governance in early human communities and who construct theories for determining why early "states", rather than alternative social arrangements, developed as they did. Given their interest in early human societies, anthropologists, while distinguishing state from society, frequently think of states merely as centralized and hierarchical systems of government or of relations of authority: "The state is a non-primitive form of government. Unlike primitive forms of government, the agencies of government by the state are usually explicit, complex, and formal."[28] While these features differentiate early states from anarchist communities, they are not sufficient for a characterization of modern states.

"States" of this general sort appear to make their first appearance in ancient Egypt, Mesopotamia, and elsewhere. In these early states we find some of the features of modern forms of social and political organization that are objects of my inquiry: distinctness from other forms of governance and from society generally; increasing centralization of political authority, increasingly determinate realms or territories, integration of a number of different communities and associations. While it would appear that in all human societies social life is regulated in part by the use of power[29] and that concentration or unequal distribution of power is very common, the emergence of the early "state" is to be found in the manner of concentration. As Lawrence Krader rightly notes,

26. Cohen, "Introduction," *Origins of the State*, p. 2.
27. As Michael Taylor reminds us, "anarchic communities did in fact survive for millennia. *Homo sapiens* lived in such communities for nearly all of his forty or fifty thousand years." Taylor, *Community, Anarchy and Liberty*, p. 3.
28. "The state is a political institution, which we define as an institution of government." Lawrence Krader, *Formation of the State* (Englewood Cliffs, N.J.: Prentice-Hall, 1968), pp. 13, vii.
29. This claim about power does not beg the question against most contemporary anarchists. See Taylor, *Community, Anarchy and Liberty*, pp. 7–10.

It is not the power itself that is at issue; rather, it is how it is attained and retained. If it is founded on brute strength or personal prestige, these may come and go, diminished by age or slander. But if the social power is founded on a continuity of organizing principles as an institution in the hands of a few, who monopolize it by force, then we are faced with a complex society of unequals, formed into a social hierarchy which is given support by monopoly of force and expression in the state ideology.[30]

For a more complete characterization of my object of inquiry, the modern state, we must look to features that are not the focus of anthropological studies.

A sense of the distinctiveness of modern states may be gleaned from a comparison with their immediate and distant ancestors, in particular the classical *polis*, the empires that followed, and the varied forms of political organization of medieval Europe. It is a commonplace that the classical *polis* was not a modern state.[31] The *polis* was an early form of political organization, increasingly urban, the origins and development of which date from approximately 800–500 B.C. Essentially a self-governing city, the *polis* was surrounded by supporting agricultural lands and engaged in trade (as well as war) with neighboring *poleis*. Population was small; Athens seems to have had about sixty thousand citizens (i.e., free adult males) in the mid–fifth century B.C., dropping to about a third of that a century or so later.[32]

As theorized by both Plato and Aristotle in its dying years, the *polis*, as well as its supporting territory, was thought to be limited in its size. Aristotle's concern was with the *polis* remaining small enough to be self-governing and self-sufficient.[33] This limitation on

---

30. Krader, *Formation of the State*, p. 16. The capacity of a form of political organization to survive changes in leadership, or in membership, is an important distinguishing mark of states. This is noted by Strayer, in the context of the emergence of modern states in late medieval Europe; see *On the Medieval Origins of the Modern State*, pp. 6–10.

31. Certainly, it is misleading to use 'state' in translations of '*polis*', if only because the former term entered our vocabulary only in the sixteenth century (see later in this section).

32. Fred D. Miller, Jr., *Nature, Justice, and Rights in Aristotle's "Politics"* (Oxford: Clarendon Press, 1995), p. 148. Mann gives figures of 30,000 citizens and a total population (including slaves) of about 330,000–350,000 for Athens in the mid–fourth century B.C. Sparta seems to have been smaller, with proportionally fewer citizens. Other *poleis* were smaller yet, and some banded together in confederacies. Mann, *The Sources of Social Power*, vol. 1, p. 224.

33. Aristotle, *Politics* VII, 4–5, 1326b2–37. The concern with a minimum size was based on the ideal of self-sufficiency (*autarkeia*). The restriction on size was influential with the classical republican tradition, and the stress on the self-sufficiency of a

size is interesting in light of the anthropologist's notion of "fission-ing" or the breaking up of communities into separate units. As I remarked earlier in this section, Ronald Cohen has argued that arresting the process of fission is one of the distinguishing marks of states (in the anthropologist's sense):

All political systems except true states break up into similar units as part of their normal process of political activity. Hunting bands, locally autonomous food producers, and chieftaincies each build up the polity to some critical point and then send off subordinate segments to found new units or split because of conflict over succession, land shortage, failure by one segment to support another in intergroup competition or hostilities, or for some other reason. These new units grow in their turn, then split again. *The state is a system specifically designed to restrain such tendencies.* And this capacity creates an entirely new society: one that can expand without splitting, incorporate other polities and ethnic groups, and become more populous, more hetero-geneous, and more powerful, with no known upper limit on its size or strength.[34]

The *polis* had the same problem that afflicted "city-states" gener-ally, the inability to expand and incorporate other groups, a feature that distinguishes it from modern states. Strayer argues that "no city-state ever solved the problem of incorporating new territories and new populations into its existing structure, of involving really large numbers of people in its political life."[35] A small size was necessary if the *polis* was to remain self-governing. The other distinguishing feature I mentioned earlier, self-sufficiency, may mislead if one thinks of the *polis* as an independent political unit in our modern sense. For individual *poleis* were not separate as our polities are, and their characteristic self-sufficiency was not that of a modern state. For the Greek *polis* was a part of a larger Greek society. The free men of the *poleis* were connected culturally (to use a modern word); they spoke Greek and distinguished themselves from *oi barbaroi*. And they were connected by various political and social ideals. Thus, Mann

polity was influential in late medieval Europe, at the time when some of the cate-gories of the modern state were being first formulated (see footnote 44).

34. Cohen, "Introduction," *Origins of the State,* p. 4 (emphasis added).

35. "Either the city-state became the nucleus of an empire (as Rome did) and so became subject to the ills of empire, or it remained small, militarily weak, and sooner or later the victim of conquest." Strayer, *On the Medieval Origins of the Modern State,* p. 11.

argues, "literacy, diplomacy, trade, and population exchanges could stabilize linguistic similarity into an enduring, shared, and extensive community for the first time in history." This collectivity, Mann notes, managed to withstand an assault by the greatest empire of the time, that of Persia. But note the difference from modern polities and confederations. The network of Greek *poleis* "seems never to have aspired to a political unity. War between city-states was not regarded as 'civil war.' Even the broadest federations were pragmatic diplomatic and military exigencies."[36]

The Greek *poleis* are to be contrasted with the most successful ancient city, Rome, and with the Italian city-republics of the Renaissance. One feature separating the Greek cities from these others is the apparent absence of a notion of secular, will-based law imposed by the polity on its citizens and subjects. The notion that the law is whatever the polity (or the prince) says seems alien to this time. The public order of the *polis* was typically understood to be one governed by law, one that was not human-made or based on the will of the ruler. Thrasymachus's conception of rule without restraint appears to be relatively novel in the history of the *polis* and was regarded by Plato and others as a challenge to an essential feature of the social, or natural, order.[37] We are still some distance from some of the central characteristics of the modern state.

In the empires that immediately succeed the *poleis* of classical Greece, the form of rule remained clanlike. The conquests of Alexander and others did not lead to the establishment of the rule or administration characteristic of modern states or even of the Roman Empire. The lack of integration within these empires prevented them from developing much political unity – certainly that characteristic of modern states. The empires' inhabitants also never developed the loyalty requisite for state unity. As F. H. Hinsley aptly notes, "if the Greek city states remained communities without distinctive state forms, these kingdoms and empires, while they evolved the forms of the state, remained states in search of communities."[38]

The matter of the *res publica* of Rome is more complex. To a high degree, Hinsley's quip about states in search of communities is true

---

36. Mann, *The Sources of Social Power,* vol. 1, pp. 224–225.
37. Plato, *Republic,* Book I. It is not surprising that the classical political thinker who most influenced Hobbes, the master theorist of the modern state, was Thucydides.
38. F. H. Hinsley, *Sovereignty,* 2nd ed. (Cambridge: Cambridge University Press, 1966), pp. 30–31.

of the Roman Empire for much of its long history. The empire's relation to the *city* of Rome and its lack of territorial integrity in the modern sense prevented its assuming our forms of statehood. The failure of this great empire to integrate other communities and to develop their loyalties meant possessing a somewhat formal unity, imposed by military means. The ruling elites of the empire were united by language and culture – they became Romanized, as it were – but their subject peoples were rather separate, both from their rules and from one another. The empire's political structure may be thought of as a "capstone government", where the ruling elites remained separated and culturally distinct from the subject communities and where government did not penetrate deeply the latter.[39] This meant that Rome, like earlier and less impressive empires, could not enlist the same loyalty that the smaller, self-governing *poleis* elicited. Further, governance of Rome's huge number of subjects was somewhat indirect, through local elites (who became Romanized). The administration of the empire did not penetrate very deeply.[40] Unlike earlier "city-states", the Roman Empire was able to expand, but the unity requisite to states of the modern variety always eluded it.

The "internal" governance of the empire was different in these ways from that typical of modern states. And the "external" relations were as well, in ways that are crucially important to our understanding of modern states. Empires such as Rome's "did not conceive of themselves as existing side by side with other such entities and as making up with these a wider system analogous to the state system. Rather, each empire saw itself as having political charge of the world as it conceived of it."[41] The empire's boundaries were not borders, but merely frontiers – the furthermost point reached by con-

39. "Chinese imperial government deserves the appellation *capstone*. The Chinese elite shared a culture, and sat atop a series of separate 'societies' which it did not wish to penetrate or mobilize." John A. Hall, "States and Economic Development: Reflections on Adam Smith," in *States in History*, ed. J. Hall (Oxford: Basil Blackwell, 1986), p. 157. See also Ernest Gellner, *Nations and Nationalism* (Ithaca, N.Y.: Cornell University Press, 1983), chap. 2, and Mann, *The Sources of Social Power*, vol. 1, pp. 282, 296–297.

40. "The empire stretched wide but not deep." Spruyt, *The Sovereign State and Its Competitors*, p. 211 n. 56. The modern state's "penetration" of its territory with law and administration is stressed by Mann (*The Sources of Social Power*, vol. 2, pp. 56–57). Poggi notes that "the political activities routinely performed within [ancient empires] were exclusively military and fiscal, and, significant as they were, they did not order social life with the purposefulness and intensity that (modern) states do." *The State*, p. 25. I discuss "direct rule" below.

41. Poggi, *The State*, p. 25.

quest (*urbi et orbi*). As Friedrich Kratochwil argues in an insightful essay, "Imperial boundaries did not operate to demarcate areas of exclusive jurisdiction on the basis of shared practices and mutual recognition of rights, but to keep the environment safe through the establishment of clients and the control of trade." Modern states, even rival ones, acknowledge one another's existence, if only implicitly through their own understanding of their boundaries and jurisdiction. This was not the case with premodern empires, especially with Rome:

The Roman Empire conceived of the *limes* not as a boundary, but as a temporary stopping place where the potentially unlimited expansion of the *Pax Romana* had come to a halt. The political and administrative domain often extended beyond the wall or stayed inside it at a considerable distance. Boundaries – i.e., legally relevant distinctions – existed only in private legal relations, where they governed property rights. The *ager publicus,* or public domain, had no boundaries; it ended somewhere, but this end was not specifiable by means of a legally relevant line. . . . The boundary was essentially a floating zone within which tributary tribes as well as Roman legions with local barbarian recruits were used to keep the peace. Other barbarian tribes were to be slowly acculturated and integrated, or subjugated and suppressed.[42]

Many features of modern states, especially juridical ones, are owed to Rome. Interestingly, the beginnings of the modern notion of "internal sovereignty" are to be found in notions surrounding the rule of the emperor starting at the end of the first century A.D., as I note later in this section. But the empire's self-conception as governor of the world prevents the development of the notion and practices of "external sovereignty".[43]

The Greek *polis* – especially Athens of the fifth and fourth centuries B.C. – and Rome are the prestatist forms of political organization most familiar to philosophers. So it is natural to compare and contrast them with our states. But it is misleading to restrict oneself to these comparisons if one seeks to discern the distinctive features of modern states. Although certain features of the *polis* and of Roman law were adapted to late medieval and early modern governance,[44]

---

42. Kratochwil, "Of Systems, Boundaries, and Territoriality: An Inquiry into the Formation of the State System," *World Politics* 39, 1 (October 1986), pp. 35–36. See also Spruyt, *The Sovereign State and Its Competitors*, pp. 16–17.
43. A point made by Spruyt, in ibid., p. 103.
44. In particular, Aristotle's conception of the self-sufficiency of the *polis* was significant. Walter Ullmann argues that our concept of the state, "understood as an inde-

the Greek *poleis* and the empire had disappeared by the time modern states were emerging. Strayer notes that "the modern state did not derive directly from any of these early examples [the *polis*, the Han empire of China, the Roman Empire]. The men who laid the foundations for the first European states . . . were far removed in time from Greece and Rome. While they learned something from Rome through the study of Roman law, and something of Greece through hints in Aristotelian treatises, basically they had to reinvent [*sic*] the state by their own efforts."[45] The distinctiveness of the modern state emerges most clearly from a contrast with the complex forms of political organization of medieval Europe.

The Roman Empire was followed in Europe, including much of the Mediterranean world, by a fragmentation of political society. In the period from about 800 to 1200, Western Europe, or Christendom, was a complicated social order in which political power was highly fragmented. Political relations between people were multifaceted, allegiances varied and overlapping, and the resulting political orders complex. Social order was not secured by centralized, hierarchical institutions, as in our societies; power and authority were decentralized. The fragmentation of political power following the disintegration of the Roman Empire is noteworthy. Our maps of Europe around the first millennium may reveal familiar names and shapes, but it is important not to read into these familiar forms of political organization, for

the emperors, kings, princes, dukes, caliphs, sultans, and other potentates of AD 990 prevailed as conquerors, tribute-takers, and rentiers, not as heads of state that durably and densely regulated life within their realms. Inside their jurisdictions, furthermore, rivals and ostensible subordinates commonly used armed force on behalf of their own interests while paying little attention to the interests of their nominal sovereigns. Private armies proliferated through much of the continent. Nothing like a centralized national state anywhere in Europe.

Within the ring formed by these sprawling, ephemeral states sovereignty fragmented even more, as hundreds of principalities, bishoprics, city-states,

pendent, self-sufficient, autonomous body of citizens which lived, so to speak, on its own substance and on its own laws . . . came about in the thirteenth century as a result of the influence of the Greek philosopher Aristotle." *Medieval Political Thought* (Harmondsworth: Penguin, 1965), p. 17.
45. Strayer, *On the Medieval Origins of the Modern State*, pp. 10–11.

and other authorities exercised overlapping control in the small hinterlands of their capitals.[46]

Medieval Europe consisted of complex, crosscutting jurisdictions of towns, lords, kings, emperors, popes, and bishops. While all were unified as part of Christendom, power was fragmented and shared by many different parties, allegiances were multiple, and there was no clearly defined hierarchy of authority. No single agency controlled, or could possibly control, political life in the ways now routine for modern states.[47] Several features are important to note. Not only was power fragmented and control of territory denied any one group or institution, but relations of authority overlapped and were not exclusive, and no clear hierarchy was discernible. In addition, feudal rule was essentially personal. In these important ways, certain characteristic features of modern governance were not to be found.

Feudalism in the period from about 800 to 1200 Strayer characterizes as consisting of "a fragmentation of political authority, public power in private hands, and a military system in which an essential part of the armed forces is secured through private contracts."[48] Rule was primarily personal in at least two senses: it was based on particular (voluntary or involuntary) relations between individuals, and governance was essentially over people rather than land. Relations between persons, many essentially promissory, laid the basis for the complex obligations between lords and vassals. Governance was also personal and not territorial. It is not so much that control of particular geographical areas was not complete or secure (though this was the case); it is that allegiances were not *territorially* determined. As Spruyt rightly emphasizes, "Feudal organization was essentially a system of rule based on mutual ties of dependence . . . inclusion in the feudal structure was not defined by physical location. That is, territory was not determinative of identity and loyalty. One's specific obligations or rights depended on one's place in the matrix of personal ties, not on one's location in a particular area."[49]

46. Tilly, *Coercion, Capital, and European States*, pp. 39–40.
47. "No single group could monopolize power; conversely, all power actors had autonomous spheres." Mann, *The Sources of Social Power*, vol. 1, pp. 397–399.
48. Strayer, *Feudalism* (Princeton: D. Van Nostrand, 1965), p. 13.
49. The "feudal logic of organization . . . is better conceptualized as organization based on personal bonds. . . . Feudalism is thus rule over people rather than land." Spruyt, *The Sovereign State and Its Competitors*, pp. 35, 40. Feudal political power is personal in another, related sense: It "is treated as a private possession. It can be

Medieval allegiances could, and frequently did, overlap. Different lords, monarchs, and emperors could have some claim over someone, and bishops and popes as well. The potential complexity of multiple allegiances was illustrated by John of Toul, in the early thirteenth century, who had four lords, each of whom he intended to honor:

> I, John of Toul, make it known that I am the liege man of Lady Beatrice, countess of Troyes and of her dearest son, my dearest lord count Thibault of Champagne, against all persons, living or dead, except for the liege homage I have done to lord Enguerran of Coucy, lord John of Arcis, and the count of Grandpré. If it should happen that the count of Grandpré should be at war with the countess and count of Champagne for his own personal grievances, I will personally go to the assistance of the count of Grandpré and will send to the countess and count of Champagne, if they summon me, the knights I owe for the fief which I hold of them. But if the count of Grandpré shall make war on the countess and count of Champagne on behalf of his friends and not for his own personal grievances, I shall serve in person with the countess and count of Champagne and I will send one knight to the count of Grandpré to give the service owed from the fief which I hold of him. But I will not myself invade the territory of the count of Grandpré.[50]

With political power fragmented thus, there was no clear hierarchy of authority. Spruyt gives the example of Henry II, king of England, who was also duke of Aquitaine, count of Anjou, and duke of Normandy. As his title to Normandy was that of duke, he was obligated to pay homage to Louis VII, king of France, which he did.[51] Given the largely customary nature of law, it would be a mistake as well to assume the existence of a single legal system, with an unambiguous hierarchy of juridical authorities.[52]

The complex social order of feudal Europe existed as part of Christendom. The Church represented a political order that claimed authority, with considerable success, over all believers. Accordingly, Christians, whatever their local allegiances, were also under the jurisdiction of the Church, that is, of popes and bishops. Like the authority claimed by Rome and by "universalist" empires gener-

---

divided among heirs, given as a marriage portion, mortgaged, bought and sold. Private contracts and the rules of family law determine the possessors of judicial and administrative authority." Strayer, *Feudalism*, p. 12.

50. Reproduced in Strayer, *Feudalism*, p. 146 (and quoted by Spruyt, *The Sovereign State and Its Competitors*, p. 39).

51. Spruyt, *The Sovereign State and Its Competitors*, p. 39.

52. See Marc Bloch, *La société féodale* (Paris: Editions Albin Michel, 1939), pp. 165–179.

ally, the Church's jurisdiction was "translocal" (to use Spruyt's useful term). It governed Christians and had no – and could not admit of any – territorial limits. The Church was not merely a "spiritual" institution as we may think of it now; it controlled considerable resources in holdings and in revenue. The pope had property and received payments from monasteries and secular rulers. And the clergy derived revenue from the tithe and other sources.[53] It was – if we may use a term that did not yet exist – a "political" force.

Christendom was a unifying force and as such may be thought analogous in some ways to our polities. But, as noted, the Church's authority was (and still is) over believers and not territorial; infidels escaped its authority, and there were no geographical limits to its jurisdiction. The importance of customary law and the local nature of important political allegiances limit its power. It is not that the Church's power was contested by "secular" rulers (though it was). Rather, its control was never intended to be as complete as with modern polities. The instruments of power did not, of course, permit this. But the different elements of medieval governance coexisted, in principle, with Christendom and its agents. Pope, bishops, monks, monarchs, lords, vassals, serfs, all were part of a single order, or better, an order of orders.[54] Further, although I have been speaking about *political* authority and organization in the Middle Ages, there is no clear distinction between the political and the rest of life. It is said that "the very term 'political' did not enter the vocabulary of governments and writers before the thirteenth century."[55] There was only one normative world, so to speak, and all – Christians, at least – were part of it. Not only does this mean that the various realms of Christendom were not separate, self-sufficient juridical domains. It means that all, including monarchs and "sovereigns", were subject to law, both customary and natural.[56]

---

53. Spruyt, *The Sovereign State and Its Competitors*, pp. 42–46.
54. I resist saying "an ordering of orderings", given that the multiplicity of allegiances and the absence of hierarchy defeat transitivity of authority and power. See the discussion of sovereignty as a transitive relation in Chapter 7.
55. "The early and high Middle Ages did not distinguish between religious, political, moral (etc.) norms, but considered only the faithful." Ullmann, *Medieval Political Thought*, p. 17.
56. Christianity also created a common identity (to use our term) for medieval Europeans. Even though most people had multiple identities, based on locale, descent, class, interests, and so on, Mann argues that the "most powerful and extensive sense of social identity was Christian. . . . Christian identity provided both a common humanity and a framework for common divisions among Europeans." See Mann's interesting discussion, *Sources of Social Power*, vol. 1, pp. 379–390.

To summarize, then, "political" organization in medieval Europe was complex, and "political" power was highly fragmented and decentralized. Allegiances were multiple, largely personal, and no clear hierarchy of political authority was discernible. Governance was not territorial; it was largely rule over persons, qua individuals or qua Christians. The complexity of relations of authority means that rule was not, for the most part, "direct" and institutions did not "penetrate" society in the ways characteristic of our states. There were no "self-sufficient" polities and consequently no "international relations". The modern state did not yet exist.

Our notion of the political as something distinct from the moral or the divine was, as I have noted, not yet present.[57] But medieval Europe was, for the most part, politically organized; that is, it makes sense to talk of the forms of political or social organization of medieval Europe, as long as we do not import too much into the term 'political'. Feudalism was one such system, part of a larger social order. In addition, there were institutions of law, commerce, and taxation. It would be misleading to think of premodern Europe as an anarchist social order, given that there was government. Further, in spite of the proprietary nature of much political power, especially lordships and kingships, most of the institutions survived changes in leadership. But governance was not yet territorial.

In the modern world, governance is territorial. Modern polities for the most part have definite and distinct territories.[58] The colors and lines on modern maps have a particular and familiar sense: within the boundaries of a state, there is a single system of governance, distinct from others operating "outside" or "externally". Today, virtually all inhabitable parts of the globe are the territory of some state. Governance is territorial in another sense, namely, that law applies to (virtually) all who find themselves within these boundaries.[59] Geography acquires a new significance, the territorialization of political

---

57. Ullmann, *Medieval Political Thought*, pp. 15–18.
58. "Indeed, in modern political thought the connection between a political society and its territory is so close that the two notions almost blend, and the same words are used indifferently to express either: thus we sometimes mean by a 'State' the territory of a political community, and we sometimes mean by 'Country' the political community inhabiting it." Henry Sidgwick, *The Elements of Politics*, 4th ed. (London: Macmillan, 1919), p. 222.
59. The 'virtually' implicitly refers to messengers and diplomats who may possess certain immunities and, most important, to lawmakers or sovereigns, who come to be understood as "above the law" (see Chapter 7).

obligation.[60] By virtue of being in a place, circumscribed by lines or markers, people acquire obligations, independently of personal relations, vows, faith, or origin.

The territorialization of governance is not compatible with the personal nature of political relations, as bonds between individuals (especially if promissory and conditional). And it is not compatible with power being understood as the personal possession of rulers.[61] One of the features distinguishing modern polities from earlier kingships is the distinction between the persons of the rulers and the office and institutions they occupy. But it is not just that there emerges a distinction between a person and roles and institutions. The polity – the state – comes to be understood as an order distinct from its agents and institutions, something reflected in the linguistic distinctions, discussed earlier, between 'state' and 'government'. The modern use of 'state' to refer to a public order distinct from both ruled and ruler, with highly centralized institutions wielding power over inhabitants of a defined territory, seems to date back no earlier than the sixteenth century.[62] The word derives from the Latin *stare*, to stand, and *status*, standing or position. '*Status*' also connotes stability or permanence, which is carried over into 'estate', the immediate ancestor of 'state'.[63] But the modern use of the word is new:

Before the sixteenth century, the term *status* was only used by political writers to refer to one of two things: either the state or condition in which a ruler finds himself (the *status principis*); or else the general 'state of the nation' or condition of the realm as a whole (the *status regni*). What was lacking in these

60. In an insightful essay, Alessandro Pizzorno sees this clearly: "What some call 'modernization of politics' is this sort of change: a process not of secularization of values – or not as a prime mover – but of territorialization of binding ties, with all its consequences." "Politics Unbound," in *Changing Boundaries of the Political*, ed. C. Maier (Cambridge: Cambridge University Press, 1987), p. 32. Spruyt stresses the territoriality of modern states in *The Sovereign State and Its Competitors*.
61. Unless the ruler identifies the realm as his (property). One possible reading of Louis XIV's alleged words "*l'Etat c'est moi*" is "the state is *mine*" ("*à moi*"). See Herbert H. Rowen, "'L'Etat c'est à Moi': Louis XIV and the State," *French Historical Studies* 2, 1 (Spring 1961), 83–98.
62. See Quentin Skinner, *The Foundations of Modern Political Thought*, vol. 2 (Cambridge: Cambridge University Press, 1978), pp. 352–358; Skinner, "The State," in *Political Innovation and Conceptual Change*, ed. T. Ball, J. Farr, and R. Hanson (Cambridge: Cambridge University Press, 1989), pp. 90–131; Dyson, *The State Tradition in Western Europe*, pp. 25–47; and Andrew Vincent, *Theories of the State* (Oxford: Basil Blackwell, 1987), pp. 16–19.
63. The French '*Etat*', originally '*estat*', and the English 'state' are derived from 'estate'. The Spanish for state, '*el estado*', preserves the etymology.

usages was the distinctively modern idea of the State as a form of public power separate from both the ruler and the ruled, and constituting the supreme political authority within a certain defined territory.[64]

The development of a new vocabulary signals a new conception of the polity, that of an order which is separate from ruler and ruled (or citizen), separate from other polities like it, and operating in a distinct territory.

The territoriality of modern rule means that all who find themselves within the polity's boundaries are, by that fact, governed. Territory becomes a jurisdictional domain.[65] Rule also becomes *direct* in a certain sense. In empires rule is typically indirect; considerable power is left to local governors and administrators. Governance is largely through intermediaries. In medieval Christendom, popes for the most part governed believers indirectly through clergy and kings. In the modern world rule comes to be direct; each and every subject is governed by the sovereign or the state, without mediation.[66] The development of direct rule in this sense is a late development, and it is related to the "penetration" of society by the state stressed by Mann and others: "The modern state added routine, formalized, rationalized institutions of wider scope over citizens and territories. It *penetrates* its territories with both law and administration . . . as earlier states did not."[67]

Direct rule and "penetration" presuppose not only territoriality of the state but also its extensive authority. The boundaries of the state – its borders – create an "inside" and an "outside". What happens "inside" is the concern of the state; no "external" authority has jurisdiction here, at least without the state's acquiescence. Not only is the state's authority *exclusive* within its realm, it is increasingly far-reaching. States – initially, sovereigns – come to claim to be the ultimate sources of political power within their realms. That is, they

<hr/>

64. Skinner, *The Foundations of Modern Political Thought*, vol. 2, p. 353.
65. "The unity of the State territory, and therefore, the territorial unity of the State, is a juristic, not a geographical-natural unity. For the territory of a State is in reality nothing but the territorial sphere of validity of the legal order called State." Hans Kelsen, *General Theory of Law and State*, trans. A. Wedberg (Cambridge, Mass.: Harvard University Press, 1949), p. 208.
66. Tilly stresses direct rule as an important feature of modern states. See his valuable discussion, *Coercion, Capital, and European States*, pp. 24–25, 103–106, 144–146.
67. "Conversely, 'citizens' and 'parties' also penetrate the modern state. The state has become a *nation-state*, also representing citizens' internal sense of community as well as emphasizing the distinctness of their external interests in relation to the citizens of other states." Mann, *The Sources of Social Power*, vol. 2, pp. 56–57.

come to claim *sovereignty*. And this becomes a distinguishing feature of modern states.

In most times it is important to have established means of resolving conflict and disagreement. In medieval societies, as in most, there were many such means, some more formal and institutional than others. But as I noted, allegiances were multiple, jurisdictions frequently overlapped, and often there were significant disagreements and conflicts among the governing bodies and persons. In the absence of an unambiguous and widely acknowledged hierarchy of authorities, resolutions might be ineffective. Without a single, ultimate source of political power within a domain, many have thought, disagreements could not be "decided", except by force. This possibility may be looked upon with alarm, especially given the ferocity of much human conflict. The more serious the conflicts between people, the more pressing the question "Who decides?" is likely to be. "To decide" a matter, in this sense, is frequently understood to mean to be "the final arbiter".[68] In Christendom this could only be God and – given that His word would require frequent interpretation – the Church. Indeed, the very notion of a *final* arbiter seemed to presuppose a cosmological hierarchy like that provided by Christian monotheism, the only model available before the distinction of values or standards of adjudication into "moral" and "political" (or "legal"). The state's answer to the question "who decides" is to put itself in the Church's place or, rather, God's place – *"le prince est image de Dieu."*[69] It, and only it, is the final arbiter, at least locally, on matters that pertain to it. To assert this, states had to contest the Church's authority. They had as well to contest the power of "internal" rivals, namely, feudal lords. Emerging from these contests is the modern notion of sovereignty: the state is the ultimate source of political power within its realm.

As I make clear in Chapter 7, it is a mistake to think that modern sovereignty is merely a restatement of old ideas about power and authority. The elements may be present in different forms, especially

---

68. The notion of arbitration here also has its ambiguities, as we shall see in later discussions of sovereignty and authority. One can "decide" a matter, "arbitrate" a dispute, or "determine" a standard or norm in either of at least two importantly distinct senses: The arbiter can ascertain the correct position (discovery) or can establish it (creation).

69. Jean Bodin, *Les Six Livres de la République*, ed. G. Mairet (Paris: Livres de Poche, 1993 [1583]), Book I, chap 8, p. 137. "All significant concepts of the modern theory of the state are secularized theological concepts." Carl Schmitt, *Political Theology*, trans. G. Schwab (Cambridge, Mass.: MIT Press, 1985 [1922]), chap. 3, p. 36.

in Roman law and in certain theological accounts of God's power. But the conception of political power that is thereby attached to a new type of political order is novel. F. H. Hinsley, characterizing the basic notion of sovereignty roughly as I have – "the idea that there is a final and absolute political authority in the community" – emphasizes that something new is coming about: "If we are to appreciate the significance of the idea we must also add this thought. With the notion of sovereignty a new or at least an altered meaning has been acquired by every element in this statement [above characterizing the notion] – by 'political authority', by 'political community', by 'final and absolute'."[70]

The concept of the modern state in fact develops along with that of sovereignty.[71] This is evident in the work of the master theorist of the modern state, Thomas Hobbes. Hobbes, of course, identified the sovereign with the monarch.[72] But sovereignty is the "Artificial Soul" of "that great Leviathan called a Common-wealth, or State, (in latine Civitas)",[73] and his notion is the one I stated, that of the ultimate source of political power within a realm.

Some moderns attribute the notion of sovereignty not to the state but to "the people" (Rousseau), "*la nation*" (the French *Déclaration des droits de l'homme et du citoyen* of 1789), or the "King-in-Parliament" (the British tradition). One reading of Louis XIV's alleged words "*l'Etat c'est moi*" would have him express a Hobbist identification of sovereignty with the monarch, without inclusion of the *parlements*.[74]

---

70. Hinsley, *Sovereignty,* p. 26.
71. See Hinsley, *Sovereignty,* p. 2. See also Gérard Mairet, *Le Dieu mortel: essai de non-philosophie de l'Etat* (Paris: Presses Universitaires de France, 1987).
72. This is not exactly true, as Hobbes identifies the sovereign with the author of law and explicitly notes that this can be a group of individuals (aristocracy) or all of the citizens (democracy), as well as a single individual (monarchy). He favors monarchy, and some commentators have plausibly argued that his case for the necessity of a sovereign more than favors monarchy. See Jean Hampton, *Hobbes and the Social Contract Tradition* (Cambridge: Cambridge University Press, 1986), pp. 105–107.
73. *Leviathan,* "Introduction," p. 9.
74. This seems to have been the view of his successor, Louis XV, who said in 1766, rebutting the claims of the *parlements,* "In my person alone resides the sovereign power . . . it is to me exclusively that the legislative power belongs." Quoted by Simon Schama, *Citizens: A Chronicle of the French Revolution* (New York: Knopf, 1989), p. 104. Louis XIV's alleged words make sense as an assertion that not merely does the monarch have no superiors (e.g., emperors, popes) but he has no peers (e.g., princes, lords, cardinals, or *parlements*). See Poggi, *The State,* p. 44. On Louis XIV, see Rowen, *The King's State: Proprietary Dynasticism in Early Modern France* (New Brunswick, N.J.: Rutgers University Press, 1980), pp. 69–71; and Poggi, *The Development of the Modern State* (Stanford, Calif.: Stanford University Press, 1978),

I shall not adjudicate these disagreements of attribution here. (For one, we should need first to determine the identity of "the people" or *"la nation"* and their relation to the state.) I shall instead tentatively accept the state's claim to sovereignty; later, in Chapter 7, I attempt to determine its plausibility.

States not only claim ultimate power within their realms, they also claim independence of one another ("external sovereignty"). In rejecting the authority of popes and emperors, sovereigns asserted the state's autonomy of other states. Not only is the state the author of its own laws – the etymological meaning of *'auto-nomos'* – the laws of others have no claim on it. With the advent of the sovereign state, relations between states or "international relations" become possible. Before this, there was no "foreign affairs" or distinction between "internal" and "external", and the modern conception of the nature of world politics as "anarchical" or unregulated was not yet possible. Once the sovereignty of states is admitted, their relations are thought to constitute a "state of nature", one that, for most early modern theorists, was beyond law. For some, to such a state, "this also is consequent; that nothing can be Unjust. The notions of Right and Wrong, Justice and Injustice have there no place. Where there is no common Power, there is no Law: where no Law, no Injustice."[75]

All who find themselves within the boundaries of a state, I have said, are under its jurisdiction and obligated to obey its laws. Members (or citizens) are obligated to obey the laws by virtue of their membership; it is *their* law. Modern states expect not only obedience but considerable loyalty. Certainly the loyalty expected of citizens is to take precedence over that formerly accorded lord, bishop or pope, or emperor. It takes precedence as well over loyalty to family or clan, though these allegiances are often projected onto the state, as the latter adapts the language of kinship ("fraternity", "nation") for its own ends.[76] Only exceptionally, at least until recently, have multiple allegiances, in the form of multiple citizenships, been permitted.

pp. 68–69, 161 n. 15. On my understanding, the state cannot be identified with a single person. Of the *roi soleíl,* I should want to say "L'Etat ce n'est pas Luy".

75. Hobbes, *Leviathan,* chap. 13, p. 90. Hegel's view is similar: "since the sovereignty of states is the principle governing their mutual relations, they exist to that extent in a state of nature in relation to one another." *Elements of the Philosophy of Right,* trans. H. Nisbett (Cambridge: Cambridge University Press, 1991 [1821]), para. 333. Varying accounts of this state of nature are the hallmark of the tradition of international relations.

76. Partisans of international order now find themselves doing the same: "the family of nations". (No one seems to talk yet of "the happy family of nations", perhaps

Just as the concepts of sovereignty and of the modern state develop together, so it might be said that the development of states and of nations is also connected, even if not simultaneous. Certainly the concepts of state and of nation are now closely tied. This is reflected in language: The word 'nation' is often used more or less equivalently with 'state' or 'country'; Adam Smith talked of "the wealth of nations", and today we have the "United Nations" and "the family of nations".[77] States have for a century or so pretended to be *nation*-states, and loyalty to states has often been assisted by sentiments of national loyalty, as I have mentioned above. And the "nationalist" view that nations are entitled to become states is one of the most influential of recent history.

Modern states and nations clearly are connected. But the relations are complex and not easy to unravel. In the first place, understanding the notion of a nation or national group (in the relevant senses) is not a simple matter. If we think for the moment of nations as societies the members of which are linked by sentiments of solidarity and self-conscious identity based on a number of other bonds (e.g., history, culture, "ethnicity", language, religion, customs), then it would seem that state and nation are not necessarily linked. Modern states require well-defined territories, but these need not be national – for instance, Canada, Switzerland, Belgium, or the former Soviet Union. Some national groups have no state – for example, Palestinians, Catalans, Tibetans, Jews before 1948, Estonians till recently. Some nations have more than one state – for example, Korea after World War II, China after 1949, the Germanies until recently, and "the Arab nation". And the homelands of some national groups straddle several states – for instance, the Iroquois, Basques, *or* the Kurds. That many of these examples – or my initial characterization of a nation – will be contentious illustrates the complexity of the issues involved.

Nationalism, as I mentioned, is often understood as the modern idea that nations are entitled to be, or should be, states. Nationalists in this sense conjoin the concepts of state and nation – sometimes without argument – and presuppose the legitimacy of states. But the concepts of state and nation should be distinguished, and the legiti-

---

because it would invite derision.) One is reminded of Mann's remark, quoted earlier, that "the importance of kinship, and its use as a symbolic model for nonkin relations, is virtually universal." *Sources of Social Power*, vol. 1, p. 197.

77. 'The family of states' does not have the same cuddly ring to it.

macy of either should not be assumed at the outset, as least in an inquiry such as this. Sentiments of loyalty to one's nation are familiar features of our political landscape, and nationality is sometimes taken to be an essential attribute of the individual. But such sentiments should not be conflated too quickly with those of loyalty to the state. Anarchist and other antistatist critics, for instance, may not wish to challenge the nation as a type of human community.[78] Indeed, anarchism and other nonstatist forms of political organization may require the sentiments of loyalty to the group provided by ties of nationality. Further, just as some moderns alienated from states may identify with a nation, so those who lack a sense of belonging to a nation – who feel at home with no national group – may identify with a nonnational state. The different kinds of estrangement should not be confused, especially at a time when these issues are taking on such importance.

There may, however, be important connections between states and nations. The mere fact that they are confused or conjoined continually in ordinary speech, and that sentiments of attachment to one or the other are often difficult to distinguish, suggests that there is more to be said. I return to these questions in Chapter 8. Even though nations often come into existence with the development of their states, they are modern forms of society that may be characterized independently of particular political institutions or statehood, and so I shall not link them by making one an attribute of the other.

States claim sovereignty and demand considerable loyalty from their subjects and citizens. Their power is considerable, and they frequently appear to resort to the use of force in securing their will. Presumably this is the source for the common characterization of states in terms of their concentrated power and their control over the use of force. Arguing that the state cannot be defined in terms of its goals or its functions, as these may be served by other, different institutions, Max Weber claims that the state must be characterized in terms of its *means*. What is unique about the state is its special use of force, thus Weber's well-known and influential definition: "A state is a human community that (successfully) claims the *monopoly of the legitimate use of physical force* within a given territory." He goes on to note that "the right to use physical force is ascribed to other institutions or to individuals only to the extent to which the state permits it. The state is

78. Some orthodox Jews in Israel do not recognize the legitimacy of the Israeli state.

considered the sole source of the 'right' to use violence."[79] According to Weber, states differ from gangs or protective agencies by claiming (successfully) for themselves two things: a monopoly of force and the sole right to determine who may legitimately use force.

It is doubtful that Weber provides, in these often cited passages, an adequate *definition* of the state.[80] Nonetheless, he does isolate an important property of modern states. His account needs qualification in a few standard ways. For one thing, it is often noted that there is a difference between *claiming* and *possessing* power; thus the emphasis on *successfully* claiming power. However, a successful claim to a monopoly of force need not be complete in order for there to be a state. Virtually all actual states exist with rival claimants.[81] A complete monopoly is probably not feasible for most states. To this extent, being a state in Weber's sense is a matter of degree, and often there are borderline cases where it is not possible to determine whether there is a state (in his sense).

I end this lengthy discussion of the concept of the modern state with a general characterization of states in terms of the features I have isolated and discussed. I should emphasize that I am not claiming that all other characterizations of the state are mistaken. Some are, but many others are not. Different characteristics of related forms of political organization may be emphasized, depending on one's explanatory or evaluative purposes. For some purposes it may

---

79. Weber, "Politics as a Vocation," in *From Max Weber: Essays in Sociology*, trans. and ed. H. Gerth and C. Wright Mills (New York: Oxford University Press, 1946 [1919]), p. 78.

80. Elsewhere, in a work less cited for these purposes, Weber expresses a more subtle and complete characterization: "Since the concept of the state has only in modern times reached its full development, it is best to define it in terms appropriate to the modern type of state, but at the same time, in terms which abstract from the values of the present day, since these are particularly subject to change. The primary formal characteristics of the modern state are as follows: It possesses an administrative and legal order subject to change by legislation, to which the organized corporate activity of the administrative staff, which is also regulated by legislation, is oriented. This system of order claims binding authority, not only over the members of the state, the citizens, . . . but also to a very large extent, over all actions taking place in the area of its jurisdiction. It is thus a compulsory association with a territorial basis. Furthermore, today, the use of force is regarded as legitimate only so far as it is either permitted by the state or prescribed by it." Weber, *The Theory of Social and Economic Organization* (Part I of *Wirtschaft und Gesellschaft*), trans. A. M. Henderson and T. Parsons (New York: Oxford University Press, 1947), p. 156.

81. Although it is not clear that organizations such as the Mafia always or usually claim the sole right to use force within a territory, certain religious sects appear to do just that. Recently, fundamentalist Islamic groups in Britain established a rival parliament, claiming not to recognize the authority of Westminster.

44

be useful to distinguish less sharply between modern and premodern forms of political organization. (For instance, differences between state, empire, principality, or *polis,* may not be important for many anthropological research projects.) By contrast, I wish to raise certain normative questions about distinctively modern forms of political organization. So these distinctions are crucial to my inquiry.

The concept of the modern state, in my sense, then, as it emerges in medieval and early modern history, is that of a new and complex form of political organization. For the purposes of my inquiry, the state is to be characterized in terms of a number of interrelated features:

1. *Continuity in time and space.* The modern state is a form of political organization whose institutions endure over time; in particular, they survive changes in leadership or government. It is the form of political organization of a definite and distinct *territory.*
2. *Transcendence.* The modern state is a particular form of political organization that constitutes a unitary public order distinct from and superior to both ruled and rulers, one that is capable of agency. The institutions associated with modern states – in particular, the government, the judiciary, the bureaucracy, standing armies – do not themselves constitute the state; they are its agents.
3. *Political organization.* The institutions through which the state acts – in particular, the government, the judiciary, the bureaucracy, the police – are differentiated from other political organizations and associations; they are formally coordinated one with another, and they are relatively centralized. Relations of authority are hierarchical. Rule is *direct* and *territorial;* it is relatively pervasive and penetrates society legally and administratively.
4. *Authority.* The state is *sovereign,* that is, the ultimate source of political authority in its territory, and it claims a monopoly on the use of legitimate force within its territory. The jurisdiction of its institutions extends directly to all residents or members of that territory. In its relations to other public orders, the state is autonomous.
5. *Allegiance.* The state expects and receives the loyalty of its members and of the permanent inhabitants of its territory. The loyalty that it typically expects and receives assumes precedence over that loyalty formerly owed to family, clan, commune, lord, bishop, pope, or emperor. Members of a state are the primary

subjects of its laws and have a general obligation to obey by virtue of their membership.

Modern states, then, are distinctive territorial forms of political organization that claim sovereignty over their realms and independence from other states. A *state system* can be thought of simply as a group of states interacting in ways, often hostile, that significantly affect the fate of each.[82]

The task now is to examine and evaluate this particular form of political organization. My characterization of some of the features of states is deliberately vague; I shall have to determine how these features should be understood. And I shall also inquire as to whether it is desirable that our forms of political organization retain these features.

2.3 ANARCHY AND OTHER ALTERNATIVES

The state as the fundamental form of political organization has swept the world. Today virtually all of the landmasses of the globe are territorial states. The state system, once European, now includes China and Japan as well as the former colonies of all the modern empires. Japan, in fact, can now be considered one of the paradigmatic states of our time, as well as one of the few to have a credible claim to be a nation-state.[83] But the global spread of the state system does not convey the full extent of the state's victory over alternative forms of political organization. The state has conquered our imaginations as well. It is not just that, for the most part, we dismiss anarchy, the main alternative we tend to think of. It is that we do not easily imagine many alternatives. We have trouble, for instance, understanding the status of various "international" bodies and often instinctively categorize institutional attempts to regulate states as themselves protostates; for instance, the United Nations was once thought of as a step toward "World Government" (which is more threatening if capitalized), or the European Union is held to be a potential federal state, a "United States of Europe".[84] Or consider our understanding of the

82. Tilly, *Coercion, Capital, and European States*, pp. 23, 162.
83. I discuss the question of nation-states in Chapter 8.
84. "There is an extraordinarily impoverished mind-set at work here, one that is able to visualize long-term challenges to the system of states only in terms of entities that are institutionally substitutable for the states." John Gerard Ruggie, "Territo-

remnants of prestatist European polities, such as Luxembourg (a grand duchy), Liechtenstein and Monaco (principalities), San Marino (a republic), or Andorra (under the joint suzerainty of the president of France and the bishop of Urgel, Spain). We commonly take these to be states. It is not thought an absurdity to consider the Vatican a state, though it has no citizenry: "It is a party to many international treaties and a member of the Universal Postal Union and the International Telecommunications Union. It would appear that by virtue of recognition and acquiescence in the context of its claims, it does exist as a state."[85] It is as if our minds, as well as the categories of our systems of law, had room only for one sort of entity or unit. When a way of organizing political association has come to dominate our practice and our thought to such an extent, it must be recognized as an extraordinary achievement.

Normatively, the state's victory is equally complete. It is common in political philosophy to assume that our societies are – must be – states, the difficult questions revolving over what shape they should take, what policies governments should implement, what ideals they should serve, if any, and the like. Some take the state to be the subject matter of modern political philosophy. Hegel's view that political science is "nothing other than an attempt to comprehend and portray the state as an inherently rational entity"[86] may be an extreme version of this view, but not all that atypical. Hegel at least had a view about history and world development that supported his

riality and Beyond: Problematizing Modernity in International Relations," *International Organization* 47, 1 (Winter 1993), p. 143.

85. Malcolm N. Shaw, *International Law*, 3rd ed. (Cambridge: Grotius Publications, 1991), pp. 167–168. "From the early years of the nineteenth century the concept of sovereignty . . . became the central principle in the external policy and the international conduct of all leading states in the European system. So much was this so that . . . the solution of all problems and the adjustment to all new developments were made to conform to it. In Europe itself these more advanced governments insisted that every political structure must be a state like themselves – so that they could not settle the international status of the Holy See without resorting to the device of establishing a Vatican city state." Hinsley, *Sovereignty*, pp. 204–205. One might think it problematic to accord the Vatican the status of statehood when the Church has not rejected its claim to authority over believers, or given that it presumably is committed to rejecting the principle of sovereignty. Hinsley argues that "a sovereign theocratic authority – a sovereign pope, for example – is a contradiction in terms." Hinsley, "The Concept of Sovereignty and the Relations Between States" [1967], in *In Defense of Sovereignty*, ed. W. Stankiewicz (New York: Oxford University Press, 1969), p. 277. For a Catholic argument against sovereignty, see Jacques Maritain, *Man and the State* (Chicago: Chicago University Press, 1961), chap. 2.

86. Hegel, *Elements of the Philosophy of Right*, Preface, p. 21 (italics omitted).

assumption of the state's rationality. Contemporary political philosophers typically do not have such a view and seem simply to take the state for granted.

Rawls, as I noted earlier, understands "the primary subject of justice [to be] the basic structure of society, or more exactly, the way in which the major social institutions distribute fundamental rights and duties and determine the division of advantages from social cooperation." These major institutions are "the political constitution and the principal economic and social arrangements."[87] In *Political Liberalism* Rawls specifies the basic structure as "a society's main political, social, and economic institutions, and how they fit together into *one unified system* of social cooperation from one generation to the next." And he indicates that he takes the basic structure to be "a modern constitutional democracy."[88] It is certainly *possible* to think of nonstatist political, social, and economic institutions that might be considered a basic structure, but it is not clear that they would necessarily constitute a single, unitary system. (I argued earlier against assuming that societies are necessarily unitary.) When one Reads Rawls's work, it seems that the framework of a modern state is simply assumed, forming the background of his account of justice.

A text of political philosophy by Will Kymlicka explores the suggestion made by Ronald Dworkin that competing contemporary political theories "do not have different foundational values. On Dworkin's view, every plausible political theory has the same ultimate value, which is equality." The conception of equality is the abstract one of treating people "as equals". Dworkin's conjecture, "the idea that each matters equally is at the heart of all plausible political theories", is the unifying idea of Kymlicka's excellent book. Leaving aside the question of the plausibility of this conjecture, what is interesting is how Kymlicka explicates this general idea of equality: "A theory is egalitarian in this sense if it accepts that the interests of each member of the community matter, and matter equally. Put another way, egalitarian theories require that the government treat its citizens with equal consideration; each citizen is entitled to equal concern and respect."[89] Presumably, then, on this view all plausible

---

87. Rawls, *A Theory of Justice*, p. 7.
88. Rawls, *Political Liberalism*, p. 11 (emphasis added).
89. Kymlicka, *Contemporary Political Philosophy* (Oxford: Clarendon Press, 1990), pp. 4–5. Kymlicka's explication follows along with Dworkin. "From the standpoint of politics, the interests of the members of the community matter, and matter equally." Dworkin, "In Defense of Equality", *Social Philosophy and Policy* 1, 1

contemporary political theories take for granted communities with citizens and governments. The possibility that states might not be justified or be the best form of political organization just does not seem to arise for Kymlicka, Dworkin, and most contemporary political philosophers.[90]

This complacency about the state is quite extraordinary. Among Anglo-American philosophers, at least, one should have thought it shattered by Robert Nozick's *Anarchy, State, and Utopia* in the mid-1970s.[91] Nozick's work may have been understood first of all as a challenge to widespread support for the political programs of welfare states. But it was just as much a challenge to the implicit statism of most political philosophers. He wrote: "The fundamental question of political philosophy, one that precedes questions about how the state should be organized, is whether there should be any state at all. Why not have anarchy? Since anarchist theory, if tenable, undercuts the whole subject of *political* philosophy, it is appropriate to begin political philosophy with an examination of its major theoretical alternative."[92] The book was widely discussed and attacked for a decade or more. How can it be that it has had so little effect on our consideration of alternatives to the state? Why is anarchism not one of the main topics of discussion in political theory?

Anarchism has not had very much influence in political philosophy. The neglect of the tradition is in some ways understandable. The practical failures of anarchist communities in the modern world are well known. The romanticism of most anarchist thinkers is an easy target for statist critics, be they liberals, socialists, or Burkean conservatives. More importantly, the anarchist tradition lacks a powerful theory. It is actually surprising to what degree the tradition survives in spite of the absence of theory. Some anarchists reject theory,

(Autumn 1983), p. 24. "Government, we say, has an abstract responsibility to treat each citizen's fate as equally important." Dworkin, *Law's Empire* (London: Fontana Press, 1986), p. 296. In this last work, Dworkin suggests that the abstract egalitarian ideal is unique to governments, or at least to collectivities. "Most of us believe, as I said, that we have no general duty to treat all other members of our community with equal care and concern in everything we do. But we believe our government, the community personified, *does* have this duty, and we might hope to find in this pervasive public responsibility some explanation of why we as individuals sometimes have that duty as well."

90. There is only one reference to anarchism in the index to Kymlicka's text, and it is to a discussion of the fact that classical liberals were not anarchists.

91. Nozick, *Anarchy, State, and Utopia* (New York: Basic Books, 1974).

92. Ibid., p. 4.

somewhat in the style of the New Left a few decades ago ("no blue-prints!"). But it is likely that, in the absence of some sort of system-atic account of how social order in the absence of a state is possible, anarchism will not receive the serious attention from political philosophers that it deserves.

The anarchist tradition has two distinct wings, each hostile to the other. The libertarian or individualist wing, introduced to many by Nozick, has experienced something of a revival, especially in the United States. The other wing, communitarian or socialist anar-chism, is more widespread in Europe than in North America in spite of the number of anarchist communities in nineteenth-century America. Both groups are anarchist in believing in social order with-out the state, but whereas one claims that stateless order and liberty are possible only in free markets, the other defends community and socialism. Genuine anarchist societies are not found merely in the writings of thinkers and novelists. Human beings, for most of the history of the species, have lived in such societies. Anarchist societies were once, and may now be, feasible.[93]

It is hard to see how a study of the state, of its nature and justifica-tions, could omit a treatment of anarchy. As Nozick puts it, "It is appropriate to begin political philosophy with an examination of its major theoretical alternative." Partisans of anarchy think stateless social order both feasible and attractive, and many think that the state is necessarily unjust. For many, that settles the case for anarchy. Most statists think anarchy infeasible, and for them, that settles the case for (some sorts of) states. It is noteworthy that both groups often appear to assume that state and anarchy are exhaustive possibilities. Certainly, if one thinks of anarchy as being social order without gov-ernment and of states as any form of government, then the two are exhaustive. But I have rejected this simple conception of states and have focused my attentions on the modern state. So I cannot take anarchy and states as exhaustive alternatives.

Historians should also have trouble thinking of state and anarchy as exhaustive. We saw how modern states differed from Greek *poleis*, the Roman Empire, and European feudalism. These were not states of the kind that interest me. Presumably, then, they can be considered

---

93. Interestingly, however, premodern anarchist communities were neither libertarian nor socialist. For the most part, they were hierarchical in many respects and com-munitarian only in a certain sense of the term. Anarchist alternatives may turn out to be varied. I come back to these matters in Chapter 3, as well as in Chapter 7, where I discuss "philosophical anarchism".

alternatives to the modern state. More interestingly, certain *features* of these old forms of political organization can constitute alternatives. Hedley Bull, for instance, speculates that it is "conceivable that sovereign states might disappear and be replaced not by world government but by a modern and secular equivalent of the kind of universal political organization that existed in Western Christendom in the Middle Ages."[94]

There were other historical alternatives that we should not neglect to consider. For the modern state did not emerge from the late Middle Ages without competitors. The great medievalist Joseph Strayer is well known for arguing that "in the centuries between 1000 and 1300 some of the essential elements of the modern state began to appear", placing the state's development earlier than many commentators do. This seems to be right, but it is a different matter to conclude, "By 1300 it was evident that the dominant political form in Western Europe was going to be the sovereign state."[95] This conclusion seems too confident and sweeping, even in hindsight. Other alternatives seem still to have been feasible. Tilly has argued against Strayer:

> In the thirteenth century, then, five outcomes may still have been open: (1) the form of national state which actually emerged; (2) a political federation or empire controlled, if only loosely, from a single center; (3) a theocratic federation – a commonwealth – held together by the structure of the Catholic Church; (4) an intensive trading network without large-scale, central political organization; (5) the persistence of the "feudal" structure which prevailed in the thirteenth century.[96]

Tilly notes that the Roman Empire was followed by the Holy Roman Empire, and reminds us not to forget about the Hapsburgs' empire or federation. The city-republics of northern Italy and the cities of northern Europe were also viable alternatives to modern states for some time.

94. Bull, *The Anarchical Society: A Study of Order in World Politics* (New York: Columbia University Press, 1977), p. 254.
95. Strayer, *On the Medieval Origins of the Modern State*, pp. 34, 57.
96. Tilly, "Reflections on the History of European State-Making," pp. 26–27. Tilly adds, in a parenthetical note, "On seeing this list, Joseph Strayer has said to me that the political federation was no more than barely possible; the theocratic federation impossible, since the church had already conceded the temporal priority of the state; the persistence of the 'feudal' structure equally impossible, because that structure was already gone by 1300."

The modern state did prevail over alternatives. But a number of important contemporary scholars – for instance, Tilly and Spruyt – argue against simple, unilinear accounts that render the state's triumph almost inevitable. Empire, city-republics (as in northern Italy), and city-leagues or federations (such as the Hanse) were early modern competitors to sovereign states. The Italian cities most resembled modern states; they were, however, less centralized, lacked the hierarchical organization of political authority characteristic of sovereign states, and their subject towns and territories were not well integrated. The empire represented a feasible alternative form of political organization, one might have thought, until Germany's unification under Bismarck. And the Hanseatic League was a significant political unit that "could raise an army, conduct foreign policy, decree laws, engage in social regulation, and collect revenue."[97] There were, then, early modern alternatives to the sovereign state, and aspects of some of these may challenge our states.

In our world there may be a number of alternatives. Some may not be appealing. The "quasi states" of Africa are states only in name, recognized as such by the international order of states.[98] There are the principalities and duchies I mentioned earlier, but they no longer represent significant alternatives. Rather, the main contemporary challenges to states may come from various developments that seem to be occurring worldwide. Growing economic interdependence, the widespread dangers represented by ecological problems (for instance, depletion of the ozone layer), and the joint nature of much military conflict (for instance, the Gulf War) make states less "self-sufficient" than they may once have been. The nature of contemporary technology makes communication, the news media, and international financial transactions difficult for governments to control, eroding some of their power. It is hard for modern states to control their borders against immigrants. With production of goods and services increasingly moved to different parts of the world, much of it

---

97. Spruyt, *The Sovereign State and Its Competitors*, p. 126. Spruyt's treatment of the Hanse is noteworthy.
98. "The enjoy equal sovereignty . . . [and] are states mainly by international 'courtesy'." Robert H. Jackson, "Quasi-states, Dual Regimes, and Neoclassical Theory: International Jurisprudence and the Third World," *International Organization* 41, 4 (Autumn 1987), p. 528. Jackson inquires into the "novel mode of establishing and preserving statehood in environments which otherwise more often discourage than encourage state-building", namely, what he calls "juridical statehood".

subcontracted, with ownership relations between companies so complex that few nonexperts can determine who controls firms, much less to what state they belong, we should expect the interests of "multinational" companies and states to be less congruent than ever before.

All these developments may erode the influence and power of states in the years to come. More significant, perhaps, are the challenges to the normative power or authority of states represented by the growth of international law, especially that of "human rights", the erosion of "external" sovereignty in the right some states are asserting to intervene in the "internal" affairs of others,[99] and the case of the European Union (EU). It is too early to say what forms the EU will take, but already it poses a challenge to the sovereignty of member states. Noting that the EU does not challenge the modern territorialization of political authority, Spruyt points out the significance of its challenges to state sovereignty: "In the sense that there is a move towards a crosscutting set of jurisdictions at the national and supranational levels, there is a change in the locus of authority. Sovereignty is no longer defined as a strict external delimitation from other claims to authority."[100] The European Court increasingly guarantees a widening set of rights to individuals, as well as to groups, and the courts of member states are authorized to enforce European law. This does not necessarily make the EU a protostate or federal "United States of Europe", as I remarked. Hedley Bull suggests that if "modern states were to come to share their authority over their citizens, and their ability to command their loyalties, on the one hand with regional and world authorities, and on the other hand with substate or sub-national authorities, to such an extent that the concept of sovereignty ceased to be applicable, then a neo-medieval form of universal political order might be said to have emerged."[101] But it is possible that the developing EU may become a continental system of political organization different in significant ways both from the system of states that has characterized the last several hundred years and from the preceding world of empires, kingdoms, and principalities of medieval Christendom.

---

99. See *Beyond Westphalia? State Sovereignty and International Intervention*, ed. G. Lyons and M. Mastanduno (Baltimore: Johns Hopkins University Press, 1995), and the issue on "Rescue," *Social Research* 62, 1 (Spring 1995).
100. Spruyt, *The Sovereign State and Its Competitors*, p. 190.
101. Bull, *The Anarchical Society: A Study of Order in World Politics*, pp. 254–255.

Already, changes both in European law and in the commercial organization of EU societies have altered the terms of political discourse and interaction. Although it is true that many of the states and republics of the former Soviet empire are breaking up in rather traditional ways, each new state attempting to assume the powers and privileges of a "sovereign state", it is no longer the case that sovereign statehood is the only conceivable ideal for nationalist independence movements within the EU. It is less clear now what great advantages would accrue to Catalonia or Corsica or Scotland, for instance, from states of their own, as opposed to greater devolution. The European Court increasingly guarantees a widening set of rights to individuals, as well as to groups. And changes in patterns of trade, facilitated by the EU, lessen the importance of state borders. Further, many European states are decentralizing and "regionalizing" political power to a considerable extent.

In other parts of the world, however, the nationalist sentiments that threaten to tear apart existing states may reinforce the state system. For what many secessionist groups demand is an old-fashioned sovereign state of their own. And in the absence of close military and commercial relations, like those binding members of NATO and the EU, the result may tragically be a replication of the old system. The European example shows the development of the European state system to be extremely bloody. Until republican and democratic institutions and traditions take root, states typically quarrel and kill. One has only to think of the failure of the imposed state system in postcolonial Africa to gain a sense of what might be at stake.

There is one change that could be important and should be mentioned. As I noted, capital and trade are increasingly international, lessening the economic powers of governments and increasing the interdependence of states. Trade partners may behave ruthlessly and borrowers may default, but few now, only fifty years after the end of the last world conflict, seem tempted by war. The growing international influence and power of Japan and Germany is especially significant, for these states are essentially nonmilitary. This feature may not survive the next several decades. (The threats from North Korea and China may well move Japan to become a military, even nuclear, power.) Nevertheless, it is significant that these two societies have achieved positions of dominance in the world by nonmilitary means. Even if we do not follow scholars such as Tilly in associating the development of states with war and conquest, the positions of Japan and Germany today suggest the possibility of a rather different state system.[102]

Hobbes wrote brilliantly about the state at an early stage of its development, and Hegel took himself to be writing about the state at a time when its essential form was in place, but there is another tradition in political philosophy, which is to write about particular forms of political organization as they are dying. The *Republic* is the classic (unintentional) example of this genre for the *polis*. It is possible that the attention being given today to the state portends that its dusk is not far ahead.

102. In Chapter 1, I referred to Kant's conjecture in "Perpetual Peace" that the establishment of republican government will tend to limit war.

Chapter 3

Social order in anarchy

3.1 SOCIAL ORDER

One reason why it might be hard to imagine modern life without states is that we are so accustomed to the goods and services secured by governments that it is difficult to think how we would manage without states. Modern governments provide us with (or subsidize the production of) goods and services as varied as protection, food, shelter, contract enforcement, roads, sanitation, space exploration, education and job training, currency and banking systems, postal services, telecommunications, radio and television, clean air and water, unemployment compensation, transportation, health care and medicine, retirement benefits, recreation facilities, parks and forests, monuments, museums, music, and painting. In most Western states, large and increasing proportions of the population receive their incomes directly from government. What would we do in the absence of modern states?

There is now a large literature devoted to showing that many, if not most, of these goods and services can be provided relatively efficiently by "the private sector", that is, by nongovernmental agencies and "markets". Much of this literature is controversial, but critics now often concede the main point that most of these goods *could* be provided by nongovernmental means, and they challenge instead the social costs, the distributional consequences, and other ethical implications of relying thus on "free markets". What remains controversial is whether we could do away completely with states and secure all that we need and want in anarchy. Many partisans of free markets, even if they dispute the view that governments must ensure the provision of most of the goods and services I listed, suppose that states are needed to provide and support the framework required for the efficient functioning of market economies.[1] Social order, they admit, may be difficult to sustain without states, if only "minimal" ones.

The view that the state, or some forms of modern government, may be necessary for social order is widely held in modern political thought. Hobbes is the best-known proponent of this view, and he probably holds the most extreme version, that "during the time men live without a common Power to keep them all in awe, they are in that condition which is called Warre". This was, for him, a condition of extraordinary insecurity, in which there could be no "Industry . . ., no Culture of the Earth . . ., no Navigation . . ., no commodious Building . . ., no Arts; no Letters; no Society; and which is worst of all, continuall feare, and danger of violent death".[2] Few other thinkers follow Hobbes in imagining that there would be no society in the absence of modern government, but the general view, that states are needed for social order, is widely held.

Social order abstractly may be thought of as consisting of two related social phenomena: stable, predictable, regular patterns of behavior, and general cooperative behavior.[3] In this sense social order is to be contrasted to the disorders that occur when social life lacks regularity and predictability and when there is little cooperation among people. Most people appear to think that some form of centralized and coercive government is necessary for social order, especially in the conditions of the modern world. Many believe that basic security of persons and possessions requires states.[4] Protection against neighbors, as well as against more distant predators, would seem to be a condition of social order, as well as of most human goods.

We may think, then, that the characteristic modern rationale for states is their assistance in securing social order and, more specifically, basic security of person and possessions. Although classical

---

1. Note the ambiguity regarding the provision of all these goods and services, to which I return in the penultimate chapter: If the provision of various goods and services is assured by nongovernmental agencies – for instance, schools, prisons, and garbage collection are "privatized" – but financing remains assured by government revenues, then in one important sense the state has not withered away.
2. Hobbes, *Leviathan,* chap. 13, pp. 88–89.
3. This is Jon Elster's conception of social order. See *The Cement of Society: A Study of Social Order* (Cambridge: Cambridge University Press, 1989), p. 1.
4. Michael Taylor understands social order to be the basic security of person and possessions and attributes this view to Hobbes. See Michael Taylor, *Community, Anarchy and Liberty* (Cambridge: Cambridge University Press, 1982), pp. 44–50, and *The Possibility of Cooperation* (Cambridge: Cambridge University Press, 1987), pp. 1, 7–8. I focus on security of person and possessions but continue nevertheless to think of social order in the broader sense just given.

political thinkers did not necessarily dispute the view that a polity of some sort was needed for social order, this was not the first good that came to their minds when thinking of the reasons for their characteristic forms of political organization. The view expressed by Socrates in the *Republic* is representative of many premodern thinkers: "I think a city comes to be, I said, because not one of us is self-sufficient, but needs many things. Do you think a city is founded on any other principle?"[5] Living in a *polis* or other political community is required because we are not self-sufficient, either as individuals or in very small groups (e.g., families). This view is, as I suggested, compatible with the modern view that states are needed for social order. But the modern view presents social order as something problematic; its assurance becomes the central problem of "politics". They may live better in the company of others, but "men have no pleasure, (but on the contrary a great deale of griefe) in keeping company, where there is no power able to over-awe them all."[6] Life in the company of others may be advantageous, but it is problematic.

The establishment of social order certainly has been a central problem for modern Europe. The image of the Four Horsemen of the Apocalypse is in some ways more applicable to the modern rather than the medieval or ancient world. Whatever the particular causes of the problematic nature of social order in the modern world, a particular and central feature of many accounts is of special relevance to my inquiry. Social order, it is widely thought, is difficult to secure because it is, to some degree, a "public" or "collective good", the benefits of which accrue to people independently of their contribution to its provision. Producing collective goods like social order thus gives rise to a "collective action problem". It is especially when social order is understood as a collective good that the principal modern rationale for states is theoretically interesting and of relevance to contem-

---

5. Plato, *Republic*, trans. G. Grube (Indianapolis: Hackett Publishing, 1974), 369b4–5. Aristotle argued that the "proof that the [*polis*] is a creation of nature and prior to the individual is that the individual, when isolated, is not self-sufficing; and therefore he is like a part in relation to the whole." Aristotle, *Politics*, trans. B. Jowett, in *The Basic Works of Aristotle*, ed. R. McKeon (New York: Random House, 1941), 1253a25–28. Thomas Aquinas concurred: It is "natural for human beings that they should live in the company of many others" given that solitary persons cannot provide for themselves. Thomas Aquinas, "On Kingship," trans. S. Ziller, C. Nederman, and K. Forhan in *Medieval Political Theory – A Reader*, ed. C. Nederman and K. Forhan (London and New York: Routledge, 1993), p. 98.
6. Hobbes, *Leviathan*, chap. 13, p. 88.

porary debates about anarchy. Michael Taylor, a critic of this rationale and a defender of anarchy, summarizes the view thus:

> The most persuasive justification of the state is founded on the argument that, without it, people would not successfully cooperate in realizing their common interests and in particular would not provide themselves with certain public goods: goods, that is to say, which any member of the public may benefit from, whether or not he or she contributes in any way to their provision. The most appealing version of this justification would confine the argument about voluntary cooperation to what are supposed to be the most fundamental public goods: goods (or services) which are thought to be preconditions of the pursuit and attainment of all other valued ends, including less basic goods, and are therefore desired by *everyone* within the jurisdiction of the state in question.

Taylor, as I mentioned earlier, thinks of social order narrowly, in terms of security of persons and possessions.

Hobbes's *Leviathan* was the first full expression of this way of justifying the state. The public goods with which he was principally concerned were social order – domestic peace and security – and defense against foreign aggression. . . . But although everyone would prefer the condition of peace and security that mutual restraint ensures to the 'war of all against all' that is the result of everyone pursuing his own interests without restraint, no individual has the incentive, in the absence of the state, to restrain himself. It is therefore rational, says Hobbes, for everyone to institute a government with sufficient power to ensure that everybody keeps the peace.[7]

This view, in one form or another, is very influential today, and not surprisingly. Not only do states appear to be the main providers of "external" as well as "internal" security. There is as well a body of theory pointing to the difficulties individuals acting alone have with collective goods.

External defense is typically ensured solely, and internal protection largely, by states. Security of person and possession is to a large degree a collective good, one whose defining characteristics are *indivisibility* (or *jointness of supply*) and *nonexcludability*. Once produced,

---

7. Taylor, *The Possibility of Cooperation*, pp. 1–2. (Taylor notes that this brief statement is a caricature of Hobbes's case and discusses it at some length in a later chapter.)

a collective good is available to everyone at no additional cost (indivisibility), and it is not feasible or efficient to exclude individuals from the benefits of the good (nonexcludability).[8] As is well known, there are problems with the efficient production of such goods. Typically, people's enjoyment of goods depends on their contribution to the goods' costs of production. Our enjoyment of "private goods" – characterized by divisibility and excludability – usually requires our contributing to the costs of production. A collective good, by contrast, can be available to people whether or not they contribute to its production; individuals have an incentive not to contribute in these cases. Consequently, in the absence of certain controls, we may expect that the quantities of collective goods produced to be less than what is desired. In the more precise language of contemporary economic and social theory, we may expect production of such goods to be *Pareto-inefficient*.[9]

Security of person and possession is to a large degree a collective good. It is true that to some degree protection of my person and possessions will not necessarily increase the security of others. And it is also true in our societies that some protection is provided on the market as a private good (e.g., fences and locks, private police). However, an important part of the service provided by public police and systems of criminal justice generally is to *deter* potential violators from harming people. And this deterrence is an indivisible nonexcludable good to neighbors and visitors. That this is so is easy to see in the case of national defense or even that of general police activities. Consider the apprehension of a thief by a private protection agency. The victims of the theft are immediately benefited; they recover their possessions. Others will also benefit insofar as these and other thieves will be deterred from robbing dwellings in that neighborhood, and this benefit is a "spillover effect" of the original victim's private protection. In addition to deterrence, there may be

---

8. There are many characterizations of collective or public goods in the literature, not all the same. There is a useful summary of the seven most common characterizing conditions in Garrett Cullity, "Moral Free Riding," *Philosophy and Public Affairs* 24, 1 (Winter 1995), 3–34. Cullity, Taylor, and others note that indivisibility, as just characterized, is not the same as *nonrivalness:* one person's enjoyment of the good does not diminish the benefits available to others. Crowded beaches and roads may be collective goods with a certain degree of rivalness. See Taylor, *The Possibility of Cooperation*, p. 7.
9. An outcome x is Pareto-efficient if and only if there is no other outcome y such that someone prefers y to x and no one prefers x to y.

the benefits that follow from incarceration of the thief – namely, incapacitation – benefits that are also indivisible and nonexcludable.[10]

Social order, or at least security of person and possessions, then, is to a considerable degree a collective good. Accordingly, to the degree that this is the case, social order may not be efficiently provided in the absence of a state. While the evils and inefficiencies of states may worry us, so may anarchy.

The argument sketched above is familiar. And it has been under attack in recent years. The main question at issue is to what extent individuals, in the absence of modern government, can provide law, cooperate one with another, and secure their persons and possessions. Much of the progress made in answering this question is owed to economic and game-theoretic models of individual interaction in conditions of anarchy. I shall review some of these arguments in this chapter.

3.2 LIBERTARIAN ANARCHY

Let us provisionally understand by anarchy the absence of a state and all forms of central government.[11] Many take anarchy to be the general alternative to the state, but I have argued this to be a mistake. There are many alternatives to the modern state. But the question of social order in anarchy is of interest even if we do not think of state and anarchy as exhaustive alternatives. So I shall examine anarchy and the possibilities that it offers, a task facilitated by the existence of interesting recent accounts concerning the workings of anarchist and semianarchist societies.

As I have mentioned, the anarchist tradition has two distinct wings, each hostile to the other. One wing, individualist or libertarian anarchism, has been undergoing a revival, especially in the United States. The other, communitarian or socialist anarchism, is more widespread in Europe. Both groups are anarchists in believing

---

10. Jean Hampton suggests that this account of the deterrence value of the criminal justice system may beg the question against most retributivist accounts of punishment, something I should not want to do.
11. One likely implication of the account I offered of the modern state in Chapter 2 is that the distinction between anarchy and state, or anarchy and government, may not be very sharp. In the end, I think the concept of anarchy may not be very useful – even if I have said that political philosophers ought to pay more attention to anarchism.

in social order without states, but whereas one claims that stateless order and liberty are possible only in a market society, the other believes that it requires community and socialism. The libertarian wing of the anarchist tradition is more inclined to theory and has some systematic accounts of society without a state. Recent libertarian anarchists argue not merely that the state is immoral but that we would be better off in its absence. So I begin with an examination of some recent libertarian arguments.

The libertarian anarchist tradition is pluralistic and imaginative, and its case against the state does not always rest on an assumption of inviolable natural rights. Indeed, libertarian anarchists, taking their cue from their sibling free-market economists, often claim simply that the costs of government greatly outweigh the benefits. Rational people, whatever we believe about their moral rights, should not be inclined to see the state as the solution to any of their problems. Without explicitly invoking inviolable rights, David Friedman boldly proclaims "that there are *no* proper functions of government."[12]

I shall call arguments such as these the "economic" case for anarchy. I do not wish to suggest thereby that the argument is not a moral (or normative) one, though some economists offering arguments of this kind in fact believe that their case is "value-neutral". The economic case for anarchy is roughly that the net costs of the state are substantially greater than the net benefits. Now, such a claim is an indictment of the state only insofar as we are or ought to be interested in net benefits. Insofar as one is able to determine, such arguments are usually quasi utilitarian: aggregate welfare or utility is at a maximum in anarchy.[13] Utilitarian arguments may leave us unmoved. But I do not want to dismiss the economic case for anarchy so easily. For it may be that if the aggregate benefits of anarchy outweigh the aggregate costs, so do the *individual* benefits. Where there is Pareto-inefficiency, there may be room for mutually advantageous cooperation.

---

12. D. Friedman, *The Machinery of Freedom*, 2nd ed. (LaSalle, Ill.: Open Court, 1989), p. 19.
13. Most contemporary economists would not talk of aggregate utility, invoking instead Pareto-efficiency or its cousin, Kaldor–Hicks efficiency. (An outcome x is *Kaldor–Hicks efficient* if and only if there is no other outcome y such that those who gain from moving from x to y could compensate those who lose. A Kaldor–Hicks improvement *with* compensation is equivalent to a Pareto-improvement.) Often economists attempt to measure benefits and costs in monetary terms, assuming perhaps that these are a rough approximate measure of welfare or of comparable utility.

The economic case for anarchy often seems to presuppose what might be called a *theory of spontaneous social order*.[14] Such a theory makes claims about certain advantageous properties of market forms of social organization. A free market is a form of social organization where goods and products and the means of production are privately owned. A theory of spontaneous social order predicts that in the absence of (much) force, theft, or fraud, the voluntary interactions of rational agents in some circumstances will bring about a social order and, in particular, one with certain admirable characteristics. Contrary to the expectations of many, from the productive activities of rational individuals in a free market emerges not chaos, but a form of civilization that can be exceptionally prosperous, creative, and interesting. The discovery of this possibility by Adam Smith and others and the development of the theory of markets represent one of the major contributions of modern European thought to social theory. As Kenneth Arrow and Frank Hahn note:

> There is by now a long and fairly imposing line of economists from Adam Smith to the present who have sought to show that a decentralized economy motivated by self-interest and guided by price signal would be compatible with a coherent disposition of economic resources that could be regarded, in a well-defined sense, as superior to a large class of possible alternative dispositions. . . . It is important to understand how surprising this claim must be to anyone not exposed to this tradition.[15]

The best developed theory of spontaneous social order is that provided by neoclassical economics. According to this well-known body of theory, a *perfectly competitive market* is a form of social organization where

1. all goods and products are privately owned,
2. the use of force and fraud is effectively prohibited,

---

14. The phrase is adapted from Friedrich Hayek, who credits Michael Polanyi: "Such an order involving an adjustment to circumstances, knowledge of which is dispersed among a great many people, cannot be established by central direction. It can arise only from the mutual adjustment of the elements and their response to the events that act immediately upon them. It is what M. Polanyi has called the spontaneous formation of a 'polycentric order': 'When order is achieved among human beings by allowing them to interact with each other on their own initiative – subject only to the laws which uniformly apply to all of them – we have a system of spontaneous order in society'." Friedrich A. Hayek, *The Constitution of Liberty* (Chicago: Regnery, 1960), p. 160.
15. Kenneth Arrow and Frank Hahn, *General Competitive Analysis* (San Francisco: Holden-Day, 1971), p. vi.

3. agents are (a) rational (i.e., utility maximizers) and (b) self-interested,[16]
4. all goods are private (none are public or collective),[17]
5. all transactions are costless,
6. agents have perfect information,
7. there is a sufficient number of buyers and sellers so that none individually can affect prices, and
8. the production functions of firms do not have increasing returns to scale.

The theory of perfect competition predicts that the outcome of the voluntary interaction of individuals in such a market will be both *stable* and *Pareto-efficient*. Further, it can be shown that the Pareto-efficient equilibria of perfect competition are in the *core*, where the core of a game is the set of outcomes that are stable, Pareto-efficient, and cannot be undermined by some new coalition.[18] Perfect competition is rather amazing.

There are different accounts of the conditions for perfect competition, but in all the conditions are rather demanding. They are not met by any existing society, or, arguably, by any feasible society. Of what use, then, are models of perfect competition? Economists frequently use such models for explanatory and predictive ends even when the conditions are not all satisfied. As long as the "real world" approximates perfect competition, they often say, the theory is useful. There are serious problems with this claim, but I shall not pursue the matter here.[19] My interest is in determining what use perfect competition is to the libertarian defense of anarchy.

16. That is, the values of individuals' utility functions do not include the preferences of others (or at least of those with whom they interact). Note that this condition is stronger than what we ordinarily take to be self-interestedness, for it excludes valuing positional goods such as rank and status.
17. That is, there are no *externalities* (i.e., uncompensated benefits or costs).
18. The reference is to the first of the two Fundamental Theorems of Welfare Economics, explained in most introductory economics texts. The sense of "stability" here is that of Nash equilibrium: an outcome (or set of strategies) is a *Nash equilibrium* if and only if no one has an incentive to change his or her behavior (or strategy) given the behavior (or strategies) of others. An accessible account of the notion of a core, as well as of basic welfare economics, is provided by Allan M. Feldman, *Welfare Economics and Social Choice Theory* (Boston: Matinus Nijhoff, 1980), chaps. 2–4.
19. Sometimes it is argued that it does not matter that the assumptions of a model are literally false as long as the derivable predictions are true. See Milton Friedman, "The Methodology of Positive Economics," in *Essays in Positive Economics* (Chicago: University of Chicago Press, 1953), pp. 3–43. Friedman's view, very influential in economics, is not widely supported by philosophers of science. A discussion

Libertarian anarchists can draw comfort from neoclassical theory only if they can tell us how the conditions of perfect competition are satisfied in a world without states. Perfect competition requires the absence of force and fraud. How is the libertarian anarchist to guarantee that? How, for instance, is fraud to be prohibited and property rights to be enforced without government?

The works of Murray Rothbard, David Friedman, Robert Nozick, and others provide an answer to these queries. They argue that basic security of person and possessions can be secured by individual action and by the use of private protective associations and agencies. In order to offer private protection as a feasible and attractive alternative to the state, libertarian anarchists argue that competition among providers of protection will produce security efficiently, or at least more efficiently than governments. However, it would be difficult to make use of the theory of perfect competition to establish this claim, as its models presuppose the existence of the very thing to be provided, namely, security of person and possession (and absence of fraud, as well as enforcement of contracts). To suppose, for the purpose of demonstration, that there exists a perfectly competitive market for protective services would be, in effect, to suppose that basic security of person and goods – at least that necessary for the existence of a perfectly competitive market for protective services – is already established. The argument would be circular.

We can be more charitable and interpret the anarchist's argument so that it presupposes less. Certainly, were there to be a perfectly competitive market for protection, then we would have the conditions for concluding that social order could be efficiently provided without government. But something like the same conclusion can be defended without such demanding assumptions. After all, various conclusions can be drawn about supply and demand without presupposing a model of perfect competition. In any case, the anarchist does not argue that the outcome of free interaction in anarchy will be Pareto-efficient *simpliciter*. The efficiency claim is relativized: Basic security of person and possessions could be provided under anarchy as efficiently as by actual states or governments. Given the inefficiency of the latter, this argument cannot be refuted easily, much less *a priori*.

of the normative implications of perfectly competitive theory would have to include a discussion of the "theorem of the second best", which shows that when some of the conditions for perfect competition are not met, attempting to satisfy them incrementally will not necessarily move the economy closer to the Pareto frontier.

Let us consider, then, the claim that private provision of protection can secure security of person and possessions relatively efficiently (that is, as efficiently as states or governments). The obvious objection to the claim that protective agencies can provide security efficiently is provided by the theory of perfect competition itself. One of the conditions of perfect competition is that all goods be private, that no good be public or collective. In a competitive market, rational individuals and firms will not produce collective goods efficiently. Such individuals face a collective action problem; insofar as they are rational, it is said, they will seek to be "free riders".

I argued earlier that basic security of person and possessions is to a great extent a collective good. It is true that protection of my person and possessions will not equally increase the security of others, and in our societies considerable protection is accordingly provided on the market as a private good (e.g., private police or investigation, nightwatchmen).[20] However, as I said, an important part of the service provided by public police and systems of criminal justice generally is to *deter* potential violators from harming people. And this deterrence is an indivisible, nonexcludable good. Insofar as social order is a collective good, we may predict that it will not be efficiently produced in a competitive market, even if all the other conditions of perfect competition are satisfied.

Libertarian anarchists are not unaware of the problem here. Their responses, however, ingenious as they may be, are not persuasive, or so I shall argue. Invariably one or more of the following suggestions is made: (1) as with other collective goods, we do not need as much security as is often claimed, for instance, by proponents of large defense expenditures; (2) we can rely to some degree on the other-regarding sentiments of individuals; (3) there are several voluntary schemes (e.g., protective associations, insurance plans) that can provide security; and (4) various technical solutions are available.[21] I shall comment briefly on each of these.

20. See Bruce L. Benson, *The Enterprise of Law: Justice Without the State* (San Francisco: Pacific Research Institute, 1990), chap. 9. Presumably, the figures would be different, for instance, for Japan, Canada, or France, than for the United States, where criminals are heavily armed.
21. See generally, Friedman, *The Machinery of Freedom*, especially chap. 34 (entitled "National Defense: the Hard Problem"); Benson, *The Enterprise of Law*; Robert C. Ellikson, *Order without Law: How Neighbors Settle Disputes* (Cambridge, Mass.: Harvard University Press, 1991); Tibor Machan, "Dissolving the Problem of Public Goods: Financing Government Without Coercive Measures," in *The Libertarian Alternative*, ed. T. Machan (Totowa, N.J.: Rowman & Allanheld, 1982), pp. 201–208;

The first claim is a partial denial of the problem. It may be true that we do not need as much security as some have claimed, but that does not address the problem of providing whatever amount of security we do need.[22] The second claim is more interesting. Some collective action problems may be resolved by other-directed sentiments, but only if the good at issue is specified without reference to these sentiments. In self-interested terms it may not be worth performing some "cooperative" act which contributes to the provision of some collective good (e.g., clean air). But if individuals do not reason in self-interested terms alone and take into account their interest in others (or the future of the planet), they may find cooperation rational. If we characterize collective action problems in terms of what it is rational for individuals to do given their actual aims (self-interested and other), then it may be argued that such a situation would not pose a genuine collective action problem. I hesitate to take a stand for or against this way of characterizing collective action problems. There are good reasons to think of such problems in terms of the easily observed payoffs to individuals (e.g., monetary benefits, years in prison); we can then be relatively certain that there is a collective action problem.[23] However, it should not go unnoticed that there are collective action problems amongst nonegoists. Problems like these are determined by *patterns* of payoffs (see Section 3.4). The requisite pattern can occur with agents of almost any sort. Further, I should note that problems of social order may be more difficult to resolve among nonegoists, especially if they are willing to make considerable sacrifices for the interests of others (e.g., kin or compatriot), are moved by considerations of relative standing (e.g., Hobbes's

Murray Rothbard, *For A New Liberty*, rev. ed. (New York: Collier-Macmillan, 1978); Anthony de Jasay, *Social Contract, Free Ride* (Oxford: Clarendon Press, 1989); and David Schmidtz, *The Limits of Government: An Essay on the Public Goods Argument* (Boulder, Colo.: Westview Press, 1991). For useful surveys of the literature, see Tom W. Bell, "Polycentric Law," *Humane Studies Review* 7 (1991/1992), pp. 1–2, 4–10, and Albert Loan, "Institutional Bases of the Spontaneous Order: Surety and Assurance," *Humane Studies Review* 7 (1991/1992), pp. 3, 17–24. Some of the "technical solutions" are discussed in Section 3.4 of this volume. See also Robert Sugden, *The Economics of Rights, Co-operation and Welfare* (Oxford: Basil Blackwell, 1986).

22. It should be mentioned in this context that some means for the private provision of security can diminish other collective goods. (For instance, locks and fences can, in some situations, undermine trust.) It is instructive here to contrast the open "public" spaces of classical European cities with their counterparts in the United States or in many Central and Latin American countries. In the latter the security of the wealthy is enhanced by distance (moving to the suburbs and traveling by automobile) and by living behind walls.

23. Schmidtz, *The Limits of Government*, pp. 60–61.

"glory"), or are fanatics of one sort or another. Without endorsing the assumption of egoism made by many economists and social theorists, I shall not linger over this way of sidestepping the problem.[24]

The third and fourth claims, however, are more interesting. The third – various voluntary schemes – runs afoul of an insight of Nozick's on the conditions for natural monopoly, which I am about to discuss in some detail. The fourth claim – various technical solutions – is addressed, in Section 3.4.

Let us focus on the libertarian anarchist's claim that there are voluntary schemes, that is, private protection arrangements, that can substitute effectively for states and governments. The general idea is that private associations or agencies, competing for associates and customers, will provide security of person and possession relatively efficiently. We are to imagine competition between firms offering a variety of protective services as a substitute for the services now performed largely by states and governments. Nozick's discussion in *Anarchy, State, and Utopia* has familiarized political theorists with the idea. But his discussion also raises a telling objection to optimism about anarchist competition between protective agencies, namely, the tendency of such markets to permit the development of a natural monopoly. The argument is simple:

Out of anarchy, pressed by spontaneous groupings, mutual-protection associations, division of labor, market pressures, economies of scale, and rational self-interest there arises something very resembling a minimal state or a group of geographically distinct minimal states. Why is this market different from all other markets? Why would a virtual monopoly arise in this market without the government intervention that elsewhere creates and maintains it? The worth of the product purchases, protection against others, is *relative:* it depends upon how strong the others are. Yet unlike other goods that are comparatively evaluated, maximal competing protective services cannot coexist; the nature of the service brings different agencies into violent conflict with each other. Also, since the worth of the less than maximal product declines disproportionately with the number who purchase the maximal

---

24. Note also that resolving collective action problems by bringing in nonegoistic interests denies one of the conditions, self-interestedness, of arguments that use perfectly competitive models. Note as well that caring about others can give rise to externalities: "An 'externality' occurs if you care about my choice or my choice affects you." Thomas Schelling, "Hockey Helmets, Daylight Saving, and Other Binary Choices," in *Micromotives and Macrobehavior* (New York: Norton, 1978), p. 213.

product, customers will not stably settle for the lesser good, and competing companies are caught in a declining spiral.[25]

The claim is that the worth of protective services is *relative* and that a natural monopoly would emerge from the competition of different private protective agencies in anarchy. Thus, in the situation envisioned by libertarian anarchists, where different agencies compete against one another to serve consumers, much as insurance companies or protection firms do in our worlds, a monopoly of sorts would emerge. Even assuming conditions of relative competitiveness, the production of protection may be a natural monopoly, with the result that a single agency emerges dominant from competition.

Some anarchists disagree. Murray Rothbard writes:

Competition insures efficiency, low price, and high quality, and there is no reason to assume *a priori*, as many people do, that there is something divinely ordained about having only *one* police agency in a given geographical area. . . . [T]here is no reason to suppose in advance that police protection is a "natural monopoly". After all, insurance companies are not; and if we can have Metropolitan, Equitable, Prudential, etc., insurance companies coexisting side by side, why not Metropolitan, Equitable, and Prudential police protection companies?[26]

Rothbard, however, provides no argument against Nozick; he merely suggests that actual competition alone can determine whether protective agencies form natural monopolies. He is right to challenge the assumption that there *must* be a single protective agency or police force in a territory, something we do tend to believe without reflection. I shall myself challenge aspects of this common belief later (Chapter 7). However, Nozick has an argument for his claim that a single agency will grow dominant and will monopolize protection in an area, and Rothbard's counterclaim seems merely to be an undefended denial.

Further, while it would be interesting (though rather difficult) to set up genuine experiments, note that something like the situation envisaged by libertarian anarchists has existed before. Indeed, people in the past have sought security through the means of private

25. Nozick, *Anarchy, State, and Utopia*, p. 17. See also Gregory S. Kavka, *Hobbesian Moral and Political Theory* (Princeton: Princeton University Press, 1986), p. 172: "There are increasing returns to scale to be obtained from specialization and by concentration of power in the areas of internal and external security."
26. Rothbard, *For A New Liberty*, p. 219.

agencies of a sort. For instance, in medieval Europe feudal lords offered security to vassals and others, who could ally themselves with the lords (and kings) best able to protect them. One could argue that feudalism was a reasonably successful alternative to the modern state for several hundred years. But the result almost everywhere in early modern Europe was virtual monopolies of political power over fairly large territories.[27] Note as well that the feudal analogues to protective agencies characteristically were not particularly solicitous of the welfare of peasants and other unfree individuals who made up the bulk of the population.[28] I return briefly to the matter of the historical record later (Section 3.5).

Although I endorse Nozick's argument, it may presuppose that power relations are fully transitive, something I challenge later (Chapter 7). So I do not want to rest my case solely on his account of the relative worth of protective services. Tyler Cowen has argued that anarchist systems of private protection tend, under the very conditions that allow for their stability, to permit agencies to exercise monopoly power and to collude. Thus, whether or not monopolist agencies *are* governments, many of the unattractive features of the latter will be shared by the former.[29]

Consider an anarchist world of competing protective agencies offering a variety of different services, that is, different systems of rules and protective services.[30] This setup is not stable unless the competing systems develop a common understanding or framework

---

27. In medieval Europe the result was complex patterns of overlapping concentrations of power. By early modern times these powers overlapped less and consequently were more concentrated. It is worth recalling how fierce was the competition among states and protostates in early modern Europe. Tilly notes that "England, France, and even Spain are *survivors* of a ruthless competition in which most contenders lost. The Europe of 1500 included some five hundred more or less independent political units, the Europe of 1900 about twenty-five." Tilly, "Reflections on the History of European State-Making," p. 15; see also pp. 38–39.

28. The point of Barbara Tuchman's book *A Distant Mirror: The Calamitous Fourteenth Century* (New York: Ballantine Books, 1978), was to console us about our times: "It is reassuring to know that the human species has lived through worse" (p. xiii). (Feudalism, it should be remembered, was past its heyday by this time.)

29. See Tyler Cowen, "Law as a Public Good: The Economics of Anarchy," *Economics and Philosophy* 8, 2 (October 1992), 249–267. See also David D. Friedman, "Law as a Private Good: A Response to Tyler Cowen on the Economics of Anarchy," and Cowen, "Rejoinder to David Friedman on the Economics of Anarchy," *Economics and Philosophy* 10, 2 (October 1994), 319–327, 329–332.

30. For instance, some might protect only against bodily injuries and threats, while others also offer protection against slander and libel. Still others might offer illiberal services, for instance, "protection" against neighbors' reading trashy novels or pornographic literature, or practicing heretical faiths.

for resolving intra-agency disputes. Without such an arrangement agencies would have to back down or resort to force in cases of conflict (that is, war). A suitable framework would be some uniform arbitration scheme or (quasi-federalist) legal system, that is, a common code for criminal standards, procedures, punishments, and the like. But this framework itself possesses monopolist power. The very arrangement that allows competing firms to avoid resorting to force permits them to exercise significant monopoly power. This in turn permits them to collude, for instance, by tacit or explicit anticompetitive conventions. Monopoly rents can be thereby secured. The ability of firms belonging to the common framework or system to exclude "outlaw" firms enables the former to exclude potential competitors. "Competing legal systems are either unstable or collapse into a monopoly agency or network."[31]

If the dominant agencies can collude successfully, they can also exploit "customers". Even if such monopolists do not yet constitute governments, it is unclear that they offer fewer disadvantages.[32] The problem of constraining firms so that they do not evolve into exploitative monopolies does not differ greatly from the problem of constraining governments. As Taylor points out, the services offered by protective agencies resemble those provided by government in one significant respect: "When we buy cars or shoes or telephone services we do not give the firm power based on force, but armed protective agencies, like the state, make customers (their own and others') vulnerable, and having given them power we cannot be sure that they will use it only for our protection."[33]

Cowen offers a general conjecture that is relevant to my overall concerns:

The protection of property rights contains both public and private good elements. The private good element allows markets to produce protection services, but the public good element implies that a monopoly firm or network will arise because of externalities in the adjudication process. The provision of protection with mixed public and private features implies that some set of

---

31. Cowen, "Law as a Public Good: The Economics of Anarchy," p. 259. Note that the normal competitive pressures that lead to the eventual breakup of cartels do not operate here, for free entry and defection are controlled.
32. Collusion among private agencies may be more likely than between governments for a variety of reasons. Cowen, "Law as a Public Good: The Economics of Anarchy," pp. 262–263.
33. Taylor, *Community, Anarchy and Liberty*, p. 65.

institutions or economic agents will enjoy monopoly power and reap economic rents.

The same contractual and cooperative relationships that overcome externalities problems in provision of the public element of protection also allow for successful interfirm collusion. Indeed, collusion itself can be thought of as a public good . . . at least for the colluding firms.[34]

Part of the explanation of the emergence of modern states may have to do with these possibilities for collusion.

From the competition of private protective agencies, then, we should expect a monopolist firm, or dominant protective agency (Nozick's term), to emerge, or at least a set of colluding dominant agencies. These agencies are not yet full-blown governments, much less states, one reason being that they do not offer protection to all the residents of its territory, in practice or even in principle. Since they are profit-making firms, they protect only paying clients; those that do not or cannot pay the fees go without protection.[35] I do not seek to justify the state by arguing, following Nozick, that dominant protection agencies gradually and legitimately become states. Rather, I invoke Nozick and Cowen's arguments that anarchist competition will lead to monopoly power as a major problem with the libertarian anarchist's claim concerning the relative efficiency of private protection. Were the dominant agency to behave as we would normally expect such groups to behave, the monopolistic feature of the competitive provision of security defeats the libertarian anarchist's case.[36]

Domination by monopolistic protective agencies may be better than many alternatives, even if the price is the monopolist's rent. Like shepherds and ancient kings, they have incentives to protect their clients so as to increase their take. If we think of the exploitation of ordinary people by the historical counterparts of these agencies as

34. Cowen, "Law as a Public Good: The Economics of Anarchy," p. 265. The conception of law as a public or collective good is a major theme of James M. Buchanan, *The Limits of Liberty: Between Anarchy and Leviathan* (Chicago: University of Chicago Press, 1975).

35. Except for the spillover protection from the enhanced security of paying clients. Natural rights libertarians cannot easily justify charging such free riders for these benefits. See Nozick's criticisms of the Hart–Rawls principle of fairness, *Anarchy, State, and Utopia*, pp. 90–95.

36. It is primarily the assumed general respect for libertarian moral rights that enables Nozick, Rothbard, and others to draw relatively peaceful pictures of anarchy. As I say later, Nozick is justified making these assumptions as his argument is meant to be *ad hominem* against natural rights anarchists (though it is not usually read thus). Anarchists attempting to defend the feasibility of stateless social order under more realistic conditions face a harder task.

a form of predation or banditry, there is an interesting explanation for the emergence of stable territorial rule. Unlike the fantastic competing firms of anarchocapitalist lore, it may be supposed that many early rulers sought to fleece their "customers" without much attention to their individual rights. However, humans are much more productive if assured some security of person and possessions, and this greater productivity could increase the revenues of predatory rulers. "Roving bandits" (such as the unemployed mercenaries of late medieval Europe or like Chinese warlords) may do less well than "stationary" predators (such as kings and feudal lords). Great gains may be had from protecting one's victims, and consequently there may be considerable advantages to the "protection" offered by stationary exploiters. As Mancur Olson argues, "uncoordinated competitive theft" is not as rewarding as "the rational monopolization of theft":

In a world of roving banditry there is little or no incentive for anyone to produce or accumulate anything that may be stolen and, thus, little for bandits to steal. Bandit rationality, accordingly, induces the bandit leader to seize a given domain, to make himself the ruler of that domain, and to provide a peaceful order and other public goods for its inhabitants, thereby obtaining more in tax theft than he could have obtained from migratory plunder. Thus we have "the first blessings of the invisible hand": the rational, self-interested leader of a band of roving bandits is led, as though by an invisible hand, to settle down, wear a crown, and replace anarchy with government. The gigantic increase in output that normally arises from the provision of a peaceful order and other public goods gives the stationary bandit a far larger take than he could obtain without providing government.[37]

Early governments may emerge, then, from the interested behavior of exploitative rulers.

As social order, or at least security, is an impure collective good, and as my case for states has much to do with the provision of such goods, I must say more about the general problems involved in their production, as well as about some of the "technical solutions" I men-

---

37. "These violent entrepreneurs naturally do not call themselves bandits but, on the contrary, give themselves and their descendants exalted titles." Mancur Olson, "Dictatorship, Democracy, and Development," *American Political Science Review* 87, 3 (September 1993), p. 568. Olson's argument is part of an account of the comparative advantages of democracies over autocracies. See also Margaret Levi's account of predatory rule in *Of Rule and Revenue*. Olson cautions against the metaphor of predation: the stationary bandit "is not like the wolf that preys on the elk, but more like the rancher who makes sure that his cattle are protected and given water" (p. 569).

tioned earlier. Some of the recent literature on cooperation in repeated Prisoners' Dilemmas is especially relevant to the question of social order in anarchy, and in Section 3.4 I suggest that it offers less comfort to anarchists than may have been thought. Next I turn my attention to "left-wing" anarchism.

3.3 COMMUNITY

Communitarian anarchism, the other wing of the tradition, has not had the revival of interest recently experienced by libertarian anti-statism, at least in North America. This may be due to the particularly romantic or utopian nature of these anarchists, as well as to the dearth of theory in this tradition. The latter, however, has been remedied to some extent by Michael Taylor's *Community, Anarchy, and Liberty,* in which it is argued that in (and only in) *community* can stateless social order be provided. It is to this argument that I turn for another defense of anarchism.

Taylor characterizes community broadly as a form of social organization where individuals (1) share beliefs and values in common, (2) engage in direct and many-sided relations, and (3) practice reciprocity.[38] To a much greater degree – albeit still a matter of degree – than in other societies, members of a community share beliefs and values in common. Which beliefs and values (e.g., ideology, religion, moral principles, recreational activities) must be so shared cannot be determined *a priori.* However, much greater agreement on these matters is to be expected in community than in modern states, given the size and increasing pluralism of the latter.

Relations between people are *direct* insofar as they are not mediated by other individuals and by institutions. In modern societies many, if not most, social relations are mediated by "middlemen" of one sort or another. In community, relations are direct to a much greater degree. Further, communal relations are *many-sided.* In modern societies most social relations tend to be specialized or confined to a few or just one dimension; for instance, we interact with shopkeepers or professionals primarily in their "public" capacities. In community, individuals tend to relate to one another through many facets of their persons.

38. Taylor, *Community, Anarchy and Liberty,* pp. 25–33.

Reciprocity, Taylor's third defining characteristic of community, refers to systems of cooperative social relations and arrangements. Individuals help one another in the expectation, often not expressed, that assistance will be reciprocated if needed. "In typical reciprocity the individual expects that his gift or assistance will be repaid; sometimes the expectation is vague and uncalculating, sometimes it must be somewhat less so. . . . If continued giving goes unreciprocated, it will usually be terminated, except where the recipient is needy or unable to reciprocate."[39]

Communities, thus characterized, must be small and stable. In modern civil society direct and many-sided relations are not possible with more than a few individuals; there are just too many people and too great a turnover in membership to sustain such relations. Reciprocity in turn requires continued relations with known individuals if the necessary reciprocation is to take place.

Anarchy I have characterized thus far as the absence of a state and all forms of central government. Taylor points out that actual anarchist societies have limited, or no, concentration of force, although anarchy does not entail the absence of force or coercion. Specifically, anarchist human communities have no centralized means of enforcing collective decisions. Further, there is an absence of political specialization, or "division of political labor". (The last two characteristics were not part of my original general characterization of anarchy.) It follows that in anarchist societies there is roughly equal participation in political functions.[40]

How, then, is social order, or basic security of person and possessions, maintained in actual anarchist societies? As I have argued, security is to a large extent a collective good. Taylor seeks to explain how it is possible for highly decentralized and stateless communities to provide this sort of good. Rejecting both libertarian anarchist accounts of stateless social order and liberal arguments for states, he develops an interesting defense of the proposition that social order without government is possible in, and only in, community. His argument is basically that the interactions of members of an anarchist community satisfy to a great degree the conditions for mutual cooperation in iterated Prisoners' Dilemmas and that we can consequently expect some voluntary collective provision of collective goods. I consider some of the game-theoretic literature later in this chapter.

39. Ibid., p. 30.
40. Ibid., pp. 4–10.

In outline, Taylor's case is that basic security can be maintained in stateless community by means of (1) various social controls, (2) education and socialization, and (3) certain structural characteristics. The last include most importantly the relations of reciprocity already mentioned. Social order, argue many anthropologists, is maintained by networks of relations of gift giving. Education and socialization include the inculcation of those beliefs and values whose commonality is a condition of community. Taylor, however, does not wish to rest too much on these means of social control.[41]

It is the third set of means that Taylor finds most important. In the absence of government or other centralized power, anarchist societies require means of social control. In actual stateless communities, these are provided, Taylor argues, by the threat of retaliation, the offer of reciprocity and the threat of its withdrawal, sanctions of approval and disapproval, and supernatural sanctions and accusations of witchcraft.[42] By such means individuals who repeatedly interact with one another can secure one another's cooperation and punish defection. Pairwise interaction in small groups, backed up by such social controls, can thus assure basic security of person and possessions and social order. These controls, however, are effective only in relatively small groups with little turnover, that is, in communities. *Contra* libertarian anarchists, only in communities can collective goods be supplied without government. Stateless social order, then, requires community. Where community is not possible or desirable, social order would seem to require government and markets.[43]

I do not wish to challenge the soundness of Taylor's argument as it is persuasive. It supports as well my criticisms of libertarian anarchism and, as I shall suggest, undermines the attractiveness of communitarian anarchy. If the collective action problems implicit in the provision of basic security effectively reduce our options to community or government, the relative infeasibility and unattractiveness of

41. Ibid., pp. 66–80. Although it is no part of Taylor's account, the exchange of women in marriage should be mentioned as one of the important structural characteristics held by many social theorists to be crucial in the maintenance of social order in stateless societies. I shall return to this point.
42. Taylor emphasizes, as do many anthropologists, the importance of "public opinion", that is, gossip, shaming, ridiculing. See especially *Community, Anarchy and Liberty*, chap. 2. Public opinion may be important in any close-knit social network, even in complex societies such as ours; see Sally Engle Merry, "Rethinking Gossip and Scandal," in *Towards a General Theory of Social Control*, vol. 1, ed. D. Black (Orlando, Fla.: Academic Press, 1984), pp. 271–302.
43. Taylor, *Community, Anarchy and Liberty*, pp. 80–94.

the former should make the case for governments or states all the stronger.

Community, as Taylor describes it, is not an altogether attractive form of social or political organization. It is not that we do not value direct and many-sided relations, or that the benefits of relations based on shared beliefs and values are negligible. Most of us would not find fulfilling a life without some such relations; virtually everyone finds them valuable. But they are to some degree available in modern civil society, without the not inconsiderable disadvantages of genuine community in Taylor's sense. Communities, Taylor argues convincingly, must be small and stable. Life in small and stable societies, however, is also one that most of us would not find fulfilling. Current migration to the city in modern society cannot be explained solely by economic factors, as a significant number of the wealthy are the first to prefer urban life to community, although they presumably have the greatest range of choices. (This is less true in the United States than in Canada and Europe, as American cities become increasingly unlivable.)

Taylor argues, again convincingly, that community requires substantial enforced leveling.[44] When one adds this feature to the picture of communal life, its attractiveness may be further diminished. The necessary egalitarianism of community, the requirement that relations be many-sided, as well as direct, and the restriction on size will generally condemn communal economies to underproductivity, as is borne out generally by actual communities. Modern society offers scope for specialization and consequent economies of scale not available to community.

Community seems to necessitate intrusions into individual privacy that most people would find objectionable. It may be true that "community *requires* privacy to be invaded only to the extent necessary for relations between people to be direct and many-sided and for the social controls characteristic of community to be effective."[45] *That* degree of interference with privacy may be considerable. Further, although only that degree of interference is *required*, how likely is it that greater interference will not occur?

44. Ibid., chap. 3.
45. Ibid., p. 159. There are further problems with individual autonomy: It is likely to be most difficult, if not impossible, to achieve in community. Taylor characterizes the concept (loosely) as requiring that autonomous individuals be rational and have preferences that are, in some sense, *theirs* (pp. 160–165).

Further still, the fact that actual communities characteristically involve pronounced inequality between the sexes should make us pause. In traditional community, as Taylor notes, the practice of exchanging women plays a significant role in the preservation of social order.[46] Other forms of sexual differentiation may be equally important, though this is a matter of controversy among anthropologists and other students of community.

It is doubtful that genuine communal life, as Taylor accurately describes it, is attractive to all or even most people today. Consider the case of Israeli kibbutzim. They must be among the most successful and attractive communities in the modern world. They have existed for a considerable length of time, at least by the standards of community longevity in the modern world. They are highly productive. Further, kibbutzim are highly respected by Israelis, so they do not suffer from the standard problems caused by a hostile environment. Yet only a very small percentage of the greater population chooses to move to or remain on a kibbutz. Given the choice, most people prefer other ways of life.[47] Setting out these facts is not intended as a condemnation of kibbutzes or similar voluntary communities, which are for the most part worthy and admirable enterprises. My point is solely that very few of us consider their attractive features to be sufficient to give up the advantages of modern civil society. This fact about our preferences and our options is made all the more striking when we recall that kibbutzes are not fully genuine communities in Taylor's sense as they exist only under the protection of a modern state.[48]

Existing communities have a problem holding on to their young members once they become aware of the advantages of other ways of life. This is an old problem, faced by many societies.[49] Knowledge of alternatives could be kept from individuals, which is what hap-

---

46. Taylor, *Community, Anarchy and Liberty*, pp. 69–71.
47. See Robert Nozick, "Who Would Choose Socialism?" *Reason* 10, 1 (May 1978), 22–23 (subtitled "The Israeli Kibbutzim Provide the Acid Test for Voluntary Socialism").
48. It is true that some of the present kibbutzim existed before the founding of the Israeli state and consequently existed at some point independently of the state. No one, however, can be particularly confident in their ability now to survive independently, given the hostility of neighboring peoples, although it is difficult to say what might have happened to these communities had the state of Israel never been founded. Presumably, if what I have to say later about "secondary state formation" processes is correct, other centralized forms of governance would have taken over British Palestine.
49. It may also be that some ways of life and "conceptions of the good life", to use contemporary jargon, are not stable in the face of multiple alternatives. Indeed, some

pens in most successful communities. That such an action would be unjust could be argued. That it is feasible, at least in the modern world, is dubious.

Without the economic and military protection of states, it is doubtful that communal life in Taylor's sense is feasible anymore. The case of Israeli kibbutzim is again illustrative. Part of the reason for the vulnerability of communities, especially in the modern world, is that states destroy many of the conditions for community, and the world today is largely one of states. But more importantly, the world today has too many people for social life to be organized communally. To be able to remain small, communities must be able to *fission* – that is, members must be able to break off and found another community. Population and space constraints today severely limit, if not make impossible, fissioning.[50]

Even *within* modern states, the opportunity for community is limited, and not simply by the hostility of the state. Today we interact with, and depend on, too many people, many more than could fit into any single community. Direct and many-sided relations are not generally possible with more than a small number of persons, and that number may be smaller in modern civil society than in community, given the occupations and ways of life of people in the former. Mobility in our societies is too great for communal stability, and the advantages of such mobility are difficult to forgo. And pluralism in basic beliefs and values characteristic of modern civil society, while often exaggerated, is still too great to sustain community.

I have argued that, to most people, genuine community does not offer an attractive alternative to the state. This argument depends on our preferences, and I naturally cannot speak *a priori* about these. Our preferences aside, genuine community is not even a feasible option in the modern world. Alone in a world of states, communities cannot survive. The difficult problem of national or, rather, communal defense returns to plague the communitarian anarchist, although the problem here has as much to do with the economies of scale of defense

possibly fulfilling ways of life may depend on participants being ignorant of alternatives. Certainly, childhood can be like that. These reflections suggest limits to the sort of neutrality between conceptions of the good or ways of life currently the rage in American political theory.

50. "Proliferation of communities by fissioning is *possible*, of course, only so long as sufficiently productive land and other resources required for subsistence are available." Taylor, *Community, Anarchy and Liberty*, p. 136; see also pp. 58, 92, 135–136, 138–139, and the discussions and references in Chapter 2 of the present volume.

than with the publicness of the good. Most political societies or states, it would appear, have formed in response to pressures from other polities. This is the process of "secondary state formation", to use the language of anthropology.[51] Community, as Taylor describes it, may simply not be feasible in the modern world, as he in fact recognizes:

> Most state formations . . . owe their development at least in part to the direct or indirect influence of already formed states. If they are not actually subjugated, colonized or absorbed by other states, the reactions of these societies to the presence of states is likely to be the same as the reactions to external threats of the societies which gave birth to the primary [or first] states. That this reaction should have been so common is little to be wondered at; but insofar as any lessons for the future can be drawn from this account of how anarchic communities first gave way to (primary or secondary) states, we can say that it inspires little optimism about the viability of anarchy in a crowded world and even less optimism about the prospects for the emergence and durability of an anarchy set in a sea of states.[52]

Taylor's acknowledged pessimism – in my view, fully justified – concerning the feasibility of community in the modern world is tempered by his defense of "partial community" in the epilogue of his book.[53] My criticisms of community do not entirely apply to partial community, nor are they meant to. One of the attractive features of some modern states may be the possibility and security of partial community, not available elsewhere in the modern world. And my purpose in examining Taylor's case for full community was not to suggest that none of its features are desirable but to argue that they are not available to us today, even in part, outside of our system of states.

3.4 GAME THEORY

The problem of the efficient provision of public or collective goods figures importantly in contemporary accounts of the state. It would

---

51. Taylor, *Community, Anarchy and Liberty*, pp. 129–139. Joseph Strayer notes, "Only the most remote and primitive peoples can do without the state. As soon as the modern world touches an area, the inhabitants must either form a state or take refuge in the shadow of an already existing one." *On the Medieval Origins of the Modern State*, p. 4.
52. Taylor, *Community, Anarchy and Liberty*, p. 139. Taylor's study is admirable for many reasons, not the least being its intellectual honesty.
53. Ibid., pp. 169–171. The notion of "partial community" here covers "a wide variety of cooperatives, collectives, neighborhood associations and other practices and projects of direct action, mutual aid and self-management."

be helpful, then, to say a little more about the problem and to discuss some of the relevant contributions of game theory. Taylor and others rely on some of these game-theoretic results, and they may have relevance to other topics I take up in this book.

The problem with the efficient production of collective goods can be explained easily, though its exact analysis is controversial. The general claim is that, typically, where people's enjoyment of goods does not depend on their contribution to the goods' costs of production, collective goods will be inefficiently provided. These are goods whose defining characteristics are *indivisibility* (or *jointness of supply*) and *nonexcludability*. As I said, once produced, they are available to everyone at no additional cost (indivisibility), and it is not feasible or efficient to exclude individuals from the benefits (nonexcludability). Given their availability to all whenever produced, each individual has an incentive not to contribute to the costs of production whenever this will not diminish his or her benefits from the goods. The provision of collective goods gives rise to a *collective action problem*.

Characterizing collective action problems is more controversial than characterizing public or collective goods. There are several attributes that have been claimed to be essential of such goods, as I mentioned earlier. I make indivisibility essential; something is a public or collective good to the extent that it is indivisible.[54] This characterization makes being a collective good a matter of degree. Its polar opposite would then be a *pure private good*, one that cannot be made available without cost to an additional person. Indivisibility is only part of the story, though. Insofar as an indivisible good is also nonexcludable, providing it efficiently poses a problem.

An early and influential analysis is offered by Mancur Olson in *The Logic of Collective Action*.[55] Let C be the total costs of producing some collective good, V_i the gross benefits to individual i, and B_i the net benefits to i from i's contribution to the production of the good ($B_i = V_i - C$). Should $B_i > 0$, or $V_i > C$, then i should find it rational individually to produce the good (disregarding strategic considerations). Thus we might explain, for instance, why individuals plant flowers

---

54. Unlike some theorists, I do not distinguish between public and collective goods. I prefer the term 'collective' as it seems to have fewer connotations that may be prejudicial to my topics (e.g., "the public interest", "the public sphere", "a public matter", "public policy", "publicly known", "in the public domain").
55. Olson, *The Logic of Collective Action: Public Goods and the Theory of Groups* (Cambridge, Mass.: Harvard University Press, 1971 [1965]), chap. 1.

in their front yards even though these provide uncompensated "spillover" benefits to others. However, should $B_i < 0$, or should $V_i < C$, as normally would be the case with significant collective goods like defense or clean air, it is then not rational for persons to produce the good individually, and we have a collective action problem. There is a temptation to be a *free rider*.[56]

One need not assume that people are self-interested and care only about themselves in order for there to be a problem with collective goods. And one need not assume a particularly controversial account of practical rationality either. The standard "economic" analysis of the problem does assume that individuals are rational in a utility-maximizing sense, leaving it fairly open that over which their preferences range.[57] As I go along, I shall signal when assumptions about rationality are likely to be controversial.

Collective action problems involve *coordinating* the actions of many agents in order to bring about outcomes that are beneficial to all of them or to avoid outcomes that are disadvantageous. There is a problem when bringing about an outcome efficiently depends on the actions of many of the people who will benefit from it. There may be coordination problems of many sorts, especially when many people are involved, time is short, and the like. With collective action problems individuals also have certain *incentives* not to coordinate or, rather, not to contribute to bringing about the outcome, and this is because the benefits they derive are not contingent on their contribution.[58]

Game-theoretic analyses of common collective action problems can be illuminating, and they have in the last few decades become commonplace in works of political philosophy. A standard game-theoretic analysis of the collective goods problem is to regard it as a multiparty or n-person Prisoners' Dilemma (PD). The analysis may be quite helpful, even if only to clarify some of the important notions involved in our understanding of these issues. But it may be mis-

---

56. I characterize free-ridership more precisely below.
57. One need not assume even that. Also, as I note later, some recent game-theorists relax the rationality assumption and assume some "irrationality" (though invariably with skeptical double quotes).
58. Some theorists characterize collective action problems in terms of the individual rationality of not contributing. But this seems to beg the question. Such a move may seem less problematic if rationality is understood as (expected) utility maximization, but even this begs certain questions against nonorthodox accounts of this conception of rationality. I shall come back to these issues.

leading as well. So, even if the basic tale is well known, it may be important to look carefully at certain features of the account.[59]

For simplicity, consider first the 2-person PD. A 2-person PD is a particular situation that arises with two individuals, each of whom is confronted with a choice between two actions (or strategies), labeled C and D, yielding four possible outcomes. In order of preference these are: (1) I choose D, the other chooses C; (2) we both choose C; (3) we both choose D; and (4) I choose C, the other chooses D. While both rank "joint cooperation" (C,C) above "joint defection" (D,D), each most prefers the outcome where he or she chooses D and the other chooses C. The dilemma may be illustrated by a simple 2 × 2 matrix:

Matrix 3.1

Beatrice

		C	D
Albert	C	3,3	1,4
	D	4,1	2,2

The numbers in the boxes represent the ordinal preferences of the two "players", Albert and Beatrice, respectively ($4 > 1$).

An outcome is in *equilibrium* (in the Nash sense) if and only if no one can do better given the *actions* (or strategies) of the others. An outcome is "optimal" or efficient in the Pareto sense if and only if no one can do better without someone doing worse. The PD is unusual in that whatever the other person does, choosing D is individually best; D *dominates* C. The collective action problem here is that the outcome of what seems to be individually rational choice, (D,D), is Pareto-inefficient, but the mutually preferred, Pareto-superior outcome (C,C) is unstable.

To generalize the 2-person PD to situations with many parties, consider a group of n individuals and suppose that the choice facing each individual is whether to contribute his or her share of the costs of producing some collective good with a ratio r of benefits to costs. Let the individual cost be 1. If n contribute, the benefit to i is $r - 1$, and if 0 contribute, the benefit to i is 0. Suppose that m contribute, where

---

59. I agree with Russell Hardin that the original tale which gives the "game" its name is unfortunate, especially insofar as it suggests that PDs are not commonplace (in one form or another). Ordinary exchange, for instance, has the structure of a PD. See Hardin, "Exchange Theory on Strategic Bases," *Social Science Information* 21, 2 (1982), 251–272.

$0 \leq m \leq n$. If m includes i, then the benefit to i is $(rm/n) - 1$. If $m - 1$ (i.e., i) contribute, then the benefit to i is $r(m - 1)/n$. Since $r(m - 1)/n > (rm/n - 1)$ by $(n - r)/n$, not contributing *dominates* contributing. This is the well-known argument of Russell Hardin showing that collective action problems with such structures are n-person PDs.[60]

Even if it oversimplifies, the PD is a useful device for understanding many, if not most, collective action problems. There is an outcome that is mutually preferred to another, but certain individual incentives need to be overcome if the second is not to occur. The PD also makes vivid a number of "solutions" that have been proposed for collective action problems. We might think of these as falling into two general categories of "internal" and "external" solutions.[61] The former take the structure of the game, including the payoffs, to remain fixed, while the latter involve various changes in people's preferences or beliefs (and expectations). External solutions in this sense would include the "selective incentives" favored by Olson in his classical analysis, the introduction of sanctions, and the like. These essentially alter the expected benefits from one's choice, effectively coordinating the different parties' actions so as to produce joint cooperation.[62] Internal solutions might include the introduction of *norms* that would have people cooperate in producing the desired goods. Norms in this sense are taken to be regularities in the behavior of individuals that act as standards for action.[63] Solutions involv-

---

60. Hardin, "Collective Action as an Agreeable n-Prisoners' Dilemma," *Behavioral Science* 16, 5 (September 1971), 472–481, and *Collective Action* (Baltimore: Johns Hopkins University Press, 1982), pp. 22–28. The result is obtained by assuming that r is a constant. Where r is not a constant, for instance, with "step" goods (see below), the dominance argument will not go through. It would be a mistake, then, to think that all collective action problems *are* PDs. In many collective action problems, there is no dominant strategy, thus no PD, as we shall see.
61. Taylor also uses the label "spontaneous" for internal solutions. *The Possibility of Cooperation*, pp. 21–24.
62. Olson's "selective incentives" include the introduction of sanctions. Their distinguishing feature is that they are "selective" accruing to persons depending on their individual choices, unlike the benefits of collective goods which accrue indiscriminately. See *The Logic of Collective Action*, esp. p. 51. Critical analyses of Olson's theory, especially his prediction that large groups are less likely to succeed in producing collective goods, are offered in Hardin, *Collective Action*, chaps. 2–3, and Todd Sandler, *Collective Action* (Ann Arbor: University of Michigan Press, 1992). The imposition of sanctions by an outside agent has been called the "Hobbesian" or the "liberal" solution to such problems after similarly named justifications of the state.
63. See Edna Ullmann-Margalit, *The Emergence of Norms* (Oxford: Clarendon Press, 1977), a work commonly associated with this solution (although it provides no account of how norms "emerge" or why individuals have reasons to follow them, qua norms). Note, however, that Ullmann-Margalit seems to assume that norms

ing norms may also include accounts of rational choice that would have rational agents make dominated or counterpreferential choices under certain conditions.[64] It is not clear, however, how useful the distinction between internal and external solutions is in the end, as some of the technical approaches I mentioned earlier in this chapter and which I shall discuss presently cannot easily be classified.

One needs, of course, to be very cautious with simple PDs and other "models" of interactive situations. Those familiar with rational choice theory and economics know not to read into the payoff numbers information that is not present. For instance, (C,C) is not to be regarded as a fair solution because all parties benefit equally (no information is provided allowing such comparisons). A 2-person game is also much simpler than an n-person one, even when n is not very large, as we shall see. And the 2 × 2 structure of the usual PDs and similar games can mislead as well. It is an artifact of limiting the agents' choices to two, which facilitates understanding but may induce some complacency. PDs can have multiple mutually beneficial cooperative outcomes, as in the "divisible PD", illustrated by the following matrix.[65]

Matrix 3.2

Beatrice

		C_1	C_2	D
	C_1	4,3	2,2	1,5
Albert	C_2	2,2	3,4	1,5
	D	5,1	5,1	2,2

are to be enforced by sanctions (pp. 22, 38). See also Elster, *The Cement of Society*, chaps. 3, 5–6. Moral norms can, of course, function to facilitate cooperation in the production of collective goods. So moral theories with plausible accounts of the rationality of moral behavior could explain how such goods could sometimes be produced.

64. I consider unorthodox and revisionist accounts of this sort in Section 5.4.
65. The divisible PD is a complex game with a bargaining problem embedded in it. See Jules L. Coleman, Douglas D. Heckathorn, and Steven M. Maser, "A Bargaining Theory Approach to Default Provisions and Disclosure Rules in Contract Law," *Harvard Journal of Law and Public Policy* 12, 3 (Summer 1989), p. 654, and Coleman, *Risks and Wrongs* (Cambridge: Cambridge University Press, 1992), pp. 106–108.

Here and elsewhere, 'cooperative' and 'noncooperative' are used to designate strategies and outcomes (or strategies pairs) in games (e.g., C,C in the PD); the terms are not used in these contexts to designate different parts of game theory.

The two cooperative outcomes (C_1,C_1) and (C_2,C_2) are Pareto-efficient (and unstable). The problem here, unlike the simple PD, is to coordinate on one of them (which is why this game is useful to represent simple bargaining problems).

Whatever the pedagogical merits of PDs, one should not assume that the collective action problem involved in the production of basic security and other collective goods is always an n-person PD. There are varieties of collective goods. Some are "incremental", like national defense or clean air: The difference between more and less of the good is a matter of degree. Other collective goods, however, are "lumpy" and come in large increments – for instance, the construction of a bridge, the election of a favored candidate, the maintenance of a truce or a ceasefire. These are "step goods".[66] In general, collective goods that are of little or no value below a certain threshold of provision (e.g., a bridge that spans 90% of the river) will be step goods.

The logic of the collective action problem faced by individuals seeking to produce a step good is different from that of a PD.[67] In the latter case, there is a dominant strategy for each agent, namely D. The standard 2-person matrix reveals this at a glance (Matrix 3.1). The ease of displaying two-dimensional matrices often tempts people to illustrate the n-person case as follows, substituting 'Others' and 'Self' respectively for our friends 'Beatrice' and 'Albert':

Matrix 3.3

Others

		C	D
Self	C	3,3	1,4
	D	4,1	2,2

Either "the others" will choose C or they won't. If they do, I am better off choosing D; if they don't, I am better off choosing D. Therefore, I should choose D whatever the others do.

Suppose, however, that $(k - 1)$ "others" choose C, where k is the number of cooperators (choosers of C) necessary for the production

---

66. Hardin, *Collective Action*, pp. 55–61.
67. See Jean Hampton, "Free-Rider Problems in the Production of Collective Goods," *Economics and Philosophy* 3 (October 1987), 245–273. See also Taylor, *The Possibility of Cooperation*, chap. 2.

of the first "step" of the collective good (CG). I may illustrate this with the following graph:

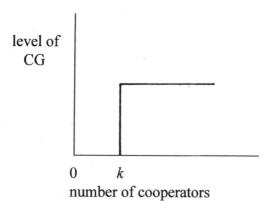

level of
CG

0   *k*

number of cooperators

Figure 3.1

If only ($k - 1$) individuals cooperate, the step good will not be produced (e.g., 90% of a bridge is not a bridge). If k choose C, the (first step of the) good will be produced. Suppose that one knows that ($k - 1$) individuals will choose C. Then it may be rational to choose C if $V_i > C_i$, where C_i is i's share of the costs of the collective good. If this is the case, it is not rational for all individuals to choose D whatever the others do. This is to say that not all individuals have dominant strategies, which entails that the collective action facing individuals seeking to produce a step good is not strictly an n-person PD.[68]

What is the logical structure of a step good collective action problem? Consider a collective action problem concerning the production of a collective step good (e.g., clearing a swamp),[69] where $n = 3$ and $k = 2$. We may represent their (ordinal) preference rankings as shown in the accompanying table, where Albert's preferences are listed first, Beatrice's second, and Carl's third.

68. When n is very large (e.g., large elections), step goods collective action problems will be like n-person PDs. See Kavka's discussion of "quasi PDs" in *Hobbesian Moral and Political Theory*, pp. 113–115.
69. This well-known example is Hume's and often is analyzed as an n-person PD. See Hume, *A Treatise of Human Nature*, 2nd ed., ed. P. H. Nidditch (Oxford: Clarendon Press, 1978 [1739–1740]), Book III, sec. 7, p. 538.

Number of Cooperators	Outcomes	Preferences
3 C:	(C,C,C)	4,4,4
2 C:	(C,C,D)	3,3,5
	(C,D,C)	3,5,3
	(D,C,C)	5,3,3
1 C:	(C,D,D)	1,2,2
	(D,C,D)	2,1,2
	(D,D,C)	2,2,1
0 C:	(D,D,D)	2,2,2

This gives us the following 2 × 3 matrix:

Matrix 3.4

Carl

	C		D	
	Beatrice		Beatrice	
	C	D	C	D
Albert C	4,4,4	3,5,3	3,3,5	1,2,2
Albert D	5,3,3	2,2,1	2,1,2	2,2,2

It is easy to show that Albert, Beatrice, and Carl do *not* face a 3-person PD. Consider Albert's reasoning. Suppose that Beatrice and Carl both choose D; in that case he should choose D (2 > 1). Suppose that Beatrice and Carl both choose C; again, he should choose D (5 > 4). However, suppose that either (but not both) Beatrice or Carl chooses C, he then should choose C (3 > 2). Albert has no dominant strategy. Hence the situation Albert and the others face is *not* a PD.

Supposing that Carl has chosen C, the problem then confronting Albert, and Beatrice, and Carl is a game of Chicken, the matrix for which is the following:

Matrix 3.5

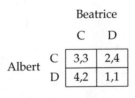

Beatrice

		C	D
Albert	C	3,3	2,4
	D	4,2	1,1

Two outcomes are both stable and Pareto-efficient: (D, C) and (C, D).[70] Similarly with step goods, as with the divisible PD, several outcomes will be Pareto-efficient. The problem is to decide which to realize.

The question for us is whether social order, or at least basic security of person and possessions, is a step good. Were it to be, then the anarchist might argue that individuals might be able to provide themselves with social order in the absence of a state. But surely it is not a step good. Deterrence – the nonexcludable, indivisible element of social order – is provided by degrees, just as clean air or general civility may be. Of course, for these and many other collective goods, there may be threshold effects. Below a certain level the value of the various increments is worth very little. Hence we may have goods whose graphs look like that in Figure 3.2.

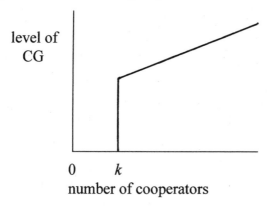

level of
CG

0   *k*
number of cooperators

Figure 3.2

Below *k* no collective good is produced. Above *k* the collective good is produced in continuous increments. In this case the collective action problem remains.

It might be argued that even if social order is a continuous, nonincremental good, it can be made into a step good. Indeed, this turns out essentially to be the trick to many analyses. To cooperate conditionally on the cooperation of a given number of others essentially is to make collective action itself into a step good. Consider one way this might be done with the provision of social order. Protective associations or agencies might announce that they will offer services to communities only if a certain number (*k*) of individuals subscribe. If

70. I am not considering equilibria of "mixed" strategies here.

fewer than k sign up, no services will be provided (and fees already paid will be refunded).[71]

It would be useful to distinguish two parts of a standard collective action problem: assurance and free-rider problems. Consider the two principal reasons not to contribute to the production of some (genuine) collective good: First, one is uncertain of the contribution of others; second, one wishes to benefit from the good without contributing to the costs of production. If the problem is thought of as a 2-person PD, the first reason is a concern to avoid one's worst outcome; the second, a concern to achieve one's best outcome. David Schmidtz labels an *assurance problem* as one that is caused by the first concern, the worry created by uncertainty regarding the contributions of others. A *free-rider problem*, by contrast, is one caused by the other reason, the wish to benefit from the collective good without paying one's share of the costs. This specification departs from the most common understandings of 'free-rider problem', but it is useful.[72]

Schmidtz proposes handling assurances problems by what he calls "assurance contracts". Potential beneficiaries of a collective good pledge support to a project to produce that good. But the pledge will be enforceable if and only if a certain level of support is reached within a certain time; otherwise, the contributions pledged are not collected. "The purpose of the contract is to give each party an assurance that his contribution will not be wasted on a public goods project that is financially undersupported."[73]

Schmidtz recognizes that his proposed resolution of the assurance problem does not resolve the overall problem of the production of collective goods. When the free-rider problem is not resolved, contributing may not even be a weakly dominant strategy.[74] Further, assurance contracts cannot generally be expected to produce collec-

---

71. See Hampton, "Free-Rider Problems in the Production of Collective Goods," pp. 271–272, and Schmidtz, *The Limits of Government*, chaps. 4 and 5.
72. Schmidtz, *The Limits of Government*, p. 56. The classic analysis of the assurance problem is found in Amartya K. Sen, "Isolation, Assurance, and the Social Rate of Discount," in *Resources, Values and Development* (Oxford: Basil Blackwell, 1984 [1967]), pp. 135–146. It is common to lump both assurance and free-rider problems (in our sense) under the latter label. I should note that economists often think of the "free-rider problem" as the rather different and essentially epistemic problem of having people reveal honestly their valuation of collective goods. This problem is solved by devising the requisite demand-revelation mechanisms.
73. Schmidtz, *The Limits of Government*, p. 66.
74. Ibid., p. 68. Schmidtz suggests some ways around this problem – for instance, assurance contracts requiring unanimity – but he does not present these as practical solutions to real collective goods problems. It is important to remember that his

tive goods efficiently.[75] Further, his proposal makes collective goods production parasitic on practices required for contractual arrangements. He argues that the latter need not be coercive and that they may emerge from the voluntary interactions of individuals. But we may remain unconvinced.[76] Last, this sort of resolution to collective goods problems is not feasible in large, impersonal societies, as I shall argue.[77]

A general worry about strategies such as Schmidtz's, as I have noted, is that the good produced may still be Pareto-inefficient. The increment provided by the conditional cooperation of k members may still be rather small, and many free riders may still remain. I do not want to overemphasize this problem, as states and other forms of political organization may, in practice, also be relatively inefficient in providing social order. More important are the strategic (and bargaining) problems associated with the transformation of continuous goods into step goods. Granted that defection dominates cooperation in n-person PDs (except under special conditions), cooperation does not dominate defection in Chicken or Battle of the Sexes games or in other bargaining problems. These situations are structurally indeterminate.[78] That is, the rationality of a particular act (or strategy) depends on a variety of contextual features of the game – for example, salience of different outcomes, bargaining power and ability, coalition formation, dispersal of information. In actual situations,

---

aim is not so much to defend anarchy as a feasible alternative to government as it is to defeat a particular and influential line of justification for the government.

75. As Schmidtz, in effect, recognizes (*The Limits of Government*, p. 68).

76. Schmidtz, *The Limits of Government*, chap. 5, argues that contract enforcement need be neither coercive nor a public good, as its benefits can be limited to particular parties. Subscription to the services of contract enforcement agencies need not be coercive if payment is voluntary. But the enforcement presumably is coercive no matter who produces it or whether it is consensual.

Schmidtz also argues that "reputation" effects may enable individuals to establish contractual practices, citing recent literature in support of his claim. I refer to this literature in footnote 96 to this chapter and express some skepticism, at least that it has much to do with what we ordinarily mean by reputation.

77. Schmidtz "admit[s] that if a society is too large or too impersonal to permit the development of reputations, premarket market failure may have no solution. But then, that very supposition suggests that the community would not remain so large and impersonal. The scope of people's interactions initially would contract to a point where people dealt only with people they could trust, perhaps in the end only with familiar faces. . . . Hence, one way or another, market forces would resolve premarket failure." *The Limits of Government*, p. 100. Note that this approach would condemn not only GATT and NAFTA, but virtually all present state-size economies.

78. Unless, of course, mixed strategies are used, in which case sets of mixed strategies may be in equilibrium, although *ex post* outcomes may not.

involving large numbers, the equilibria attained may be very inefficient. Chicken games can be particularly vicious.[79]

The game-theoretic analyses most supportive of anarchist social order involve dynamic contexts where agents interact repeatedly one with another. The analyses I have been discussing are implicitly *single-play*. In a single-play PD, where all parties choose simultaneously, D ("defection") is the dominant strategy, and most rational choice theorists think it rational. If the game is repeated, however, then under certain conditions it is rational to cooperate. Results from repeated games are now often invoked by partisans of anarchist social order, as seen in the following look at some of this literature.

In their classic text, *Games and Decisions*, R. Duncan Luce and Howard Raiffa argued that it could be rational for two players to cooperate in a series of repeated PDs but that the cooperative outcome was "a sort of quasi-equilibrium" and rather unstable. For were the series of PDs of finite length and were this known to the players, the noncooperative outcome would be the equilibrium outcome. The argument is simple. A repeated or iterated PD is a series of PDs. Suppose that the series is finite in length and that the players know when it will end. Then it is rational for each to choose D whatever the other chooses. Let the series be of duration d. Then it is rational for each to defect on $(d - 1)$nth play, given that each expects the other to defect on the last play. Anticipating this, it is rational for each to defect on the $(d - 2)$nth play. And so on. The reasoning seemed without flaw to Luce and Raiffa, yet the recommendation of game theory did not strike them as entirely "reasonable".[80]

Suppose instead that the series is infinite or, more realistically, of "indefinite" or unknown length. Suppose as well that agents *discount* future payoffs to some degree; the worth to them of a benefit in the future is less than its worth today. The outcome (or strategy set) where all choose D will still be in equilibrium (for any discount rate). But a variety of cooperative outcomes will also be sustainable. If

79. Especially when agents are able to commit (or "precommit") themselves to certain strategies. Peter Danielson, in his study of the rationality of moral cooperation, notes, "While the PD is a deep and difficult problem, it turns out to be especially favourable to a moral solution by means of communication, commitment and an opportunistic minimal morality." It is another matter with games like Chicken, where aggression and threatening behavior can pay. Peter Danielson, *Artificial Morality: Virtuous Robots for Virtual Games* (London and New York: Routledge, 1992), p. 163.
80. R. Duncan Luce and Howard Raiffa, *Games and Decisions* (New York: Wiley, 1957), pp. 97–102.

players adopt any of a number of conditional strategies – sequences of strategies for the individual games – cooperation may be expected.

Agents may adopt the strategy Tit for Tat, which would have them choose C in the first round of a 2-person PD and then in the second match whatever the other player did in the first. Agents who choose D are in this way "punished" on the next round. This strategy was popularized in Robert Axelrod's famous computer simulations or tournaments. Inviting game theorists to submit strategies for a computer-run series of PDs, where players (or programs) would be paired off randomly and scored, Tit for Tat, submitted by Anatol Rapoport, outperformed all the other strategies.[81]

In a footnote Axelrod expresses the hope that "it is possible that the results from pairwise interactions [in iterated PDs] will help suggest how to undertake a deeper analysis of the n-person case as well".[82] A variety of other results are involved in attempts to do just that. Michael Taylor's defense of communitarian anarchy, already discussed, alludes to his earlier work on repeated games.[83] There he considers a generalization of T for an n-person PD, T_m: choose C in the first game, and thereafter choose C if and only if at least m other players chose C in the preceding game (where $n \geq m > 0$). Then cooperation can be rational for all or merely some players under certain conditions.[84] Two general conclusions may be drawn: (1) Universal conditional cooperation $(T_m, T_{m'} \ldots, T_m)$ is stable when each player's cooperation is conditional on that of *all* of the other players and discount rates are not too high, and (2) universal conditional coopera-

81. Robert Axelrod, *The Evolution of Cooperation* (New York: Basic Books, 1984). Tit for Tat (T) is also *evolutionarily stable* in the sense that a group of individuals using T within a larger group will continue to use T and the others will convert to T if they wish to do better. Although Axelrod's studies do not enable us to say that any strategy is "best", we do learn that the best strategies are "nice" (it does not choose D first), "forgiving" (it does not punish very long), and simple. It should be noted that payoffs in the study were symmetrical and constant for the series.

82. Ibid., p. 216. In a later footnote (p. 221), Axelrod cites work by Robyn Dawes showing that "the n-person case is qualitatively different from the two-person case in three ways. First, the harm caused by a defection is diffused over many players rather than focused on one. Second, behavior may be anonymous in n-person games. Third, each player does not have total reinforcement control over all the other players since the payoffs are determined by what many different players are doing." See also Hardin, "Individual Sanctions, Collective Benefits," in *Paradoxes of Rationality and Cooperation*, ed. R. Campbell and L. Sowden (Vancouver: University of British Columbia Press, 1985), pp. 339–354.

83. *The Possibility of Cooperation*, a revised edition of *Anarchy and Cooperation* (London: Wiley, 1976).

84. See Taylor, *The Possibility of Cooperation*, pp. 85–88.

tion among a proper subset S of the whole is stable provided some of the members of S cooperate conditionally on the cooperation of all of the members of S. Taylor concludes tentatively that "it has been shown that *under certain conditions* the Cooperation of some or all of the players *could* emerge in the supergame *no matter how many players there are.* The question arises, whether these conditions are likely to be met in practice."[85] The crucial conditions are that the group be small, that it be possible to monitor individual defection, and that the benefits of defection in an ordinary game be small relative to the (discounted) benefits of future cooperation.

The logic of the overall argument is quite simple. Let k be the minimum number of individuals who choose to cooperate such that the benefits from mutual cooperation are worth the costs. (1) Suppose that $k = n$. Then it is worth cooperating if and only if all of the other players cooperate. (2) Suppose that $k < n$. Consider first (a) the case where $(j - 1) = k$, where j is the number of players choosing C. This is the case where one additional player is needed in order to make cooperation worthwhile. It then may be worthwhile to cooperate, depending on certain strategic considerations. (b) If, on the other hand, $(j - 1) > k$ or $(j - 1) < k$, there are either too many or too few cooperators to make it worthwhile to choose C. Taylor's argument that mutual cooperation can be stable in n-person iterated PDs, given the above conditions, is roughly this: If the defection of a single individual makes the others worse cooperating than if all defected, then mutual cooperation can be stable. This case is effectively that of a step good. If some can defect, leaving the remaining cooperators in a position where they are still better off continuing to cooperate than defecting, then the set of cooperators is quickly reduced to the minimum number. In effect, the group of cooperators shrinks until it reaches the point at which unanimous cooperation is necessary for the production of the good.

We can now appreciate the importance of Taylor's initial conditions. Suppose that payoffs to players are not symmetrical. Then it is possible that there is no *particular* size for the residual group. Suppose that the discount rates of players are not identical. Then decisions to defect will be reached at different times. Suppose in general that the defection process is not orderly. Then the minimum number

85. Ibid., p. 104.

of cooperators necessary for production of the good may be overshot and the good not produced at all.[86] Even supposing that none of these conditions holds, we can expect only a minimum amount of the collective good in question to be produced voluntarily, and no more.

It is important that these series of PDs be infinite in length or, if finite, of indefinite length. Finite but indefinite series are probably to be preferred for representing the interactions of mortal beings. But there can be significant differences between them and infinite series. Recall Luce and Raiffa's original argument that there are only unco-operative equilibrium outcomes in iterated PDs of known duration. Gregory Kavka has suggested that, in some interesting cases, it may not matter if the series is of indefinite length if it is known that there is a specific and definite number of plays. In such a case it may be that only uncooperative equilibria exist.[87] There is a theorem owed to John Carroll that in finitely, but indefinitely, iterated PDs (or bounded iterated PDs) only uncooperative equilibria exist.[88] Carroll associates with every iterated game a particular function, $p(t)$, which is to represent the probability that a particular game t is the last. Minimally informed rational agents will be certain, for instance, they will die, so it does not seem realistic to represent their expected payoffs in repeated PDs as an infinite sum of discounted winnings.

The results of Taylor, Axelrod, and others for PDs are instances of a more general "folk theorem", so called because of its unwritten and obscure origins.[89] There are now many different versions, with different proofs. The basic theorem says roughly that any number of cooperative outcomes may be sustained by various combinations of strategies in infinite or indefinite series of games (not just PDs). There are, then, many cooperative outcomes (or sets of strategies) that are Nash equilibria in such games. To state the basic theorem more pre-

---

86. See Michael Laver, *The Politics of Private Desires* (Harmondsworth: Penguin, 1981), pp. 54–56. Laver also notes that Taylor's solution does not work with certain kinds of collective goods: namely, those requiring large-scale capital investment, where a commitment of a future flow of resources is required.
87. See Kavka, "Hobbes's War of All against All," *Ethics* 93, 2 (January 1983), 302, and *Hobbesian Moral and Political Theory*, pp. 130–131.
88. See John Carroll, "Indefinite Terminating Points and the Iterated Prisoner's Dilemma," *Theory and Decision* 22 (1987), 247–256, and "Iterated N-Player Prisoner's Dilemma Games," *Philosophical Studies* 53 (1988), 411–415.
89. It appears to date back to the late 1950s. See Robert J. Aumann, "Game Theory," in *Game Theory, The New Palgrave: A Dictionary of Economics*, ed. J. Eatwell, M. Milgate, and P. Newman (New York and London: Norton, 1989 [1987]), p. 20.

cisely, we need to find the *minimax point* for a game, the set of payoffs for each agent that are the lowest for each that the other(s) could impose (in retaliation for uncooperative action). Consider, then, the set of feasible outcomes are Pareto-superior to the minimax point. The theorem says that any of these can occur as the result of a Nash equilibrium of individual strategies in an infinite or indefinite game, provided discounting of the future is not too great.[90]

For most of the folk theorems, cooperation depends on players sanctioning or ostracizing defectors. Other versions introduce some uncertainty, for instance, about the payoffs or rationality of others. It is hard to know what to conclude about cooperation between humans from this recent literature. The sanctioning strategies required to sustain cooperation can be very complex, and they can unravel quickly if enough agents do not carry through on threats to punish. It may often be worthwhile for a subset of agents to "renegotiate" rather than carry through a set of conditional strategies.[91] The credibility of threats is one problem.[92] In addition, the agents, especially if numerous, may not know what strategies others are using and therefore may not be able to coordinate sanctioning behavior. For instance, some may be using Tit for Tat while others play the "Grim Trigger" strategy, which would have one choose D *forever* in response to D. Given that both strategies are behaviorally indistinguishable in the first game after a defection, it is unclear how agents are to know which is being played.[93] The equilibrium outcome may end up being uncooperative and inefficient.

The folk theorems reveal that the number of cooperative outcomes that can be sustained by sets of suitable strategies can be very large. Normatively, the theorems do not decide much. Descriptively, the multiplicity of cooperative equilibria threatens to make the theory of repeated games useless for explanatory purposes. If virtually any

90. Accessible accounts of the folk theorem may be found in Shaun P. Hargreaves Heap and Yanis Varoufakis, *Game Theory: A Critical Introduction* (London and New York: Routledge, 1995), chap. 6, and James D. Morrow, *Game Theory for Political Scientists* (Princeton: Princeton University Press, 1994), chap. 9. A more difficult account and survey is in Drew Fudenberg and Jean Tirole, *Game Theory* (Cambridge, Mass.: MIT Press, 1992), chap. 5.

91. Morrow, *Game Theory for Political Scientists*, pp. 268, 278–279, 291. The literature on renegotiation is complicated; see Fudenberg and Tirole, *Game Theory*, pp. 174–182.

92. The credibility of commitments generally is problematic for the received conception of practical rationality, which is future-oriented and does not easily allow for backward-looking considerations like intentions, threats, promises. I return to some of the issues about rationality in Section 5.4.

93. Morrow, *Game Theory for Political Scientists*, pp. 267–268.

arrangement can be sustained by some set of strategies, then one cannot explain how a particular arrangement came about without reference to various contingent features of the historical or cultural context in question.[94] From the structure of a repeated game alone nothing guarantees a particular outcome, much less a cooperative one.[95]

It is not clear what conclusions about anarchist social order should be drawn from contemporary game theory. Certainly, Taylor and others are right in thinking that game theoretic models show Hobbists wrong in thinking social order in anarchy *impossible*. And there may be reason to believe that governments often provide less assistance to cooperation than might have been thought. But beyond that, it is unclear if anarchists can draw much comfort. Game-theoretic models show how cooperation in repeated games is possible but also how it can quickly unravel, especially in the presence of uncertainty.[96] In addition, the experimental literature does not always support the initial predictions of game theorists; there is often much more cooperation in experimental situations than might be predicted.[97] To know whether it is safe to dismantle our states, it might

94. See John Ferejohn, "Rationality and Interpretation: Parliamentary Elections in Early Stuart England," in *Economic Approaches to Politics*, ed. K. Monroe (New York: HarperCollins, 1991), esp. pp. 283–285.

Note as well an analogous problem with normative contractarian theory: Virtually any arrangement can be shown to be mutually advantageous and the object of a hypothetical "social contract" from *some* prior baseline. In the absence of some way of determining the appropriate baseline, contractarian theory is indeterminate in its normative implications.

95. In fact, "there is still no guarantee that a Nash equilibrium will surface even if it exists and it is unique." Hargreaves Heap and Varoufakis, *Game Theory*, pp. 192–194.

96. I have not discussed the recent literature that shows how cooperation can be sustained if there is some small uncertainty about the payoffs or even the rationality of others. For instance, if agents believe there is a possibility that others might not be rational, it may pay to cooperate, even in a finite series, if only to lead others to believe one is not rational. The literature is thought by many to show the importance of "reputation" in certain contexts. The interpretations many give, however, are problematic, evidenced perhaps by the liberal use of double quotes around key terms (e.g., "reputation", "irrationality"). For a very accessible introduction by one of the pioneers of this literature, see David M. Kreps, *Game Theory and Economic Modelling* (Oxford: Clarendon Press, 1990), esp. pp. 65–90. For some of my concerns, see Morris, "What Is This Thing Called 'Reputation'?" *Business Ethics Quarterly*, special issue on "Game Theory and Business Ethics" (in press).

97. Here, too, the literature is now vast. See Hargreaves Heap and Varoufakis, *Game Theory*, chap. 8. See also Robert H. Frank, Thomas Gilovich, and Dennis T. Regan, "Does Studying Economics Inhibit Cooperation?" *Journal of Economic Perspectives* 7, 2 (Spring 1993), 159–171.

be prudent to supplement the formal models of game theory with some history and common sense.

3.5 HISTORY OF THE WORLD

The case for anarchist social order in the modern world, though not without merit, is implausible. Some libertarian anarchists concede that stateless social order is not likely to succeed in the absence of general respect for individual rights.[98] Few societies, presumably, can function or even survive if most people do not respect the most basic social conventions. But few societies have as their most basic conventions the particular norms that individualist libertarians prescribe (or, for that matter, that egalitarian anarchism requires). Even if one can normally count on most people behaving decently most of the time, some can be expected not to do so, and they cannot always be easily identified in advance. In a crowded world, where single individuals can blow up buildings and kill several hundred people with relative ease, or where groups can massacre hundreds of thousands using only machetes, it is hard to be very confident about anarchist social order.

Anarchists might urge that we try anarchy and put our skepticism to the test. But stateless social order in different forms has been tried. In my sense there were no states in premodern times, and government in medieval Europe was not typically strong or centralized. The result of this "experiment" was the birth of sovereign states and their displacement of all other forms of political organization in all areas of concentrated human settlement on the globe.[99] Most of the decentralized, noninstitutional forms of cooperation that we are familiar with take place in states. These are really experiments in *semi*anarchy. Kibbutzim are protected against hostile neighboring states and peoples by the Israeli army, and farmers in Shasta County can resolve some of their local disputes by themselves with little fear of losing

---

98. Friedman, *The Machinery of Freedom*, p. 123, and "Law as a Private Good," p. 326; Rothbard, *For a New Liberty*.
99. I should have said "virtually all", as Vatican City and the Principality of Monaco are not genuine states. (Even though Monaco is a member of the United Nations, its minister of state [prime minister] is picked from a slate of three candidates chosen by the president of France.) The *ideological* victory of the state is so great, as I have said, that most remnants of premodern forms of organization are now thought of as states.

their property to invaders from elsewhere.[100] States can provide assurance that the larger social framework will not unravel and thus facilitate semianarchy.

Anarchists may complain that Lebanon, Yugoslavia, Rwanda, or the South Bronx are not fair models for the likely failures of anarchy. For states contributed to the troubles of these societies. In a world without states, it may be claimed, collapse of social order on the scale visited on these countries would not be possible. I am not convinced by this reply. For one thing, the killings in Rwanda, at best a "quasi state",[101] as well as those of Pol Pot, were not carried out by states. But suppose it is true that these horrors would not take place in a world without states. This fact would not be a reason for the inhabitants of any particular state unilaterally to dismantle their governments and armies and territorial boundaries. Anthropologists explain the development of most premodern "states" through the process of "secondary state formation". The choice facing a group with no centralized means of social control and defense often has been to acquire some or be swallowed up by another group.[102] The same alternatives surely face contemporary anarchist communities.

Anarchists are sometimes tempted to argue that a stateless North American continent would be less tempting a target for conquest, as it would be difficult to control and exploit without the institutions of government. Again, this is incredible. The continent was, after all, conquered several centuries ago, and its more than 15 million inhabitants were killed or subjugated. Many inhabitants of another stateless continent were enslaved (or killed) by the same conquerors. The evidence of history is more telling than the economic or game-theoretic models of contemporary anarchists.

Since the time of written records, in most places where humans have lived together, there have been concentrations of power, that is, individuals and groups wielding considerable power over others. The world of anarchically interacting individuals depicted by contemporary theorists seems remote even from the social conditions of

100. The fascinating tale of the Shasta County farmers is told in Ellikson, *Order Without Law: How Neighbors Settle Disputes.*
101. See Jackson, "Quasi-states, Dual Regimes, and Neoclassical Theory."
102. See the discussions in Chapter 2. It is interesting how there are no states (in my sense) today that are surrounded on all sides by another, single state (a fact brought to my attention by Alexei Marcoux). Presumably, "doughnut" states cannot resist filling in their holes.

premodern Europe. There, as elsewhere, before the development of modern states, individuals and groups amassed power and dominated and exploited others. Few behaved as the protective agencies of contemporary anarcholibertarian lore. Viewed from this perspective, the modern state at times may seem to be an improvement. For while the power of government is greater, in most Westerns states at least, it is also constrained and tamed, unlike the concentrated powers of earlier times. Although the scope of governance and the power of the state today may be greater than ever before, it is also the case that republican or democratic states typically rely less on force than did earlier forms of rule. In these states there is greater sharing of power today than in the past, even compared to the classical republics, where citizens formed a very small subset of the subject populations. Everywhere the power of bureaucratic rule may have increased. But it, too, has been tamed by procedural means. Noting some of these changes, Poggi claims that it is difficult

not to acknowledge both the considerable factual efficacy and the moral superiority of the principles, however imperfectly implemented, inspiring the construction of modern administrative systems. I am thinking, again, of the notion of conflict of interest as disqualifying office-holders and invalidating their acts; of the practice of competitive examinations for appointments to public office; of the auditing of the expenditure of agencies on the part of a central treasury on the basis of regular budgets; of the equality of citizens before the law; of the expectation that office-holders will operate on the basis of the law, their superiors' directives, and their own 'science and conscience'; of the systematic allocation of competences to offices and of their subordination to ultimate political decision-makers.[103]

The power of the *arbitrary* especially has been reduced and contained by the modern state, at least in its constitutional and democratic forms.[104]

There have been considerable costs to the state's sweep of the globe. The horrors of World War II are a reminder of what the state makes possible. But, as I have said, many humans prove capable of

---

103. Poggi, *The State*, p. 76; see generally pp. 72–79.
104. See ibid. For a conception of political freedom that makes the control of arbitrary power essential, see Philip Pettit, "Freedom as Antipower," *Ethics* 106, 3 (April 1996), 576–604, and *Republicanism: A Theory of Freedom and Government* (Oxford: Clarendon Press, 1997).

atrocities without the aid of powerful centralized government; the massacres of Rwanda, Bosnia-Herzegovina, and Kampuchea are reminders of this. Rather than attempt the impossible task of exhaustively comparing the horrors of states and nonstates, we might instead examine the conditions for justified states and determine in what ways their just powers correspond to their self-image.

Chapter 4

Legitimacy

4.1 LEGITIMATE STATES

When are states *legitimate?* What is the basis of their claimed *legitimacy?* These questions are *evaluative* or *normative*. By contrast, we might wish to know whether a particular state is regarded as legitimate, just as we might want to learn whether a particular novel is thought to be good or whether a candidate for office is believed to be corrupt. These queries are primarily nonnormative and are answered by discovering people's beliefs or attitudes. The broadly sociological accounts, derived from Weber and still influential, that would have us understand the state's legitimacy in terms of the attitudes of subjects are nonnormative in this manner.[1] My primary concerns in this essay are normative, so these sorts of accounts are beside the point. But they are also inherently problematic, as has been pointed out frequently in the philosophical literature: "Attempts to explain the notion of legitimacy of government in terms of the attitudes and beliefs of its subjects have a difficult time avoiding the reintroduction of the notion of legitimacy when it comes time to explain the precise content of the subjects' attitudes and beliefs."[2] Legitimacy may depend on people's attitudes, but the first question is what attitudes *ought* we have.

1. "A legitimate authority is one which is recognized as valid or justified by those to whom it applies. It is recognized as lawful, just or rightful." Vincent, *Theories of the State*, p. 38. See Weber, *Sociological Writings*, ed. W. Heydebrand (New York: Continuum, 1994), pp. 9–13, 23–24, 28–32, and David Beetham, *The Legitimation of Power* (London: Macmillan, 1991), chap. 1.
2. Nozick, *Anarchy, State, and Utopia*, p. 134n. Green notes, "It is absurd to say, as some political scientists do, that a state is legitimate if it is believed to be legitimate by its citizens; for what are we to suppose they believe in believing *that?*" *The Authority of the State*, p. 5.

'Legitimacy' and its cognates have a variety of related but different senses. The word is derived from the Latin *lex* and has the same root as 'legislation'. One sense of 'legitimate' is being in accordance with law, or lawful (legality). Closely related to this would be the more general notion of being in accordance with the established rules or procedures relevant to the matter at issue. In this sense, being the monarch's firstborn son might be a condition for being the legitimate heir to the throne, or election might be a condition for office. Similarly, being in accordance with the rules of logic might be necessary for a legitimate deduction or with the rules of chess for a legitimate move. These senses of 'legitimate' are largely procedural and are similar to the primary sense of 'legal' (being in accordance with the law). Note that legitimacy in these procedural senses need not make essential reference to the beliefs or attitudes of subjects; in principle something could be in accordance with accepted rules or procedures although few subjects realize this, and it could be that people believe erroneously that something is legitimate in this sense.

I have dubbed these senses of the term "procedural", and they seem to be very common. Often when something is claimed to be legitimate, this seems to be what is meant. But there is an ambiguity that needs to be drawn out. One might say that something is legitimate in a procedural sense; this is, in the context at least, what 'legitimate' *means*. One might also think that procedural considerations establish when something is legitimate; legitimacy is then what is conferred by the satisfaction of certain conditions. In this case, 'lawful' and its cognates are not the meaning of 'legitimate'; legitimacy is a property of those things lawful. The question would then be what property?

In some contexts, the legitimacy of states is thought to depend on recognition by other states or bodies of states (e.g., the United Nations).[3] Legitimacy here is something conferred by others. This is different from more procedural accounts, as recognition may be independent from legality. It is also more clearly normative, as international recognition confers rights, duties, and liabilities, as well as a certain status. Recognition has legal implications in international, as well as municipal, law.[4] But there is considerable ambiguity and obscurity here, the sources of which are not unrelated to common

---

3. See A. John Simmons, *Moral Principles and Political Obligations* (Princeton: Princeton University Press, 1979), pp. 41, 197.
4. See Shaw, *International Law*, chap. 7.

confusions about states and other matters that we are taking up. Often to be recognized both as a state and to be called legitimate amount to the same thing. And sometimes it is thought that something is a legitimate state if it is simply accepted as such, as if it were membership in a club at issue and recognition conferred membership.[5] Legitimacy here seems tied to stability and effective control: A state is legitimate in this way if it is organized territorially, has a central government that maintains effective control, and the like. The normative questions as to what sorts of states ought to be recognized and accorded the status and privileges of states in international law remain to be addressed.

Legitimacy of the sort relevant to this essay is both a normative and a substantive notion. While lawfulness may be an important attribute of legitimate states or governments, it is hard to believe that it confers the normative and substantive status we seem to be thinking of when attributing legitimacy. A state or government may be legitimate in a procedural sense by being lawful or by functioning in accordance with its rules or procedures. This would be a type of consistency, an attribute presumably of the "rule of law". This need not be trivial and should not be belittled, for lawfulness even in a system of bad laws may reduce considerably the amount of arbitrary power wielded over subjects. But it is not the sort of legitimacy we wonder about when we raise the questions central to this inquiry. These require a substantive notion.

What is it, then, for a state to be legitimate in a substantive sense? I do not ask what sorts of considerations would legitimate a state; we shall come to that later. I ask what it is for a state to be legitimate. Suppose we think that consent of the governed is sufficient for legitimacy; then what is it that a state possesses when it has secured the consent of the governed? Or suppose that we think that securing certain benefits contributes to legitimacy; what is it that states have when these benefits are assured to subjects? Legitimacy in this substantive sense seems connected to justification.

---

5. Still, one usually has to be an entity of a certain sort to be a candidate for membership in a club; birds or books could not be members of a chess or wine club. As we have seen, common conceptions of a state have to be very diluted if Andorra, the Vatican, and the "quasi states" of Africa can all be regarded as states. The view that something is a state if recognized as such is probably nominalist in appearance only; birds or books would not be states even if "recognized" as such. One source of confusion in these contexts is due to thinking that notions like 'to recognize as' or 'to determine or decide that' do not presuppose independent facts of the matter.

4.2 JUSTIFICATION

If a state is legitimate, it has a certain status. At the least, presumably, its existence is permissible; it may also have a (claim)right to exist. States *rule* and claim certain powers, liberties, and rights related to governance. Legitimacy may also confer these on a state.

My general characterization in Chapter 2 has it that a state is the form of political organization of a society. A state exists when the political institutions and relations of the residents of a particular land are organized in certain ways and certain powers are claimed and are recognized by significant bodies of people:

1. *Continuity in time and space.* The institutions of the state endure over time, surviving changes in leadership, and governing a definite and distinct *territory*.
2. *Transcendence.* The state constitutes a unitary public order distinct from and superior to both ruled and rulers, one capable of agency.
3. *Political organization.* The institutions through which the state acts (e.g., the government, the judiciary, the bureaucracy, the police) are differentiated from other political organizations and associations, are formally coordinated one with another, and are relatively centralized. Relations of authority are hierarchical. Rule is *direct* and *territorial*; it is relatively pervasive and penetrates society legally and administratively.
4. *Authority.* The state is *sovereign*, that is, the ultimate source of political authority in its territory, and it claims a monopoly on the use of legitimate force within its territory. Its jurisdiction extends directly to all residents of that territory. In its relations to other public orders, the state is autonomous.
5. *Allegiance.* The state expects and receives the loyalty of its members and of the permanent inhabitants of its territory, a loyalty that assumes precedence over that formerly owed to family, clan, commune, lord, bishop, pope, or emperor. Members of a state are the primary subjects of its laws and have a general obligation to obey by virtue of their membership.

A legitimate state, we might suppose, is one that has these properties permissibly or even by (claim)right.

I think, however, this is not the best way to proceed. For the characterization I proposed of states is ideal in many respects, and it may

105

turn out that no state in fact has all the properties and powers enumerated. One of the hypotheses we must keep open is that only some of these attributes are justified or possessed by legitimate states and even then not to the extent usually claimed. Our states pretend to, or aim for, a certain ideal and status, and the object of this inquiry is to determine the truth of the matter. It may be that states overreach, that some of their normative powers and authority are often justified, but not others. That is, in fact, what I shall argue.

I shall say, then, that a state exists to the extent that a territory and its inhabitants are organized politically as just stated, and when many of the state's powers related to governance are acknowledged by significant bodies of people. A legitimate state is minimally one that has a liberty to exist. It would be surprising to discover that legitimacy did not also confer a (claim)right. I shall take these to be minimally senses of legitimacy. Presumably there will be more, some sort of entitlement to rule and to some sort of authority.

What is it to establish minimal legitimacy? It is hard to draw much of a distinction between securing legitimacy and *justification,* or, rather, the two seem closely connected: A state is legitimate insofar as it is justified. We might think of substantive legitimacy in these contexts as *justified governance.* To show a state to be legitimate, then, would be to justify its existence and (some of its) powers. This may be helpful but only if we become clear about justification. What is it to justify something?

Broadly, to justify something is to show it to be just or right, to be reasonable, or to be warranted; it is to validate or vindicate. In epistemic contexts, justification pertains to beliefs or statements. For practical matters, it is principally acts or powers that are called upon to be justified.[6] To justify a state, then, might be to show its powers to be just (or right) or reasonable.

Some thinkers believe that we need states or at least strong centralized government in part because people do not agree sufficiently on justice or other central moral norms or ideals. For them, states and systems of law are to replace justice as means of ensuring order. On this view, it would seem that justification could not take the form of showing the state to be just or right. A similar claim might even be made about reasons or at least the reasonable: We do not agree very

---

6. In law, justification can as well show someone to be innocent (i.e., without guilt or fault) or to be excused. These sorts of justification are not central to my concerns.

much about what is reasonable, so there is a need for institutions to determine this for us. I consider these sorts of positions in the next chapter. For now, note that some influential accounts of justification concede the claim about disagreement but make it the starting point of their view. Rawls's rather pragmatic account of justification makes disagreement central. For him,

> justification is argument addressed to those who disagree with us, or to ourselves when we are of two minds. It presumes a clash of views between persons or within one person, and seeks to convince others, or ourselves, of the reasonableness of the principles upon which our claims and judgments are found. Being designed to reconcile by reason, justification proceeds from what all parties to the discussion hold in common.[7]

On this view, disagreement about some matters makes justification necessary, and agreement about others makes it possible.

Justification may well be contextual, at least in the sense that it addresses doubts or questions that are evident in the context that is relevant. Calls for justification often arise when someone challenges another to justify some act or claim. But we may also simply wonder whether some ancient practice was justified or whether a hypothetical one would be. In all these cases the context should reveal what matters may be problematic and in need of justification. But the contextuality of justification does not require that the standards appealed to be accepted in fact by the parties addressed. Justification may be "designed to reconcile by reason", but it need not address the concerns of the unreasonable and cannot be expected to persuade those who are not rational.[8] It remains a normative matter and so cannot be understood solely in terms of unconstrained agreement.

Justification typically is dialogic or reactive, and Rawls's pragmatic account emphasizes this. We offer justifications most often in response to skeptical challenge. But this need not be. We might examine, for instance, a constitutional order and inquire into its hierarchical structure, wondering how the different parts connect with and

---

7. Rawls, *A Theory of Justice*, p. 580.
8. See Gerald F. Gaus, *Value and Justification: The Foundations of Liberal Theory* (Cambridge: Cambridge University Press, 1990), pp. 16, 21–22, 327. "To justify a position or action is to give reasons for its acceptance or performance which a *reasonable* person *ought* to find persuasive." Virginia Held, "Justification: Legal and Political," *Ethics* 86, 1 (October 1975), 1–16 (emphasis added).

authorize one another. Or we might just be curious as to the nature of the justification of some institution or practice. Related to its typical reactive nature, justification is often thought to be "public" in the sense of being accessible to all, or at least aspiring to be so. Accordingly, it may be urged that we dispense with "appeals to inner conviction or faith, special insight, secret information, or very difficult forms of reasoning".[9] But as desirable as this might be sometimes, it is not clear that publicity is a requirement for the justification of states. After all, the relevant facts may be relatively inaccessible; and the reasoning required, difficult. It is hard to see how one could rule this out in advance, except perhaps by an insistence that a central concern should be social stability.[10] Since my primary concern is with understanding and evaluating the state as a form of political organization, the value of stability does not enter in at this stage of inquiry.[11]

Even if justification need not be contextual, reactive, or public in many of the ways it is often held to be, it has *objects* as well as *audiences*. The former is that which is to be justified (e.g., the state's authority, its right to impose sanctions), and the latter is those to whom something is to be justified (e.g., the members of the state, those subject to its authority, "the international community"). The audience is the set of persons to whom the justification is addressed or aimed at. Something may be justified even if the relevant audience does not realize this, or so I am allowing at this stage.[12] The usual view is that the justification of a state must be to its members or, more generally, its subjects: "The task of discovering the conditions of

9. Stephen Macedo, *Liberal Virtues: Citizenship, Virtue, and Community in Liberal Constitutionalism* (Oxford: Clarendon Press, 1990), p. 46.
10. A concern with stability is, of course, central to Rawls's enterprise. See *Political Liberalism*, pp. xvii–xviii, 142–143. On his view, "A conception of political legitimacy aims for a public basis of justification and appeals to public reason" (p. 144). Gaus argues that "overwhelming evidence indicates fundamental divergences between commonsense-sanctioned inferences and normatively appropriate inferences. Consequently, Rawls's and Macedo's populist theory of public reason can generate arguments that are widely accepted but are not justificatory". Gaus, *Justificatory Liberalism: An Essay on Epistemology and Political Theory* (New York: Oxford University Press, 1996), p. 136. "Legitimacy is not the same thing as stability. A legitimate system may be unstable. . . . An illegitimate system may be stable." Thomas Nagel, *Equality and Partiality* (New York: Oxford University Press, 1991), p. 35.
11. Except with regard to considerations of effectiveness (see Section 4.3).
12. My view of political justification is the analogue to externalism in the theory of knowledge. A state may be justified, and the relevant audiences (in my sense) may not know this.

legitimacy is traditionally conceived as that of finding a way to justify a political system to everyone who is required to live under it."[13]
(Since full members and mere subjects will typically have different
burdens and benefits, the objects of justification will differ as well.)
According to some – Hobbes, for instance – nonsubjects need not be
addressed; no justification is owed them. Some persons, then, may
lack *standing* with regard to matters of justification. Their interests
and concerns need not be considered when determining the justification for the matter at hand. Thus, some may argue (or assume) that
the justification of a particular state need have its subjects as audience but not people elsewhere.

The matter of audience, in this sense, is complex, and some of the
issues are addressed in Chapter 9, where I consider questions about
membership. These are questions about standing, as well as about
justice. If the scope of justice is narrow, then the audience of justification may not be very large. But if its scope is broad or its distributive implications of a certain kind – for instance, the earth is held in
common by all humans – then the audience may approach univer-
sality. Centuries ago when the affairs of people in one state did not
much affect those far away, it may have been more reasonable to
assume that states are to be justified primarily to their subjects. But
today this common assumption may need to be questioned.[14]

What are the objects of justifications of the state? Here much
depends on the relevant analysis. Political thinkers who stress the
state's alleged monopolization of "legitimate" force focus on justifications of force. What is especially problematic on these accounts is
the state's denial of the right to use force to anyone not authorized.
The obligations of members and subjects to the state are also stressed
by many. For these theorists "the goal of justification of the state is to
show that, in principle, everyone within its territories is morally
bound to follow its laws and edicts."[15] As we saw in Chapter 2, however, the state's claims about force and the obligation to obey law are
not exhaustive of the powers and attributes of states. The state's
authority, in particular its territoriality and its claim to sovereignty, is

13. Nagel, *Equality and Partiality*, p. 33.
14. A few centuries ago, or even before (when, in Locke's words, "all the World was
America"), the establishment of states or other polities often affected others in
ways that should have been considered by political thinkers and actors.
15. Jonathan Wolff, *An Introduction to Political Philosophy* (Oxford: Oxford University
Press, 1996), p. 42.

equally in need of justification. As I argued, these are features distinctive of modern states. States are also agents – that is, entities capable of action – and they seem able to make commitment for their members and to speak for them. The latter may be held collectively responsible for their state's actions, at least if the latter has a republican or democratic form. So there may be many objects of justification. And it is possible that one may fail to justify some of these (e.g., the state's sovereignty) but not others (e.g., its use of force).

What might be concluded from a justification of some of a state's powers and attributes? At the least, presumably, that these are *permissible.* They may also be *just* or something to which the state has a *claim right.* Members and other subjects may be shown to have an *obligation* to obey their state and to support it in other ways. Nonmembers may also have obligations to respect other legitimate states. We may learn as well that legitimate states are authorized to act and speak for their members. Or it may be that justified states are those that subjects have reasons to support and obey, or reasons to approve. Alternatively, the justification of states may not take into consideration justice or other moral virtues; perhaps all it can show is that subjects and possibly others have reasons to support and obey it.

Justifications of states may simply be sets of reasons that support conclusions like these. The complexity of my account of the nature of modern states should caution us about specifying conditions in advance. A "complete justification" of a modern state may very well be a justification of all of the features I mentioned to all relevant audiences. Such a justification would vindicate the state's self-image. But it would be too much to require this, or even to expect it. Some features of states may be justified to some audiences in various contexts and times but not others. And some features may not be acceptable, whatever the situation. I suggested earlier that we might think of substantive legitimacy in terms of justification. Legitimacy then becomes something that allows of degrees. There is no such thing, then, of legitimacy *simpliciter.* A state is legitimate to the extent that its powers and attributes are justified to the relevant individuals.

My inquiry is motivated by a number of concerns and worries, which I have already detailed: the evils of states, their unusual and distinctive properties, and certain aspects of their modernity. An account of their legitimacy presumably should address these concerns. It may be, however, that states can be legitimate or justified but still commit some of the horrors with which we have become familiar. If this is true – as it may be if the influential Hobbist or "realist" tradition is right – we may want to reopen the matter of justification.

4.3 EFFICACY

The Count of Paris still claims the French throne. Some agree with him and think that he has a *right* to rule as king of France, but they presumably do not think he governs. Similarly, we do not suppose the government of the People's Republic of China to rule Taiwan or the latter's government the mainland, whatever we think of the merits of their respective claims. And before the peace accords, even if we thought the Palestine Liberation Organization's claim to speak for Palestinians in the territories occupied by Israel had merit, we did not believe the PLO to be a government. Something cannot be a political authority or power, or at least the government of a state, if it is not relatively *effective*. Efficacy is a necessary condition of governance, or so it would seem.

Hobbes has sometimes been read as claiming that effective rule is sufficient for legitimacy. And his account of the second means of establishing a state, "sovereignty by acquisition", may suggest something close to this.[16] Hobbes's account is complex and requires more than efficacy for legitimacy. But he and members of the "realist" tradition do place considerable importance on effective power. And something seems right about this. Rulers and governments that are not obeyed and that lack the means to impose their will are not merely ineffective; they do not rule or govern.

Insofar as this is so, it is hard to see how it could be a conceptual truth. Rather, it would seem to have to do with some of the reasons why governments and states might be desirable. Suppose that in modern conditions states are needed to secure order and to assist in the provision of certain collective goods, as suggested in Chapter 3. Or suppose that states are needed to force the recalcitrant and unruly to act justly and to punish wrongdoers, offering assurance thereby to the just. Then ineffective states would not be very useful. I agree here with Raz, who shares

the belief that a legitimate political authority is of necessity effective at least to a degree. But this is a result of substantive political principles (e.g. that one

16. Hobbes, *Leviathan*, chap. 20.

of the main justifications for having a political authority is its usefulness in securing social co-ordination, and that knowledge and expertise do not give one a right to govern and play only a subordinate role in the justification of political authority). It is not entailed by a conceptual analysis of the notion of authority, not even by that of the concept of political authority.[17]

I shall take minimal efficacity, then, to be a necessary condition of a legitimate state.

An efficacy requirement, it should be noted, can curtail the "externalism" of justification. I have noted that something could be justified even if the relevant audience does not realize this, and I rejected the view that political justification had to be public. Power could be justified, on this view, without most people being aware of this. But if efficacy is a condition for justified *authority*, then most people subject to the authority must *believe* it is justified, even if they do not know that it is. For authority probably cannot be effective if subjects do not regard it as authority (as opposed, say, to mere power). And to regard something as authoritative involves taking it to be justified, even if, in fact, it is not.

The point here is a general one about certain normative concepts, and it is what it missed by the broadly sociological accounts of legitimacy that understand it in terms of nonnormative facts about people's beliefs.[18] According to the account of political authority that I accept, a state *claims* authority when it intends its directives to be authoritative (i.e., to provide reasons for action of a certain kind). A state's authority is *recognized* by someone when that individual so treats its directives. The authority of a state *exists* when its claim to authority is generally recognized; its authority is then *de facto*. (*De facto* authority is necessary, but not sufficient, for justification.) To claim or to recognize authority, in these senses, is to regard it as justified. Something cannot be a *de facto* authority without being regarded as legitimate or justified by a significant proportion of the population.[19] To regard something as justified is not, of course, for it to be so. A state has legitimate authority only insofar and to the extent that its claim is justified. By contrast, political power, of a

---

17. Raz, *The Authority of Law*, pp. 8–9, and *The Morality of Freedom*, pp. 56, 75–76. See also Raz's criticisms of Austin and Kelsen's accounts of law in *The Concept of a Legal System*, 2nd ed. (Oxford: Clarendon Press, 1980 [1970]), chaps. 2 and 5.
18. See footnotes 1 and 2, above.
19. This can be weakened. See Raz's discussion in *The Authority of Law*, pp. 9, 28–29.

causal sort, need not be thought to be justified in order to be so. It is possible in most political contexts that the efficacy of (mere) power will depend on its *de facto* acceptance; regimes that rule by force alone, even if relatively effective, are usually very unstable. And the state's power should be kept in mind, as it may be justified even if its authority is not.

Chapter 5

Reasons

5.1 RATIONAL JUSTIFICATION

A state, I suggested, may be justified in one sense if it provides the relevant people with reasons to respect its laws and to support it in various ways. If justice and other moral elements are excluded from this account of reasons, then we might call this a kind of *rational justification* of a state. As I said, some political thinkers believe this is the sort of justification that is called for by states. Sovereign states, on their view, may be needed for social order, especially when people have incompatible views about justice. And where there is little agreement about justice and other moral matters, the latter cannot be the basis for legitimation. "Realist" accounts of legitimacy may be understood thus.[1] This sort of position may be most plausible if it is seen as derived from some kind of skepticism about morality or "right reason".[2] It is possible to read Hobbes this way. We could understand the Hobbist Sovereign to be an arbitrator made necessary by disagreement and conflict:

as when there is controversy in an account, the parties must by their own accord, set up for right Reason, the Reason of some Arbitrator, or Judge, to whose sentence they will both stand, or their controversie must either come to blowes, or be undecided, *for want of a right Reason constituted by Nature;* so

1. I am thinking of the realist tradition, especially influential in international relations. See, for instance, Hans J. Morgenthau, *Politics Among Nations,* 5th ed., rev. (New York: Knopf, 1978 [1948]). The tradition has many different strands, and it is hard to lend it a single account of justification or legitimacy.
2. It may be a mistake, for this reason alone, to interpret Rawls's recent works as attempting to develop an account of legitimacy of this sort, even though he is clearly impressed by the differences among reasonable "comprehensive doctrines". See *Political Liberalism,* pp. xvi–xxviii, 62–63.

is it also in all debates of what kind soever: And when men that think themselves wiser than all others, clamor and demand right Reason for judge; yet seek no more, but that things should be determined, by no other mens reason but their own, it is as intolerable in the society of men, as it is in play after trump is turned, to use for trump on every occasion, that suite whereof they have most in their hand.[3]

The good, for Hobbes, is desire-based and agent-relative. The goods of different people may consequently conflict, and there is no "common Rule of Good and Evill, to be taken from the nature of the objects themselves", to which appeals can be made.[4] We can also read Hobbes as denying the existence of justice before the establishment of civil law, excluding justice as a necessary part of justification.[5] Other readings, especially those making use of earlier texts or giving a theological interpretation of *Leviathan*, may be different. Accuracy of interpretation, however, is not the issue. Rather, the point is that this sort of "realist" account of the purpose and justification of states cannot appeal to justice; these theorists have available only what I have called rational justification.

A state is rationally justified, I shall say, to the extent that the relevant people have sufficient reasons to respect its laws and to support it in various ways. I leave open for now what sorts of reasons may be involved, what support of states is called for, as well as who the relevant individuals are (e.g., members, subjects, all affected). I consider in this chapter to what extent states can be justified thus, and whether there might not be more to substantive legitimacy than rational justification.

5.2 PRACTICAL RATIONALITY

The nature and extent of rational justification will depend on the nature of reasons and of practical rationality. So I need to discuss

3. Hobbes, *Leviathan*, chap. 5, pp. 32–33 (emphasis added).
4. "[W]hatsoever is the object of any mans Appetite or Desire; that is it, which he for his part calleth *Good* ... these words of Good, Evill, and Contemptible, are ever used with relation to the person that useth them". Hobbes, *Leviathan*, chap. 6, p. 39.
5. "To this warre of every man against every man, this also is consequent; that nothing can be Unjust. The notions of Right and Wrong, Justice and Injustice have there no place. Where there is no common Power, there is no Law: where no Law, no Injustice. . . . It is consequent also to the same condition, that there be no Propriety, no Dominion, no *Mine* or *Thine* distinct". Hobbes, *Leviathan*, chap. 13, p. 90.

matters that have been raised only implicitly. We should expect different accounts of rationality to support different conclusions about the state. Hegel's endeavor, mentioned earlier, "to comprehend and portray the state as an inherently rational entity", presupposes a conception of reason alien to most invoked today. Very different, largely instrumental and maximizing conceptions are now dominant in Anglo-American political and social theory. These are, for instance, typically presupposed by the economic and game-theoretic accounts of cooperation discussed in Chapter 3. As I make clear on a number of occasions in the chapters that follow, much turns on the particular account of reasons adopted. I need for now to clarify the general conception of practical rationality that is to be invoked for rational justifications of states.

The rational choice conception influential in contemporary social and political theory would have us understand practical rationality as the maximization of (expected) utility or, more generally, the maximization of (expected) value. In principle the values to be maximized could be almost anything, as long as they have a certain structure and provide the agent with reasons for action.[6] In practice, social scientists and political theorists tend to assume that reason is solely instrumental and that utility measures desire- or preference-based values.[7] In some contexts, especially in economics, it may even be assumed that agents are solely self-interested. For my purposes it is best to think of rational choice conceptions of rationality abstractly, without importing any special assumptions about people's motivations. Rational agents, on this general view, are able to rank the options or alternatives among which they must choose. Their rankings must be weak orderings and, for contexts of risk, conform to the other axioms of expected utility theory. An agent acts rationally insofar as his or her choices maximize expected utility (that is, the expected value of the utility function representing his or her rankings). I say more about the theory when necessary. For now, note that it is not, as often claimed, empty or trivial. Humans can fail to be rational by the standards of this account.[8]

---

6. The structure is determined by the conditions or axioms that order the agent's rankings of options.
7. In practice, social theorists often confuse reasons and motives as well. We must not do this, as motives are primarily explanatory.
8. "The content of the theory is absolutely clear and precise; it is laid down in the axioms. Utility theory says that a person's preferences conform to the axioms. It says nothing more and nothing less." John Broome, "Deontology and Economics,"

Rational choice accounts of rationality may be thought to be special cases of a more general conception, which I shall call the "balance of reasons" view. On this view, one's choices should be determined by the weight or balance of reasons. Consider a very simple choice between two alternatives, one of which is supported by a single reason, whereas the other is not supported by any. One acts rationally by choosing the alternative supported by the reason. But this is uncommon, most decision problems confronting the chooser with many reasons, some of them conflicting, and with reasons supporting more than one alternative. In this more common situation, one should assess the reasons comparatively, determining their relative weight. One acts rationally insofar as one acts according to the *balance of reasons*, choosing the alternative recommended by the weight of reasons.[9]

The language of weights and measures may suggest that all reasons will be *comparable*, in other words, that one particular reason should always be greater (i.e., weightier) than, equal to, or less than another. It may suggest as well that they must be *transitive*: If reason A outweighs reason B, and B outweighs C, then A outweighs C. A set of comparable and transitive (and reflexive) reasons constitute an ordering. People often assume that reasons are ordered, but this need not be. It may be that some reasons are not fully comparable, or it may be that some are not transitive.[10] Rational choice accounts of the balance of reasons usually assume an ordering.

It is very common, especially in the social sciences, and in philosophy as well, to think that practical reason is (only) instrumental. On this view, reason can advise only about the means we should take in pursuit of our ends; it must be silent about the ends. If we think of our ends as being determined, say, by our passions, then these

Economics and Philosophy 8, 2 (October 1992), 279. There are now numerous introductions to expected utility theory, many of which give accessible and competent presentations of the axioms and theory. For a useful collection of reference articles from *The New Palgrave Dictionary of Economics*, see *Utility and Probability*, ed. J. Eatwell, M. Milgate, and P. Newman (New York: Norton, 1990 [1987]).

9. Raz calls this the intuitive conception of practical rationality. Raz, *Practical Reason and Norms*, 2nd ed. (Princeton: Princeton University Press, 1990 [1975]), p. 36.

10. The thesis of value incommensurability has been defended in recent years by Raz. See *Morality of Freedom*, chap. 13. See also *Incommensurability, Comparability and Practical Reasoning*, ed. R. Chang (Cambridge, Mass.: Harvard University Press, 1997). For discussions of intransitivities, see Thomas Schwartz, *The Logic of Collective Choice* (New York: Columbia University Press, 1986), pp. 113–115, and Gregory S. Kavka, "Is Individual Choice Less Problematic than Collective Choice?" *Economics and Philosophy* 7, 2 (October 1991), pp. 153–157.

can be contrary to reason only so far as they are *accompany'd* with some judgment or opinion. According to this principle, which is so obvious and natural, 'tis only in two senses, that any affection can be call'd unreasonable. First, When a passion, such as hope or fear, grief or joy, despair or security, is founded on the supposition of the existence of objects, which really do not exist. Secondly, When in exerting any passion in action, we chuse means insufficient for the design'd end, and deceive ourselves in our judgment of causes and effects. Where a passion is neither founded on false suppositions, nor chuses means insufficient for the end, the understanding can neither justify nor condemn it.[11]

Contemporary rational choice theorists often understand decision theory, in accounting for instrumental choice, to exhaust the study of practical reason.[12] This is a mistake. It may be that rationality is instrumental (only). But rational choice theory need not pronounce on this. The ends one pursues may be rationally assessable, or they may not. Decision theory per se does nothing to settle the question. Maurice Allais may well insist that it "cannot be too strongly emphasized *that there are no criteria for the rationality of ends as such other than the condition of consistency.*"[13] But as long as our ends have the requisite structure, rational choice theory does not pronounce on their content, origin, or source.

Sometimes theorists adopt a purely instrumentalist account of practical rationality out of a desire to invoke "weak" assumptions. Occasionally, this is to avoid begging substantive questions. Or it may be to make one's argument as strong as possible, by deriving one's conclusion from weak premises. If we think of an instrumentalist account of practical reason as one which asserts that reason is *only* instrumental, then, in one important way, adopting the account is not invoking a weak assumption, as it excludes certain positions. Formally, an assumption A is weaker than another B if everything entailed by A is also entailed by B, but some implications of B are not implications of A. In this sense, instrumentalism about reason can be a relatively strong assumption, as it rules out a variety of important alternatives. I argue this briefly while explicating some concepts

11. Hume, *A Treatise of Human Nature,* Book II, Part III, sec. 3, p. 416.
12. The study of merely instrumental choice has turned out, unexpectedly, to be very complex and controversial.
13. He adds: "Ends are completely arbitrary." Allais, "The Foundations of a Positive Theory of Choice Involving Risk and a Criticism of the Postulates and Axioms of the American School," in *Expected Utility Hypotheses and the Allais Paradox,* ed. M. Allais and O. Hagen (Dordrecht: D. Reidel, 1979 [1952]), p. 70.

about value that will be useful for my treatment of justification and for other issues taken up later.

Something may be valuable as an end, as a means, or as both. We distinguish accordingly between *ultimate* (or "intrinsic") and *instrumental* value. Focusing on ultimate value, here are a few distinctions adapted from the literature. Some think that judgments expressing ultimate values can be true or false, and others deny this. On most accounts, if they can have truth values, these can be known. Let me distinguish, then, between *knowable* and *unknowable* value. One believes value to be knowable if one thinks that some judgments of value are true and this can (in principle) be established. Many deny that judgments of ultimate value are knowable in this sense.

This last distinction has both semantic and epistemic elements. The next distinction is metaphysical. It is sometimes held that value properties are, so to speak, in the eye of the beholder, even if they are knowable in my sense. Some think of them as "projected" onto the world by valuers. There is a debate, then, about the nature of valuing and the respects in which it is analogous to seeing or to cognizing in presupposing an object independent of the valuer's mental states (e.g., desires, passions). A value is *inherent* insofar as it exists independently of the mental attitudes of valuers. Values dependent on desires and tastes are *noninherent*.[14] Note that denying the inherent nature of values does not commit one to denying that they are knowable. One reason the terms 'subjective' and 'objective' are unhelpful in these contexts is that their use often implicitly conflates this pair of distinctions.

The last important distinction figures prominently in recent philosophy. It concerns the possible *relativity* of value. Suppose that some ultimate values are both knowable and inherent. The question, then, is whether these values are reasons for all valuers or merely for some, namely, those *to* whom they are values. Something has *agent-relative* value insofar as it has value only from particular perspectives, those of the particular valuers *to* whom it is valuable. By contrast, something has *agent-neutral value* insofar as it is valuable *from*

---

14. Sometimes the term 'intrinsic' is used for what I call inherent. This is confusing, as 'intrinsic' is also commonly used for ultimate, noninstrumental value. Note that this characterization of inherent value is somewhat crude and may not be adequate for all purposes. For one thing, it is hard to know how one should classify values that belong to a Kantian phenomenal world. Also, we might want to distinguish between values that depend on the mental attitudes of a single individual and those dependent on many people, the latter being intersubjective in a sense. The wrongness of violating certain norms may be a noninherent value, but it would be one dependent on the attitudes of groups, not mere individuals.

the perspective of all or, rather, any valuer. Suppose that the value of *x* is a *reason* for action. Then agent-relative values are reasons only to some, namely, those *to* whom they are values; agent-neutral value, by contrast, are reasons for all valuers.[15] The key notion seems to be that of *perspective: to* whom, or from what perspective, is something valuable? Some thinkers understand value to be relative, in certain respects, to individuals, while others have affirmed the independence of (at least some) value from particular perspectives.[16]

Some philosophers have claimed that the cessation of pain, for instance, is an agent-neutral value; all rational agents have a reason to act so as to diminish pain, no matter whose pain it is. (The reason need not, according to this view, be a *sufficient* reason so to act; other values may have priority or greater strength.) Without presupposing that values always are reasons *to act*, it might instead be said that someone's pain provides anyone with reasons to wish to see it diminished. Others have denied this thesis (e.g., about pain), arguing that value is always agent-relative. It is simple to defend this from positions that assert the noninherent nature of the value in question; for these usually entail the agent-relativity of that value. Recently, however, a number of philosophers have denied the agent-neutrality of value while rejecting "subjectivist" theses about value. So it is important not to confuse this distinction with the others.

Putting these distinctions together, we have a number of different positions. The first I shall call *subjectivism*. It is the view that no value is inherent and no value is agent-neutral.[17] Another position is *realism:* At least some value is inherent.[18] Two varieties of "realism" must

15. A value *to* A need not be a value *for* A, that is, a self-interested value. In other words, the preposition 'to' is used to indicate the self as subject; the preposition 'for', the self as object.
16. The contemporary distinction is usually traced to Thomas Nagel. See *The Possibility of Altruism* (Princeton: Princeton University Press, 1978 [1970]), pp. 90–95, and *The View from Nowhere* (New York: Oxford University Press, 1986), pp. 152–153, 158–159. See as well Derek Parfit, *Reasons and Persons* (Oxford: Clarendon Press, 1984), p. 143.
17. "Value is then not an inherent characteristic of things or states of affairs, not something existing as part of the ontological furniture of the universe in a manner quite independent of persons and their activities. Rather, value is determined, that is, created or determined through preference. Values are products of our affections." David Gauthier, *Morals by Agreement* (Oxford: Clarendon Press, 1986), p. 47; see also pp. 24–26.
18. Readers familiar with the literature will know this is one of many different senses of the term. For guidance to the complicated contemporary debates, see *Essays on Moral Realism*, ed. G. Sayre-McCord (Ithaca, N.Y.: Cornell University Press, 1988), esp. the editor's introductory essay.

be distinguished, depending on the position adopted on the matter of agent-neutral value. Some affirm, while others deny, the existence of such value. The latter are *agent-relative realists* and assert that no value is agent-neutral. Others accept *agent-neutral realism* and claim that at least some agent-neutral value exists.[19]

In the way I have constructed these positions, no proponent need deny *some* value to be noninherent. Few contemporary thinkers seem to deny that *some* value is agent-relative. The debates tend to be about whether there is *any* inherent value, whether *any* such value is agent-neutral, and how agent-neutral value should be weighed with agent-relative value. We may arrange the positions we have characterized in matrix form in terms of their existential commitments:

	Value		
	knowable	inherent	agent-neutral
subjectivism	no	no	no
agent-relative realism	yes	yes	no
agent-neutral realism	yes	yes	yes

The way these positions are constructed allows us to order them in terms of weakness. In terms of contemporary controversies about value and reason, the position I have labeled "subjectivist" is *not* the weakest, for it begs a number of substantive questions. In this sense it is not a weak position; and it is not uncontroversial. Theorists may urge its acceptance because they think it true, but it is another matter to defend it as a weak assumption. These controversies about value may not, in the end, greatly affect general questions about the legitimacy of states. But they will have implications, for instance, for the justification of particular government activities such as the redistribution of wealth and efforts to protect people against their own bad judgment (see Chapter 9).

Let us return to practical reason. All three positions on value are compatible with the general balance of reasons account of rationality.

19. Nagel and Parfit adopt different versions of agent-neutral realism. By contrast, Philippa Foot, Eric Mack, and many neo-Aristotelians would appear to be agent-relative realists. See Foot, "Utilitarianism and the Virtues," *Mind* 94 (1985), 196–209; Mack, "Agent-Relativity of Value, Deontic Restraints, and Self-Ownership," in *Value, Welfare, and Morality*, ed. R. Frey and C. Morris (Cambridge: Cambridge University Press, 1993), pp. 209–232; and Miller, *Nature, Justice, and Rights in Aristotle's "Politics,"* pp. 131, 375–376.

Suppose we accept a version of agent-neutral realism. Then we act rationally insofar as we act on the balance of the relevant agent-neutral and agent-relative (if any) reasons. We could also fit this into a rational choice framework if we assume comparability of reasons or values: We act rationally insofar as we maximize the weighed sum of agent-neutral and agent-relative value.[20] The source and content of the values may differ depending on the position we adopt, but the structure of practical reason may stay the same. I shall not, then, pronounce on the issues dividing partisans of these different positions unless I must. I conjecture that they will matter less for the general, abstract questions of legitimacy than for the justification of concrete programs and arrangements.[21]

5.3 REASONS FOR STATES

A rational justification of a state is provided when the relevant people have reasons to respect its laws and to support it in various ways. More broadly, they may have reasons to do their part in supporting and maintaining the state. It is not clear that an account of "doing one's part or one's share" can be given without bringing in the moral reasons that rational justifications are supposed to circumvent, so I shall concentrate on reasons to obey the state's laws.

A rational justification, on one interpretation, is supposed to avoid moral reasons which are said to be something about which there is insufficient agreement on which to base a society or legal order. There is an ambiguity regarding the nature of the reasons which can make up a rational justification. A state or political organization may provide nonmoral reasons to all involved, or it may provide reasons to each individual including some that persons take to be moral. In the first case, no moral reasons enter at any point in the justification; in the second, any individual's moral reasons can come in but only

20. Some adjustments might have to be made if, for instance, only a lexical ordering of alternatives is available.
21. See Chapters 7 and 9. Consider the analogous question of the implications of different accounts of the reliability of divine revelation on issues having to do with forms of political organization. It is not clear that certain controversies here could be sidestepped. Remarks made in Chapter 1 about instrumentalism regarding the state may effectively rule out certain classical theocentric conceptions of the state . that appear to be experiencing a revival in some parts of the world.

as reasons for that person.[22] It may be important to distinguish these two cases at different points.[23]

Are states often rationally justified? Consider any well-organized, stable state with a functioning legal system and a relatively efficient government. Abstract away any special problems that might ordinarily threaten a rational justification, for instance, arbitrariness of rule, systematic exploitation, or extreme poverty. We may suppose that the legal system prescribes sanctions for disobedience.[24] These sanctions – as well as the threatened use of force – are reasons for action. Abstract away these sorts of reasons. Is this hypothetical state likely to be rationally justified? Most likely not. If we do not consider the reasons provided by sanctions, many people are likely not to have reasons to obey the laws in many or even most instances. Although most people might refrain from homicide in the absence of sanctions, few would have reasons to pay most taxes or parking fees, to obey complex safety or health regulations to the letter, or to spend several years in the military, possibly risking their lives.[25]

The motivating idea behind rational justification is the infeasibility of moral justification given moral disagreement. Presumably, then, one of the main reasons for wanting a state and legal system would have to do with the need for sanctions and enforcement of rules. These address the free-rider and assurance problems in situations that are structured like PDs. Is our hypothetical state likely to be rationally justified if the reasons provided by sanctions are also considered? Would people then have reasons to pay their taxes, to obey complex and burdensome regulations, or to risk their lives in military service? I leave aside for now whether the reasons provided by sanctions are of the right kind for justification. The question is whether people would have reasons to obey the state's directives. Taking into

---

22. They are "preferences" in the somewhat technical sense of rational choice theory.
23. In any case, I come back to question the distinction between rational and moral justifications of states.
24. Note that sanctions are penalties and need not involve force. Sanctions and force (and violence) are so often confused that one needs to make clear the distinction among them. Most sanctions in law involve the imposition of duties (e.g., to pay a fine) or the withdrawal of rights (e.g., to one's liberty). Force typically enters in to ensure compliance with laws, including sanctions. See Raz, *Practical Reason and Norms*, pp. 154–159 (and the discussion in Chapter 7).
25. This last example is dated, at least in the West, where most states have abolished mandatory military service. But historically such service was one of the main demands states made on males. I discuss obedience to the law in Chapter 7 as well.

account sanctions and enforcement would increase the amount of rational obedience and make it more likely to be justified. But some people will probably still fail to have reasons to respect all of the laws, and most people even will have reasons to disregard some of the laws at least some of the time. I need not suppose that the laws in question are undesirable in any way. But there are limits to the capacity of any state efficiently to enforce all laws. And the necessary generality of laws constrains their effectiveness. Consider a simple example. There are good reasons for wanting rules requiring drivers to stop at certain intersections. But few people believe they have reason to come to a complete stop at a stop sign in a deserted, well-lighted area where no other vehicles or persons are visible. The law will say clearly that we are obligated to come to a complete stop even in such circumstances, and will authorize the police to sanction violators. But it seems unlikely that we do have reasons, especially when the probability of apprehension is negligible. (I return to this sort of case and the issues raised when I discuss sovereignty and authority in Chapter 7.)

Free-rider and assurance problems are likely to persist, even if sanctions are taken into consideration. Even relatively efficient governments cannot effectively impose and administer sanctions for all laws. So there are likely to be free-rider problems (e.g., I prefer not to pay my taxes or to curb my polluting activities even if everyone else does). If it is known that there are many potential free riders, whatever assurance problems there are will be more severe. It is doubtful that all will have reasons to obey the law, even if sanction-based reasons are taken into account.[26] This may seem counterintuitive. One may think that most stable social orders could not exist were not most people to go along. But "going along" and obeying the law are not the same. And states are constrained by what subjects are willing to put up with. Most states choose not to enforce some laws and not to make laws governing certain things, for fear of massive disobedience. In addition, forced compliance with some laws owes as much to general social pressure as to state enforcement (e.g., conscription in World Wars I and II).

A Leviathan or totalitarian state may be relatively successful in sanctioning and enforcing its laws. But the consequence of its success

---

26. Sanction-based reasons are of the wrong sort, at least given the state's self-image. We are supposed to obey the law because it is the law, not because of sanctions or force. Law for Hobbes is command, and this is "where a man saith, *Doe this*, or *Doe not this*, without expecting other reason than the Will of him that sayeth it." *Leviathan*, chap. 25, p. 176. I take up in Chapter 7 some of the issues raised here.

may well be tyranny. If this is the price of rational justification, we may certainly query the desirability or relevance of this kind of "legitimacy". Indeed, in *what* sense would a reason-providing tyrannical state be *justified?* One starts to lose grip of the notion of justification – even our constructed notion of rational justification – when one thinks of the possibility of a tyrannical state being rationally "justified" by virtue of its efficient enforcement of the law. Tyranny is likely to be unjust on most people's understanding of justice. So, if people's individual views of justice are included in their reasons to support the state – one of the two alternatives I have just mentioned – then surely some will lack reasons to support a tyrannical state. Rational justification seems either unlikely or no justification at all. There is more to be said about rational justification, especially if our notions of rationality are enriched and other normative (but not necessarily moral) considerations are brought in. But the simple kind of rational justification I have been considering does not seem promising.

A rational justification, as I understand it, is a simple conditional: A state is justified *if* there are reasons to obey for all (or most) people. The failure of rational justification would not entail that a state is not justified if there are no reasons for all (or most) people. It may still be justified, even if there are no reasons for all to obey. Now it may be that rational justification, in light of anticipated free-rider and assurance problems, should be understood not in terms of obedience. Rather, perhaps states are rationally justified if the relevant people have reasons to approve or endorse them. Approval or endorsement would not necessarily yield reasons to obey, but it might distinguish certain states from forms of rule and organization we think illegitimate (e.g., tyranny, the Mafia). For instance, we could fail to have reason to come to a complete stop at a deserted intersection, but we might approve or endorse the police officer's issuing a ticket were we apprehended.

Rational justification seems more likely for our hypothetical state if it has to do with approval and endorsement. But the question would then be, To what extent are these notions nonmoral? Would rational justifications of this sort circumvent the moral disagreement that is thought to make them necessary? I think this alternative notion of rational justification ought to be explored. But I wish to raise a number of other issues first. In the end, I suggest that justification must make reference to some moral virtues (i.e., justice), so I shall not want to pursue this alternative view of rational justification. But it seems much more promising that the original one I have been considering.

Many political theorists have thought that states would be justified were they to be the object of a suitable hypothetical collective agreement or choice. It may be best to read Hobbes's own account as requiring hypothetical agreement, although other readings are possible. Certainly, Kant's account, as well as those of Rawls and many contemporary theorists, invokes hypothetical agreement.[27] Now, hypothetical choice may justify, but it does not do so by committing the choosers in the ways consent normally does. For hypothetical consent is not consent; it is instead some sort of heuristic device for determining principles of evaluation.[28] Can hypothetical agreement reveal reasons that we may have to support a state? It may, but establishing that it does would require discussion of many controversial matters.[29]

27. Kant, "On the Common Saying: 'This May be True in Theory, but it does not Apply in Practice'," in *Kant: Political Writings*, p. 79; Rawls, *A Theory of Justice*, pp. 12, 21, 120, 167, and 587.
28. See Raz, *Morality of Freedom*, p. 81n. ("Theories of hypothetical consent discuss not consent but cognitive agreement."); Morris, "The Relation of Self-Interest and Justice in Contractarian Ethics," *Social Philosophy and Policy* 5, 2 (Spring 1988), 121–122, and "A Contractarian Account of Moral Justification," in *Moral Knowledge? New Readings in Moral Epistemology*, ed. W. Sinnott-Armstrong and M. Timmons (New York: Oxford University Press, 1996), pp. 219–220; Gaus, *Value and Justification*, pp. 19, 328; and Simmons, *On the Edge of Anarchy: Locke, Consent, and the Limits of Society* (Princeton: Princeton University Press, 1993), pp. 78–79. According to Simmons, hypothetical contract theory bases "our duties or obligations not on anyone's actual choices but on whether our governments (states, laws) are sufficiently just, good, useful, or responsive to secure the hypothetical support of ideal choosers . . . the 'contract' in hypothetical contractarianism is simply a device that permits us to analyze in a certain way quality of government".

David Gauthier, it should be noted, disagrees with this understanding of hypothetical consent. He grants "that it isn't actual consent; nevertheless, it serves in place of actual consent, when that is in principle unavailable." For instance, when evaluating an institution that preexists "those regulated by it, *ex ante* consent is ruled out. So one considers the next best thing – a justification in terms of what persons would have consented to, had they been in a position to establish institutions regulating their interactions" (personal correspondence).
29. The literature here is enormous. The sort of hypothetical contractarianism relevant to questions of rational justification would be the "Hobbesian" sort. Perhaps the best version of this type of theory, after Hobbes's own, is J. Buchanan, *Limits of Liberty*. See Thomas Christiano, "The Incoherence of Hobbesian Justifications of the State," *American Philosophical Quarterly* 31, 1 (January 1994), 23–38, for a general argument that certain types of hypothetical agreements do not succeed. See also Jody S. Kraus, *The Limits of Hobbesian Contractarianism* (Cambridge: Cambridge University Press, 1993), for another argument, that "the problem of collective action poses a formidable, if not insurmountable, barrier to the success of Hobbesian contractarianism" (p. 38).

If actual consent is not required for justification, it is unclear what relevance collective action problems have to attempts to *justify* states in terms of what they accomplish or in terms of the benefits they provide. The latter is what David Schmidtz has called a "teleological" justification, and he argues rightly that "a government can be teleologically justified even if collective action problems would

Hypothetical agreement may also reveal reasons we may have to approve or endorse a state. But it may, in the end, do no better than other devices for providing reasons that alleviate free-rider and assurance problems, at least as long as we remain content with the conception of practical rationality I have presupposed thus far.

5.4 RATIONALITY REVISITED

According to the received view, rationality in action is the maximization of (expected) utility or, more generally, the maximization of (expected) value. I suggested this account is a special case of a more general, balance of reasons view: One acts rationally insofar as one acts according to the balance of reasons, choosing the alternative recommended by the weight or preponderance of reasons. The orthodox rational choice account, as well as most versions of the balance of reason view, would have us choose in a forward-looking manner. We are always to do what is likely to maximize utility given the options available to us at the point of choice. Rational choice is always, as it were, from the standpoint of the present.[30] On this understanding, backward-looking considerations such as intentions, resolutions, plans, or commitments are problematic unless there are forward-looking, future-oriented reasons for taking them into account.[31]

The received theory recommends what David Gauthier has called "straightforward maximization": A rational agent is one who, at every decision point, chooses the course of action that he or she believes promises greatest preference satisfaction. Straightforward maximizers, as contemporary decision theory makes clear, can choose in very complicated ways, depending on the context of choice,

prevent the sign of its justification [e.g., consent] from materializing." Schmidtz, "Justifying the State," *Ethics* 101, 1 (October 1990), 95, and *The Limits of Government*, p. 8. If an account of a state is *normative* (e.g., justificatory), it is not clear that it need be concerned also with *explaining* the state's emergence. But see Hampton, "The Contractarian Explanation of the State," in *Midwest Studies in Philosophy*, vol. 15, ed. P. French, T. Uehling, and H. Wettstein (Notre Dame, Ind.: University of Notre Dame Press, 1990), pp. 344–371. I say more about these issues in Chapter 6.
30. As Bernard Williams puts it, "The correct perspective on one's life is *from now*." Williams, "Persons, Character, and Morality" [1976], reprinted in *Moral Luck* (Cambridge: Cambridge University Press, 1981), p. 13.
31. Utilitarianism and other consequentialist moral theories usually share this future-oriented feature of received accounts of rationality. These moral theories notoriously have difficulty taking seriously backward-looking notions like intention and commitment (and, for instance, retributive accounts of punishment).

adopting strange procedures and randomizing devices. What they may not do is to choose *counterpreferentially;* that is, they cannot rationally choose a course of action that, *at the time of choice,* is less preferred to another.[32] Backward-looking considerations (e.g., intentions, resolutions, plans, commitments) that are not reflected in an agent's occurrent preferences may not be rationally acted on.

Agents who cannot rationally choose counterpreferentially face free-rider problems in collective action dilemmas that are relatively intractable. Recall the distinction introduced in Chapter 3 between "internal" and "external" solutions to collective action problems. The former take the structure of the game, including the payoffs, to be fixed; the latter involve changes in people's preferences or beliefs through "selective incentives", sanctions, and the like. External solutions alter the expected benefits from one's choice, effectively coordinating the different parties' actions so as to produce joint coopera-tion. The introduction of *norms* that would have people cooperate in producing the desired goods counts as an external solution if these are understood to change people's preferences. If norms do not operate in this way, the puzzle is to explain how they can effect coopera-tion among rational individuals. It is hard to see how one could do this on the received conceptions of rationality.[33]

The difficulty may be better understood by looking at a sequential choice problem. Consider a simple exchange problem where only one agent (Albert) has the preferences constitutive of a PD:

Matrix 5.1

		Beatrice	
		C	D
Albert	C	3,4	1,3
	D	4,1	2,2

Albert's reasoning, on the received view, is as before: Whatever Beatrice does, his "best reply" is to choose D (D is the dominant act or

32. 'Preference' here is used in the broad technical sense current in rational choice the-ory. Our preferences in this sense are reasons for action. Many theorists, implicitly at least, think of preferences as *whatever* yields reasons, but, as I shall suggest, this is a significant error.
33. Jon Elster notes that he has "come to believe that social norms provide an impor-tant kind of motivation for action that is irreducible to rationality or indeed any other form of optimizing mechanism." Elster, *The Cement of Society,* p. 15.

strategy). By contrast, Beatrice's situation is different. Her best reply to Albert's choice of D is also to choose D. However, should Albert choose C, she should as well. This differs from the PD because Beatrice here has no dominant strategy. She still faces an assurance problem.

Consider now a sequential version of the situation just described, one where Albert must act first. Assuming complete information, he should choose C, and the outcome will be Pareto-efficient. Suppose instead that Beatrice chooses first. What should she do? This second situation is illustrated by the following decision tree (where the order of the utility values remains alphabetical):

Tree 5.1

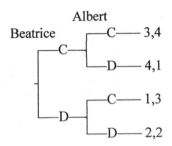

If Beatrice knows Albert to reason in accordance with the received view, she should choose D, for she would expect him so to choose, whatever her choice. Suppose instead that Albert is able to form plans and to act on them. Realizing that Beatrice's expectation that he will choose D will lead her to do the same, he may form the plan to do C conditional on her choosing C, and so informs her. Supposing that Albert can so commit himself and that he can do so credibly, he and Beatrice can secure for themselves the otherwise elusive (C,C) outcome. For once she is assured that he will choose C, doing the same is rational for Beatrice. Such a commitment, however, in the end may not be feasible. For, after securing Beatrice's choice of C, Albert must, if he is rational, choose D. He cannot rationally so commit himself, or act on such a plan, or comply with such an intention, on the received view of rationality. It seems it is Albert's very rationality (on the received view) that prevents him from cooperating.

The issues are quite complex and cannot be adequately treated here. The point I wish to make is that the orthodox conception of

rationality cannot lead agents to act on backward-looking considerations such as intentions, plans, resolutions or commitments, except
insofar as the value of these is included in the individual's preferences (or the value of acting on them, for instance, in iterated contexts, is calculated in the expected payoffs). But agents who reason
this way will be able to address their free-rider problems (and associated assurance problems) only through external devices. This suggests that states populated by such individuals will face free-rider
(and assurance) problems and, I think, in the end, that most people
will not generally have the reasons to obey the law that states claim
they have.

A small number of contemporary theorists, puzzled by the conclusion that rational agents do poorly in certain situations, have
developed alternative accounts. Struck by the fact that these agents
(e.g., Albert in the example just given) do poorly *because* of their
alleged rationality, these thinkers offer revisionist accounts according to which cooperation can be rational under certain conditions not
allowed by the orthodox view. They contrast straightforward maximizers, who maximize at every decision point or node, with more
"resolute" choosers, who can act on backward-looking considerations that are not already built into their expected utilities.[34] Borrow-
ing from Parfit, let us distinguish between the *aim* of rational choice
(e.g., preference satisfaction, doing well) and the *decision* or *choice*
rules recommended by rationality (e.g., maximize expected utility,
follow rational plans).[35] Partisans of the orthodox account seem, in

34. 'Resolute choice' is from Edward F. McClennen, *Rationality and Dynamic Choice:
Foundational Explorations* (Cambridge: Cambridge University Press, 1990). David
Gauthier's protagonists once went under the name of "constrained maximizers";
see "Reason and Maximization" [1975], reprinted in *Moral Dealing*, pp. 209–233,
and *Morals by Agreement*, chap. 6. Straightforward maximizers accept, and resolute
choosers and constrained maximizers reject, a *separability* condition on dynamic
choice: For any sequence of choices, choice at any decision point should be made
in abstraction of past choices, as if choosing anew. See *Rationality and Dynamic
Choice*, chaps. 7 and 12. This condition is implicit in the requirement that a solution
to a dynamic game be a subgame perfect equilibrium. I adopt McClennen's term
'resolute choice' for all such revisionist accounts. Resolute choice may be understood as an "indirect" approach to choice and thus to resemble moral analogues
such as indirect consequentialism. For the latter, see Peter Railton, "Alienation,
Consequentialism, and the Demands of Morality," *Philosophy and Public Affairs* 13,
2 (Spring 1984), 134–171, and L. W. Sumner, *The Moral Foundations of Rights* (Oxford: Clarendon Press, 1987), chap. 6.
35. Parfit, *Reason and Persons*, p. 3. Danielson distinguishes between "the *criterion* of
success" and "various *theories* or *conceptions* of rationality purporting to tell a

effect, to assume that the two are the same or at least that their structural principles are isomorphic; "maximize expected utility" is both the aim and the choice rule prescribed by practical reason. The revisionists, by contrast, suggest that the decision rules need not take the same form as the aim, that resolute choice may be rational even if the rational aim is maximum preference satisfaction.

These revisionist theories are controversial, and the issues they raise cannot be adequately treated here. My concern is the implications of these accounts for the matter of the rational justification of states. If it is rational to choose counterpreferentially under certain conditions (e.g., when assurance is provided), the free-rider problems, which would otherwise make reasons to obey unlikely, may be more tractable. This will make rational justifications of states more promising than I suggested earlier.

The diminution of free-rider problems will in many situations reduce assurance problems. Interestingly, there is an unexpected effect that large numbers can have in these contexts. In the usual account, except in economic analyses where strategic considerations are disallowed, large numbers of agents make collective action more difficult.[36] Given that resolute choosers are willing to cooperate conditionally on the cooperation of others, even in noniterated situations, learning that a sufficient number of others have cooperated should be sufficient to elicit their cooperation. Their concerns about assurance are addressed by information about the number of cooperators. They might, for instance, pay their fair share of taxes on learning that a high percentage of the population does the same regularly. Resolute choosers should be able to cooperate independently of the sorts of conditions required for cooperation among straightforward cooperators in repeated games.[37] This advantage of resolute choosers does not, by itself, establish that counterpreferential is ever rational. Establishing that is considerably more difficult and involves issues not directly pertinent to the matter of the justifications of states.

Rational choice accounts are, as I have said, special cases of a more general balance of reasons view: One acts rationally insofar as one

---

player how to select instrumentally successful acts". Danielson, *Artificial Morality*, pp. 62–63.

36. Olson, *The Logic of Collective Action*, chap. 2, and Sandler, *Collective Action*.

37. I owe this argument about large numbers to Edward McClennen.

acts according to the balance of reasons, choosing the alternative recommended by the weight of reasons. The separability assumption
already mentioned is also implicit in many intuitive balance of reasons accounts.[38] But the general balance of reasons account can be
developed so as to allow for commitment and intention, as Joseph
Raz effectively has done. We have been implicitly focusing on first-
order reasons to act (or to refrain from acting). Clearly, many reasons
are of this sort. But some reasons are second-order reasons to act (or
to refrain from acting) for a reason.[39] Raz understands an *exclusionary reason* to be a second-order reason to refrain from acting for a reason. For example, the directives "Do this because he said so" or
"Don't do this out of devotion to her", when authoritative, would be
exclusionary reasons.[40] On Raz's view, second-order reasons are not
simply added to our first-order reasons and weighed along with
these; to the contrary, they are reasons that bypass normal considerations of weight. In effect, exclusionary reasons are reasons to disregard the balance of reasons: "exclusionary reasons exclude by kind
and not by weight. . . . Their impact is not to change the balance of
reasons but to exclude action on the balance of reasons."[41] Suppose
the weight of reasons favors doing some act A, but we have committed ourselves, for good reason, to act otherwise. Our commitment, on
this view, is a reason for us so to act and a reason not to act on the
(balance of) reasons favoring A.[42]

---

38. It is this that makes intentions, plans, and commitments problematic for many theorists. The counterpart controversies in ethics concern promises, retributive punishment, and the like. For a conception of intention with similarities to these revisionist rational choice theories, see Michael Robins, *Promising, Intending, and Moral
Autonomy* (Cambridge: Cambridge University Press, 1984). For some critical worries about accounts such as these, see Michael E. Bratman, "Toxin, Temptation, and
the Stability of Intention," in *Rational Commitment and Social Justice: Essays for Gregory Kavka*, ed. J. Coleman and C. Morris (Cambridge: Cambridge University Press,
in press).
39. Second-order reasons are not usually explicitly integrated into formal, rational
choice accounts, but they can be. See Richard C. Jeffrey, *The Logic of Decision*, 2nd
ed. (Chicago: University of Chicago Press, 1983 [1965]), Appendix.
40. See *Practical Reason and Norms*, chap. 1, and *The Morality of Freedom*, chaps. 2 and 3.
41. Raz uses the notion of exclusionary reasons to understand the concept of legal and
political authority, and specifically the difference between an order and a request:
"Valid orders are not necessarily more weighty or important reasons than valid
requests. . . . The difference is not in importance but in mode of operation." *The
Authority of Law*, pp. 22, 23. In Chapter 7, I make use of his account of authority.
42. A *moral* reason, we might argue, includes an exclusionary reason. Moral reasons
would have us act in a particular way and refrain from acting differently for other
reasons. On this view, the reasons provided by obligations are reasons to do the
obligatory act and second-order reasons not to act on (otherwise valid) reasons to

We may think of resolute choosers as agents to whom rational commitments, plans, intentions, and other backward-looking considerations provide second-order reasons to act counterpreferentially or not to act on the balance of reasons. Rational agents of this sort presumably would find more reason to obey the directives of our hypothetical well-organized stable state, with a functioning legal system, and relatively efficient government. It may well be that rational justification will be much easier to secure for these sorts of agents. At the same time, populations of resolute choosers should face fewer free-rider problems. If it is these difficulties that states are supposed to be especially well-placed to address, the appearance of resolute choosers may diminish the need for states. Individuals able to refrain from acting on the balance of reasons may be able to rely less on states and political constraints; many of the reasons for which we might want states might not apply to them. To some extent, then, from the perspective of these revisionist theories of practical reason, it may be our imperfect rationality that makes us depend so on states for social order.

Reflecting on the costs of political constraints, David Gauthier stresses the social advantages of rational cooperation:

Even if we suppose that power does not corrupt, so that the sovereign is the perfect instrument of his subjects, acting only in their interests, yet each would expect to do better if all would adhere voluntarily to their agreements, so that enforcement and its costs would be unnecessary. We pay a heavy price, if we are indeed creatures who rationally accept no internal constraint on the pursuit of our own utility, and who are consequently able to escape from the state of nature, in those circumstances in which externalities are unavoidably present, only by political, and not by moral, devices. Could we but voluntarily comply with our rationally undertaken agreements, we could save ourselves this price.

Gauthier suggests that political institutions might serve different purposes for rational agents able to constrain themselves:

We do not suppose that voluntary compliance would eliminate the need for social institutions and practices, and their costs. But it would eliminate the need for some of those institutions whose concern is with enforcement. Authoritative decision-making cannot be eliminated, but our ideal would be

do something else. These are "protected reasons". Raz, *The Authority of Law*, p. 18. Kant's categorical imperative excludes acting on certain maxims but leaves open which ones remaining should determine one's actions.

a society in which the coercive enforcement of such decisions would be unnecessary. More realistically, we suppose that such enforcement is needed to create and maintain those conditions under which individuals may rationally expect the degree of compliance from their fellows needed to elicit their own voluntary compliance.[43]

I shall follow up some of these conjectures about rational authority in Chapter 7 and we shall see, in chapters to follow, that the nature and functions of justified states depend on the nature of our rationality. I shall also rethink and characterize anew the conception of a rational justification.

5.5 TYRANNY, SLAVERY, AND OTHER EVILS

Let us suppose that some well-organized, stable state, with a functioning legal system and relatively efficient government, is rationally justified. We may suppose it to be populated by resolute choosers or by straightforward maximizers. Suppose as well that members of this state generally have no ground for complaint about the way in which they are treated by others and by the institutions (e.g., the state is not a tyranny). Everyone – members at least – has reasons to obey the directives of the state, or at least most of these. I have supposed that the state is rationally justified and have said nothing about morality. Presumably the state could be unjust; rational justification per se does not exclude this. Were the members of the state to exploit systematically a group of nonmembers – enslave them, for instance – most of us would regard this as unjust. It might be in the interests of the state to commit extraordinary injustices, perhaps in the course of fulfilling an imperial mission.[44] It may be that such societies are often in the grips of a pernicious myth about destiny and their place in history, and that this fact vitiates the rational justification, but I shall ignore this possibility for now. The question is to determine what follows from mere rational justification.

43. Gauthier, *Morals by Agreement*, pp. 164–165.
44. Recall Nagel's view, quoted in the preceding chapter: "The task of discovering the conditions of legitimacy is traditionally conceived as that of finding a way to justify a political system to everyone who is required to live under it." We might say that nonmembers do not, in the relevant sense, "live under" the rule of this exploitative state; they are, as it were, in a Hobbesian-state-of-nature relation to it. We do not seem entirely to reject this sort of view; we may not, for instance, think that our state need be justified to tourists, illegal immigrants, or diplomats.

It is possible, depending on our account of justice, that a rationally justified state that commits gross injustices against others is one that its members have reason to support. It is not likely that this conclusion can be upheld, except perhaps by certain conventionalist and Hobbist accounts of justice. But I shall grant it for now. Are nonmembers obligated to respect its independence or sovereignty? Does the state have a *title* to its territory? Presumably not. The mere fact of rational justification does not secure the sorts of claims that states characteristically make against one another. The victims of this hypothetical state have no obligations, much less reasons, to respect it and its members. Others who care about justice may not either.

The matter may be more complicated than I am suggesting. There are occasions where we may have reasons as well as duties to deal with murderous tyrants (e.g., the alliance with Stalin, détente with the Soviet Union, recognition of and diplomatic relations with the People's Republic of China). But this should not lead us to overlook the fact that mere rational justification, without justice, will not support the full set of claims that states make regarding their territorial independence and sovereign rights. A grossly unjust but rationally justified state may be one whose independence we have no duty to respect, temporary consequential considerations aside. Such a polity may very well be a state – a unitary, territorial form of political organization, with hierarchical and direct rule. But only its members have reasons to obey its directives and to support it. As I argue later, it will lack authority – and internal sovereignty – as the reasons for obedience are of the wrong sort. Its independence – or external sovereignty – is not something we have reason, much less are obligated, to respect. Its "right" to govern its territory and to make laws is a mere Hohfeldian liberty to nonmembers – indeed, it may not even be that insofar as it has a duty to desist.

I return to these issues and the matter of rational justification in Section 6.7. For now it seems that rational justification alone, without justice, falls short of supporting the substantive legitimacy that states claim and that we might think they sometimes possess. If mere rational justification can "justify" tyranny or slavery, it may not be worth much.

Chapter 6

Justice

Remota iustitia, quid sunt regna nisi magna latrocinia? – Augustine

6.1 MORAL JUSTIFICATION

Broadly, to justify something is to show it to be just or right or to be reasonable. To show we have reasons to obey and support a state might provide a rational justification. I have argued that it is unlikely that many states are such as to provide virtually all subjects with reasons to obey virtually all laws, even if we take sanctions to provide reasons of the relevant sort (and I defend this again in Chapter 7). Perhaps states that do offer most subjects reasons may nevertheless be tyrannical or capable of committing various evils. It is unclear, therefore, that rational justification is the sort we should seek. It would seem that some species of moral justification is what is needed.

One motive for rational justification is the conviction that the degree (or the nature) of modern moral disagreement would vitiate moral justification. Accordingly, we should want states to provide authoritative norms and decisions in the absence of moral agreement. I return to this idea in the next chapter and interpret it differently than I did in Chapter 5. For now, I assume that it is possible for a state to be evil and yet to be rationally justified.[1] Even if there is considerable moral disagreement in modern times, sufficiently impressive for us to be skeptical of the power of much moral justification, it need not be the case that we should wish to eschew all moral justification. Maybe there is considerable disagreement about

---

1. As I note in Chapter 7, this possibility excludes certain positions regarding the relation between reasons and morals.

moral matters generally, but there is some substantive agreement as well. Members of a society may disagree about abortion but agree that murder is wrong and that the intentional killing of adult humans is normally murder. Or they may disagree about important questions of faith but agree that no believer should be persecuted or forced to convert. In fact, it is unlikely that a society, whatever its structure, can survive general disagreement about all moral matters. So there should always be some norms or ideals on which there is considerable agreement, if only at the level of abstract principle. Even if there is much disagreement about the whole of morality, there may be sufficient agreement about some parts.

There certainly is considerable disagreement about justice, especially distributive justice. There may be a consensus today that slavery is (very) wrong and that persons have certain basic rights: for instance, not to be killed or not to be restricted in their liberties without cause. But there is less agreement about the scope of these rights and about the relative strengths of rights of property. So it is not clear that it would be useful to invoke a favored account of justice in my evaluation of states. Rather, I shall try to bypass contemporary controversies, at least for now. It is mostly with regard to questions about the just functions of government (see Chapter 9) that the differences between rival accounts become especially important. For now, I restrict myself to general considerations of justice.

"Justice is the first virtue of social institutions, as truth is of systems of thought."[2] A state is justified, we may think, insofar as it respects justice. This would accord with the etymology of 'justification'. It may also accord with traditional accounts of the virtue of justice. We must nevertheless consider why justice should be a requirement of justification and legitimacy. Part of the answer depends on why we should care about justice, and this is a complicated subject that I address in Section 6.5.

What must a state do to be just? A just state presumably is, first of all, one that respects the constraints of justice. Justice imposes constraints on the behavior and intentions of persons and, presumably, institutions. I suppose that many of these constraints take the form of moral rights and duties. States, then, must respect the moral rights of individuals and fulfill duties owed to individuals.[3]

---

2. Rawls, *A Theory of Justice*, p. 3.
3. Perhaps there are duties to nonindividuals (e.g., peoples, corporations) as well as to nonhumans. The latter will not essentially concern us in this essay, though the for-

It is not clear what sort of constraint this condition imposes on states until the nature and content of our moral rights and duties are specified. It is likely that, on most accounts, our moral rights block the sorts of atrocities found on lists of the evils of states. We may suppose, at least for the time being, that we each have moral rights to our lives, liberty, and possessions, though, as I said, the difficult questions concern their nature and scope. It is not particularly controversial to say of the regimes of Nazi Germany, the former Soviet Union, China, Iraq, and so on that they violated the rights to life, liberty, and possessions of many. What is disputed is the specification of these rights, their nature and exact content. As I shall suggest, partisans and critics of moral rights alike often assume a particular specification, one that makes the development of the state problematic.

States typically claim sovereignty and exclusive rights to use force. Individuals are not supposed to use force without the state's permission. It is often argued that states have the particular task of ensuring that we do not individually need to use force (e.g., to protect ourselves). If this is true, states may consequently have the provision of justice as one of their main tasks. Restrictions on one's capacity to use force might not be advantageous or justified except as part of a package that offered one better protection. Justice may then require states not only to respect the constraints of justice but also to provide justice. What might be involved in a state's provision of justice? Typically states enforce laws, adjudicate disputes, and provide mechanisms for collective decisions (e.g., contracts, corporate law, local governments, parliaments); they also seek to effect distributive justice. We may expect that their justification depends on their provision, to some degree, of such services (see Chapter 9).

We may require, then, of states that they respect and provide justice. Suppose we say that a state is justified insofar as it is just. This requirement, by itself, would elicit few objections from most political philosophers. "Political realists" and some others, as we have seen, might object; they might claim that states can be justified even if unjust. I come back to the distinction between rational and moral justification in Section 6.5. At present, I address a possible implication of this requirement on states, namely, that no state is, or could be,

---

mer is of some importance for my inquiry. States are not individuals, and they claim to be the bearers of rights (e.g., those of sovereignty) and the object of duties. I begin with the rights and duties of individuals for methodological reasons alone. Some of the rights and liberties of nonindividuals are discussed in Chapters 7 and 8.

thereby justified. For it may be that the constraints of justice are such as to fill up all of moral space or at least leave no room for the state's exercise of its functions or even for its existence. For instance, should we possess indefeasible (or "virtually indefeasible") natural rights to our lives, liberty, and possessions, it is doubtful that the state may do much, if anything, without violating our (moral) rights. Essentially this is the criticism of states offered by many American libertarian anarchists. An answer to this criticism must be given, and it is provided by any account of justice that denies that our moral rights are strong enough to prevent the just emergence of a state. Among contemporary accounts of justice, contractarian and consequentialist theories most easily satisfy the justice condition.

6.2 NATURAL RIGHTS

It has been said that "individuals have rights, and there are things no person or group may do to them (without violating their rights)."[4] This may be true – perhaps trivially so. The virtue of justice is the source of moral rights; so we may suppose that respect for justice requires respect for the moral rights of individuals.

We may think, then, that respect of individual rights is a condition for the justifiability of a state. It may, however, be excessively strong, a condition no feasible state could satisfy. For if individuals have rights, some contemporary libertarians argue, it is unclear that there is much, if anything, for states to do qua state. Robert Nozick rightly asks, "Individuals have rights. . . . So strong and far-reaching are these rights that they raise the question of what, if anything, the state and its officials may do. How much room do individuals' rights leave for the state?"[5] States claim various powers and rights (e.g., sovereignty, control of force). But whence these rights and powers? If individuals possess rights to liberty, how is it possible for states to monopolize legitimate force, without violating these rights? Consider that for states to pursue justice, they must use resources, typically taken from citizens and others – that is, taxation. But if individuals have rights to their possessions, whence the right to tax?

It could be argued, following Hobbes, that the moral (claim) rights of individuals come into being with the establishment of a state (or

4. Nozick, *Anarchy, State, and Utopia*, p. ix.
5. Ibid.

government), that before this they have no such rights (or duties). But this seems implausible.[6] What then is to be said against the libertarian anarchist?

Nozick claims: "Individuals have rights, and there are things no person or group may do to them (without violating their rights)." From this seemingly innocuous premise, a case can be made against states: They cannot exist without violating these rights. Therefore states cannot be legitimate.[7] I shall examine the premise of such an argument, namely, that we have certain moral rights, and in so doing discover what must be claimed about the moral rights of individuals if these are to leave room for the state.

In order for moral rights to block the legitimacy of states, they must precede the establishment of the state and be quite strong. It is no accident that libertarian critics of states often look to seventeenth- and eighteenth-century natural rights moral theory to defend their position. What, then, are natural rights?[8]

It turns out there is no simple, much less uncontested, answer to this question. Proponents of natural rights differ one from another on significant matters of doctrine. And the language of natural (and human) rights has been so widely appropriated that it is no longer clear what precise content it has. Still, so-called natural rights libertarians are sometimes clearer and more in agreement in their accounts than are other "rights theorists". In any case, it is not labels but doctrines that are important. I shall develop an account of natural rights that attempts to capture much of what many libertarians mean and to articulate an interesting position regarding justice. Later this position will be contrasted with another, to be labeled "seminatural rights". As both of these positions will consist of largely separable conditions, alternative positions can easily be constructed and

---

6. The plausibility of this position – that rights (and duties) presuppose the existence of a state or government – is typically due to making sanctions an existence condition of rights (and duties). This condition is widely rejected by contemporary moral and legal theorists. But even if one were to accept a sanction condition for rights and duties, it should be recalled that modern states are not the only enforcement agency. I discuss a "Hobbesian" position in Section 6.3.

7. "[L]aws and institutions no matter how efficient and well-arranged must be reformed or abolished if they are unjust." Rawls, *A Theory of Justice*, p. 3.

8. Parts of what follow borrow from Morris, "Natural Rights and Public Goods," in *The Restraint of Liberty, Bowling Green Studies in Applied Philosophy*, vol. 7, ed. T. Attig, D. Callen, and J. Gray (Bowling Green, Ohio: Bowling Green State University, 1985), pp. 102–117, as well as L. W. Sumner, "Rights Denaturalized," in *Utility and Rights*, ed. R. Frey (Minneapolis: University of Minnesota Press, 1984), pp. 20–41, and *The Moral Foundations of Rights*, chap. 4.

their implications determined. My purpose will be less to explicate widely held positions than to determine what characteristics of rights (and duties) threaten to make all states unjust.

What then are natural rights? They are first of all *rights*, that is, claim rights as opposed to mere liberties. Someone has a (claim) right to *x* only if some other individual or institution has a duty to the first with regard to *x*.[9] Furthermore, natural rights are a species of *moral*, not *legal* rights. Most importantly, natural rights are moral rights that are *natural*. This is the crucial attribute; what does it entail? According to early modern philosophers, natural rights are those rights that humans possess in a *state of nature*. But this may be to explain the unclear with the opaque. For many of these thinkers, a state of nature is that situation in which humans find themselves in the absence of government or even society. For Hobbes, states of nature are asociable and nasty. By contrast, Locke thought them to be sociable, albeit increasingly inconvenient, states of affairs. Part of their disagreement lies in the fact that Locke believed humans possess certain moral duties and (claim) rights in the state of nature and that these would generally be respected, whereas for Hobbes, the "right of nature" is but a mere liberty.[10] Each theorist uses the notion of a state of nature to set out his distinctive moral position, as well as his conception of human nature.

States of nature are what exists prior to government and the state. What is meant by this? The state for most modern political thinkers is a product of convention.[11] Some of the moral rights that exist in states of nature are thus *prior to convention*. These rights (and correlative duties) may then *constrain* states. Further, it was widely thought that such rights are *independent of convention*. Thus, they may be invoked as a standard against which to assess the state and society, law and custom. Indeed, this independence of convention must

---

9. This (partial) analysis of a claim right is now standard in the literature, though some contest it. Typically, unless I specify otherwise, I shall speak simply of rights; Hohfeld's "privileges" and Hobbes's "right of nature", for instance, I shall refer to as (mere) liberties. Duty, when tied to rights, is a relational notion: Someone has a duty to someone else with regard to something. Unlike many theorists, I do not distinguish duties from obligations in these contexts.

10. "The RIGHT OF NATURE . . . is the Liberty each man hath, to use his own power, as he will himselfe, for the preservation of his own Nature; that is to say, of his own Life; and, consequently, of doing any thing, which in his own Judgement, and Reason, he shall conceive to be the aptest means thereunto. . . . By LIBERTY, is understood, according to the proper signification of the word, the absence of external Impediments". Hobbes, *Leviathan,* chap. 14, p. 91.

11. As remarked in Chapter 1, Hegel is a notable exception.

account at least in part for the popularity of appeals to natural rights. (Sometimes this seems to be all that is involved in appeals to such rights.)

If prior to, and independent of, convention, natural rights must be possessed by virtue of some natural or nonconventional property of their possessors. Thus, it is usually claimed that possession of such rights is by virtue of possession of certain natural attributes – for instance, rationality and self-consciousness. Possession of such rights depends not on social convention or status but solely on the sort of creature that one is.[12]

Summarizing my account so far, we may say that natural rights are (1) moral (2) claim rights, that are (3) natural, that is, (a) possessed in a state of nature, (b) prior to and (c) independent of convention, and (d) held by virtue of possession of some natural attribute.[13]

Thomas Jefferson and others have claimed it is *self-evident* that we have certain rights. Although appeals to self-evidence are now out of fashion,[14] the moral rationalism implicit in such appeals is still an important part of the natural rights tradition. Typically, natural rights theorists have been moral rationalists, committed to the view that moral truths are discoverable by human reason. This is important, as skepticism about natural rights is often closely tied to skepticism about moral rationalism or moral realism. We could add, then, a further characterizing condition to my account of natural rights: (e) known by reason. Some may object to adding an epistemic condition to an analysis of the *content* of a type of moral claim, which would amount to mixing up levels of discourse.[15] I cannot think of a single

---

12. In one sense, possession of such rights depends on birth. But in the classical sense, where 'birth' designated class membership, natural rights, attributed to all humans or persons, were weapons against the privileges claimed by aristocracies.

   Fred Miller usefully distinguishes rights that are natural in the sense of being based on natural justice from ones that are prepolitical. See *Nature, Justice, and Rights in Aristotle's "Politics,"* p. 88. I prefer to think of "states of nature" as prior to government and law because the notion of "political" is so imprecise and variable. But his distinction is effectively preserved in my characterization of natural rights.

13. See also the contrasts John Simmons draws in his account of Lockean natural rights, *The Lockean Theory of Rights* (Princeton: Princeton University Press, 1992), pp. 89–94.

14. Hillel Steiner, however, believes that certain truths about rights are conceptual, and he thinks of this as a kind of self-evidence (personal communication).

15. Although I do not wish to draw a sharp distinction here between normative and metaethics, much less to claim that the latter must been neutral between accounts of the normative, it may be well to regard this condition as more problematic than others. See Thomas Hurka, "Sumner on Natural Rights," *Dialogue* 28 (1989),

natural rights theorist who does not believe that such rights are known by reason. The moral rationalism of the tradition is often stressed by defenders and opponents alike. But I shall not insist on retaining this characteristic.

What natural rights do we have? Tradition provides different answers to this question, and it is difficult to evaluate these in the absence of coherent and clear criteria for the identity of natural rights. It is usually assumed that we have natural rights to our lives, liberty, and possessions. I shall simply follow tradition here and assume that if we have any natural rights, we have these three rights. I shall not, however, require that these be part of the characterization of natural rights, for it is certainly possible that our basic moral rights are other than these three.

Further, it is often also claimed that natural rights are *absolute* or *indefeasible.* A right (or a duty) is absolute in this sense if it binds always, *whatever the consequences,* and it is defeasible if it is not absolute. Absolute rights or duties may *never* be overridden.[16] I shall not, however, characterize natural rights as absolute. Few natural rights theorists or other moral philosophers today believe that rights or duties are absolute in this sense. It is at the least conceivable that such rights sometimes be justly overriden.[17] There is, however, something special about natural rights that is not yet captured by my

---

117–130, where it is argued that expressivists could be natural rights theorists. To my knowledge, none are, but Hurka's point seems right.

16. It would be useful to develop a notion of "virtually absolute" for duties that are *almost always* indefeasible. Nozick seems not to believe our rights to be absolute or indefeasible in my sense. See Nozick, *Anarchy, State, and Utopia,* p. 30n.

17. A right's being indefeasible or its being "basic" (see below) should not be confused with its inalienability. A right is *inalienable,* I shall say, if it cannot be alienated. That is, someone who possesses an inalienable right lacks a power that is conjoined to many rights. Property rights are typically alienable in this sense, whereas voting rights are not. Inalienability is a property often attributed to certain rights by natural law or natural duty theorists for whom rights are not basic (see footnote 21) and for whom certain duties are indefeasible. (Jefferson's reference to inalienable rights in his draft of the Declaration of Independence may suggest that he is best read as a natural duty theorist.) I shall not attribute inalienability in this sense to natural rights; few libertarian thinkers do so.

A right's being alienable should not be confused with its being *forfeitable.* If a right is possessed by virtue of one's nature (e.g., rationality, self-consciousness, species membership), it is possible that it cannot be forfeited except by loss of that nature. It may, therefore, be difficult to defend the death penalty (as opposed to the right to kill in self-defense) if people have the right to life by virtue of their nature, it being implausible that people lose their humanity or rationality (in the relevant sense) by committing a crime. See L. W. Sumner, *Abortion and Moral Theory* (Princeton: Princeton University Press, 1981), pp. 110–111.

account and that risks being omitted should one agree in not insisting on indefeasibility. Although some disagree, it would seem that other moral traditions can make use of the notion of moral rights. Certainly contractarian moral theory can support moral rights; more controversially, I would claim that utilitarianism can as well.[18] The mere attribution of moral rights to individuals, even in a state of nature, does not make one a member of the natural rights tradition. A distinguishing feature of natural rights theories is the *place* accorded such notions in the structure of the theory. Natural rights theories, I suggest, understand natural rights to be *basic*. Without necessarily assuming foundationalism, conceive of the structure of a moral theory as hierarchical, some moral notions and principles being explanatorily prior to others. Then a right (or duty) is basic if and only if it is not dependent on any other *moral* property or relation. A basic moral right must be grounded on some nonmoral property or relation. A natural rights theory, I am suggesting, takes certain rights to be basic.[19]

I shall then add a further condition to my characterization of natural rights. In addition to the conditions above, natural rights are basic. Summarizing: *Natural rights are (1) moral (2) claim rights that are (3) natural, that is, (a) possessed in a state of nature, (b) prior to and (c) independent of convention, (d) held by virtue of possession of some natural attribute, and (4) basic.*

A full defense of my analysis would require more space than available here, and judging by the literature, it might not be an easy matter to reach agreement. My purpose, in any case, is less to explicate widely held positions than to determine what characteristics of rights (and duties) threaten to make all states unjust. I should, however, note what will strike many as a strange consequence of my characterization, namely, that many thinkers, normally categorized as natural

---

18. See Sumner, *The Moral Foundations of Rights*. A variety of positions on these matters is defended in *Utility and Rights*.
19. Taking certain rights to be basic in this sense does not entail that they are absolute, though this is often claimed as well. One might argue a defeasible but basic right is not overrideable except by another basic right, for the overriding considerations cannot have their source in a less basic right. Note an important implication of this feature of natural rights. If such rights are basic, then if they are defeasible they may be overridden only by other basic rights. Hence, they may function much like absolute rights, depending on the nature of the defeasibility conditions. I am indebted here to conversations some time ago with Wayne Sumner and Peter Danielson.

rights theorists, will not be. Locke, for instance, will not be a natural rights theorist on my account, nor will Catholic thinkers such as John Finnis. For they may be best interpreted as denying that rights are basic in my sense. Rather, their theories are better understood as duty-based or law-based, where one of these concepts is basic instead of that of rights.[20] If this implication of my analysis is troublesome, then the condition of basicness can be bracketed, for it will figure in my argument at only one point.[21] In any event, I propose to consider a particular natural rights libertarian case against the state, and for this the account should serve adequately. Taxonomies and analyses are, to a large extent, to be judged by reference to the purposes they are intended to serve.

The crucial premise of the natural rights libertarian argument against the state is the claim that states violate the natural rights of individuals. This claim does not seem to be difficult to establish once it is granted that we have natural rights (in my sense) to our lives, liberty, and possessions. States claim control of the legitimate use of force within a territory, refuse to recognize rival claims, and forbid others to act on any rights other than those that they recognize. Further, states characteristically appropriate part of the wealth of their subjects in order to finance their activities and often conscript their

---

20. See Locke, *Second Treatise*, chap. 2, para. 6. John Finnis claims that "when we come to explain the requirements justice, which we do by referring to the needs of the common good at its various levels, then we find that there is reason for treating the concept of duty, obligation, or requirement as having a more strategic explanatory role than the concept of rights." *Natural Law and Natural Rights* (Oxford: Clarendon Press, 1980), p. 210.

21. The term 'natural rights' is used often broadly and loosely. And my distinction between "natural rights" theories and what we may call "natural duty" or "natural law" theories may strike many as esoteric. It may be crucial, however, to understanding the individualism implicit in the natural rights tradition, especially in the United States. By contrast to the latter, many eighteenth-century thinkers were transitional, I suggest, halfway between medieval natural law and more modern, individualist ways of understanding justice. Further, although the issue dividing our "natural rights" and "natural duty" theorists may not be very important for some of the issues we are considering here, in practical ethics the distinction is important. Suppose that we have a right to life and that it is derived from a more basic duty not to kill (i.e., a natural duty). Suppose also that it is very stringent, e.g., indefeasible (or virtually so). Then it would seem that the right that correlates with the duty not to kill – some but not all duties correlate with rights – would be *inalienable* (i.e., could not be alienated or waived by the right-bearer). By contrast, individualist natural rights theorists typically understand our natural right to life as alienable, just like our rights to liberty and to our possessions. The respective positions on the permissibility of suicide would be different.

members (and others) to fight wars. They imprison and often take the lives of those who resist their authority. If we have natural rights to life, liberty, and property, they are frequently violated by states.[22]

States frequently violate these natural rights. *Must* they do so? Were a state to respect the natural rights of individuals, then it would not necessarily be illegitimate. Suppose a state were based on the consent of the governed ("to secure these rights, governments are instituted among men, deriving their just powers from the consent of the governed"). It would not violate the natural rights of individuals and thus might be legitimate.

If we have natural rights to life, liberty, and property, consent justifies a state only if genuine – that is, explicit, voluntary, and informed. For the natural rights theorist, hypothetical consent "is not worth the paper it's not printed on".[23] *Contra* Hobbes, involuntary "consent" is not *consent*. And uninformed consent does usually not bind. At the very least, the standard sorts of restrictions that govern legal consent have to be applicable for consent to confer legitimacy. The more significant the transaction, the more restrictions; conditions on the consent required for, say, selling a house or marriage need to be more restrictive and explicit than those regarding buying a daily newspaper. Further, the explicit, voluntary, and informed consent of the governed would have to be unanimous. Suppose it were not unanimous. Then some individuals would be "independents", outside the jurisdiction of the state.[24]

No existing state comes close to satisfying these conditions. The United States of America, often said to be founded on the consent of the governed, is a constitutional order to which few, if any, (living) citizens can be said to have genuinely consented in the required sense. To avoid this objection, Jefferson insisted that every generation rewrite the Constitution. But this would not solve the problem, even if we were to assume that generations come into existence and die off all at once. There is no feasible way of securing the genuine consent of an entire generation. Consider that the present U.S. Constitution did not even obtain the unanimous consent of the committee that drafted it (without the authority to do so), much

---

22. I leave until Chapter 7 the matter of the state's claim to sovereignty.
23. I thought this quip to be Nozick's, but I cannot find the reference. As I noted in Chapter 5, hypothetical "consent" is not consent.
24. I consider consent in greater detail in Section 6.4, and questions of authority and obligations to obey in Chapter 7.

less that of the special conventions created for purposes of ratification.

Focusing on the American experience of constitutional convention is perhaps a mistake. Simultaneous and joint consent is but one way to secure the requisite agreement. Perhaps a legitimate state can emerge, "as if by an invisible hand", from the voluntary actions and pairwise consent of individuals. A state need not be established by a consensual constitutional convention in order to be consistent with the natural rights of persons. Or so we may interpret Part I of Robert Nozick's *Anarchy, State, and Utopia*.

The libertarian anarchist claims that any state violates the natural rights of individuals and is consequently illegitimate.[25] To evaluate this claim, Nozick grants the libertarian anarchist his or her "optimistic" assumptions concerning a "Lockean" state of nature: natural rights, general compliance, and so on.[26] Against the anarchist Nozick claims that a (minimal) state *can* arise without violating the natural rights of individuals. His defense of this claim consists in the development of a plausible story of the emergence of a minimal state that does not violate anyone's natural rights. The tale has five stages. (1) We begin in a Lockean state of nature where individuals have certain basic rights (life, health, liberty, possessions, punishment). (2) Problems caused by private enforcement of these rights and the inability of some to defend themselves lead to the emergence of *private protective associations*. These agencies offer their protection services at a price. (3) Protection is a special kind of good, however, and competition between the agencies leads to the emergence of a *dominant protective association*. The claim here is that the protection of the strongest protective agency is better than that of its rivals, and that the stronger it becomes, the better its product. Free competition leads not to a plurality of agencies but to a *natural monopoly* of one.[27] (4) The dominant protective association eventually acquires a monopoly of force within a territory, having put its competitors out of business. The dominant agency is now an "ultraminimal state", protecting its clients within a defined territory. It is not yet a state, as it only protects paying clients; it does not protect "independents".

---

25. Nozick, *Anarchy, State, and Utopia*, p. 6. Nozick does not always specify that the rights in question are natural. Further, I should mention that neither he nor his anarchist opponents necessarily subscribe to the account of natural rights I have offered.
26. Nozick, *Anarchy, State, and Utopia*, pp. 10–12.
27. Ibid., p. 17. This part of Nozick's story was presented in Chapter 3.

The argument so far is that the transition between these various stages of our story are morally permissible. A protective association can become dominant and then an ultraminimal state without violating anyone's rights. The transition to (5) the emergence of a state is not only morally permissible but morally required given the dominant protective agency's dominant position. The argument is extremely complicated, and I shall not reproduce it here. (See Section 6.8.)

The consensus in the literature is that Nozick's impressive argument is, at best, very problematic. More important, even if it were effective against the libertarian anarchist's claim that *no* state can arise without violating the natural rights of individuals, Nozick's tale would not rebut the contention that *all existing* states and *virtually all feasible* states are illegitimate (if we have natural rights). The justification of any particular state, on his view, must turn on *that* state's history, from its emergence from the rights-respecting interactions of individuals.[28] The fastest and simplest route to defeating the legitimacy of states, it would appear, is via natural rights. If we have natural rights to our lives, liberty, and property, it is difficult to see how a state could exist without violating these rights; it is hard to see how feasible states could be legitimate.

The failure of Nozick's argument, as well as its extraordinary complexity and ingenuity, should alert us to the difficulty of justifying the state once we have assumed that individuals have natural rights. (I say more on this in Section 6.8.) The ends that Nozick has to go in his attempt to justify the (minimal) state are an indication of the moral force of natural rights, and I take this as one of the important lessons of his book. Little wonder, then, that proponents of rebellion and writers of revolutionary pamphlets mix their calls to the barricades with references to natural rights. The libertarian anarchist may well be right in believing that the road to the state, even the classical liberal democratic state, is blocked by these rights.

The central premise of the libertarian anarchist's argument asserts the existence of natural rights. Those who reject natural rights can defeat the libertarian anarchist with considerably less trouble than Nozick.

---

28. The view of distributive justice natural rights theorists like Nozick are constrained to hold is *historical:* "whether a distribution is just depends upon how it came about." Ibid., p. 153.

6.3 HOBBESIAN CONTRACTARIANISM

If natural rights threaten to condemn most states, Hobbes's "social contract" threatens to justify virtually all of them. It may be, as Nozick says, that individuals "have rights, and there are things no person or group may do to them (without violating their rights)." But if they have no rights prior to the state, and if the only rights they have are those recognized by the state, then their rights pose no threat to the state.

According to Hobbes the only "right" humans have by nature is "the Liberty each man hath, to use his own power, as he will himselfe, for the preservation of his . . . own Life". In the condition of nature, "a condition of Warre of every one against everyone . . . every man has a Right to every thing". This right, Hobbes makes clear, is a mere liberty, the absence of contrary duties or obligations.[29] The claim-rights of humans thus do not stand in the way of the emergence of states; indeed, no part of justice does:

> To this warre of every man against every man, this also is consequent; that nothing can be Unjust. The notions of Right and Wrong, Justice and Injustice have there no place. Where there is no common Power, there is no Law: where no Law, no Injustice. . . . It is consequent also to the same condition, that there be no Propriety, no Dominion, no *Mine* and *Thine* distinct; but onely that to be every mans, that he can get; and for so long, as he can keep it.[30]

Bentham's view of natural rights is similar to Hobbes's, even if his moral theory is very different. In his famous attack on the *Déclaration des droits de l'homme et du citoyen* of the French Assembly of 1791, he heaps scorn on partisans of natural rights:

> There are no such things as natural rights – no such things as rights anterior to the establishment of government – no such things as natural rights opposed to, in contradistinction to, legal. . . .
> [L]iving without government [is] to live without rights . . . no government, and thence no laws – no laws, and thence no such things as rights – no security – no property.[31]

29. Hobbes, *Leviathan*, chap. 14, p. 91.
30. Ibid., chap. 13, p. 90. I should mention that this reading of Hobbes, while not uncommon, is not universally accepted.
31. Jeremy Bentham, "Anarchical Fallacies," in *Human Rights*, ed. A. I. Melden (Belmont, Calif.: Wadsworth, 1970), p. 31. On Bentham's general analysis of a right, see

It could be argued, following Hobbes and Bentham, that the (claim) rights of individuals come into being with the establishment of a state (or government), that before this, they have no such rights. But this seems implausible, and few philosophers adhere any longer to such a view. As I noted earlier, the plausibility of this position is typically due to making sanctions an existence condition of rights ("Covenants, without the Sword, are but Words, and of no strength to secure a man at all"). This condition is widely rejected by contemporary moral and legal theorists. But even if one were to accept a sanctions condition for rights and duties, it should be recalled that modern states are not the only enforcement agency. Rights, and norms generally, can be enforced by nongovernmental bodies, as we saw in Chapter 3.[32]

The view that all rights are "positive" is no longer widely held in political and legal theory. It was always a curiosity that the view singled out rights and exempted other norms (e.g., duties) from dependence on state enforcement. It seems hard to contain the nihilism of such a position. Sometimes this position may just be a confused statement of a more plausible view that the state is the ultimate or final judge of what our rights and duties are. This view, discussed in Chapter 7, need not pronounce on the origin of our rights; it could be compatible with the position that they are natural. It merely posits the state as having the power to ascertain and interpret the scope of these rights. Its determinations are then binding, even if mistaken.

The "Hobbesian" view of rights may well be implausible, but it contains an interesting idea, which may be of importance in understanding the relation between prior rights and states. Utilitarian accounts of rights understand these to serve the general advantage of society (or humankind), as Bentham noted: "That in proportion as it is *right* or *proper,* i.e., advantageous to the society in question, that this or that right – a right to this or that effect – should be established or maintained, in the same proportion it is *wrong* that it should be abrogated".[33] But the particular flexibility of utilitarianism in this

---

Gerald J. Postema, *Bentham and the Common Law Tradition* (Oxford: Clarendon Press, 1986), pp. 321–324, 416–418.

32. Hobbes's position is more complex than may at first appear. Covenants in the condition of nature are valid if there is no reasonable suspicion that the other party will defect. Were another to perform first, perhaps irrationally, one may be bound to do one's part consequently, even in the absence of a Sovereign enforcer. See *Leviathan,* chap. 14, esp. p. 96.

33. Bentham, "Anarchical Fallacies," p. 32. See, of course, the last chapter of Mill's *Utilitarianism.*

regard is precisely what worries so many critics. When Rawls affirms that "justice is the first virtue of social institutions", he puts forward an antiutilitarian position: "Each person possesses an inviolability founded on justice that even the welfare of society as a whole cannot override. [Justice] does not allow that the sacrifices imposed on a few are outweighed by the larger sum of advantages enjoyed by many."[34] There is more to be said in defense of utilitarian accounts of justice and rights,[35] but I shall focus instead on contractarian accounts.

Contractarianism is a tradition or a family of views that seek to justify morality or political institutions by reference to rational agreement. The general idea is that a morality or a form of political organization (e.g., a state) is to be justified by being shown to be the outcome of the rational agreement of the individuals over whom it has authority. There are so many different accounts of the relevant agreement – even some that effectively replace agreement with conventions – that it is unclear whether all really have much in common.[36] Contractarianism may be moral or political (or both). *Moral contractarianism* is the attempt to justify morality, or part of morality (e.g., justice), by reference to agreement. *Political contractarianism* is a normative (usually, albeit not necessarily moral) theory of political institutions (e.g., the state, law). The latter might be taken to be relevant to the theory of the state, but it is moral contractarianism that is the source of the moral rights relevant to my present concerns.[37]

We may think of certain of the rights that might be supported by a "Hobbesian" contractarian account of justice as derived from norms, adherence to which is mutually advantageous. So it may be that norms guaranteeing each a right not to be harmed in his or her per-

---

34. Rawls, *A Theory of Justice*, pp. 3–4.
35. See Sumner, *The Moral Foundations of Rights*.
36. This is especially true about recent contractarianism. Will Kymlicka thinks, "in a sense, there is no contact tradition in ethics, only a contract *device* which many different traditions have used for many different reasons." He rightly notes, "It is often said that all contract theories ground morality in agreement. But only the classical theorists actually grounded obligation in agreement. For modern theorists, agreement is just a device for identifying the requirements of impartiality or mutual advantage, which are the real grounds of obligation." "The Social Contract Tradition," in *A Companion to Ethics*, ed. P. Singer (Oxford: Blackwell Reference, 1991), pp. 196, 195.
37. A political contractarian theory intended to provide a normative but nonmoral account of political institutions would offer a rational justification. It is possible to read Hobbes thus, depending on what one makes of his "laws of nature". Among contemporary theorists, James Buchanan comes closest to this sort of account. See his *Limits of Liberty*, as well as *The Calculus of Consent* (Ann Arbor: University of Michigan Press, 1962), written with Gordon Tullock.

son or possessions are mutually beneficial.[38] In an account such as Gauthier's, these may be rights that emerge to constrain the prebargaining stage of contractarian morality.[39] Such rights are conventional in one sense, as they are ascribed to individuals only insofar as certain conventions or norms are in force.[40] But they can very well exist in a state of nature, before agreement on general principles of justice and the like. In these respects they can be thought of as *natural*. They may also be thought to be natural in another way, as noted by Hume in his discussion of the "artificiality" of justice:

When I deny justice to be a natural virtue, I make use of the word, *natural*, only as oppos'd to *artificial*. In another sense of the word; as no principle of the human mind is more natural than a sense of virtue; so no virtue is more natural than justice. Mankind is an inventive species; and where an invention is obvious and absolutely necessary, it may as properly be said to be natural as any thing that proceeds immediately from original principles, without the intervention of thought or reflexion. Tho' the rules of justice be *artificial*, they are not *arbitrary*. Nor is the expression improper to call them *Laws of Nature*; if by natural we understand what is common to any species, or even if we confine it to mean what is inseparable from the species.[41]

In these senses, some contractarian rights can be natural, even if they are not independent of convention. If we recall the characterization of a natural right offered in Section 6.2, these rights are similar even if conventional. Natural rights I characterized as (1) moral (2) claim rights, that are (3) natural, that is, (a) possessed in a state of nature, (b) prior to and (c) independent of convention, (d) held by virtue of possession of some natural attribute, and (4) basic. Contractarian rights can satisfy many of these conditions, with some modifications, except for (c). We may think of them as "seminatural rights" and characterize them as (1) moral (2) claim rights that are (3) natural, that is, (a) possessed in a state of nature, (b*) prior to and (c*) inde-

---

38. On some accounts such norms can be sustained essentially through pairwise and small group interaction. See Sugden, *The Economics of Rights, Co-operation and Welfare*, as well as Loren E. Lomasky, *Persons, Rights, and the Moral Community* (New York: Oxford University Press, 1987), chap. 4.
39. See *Morals by Agreement*, chap. 7. In these sorts of theories, principles of justice issue from hypothetical rational choice in an initial or original bargaining position.
40. "Conventions" in this essay are not restricted to coordination games, as in much of the literature.
41. Hume, *Treatise of Human Nature*, Book III, Part II, sec. 1, p. 484.

pendent of government or law, (d*) held by virtue of possession of some natural attribute and certain conventions, and (4) basic.[42]

Bentham was mistaken in his implicit assumption that if there are no natural rights, then all rights are dependent on government ("there are no such things as natural rights – no such things as rights anterior to the establishment of government – no such things as natural rights opposed to, in contradistinction to, legal"). This does not follow; in the absence of natural rights there could be "seminatural" ones. I suggested that the main lesson of Nozick's *Anarchy, State, and Utopia* is the difficulty of justifying states from the assumption of natural rights, all the more so if such rights are thought to be "virtually indefeasible" or even stronger. One might infer that rejecting natural rights would make the task of justifying states much easier, even if not as simple a matter as Hobbes had hoped. But seminatural rights might pose a similar threat to states.

The significant difference in this respect between natural rights and contractarian seminatural ones turns on the fact that the latter are designed to be mutually beneficial. Suppose a particular arrangement, practice, or state is mutually beneficial for everyone in a certain area (a strict Pareto-improvement over the status quo). If people are understood to possess natural rights, then consent is required for instituting the new arrangement or practice. If unanimous consent of all concerned is not obtained, for whatever reason – for instance, some hold out for strategic reasons – the arrangement is blocked. The natural rights may well be overridable – for instance, to avoid moral catastrophes.[43] But it is not clear, especially if the rights are "basic", that they will be overridable merely by considerations of mutual benefit. Natural rights theorists often are critical of abridgments of property rights in the public interest (e.g., eminent domain), and not just because these powers are likely to be abused.[44] Nozick concludes

---

42. See Morris, "Natural Rights and Public Goods." The conditions for the possession of such rights (condition d*) can be more complicated than is usually suggested in the literature. For some of these complications, see Morris, "Moral Standing and Rational Choice Contractarianism," in *Contractarianism and Rational Choice: Essays on David Gauthier's "Morals by Agreement,"* ed. P. Vallentyne (Cambridge: Cambridge University Press, 1990), pp. 76–95, and "A Contractarian Account of Moral Justification."
43. See Nozick, *Anarchy, State, and Utopia*, p. 30n.
44. "The power of eminent domain, the power of the state to seize property against the will of its rightful owner, whether accompanied by the payment of compensation or not is wholly unjustifiable ... the right to property stands on higher moral ground than considerations of efficiency." Ellen Frankel Paul, *Property Rights and*

his attack on a well-known principle by noting that "even if the principle [of fairness] could be formulated so that it was no longer open to objection, it would not serve to obviate the need for other persons' *consenting* to cooperate and limit their own activities."[45]

Natural rights may require consent for mutually beneficial arrangements, but it is not clear whether contractarian seminatural rights would. The rationale of such rights is mutual advantage. Consequently, perhaps they would be overridable by mutually beneficial practices that could not efficiently secure the consent of all involved. This presumably would be the contractarian rationale for practices or powers like eminent domain. Similarly, a well-known "economic" analysis of tort law – liability and compensation in torts as enabling efficient transfers in the absence of contract (i.e., consent), when transaction costs are high[46] – may be adapted easily by contractarian accounts. Accordingly, the rights that protect our liberties and possessions may be overridable when mutually advantageous arrangements cannot efficiently secure general agreement.[47]

If contractarian seminatural rights are overridable by such considerations, they need not require consent as a condition of the justification of states. So we should expect states that are mutually beneficial not to be blocked by contractarian seminatural rights. Some prior rights, then, leave room for states. It is important to note that this result is not ad hoc. For contractarians, in effect, think both of justice and of states as means of resolving collective action problems involving security and other collective goods. That contractarian seminatural rights, then, leave room for states should be no surprise.[48]

Eminent Domain (New Brunswick, N.J.: Transaction Books, 1987), p. 255. These powers are likely to be abused or, rather, to be used in ways that are not mutually beneficial. This is what makes the theory of institutional design so difficult (see Chapter 9).

45. *Anarchy, State, and Utopia*, pp. 90–95 (italics in original).

46. For an accessible but critical presentation of the economic analysis of torts, see Coleman, *Risks and Wrongs*, Part III. See also Richard A. Posner, *Economic Analysis of Law*, 4th ed. (Boston: Little, Brown, 1992), pp. 252–254.

47. In relation to this line of thinking, see Coleman's interesting reinterpretation of the well-known Calabresi–Malamed accounts of liability and property rules, *Risks and Wrongs*, pp. 338–340.

48. Of course, some other theories of justice – for instance, utilitarian or natural duty theories – may do the same. Further, the matter of the emergent normative properties of the state may already appear less mysterious. Contractarianism is a type of constructivism; moral properties are constructed out of prior elements by convention. So, insofar as the possession of certain normative properties by certain collective entities (e.g., communities, states, corporations) is needed to resolve cer-

6.4 CONSENT

Natural rights, I have claimed, constrain states by requiring them to secure the consent of the governed. This is, in effect, to assume that rights protect choices. It is now common in the literature on rights to distinguish between choice (or will) accounts and interest (or benefit) accounts. The latter understand rights to be protected interests or benefits, where the former conceive of them as protecting choices. In one case, the correlative duties protect interests or guarantee benefits; in the other, the duties (and accompanying powers) protect choices. I have, in effect, assumed that natural rights libertarians favor choice or will accounts of rights.[49] Consent would effect (limited) alienation or suspension of our rights and thus be a condition of justified state interference. However, it may be that our fundamental rights are best construed as protecting interests or benefits. On this interpretation they would not block states, at least as easily as choice-protecting rights. We could then argue that "to secure these rights, governments are instituted amongst men" and that (the) people may alter or abolish governments that become "destructive of these rights", while omitting the condition that governments derive "their just powers from the consent of the governed".[50]

My object is not, as I have said, to put forward the most plausible account of natural rights or the best interpretation of particular natural rights theorists. Rather, I have sought to determine what sorts of

---

tain collective action problems, collective or corporate rights may be justified. I take up some of these matters in Chapter 7.

49. Many are best interpreted thus (cf. Nozick's remarks quoted above). See also Hart, "Are There Any Natural Rights?" *Philosophical Review* 64, 2 (April 1955), 175–191. Simmons does not attribute to Locke a choice account (*The Lockean Theory of Rights*, pp. 92–93), and Miller rejects such an account for Aristotle (*Nature, Justice, and Rights in Aristotle's "Politics,"* esp. pp. 115–117), two classical authors often invoked by contemporary natural rights thinkers. It should be noted that the common distinction between benefit and choice accounts of rights and the classification of theorists are not as simple as may appear. Raz is often cited as a benefit theorist (see *Morality of Freedom*, chap. 7), but his account does not fit the standard taxonomy neatly. See Morris, "Well-Being, Reasons, and the Politics of Law," *Ethics* 106 (July 1996), 822. For a lucid discussion of the differences between benefit and choice accounts of rights, see Sumner, *The Moral Foundations of Rights*, chap. 1, esp. pp. 45–53.

50. From the second paragraph of Jefferson's draft of the Declaration of Independence. I should mention the possibility that one of the interests protected by interest-protecting rights might be autonomy, as David Copp pointed out to me. In this case, consent might be a condition for abridging this right, even if it is construed as an interest- or benefit-protecting right.

prior rights threaten to condemn virtually all states. I do not find plausible most theories of the sorts of rights I have identified as "natural" (as opposed to the "seminatural" kind). But, as many of my conclusions about states will be rather skeptical, I need not spend time arguing against natural rights theorists. Much of their skepticism about states may be warranted, even without their premises.

At the same time, it is clear one may be a consent theorist without endorsing any special claims about people's natural rights. In the opening chapter, I contrast consensual accounts of states with mutual advantage (and Paretian) theories, and I suggest that many important contemporary controversies turn on the differences between the two traditions or perspectives. I cannot resolve these differences in this essay. Even if I favor mutual advantage accounts, I do not want to beg the question – or too many questions – against consent theorists.

Consent can be a necessary condition for legitimacy, merely a sufficient one, or both. Assuming that consent could suffice to legitimate only (reasonably) just governments or states, I shall think of *consent theory* as affirming both the necessity and the sufficiency of consent to legitimacy.[51] The claim that consent is sufficient is the less controversial of the two.[52] It is the claim of its necessity that is of greater concern here, and I shall take it to constitute the core of consent theory or *political consensualism*. Many partisans of consent have as well affirmed the consensual legitimacy of some states or types of states (e.g., republics or democracies), but this need not be part of the *theory*. Consent theory is a normative account, and it is possible that all actual states fail to satisfy its conditions for legitimacy.[53] This is also what many contemporary consent theorists in fact claim.

Consent is to be distinguished from consensus or general agreement. Most forms of political organization depend to some degree on consensus or agreement. But consensus has to do largely with shared

---

51. See Simmons, *Moral Principles and Political Obligations*, p. 57, and *The Edge of Anarchy*, pp. 197–198; Green, *The Authority of the State*, pp. 161–162; and Harry Beran, *The Consent Theory of Political Obligation* (Beckenham: Croom Helm, 1987).
52. Raz argues that consent binds only when certain conditions are met and that these do most of the justificatory work. See *The Morality of Freedom*, chap. 4, esp. pp. 93–94.
53. See Green, "Law, Legitimacy, and Consent," *Southern California Law Review* 62, 3 and 4 (March–May 1989), p. 808. (Just because most have not satisfied the theory's conditions for legitimacy, "consent theory is not therefore a failed explanatory hypothesis. It is a critical theory of the conditions under which we would have such an obligation.")

beliefs (or values). Sometimes terms like these are used to suggest more, but they essentially refer to agreement in belief, thought, or value. Consent, by contrast, involves the engagement of the *will* or commitment.[54] Something counts as consent only if it is a deliberate undertaking. Ideally, an act is one of consent if it is the deliberate and effective communication of an intention to bring about a change in one's normative situation (i.e., one's rights or obligations). It must be voluntary and, to some degree, informed.[55] Consent can be express (direct), or it can be tacit or implied (indirect). Both are forms of *actual* consent.[56] By contrast, as I have noted, (nonactual) "hypothetical consent" is not consent.

Consent theory should be seen as a distinctive philosophical position, one standing in opposition to other traditions which find the polity or political rule to be natural or would see government and law as justified by their benefits. The mutual advantage, Paretian tradition and different types of consequentialism seek to base legitimacy in what the polity does for its subjects and others. Yet other, more "participatory" accounts might require active involvement by citizenry for legitimacy. Political consensualism should not be conflated with these other traditions, however closely associated they may be historically, and should certainly not be confused with other allegedly "consensual" theories that base legitimacy on consensus or agreement.

The conclusion of contemporary consent theorists seems to be that virtually no states satisfy the account's conditions for legitimacy. It is simply that few people, "naturalized" citizens and officials aside, have explicitly or tacitly consented to their state. It is implausible to interpret voting in democratic elections as expressing the requisite

54. My brief account borrows especially from Simmons's writings. Like him, I understand intention to be essential to consent and do not follow Raz in taking belief to be central. See esp. Simmons, *On the Edge of Anarchy*, p. 70n., and Raz, *Morality of Freedom*, p. 81. Bernard Boxill agrees that someone cannot consent unknowingly but rejects the intentionality condition. See "On Some Criticisms of Consent Theory," *Journal of Social Philosophy* 24, 1 (Spring 1993), 83–85. There is a very useful discussion of this sort of view in Green, *The Authority of the State*, pp. 163–165.
55. The precise normative conditions will depend on the particular moral or legal theory invoked, as well as the account of the will. Hobbes notoriously allows for the establishment of Sovereignty by Acquisition, by force, and holds covenants entered into by fear to be obligatory. But his moral theory is radically conventionalist, and his account of the will eliminativist ("In Deliberation, the last Appetite, or Aversion, immediately adhaering to the action"). See *Leviathan*, chap. 20, p. 138, chap. 14, p. 97, and chap. 6, p. 44.
56. Simmons's writings can be recommended for accounts of tacit or implied consent.

consent, and mere residence and the like do not seem to be credible as the sort of engagements of the will required by consent theorists for obligation. Consequently, most people may not have the general obligation to obey the laws of their states that they are commonly thought to have. In Chapter 7, I discuss the matter of obligations to obey, as well as related questions about authority. So I shall not pause to interpret this skeptical conclusion here. For now I merely note, and endorse, the virtual consensus in the contemporary literature about the implications of consent theory.[57]

6.5 JUSTIFICATION REVISITED

I suggested that a just state respects the constraints of justice (e.g., the rights of subjects and others). It may as well be required to provide justice (e.g., enforce laws, adjudicate disputes, provide mechanisms for joint or collective decisions, ensure distributive justice).[58] I have argued that the rights of individuals need not threaten the legitimacy of all states, unless they are construed as choice-protecting natural rights (or virtually indefeasible basic rights). Some moralists do so construe them, and they should find themselves committed to "philosophical anarchism", the position that (virtually) no existing or feasible state is legitimate. But acceptance of rights such as these is not widespread among theorists. I shall assume that our rights do not stand in the way of states. It would take me far afield to defend my skepticism regarding choice-protecting natural rights (or virtually indefeasible basic rights); as some of my conclusions are similar to these philosophical anarchists, perhaps it is not necessary that I do so.

We still need to ask why justice is a condition for the legitimacy of states. One question is why the virtue of justice should be singled out and privileged over others (e.g., benevolence). The most important question is, Why should justice figure so centrally in our concerns with states? What hold does justice have over us that satisfying its requirements is a condition for legitimate states? The first reason has to do with the apparent failure of rational justifications: They seem to

---

57. Not everyone agrees. Boxill claims, "The criticisms of Simmons and others against consent theory are specious" (cf. his criticism, just noted, of the intentionality condition). It seems, however, that the important suggestion is that consent has to do with assumed and collective responsibility. "On Some Criticisms of Consent Theory," pp. 81, 99–100. I return briefly to this interesting idea in the next chapter.
58. I say more about the latter in Chapter 9.

be able to accord legitimacy to evil states. But the main answer to these queries lies in the nature of the particular virtue of justice.

Justice is the particular moral virtue that is concerned with what is *owed* or *due* to individuals. As I have noted, it is the virtue to which individuals appeal when they claim that to which they have a *right*. But the domain of justice, in the broad sense, is not exhausted by that of rights. Justice in this sense "covers all those things owed to other people: it is under injustice that murder, theft and lying come, as well as the withholding of what is owed for instance by parents to children and by children to parents, as well as the dealings which would be called unjust in everyday speech."[59] Although recent discussions of justice have focused largely on principles of distributive justice, the issues raised by states pertain to the broad virtue of justice.

Most moral philosophers since Plato have thought justice and practical reason to be closely connected – specifically, someone required by justice to do or to refrain from doing something has a reason to comply. The assumption that moral requirements are reasons goes by the name of (moral) *internalism*.[60] If this assumption is correct *and* the scope of justice is universal, it would seem that the reasons individuals would have to act justly would hold as well for states (and other corporate or collective agents). Different theories of justice will offer different accounts of these requirements and the reasons they apply to agents. Some may also relax the requirements of certain norms of justice for some or exempt others – for example, people who hold certain positions of responsibility, such as heads of state and physicians.[61] But it is doubtful that plausible theories would completely exempt states and their agents from all norms of justice. There may very well be special justifications for dissimulation and lying that apply to states and officials but not to ordinary individuals. If states have distinct powers and privileges, then they may correspondingly be able to override certain ordinary duties (e.g., against using force). But there should be no need to exempt

---

59. Philippa Foot, "Moral Beliefs" [1958], in *Virtues and Vices* (Berkeley and Los Angeles: University of California Press, 1978), p. 125.
60. I formulate internalism in terms of reasons as opposed to motives, as the assumption I have in mind is normative and not psychological. I discuss some of the varieties of internalism in "A Contractarian Account of Moral Justification."
61. In professional ethics a social position may be "strongly role-differentiated" if special professional norms are applicable to it, permitting or requiring occupants to ignore certain moral considerations that would otherwise apply – e.g., norms requiring truth telling. Alan H. Goldman, *The Moral Foundations of Professional Ethics* (Totowa, N.J.: Rowman & Littlefield, 1980), p. 260.

states from the standard constraints of justice, especially respect for the basic rights of individuals. It is not credible, given what we know about the corrupting effects of power, that we would rationally agree to exempt states from *all* of the major constraints of justice. To adapt an argument of Locke's:

> ... as if when men quitting the state of nature entered into society, they agreed that all of them but one, should be under restraint of laws, but that he should still retain all the liberty of the state of nature, increased with power, and made licentious by impunity. This is to think, that men are so foolish, that they take care to avoid what mischiefs may be done them by *pole-cats*, or *foxes;* but are content, nay, think it safety, to be devoured by *lions*.[62]

The very same reasons that make it desirable that individuals be constrained by justice make it equally desirable that states be so constrained. All the harms that other individuals can do us, states can do worse. Insofar as we have reason to seek protection from others, we have reason to seek protection from states.[63]

If the constraints of justice are reasons and apply to all agents, including states, then the distinction I made earlier between rational and moral justifications is more complicated than I made it seem. I said a state is rationally justified if it provides the relevant people with nonmoral reasons to respect its laws and to support it in various ways. I mentioned an ambiguity about the reasons alleged to be nonmoral. One difficulty with many "realist" accounts of justification is the opacity of the relevant moral-nonmoral distinction(s). I shall try to sidestep this problem as long as possible. Suppose that there is little disagreement about justice among a group of people and that their beliefs are largely veridical. Suppose as well that their state is more or less just. Then, assuming other conditions we may add are satisfied, they have reasons to respect the state's laws and to support it in various ways. Moral justification, under certain assumptions (e.g., internalism), turns out to be a species of rational justification.

Suppose instead either that the internalism assumption must be relaxed or that the constraints of justice do not bind all. Then moral

---

62. Locke, *Second Treatise of Government*, chap. 7, sec. 93.
63. The issues raised here are more complicated than the attention I am giving them. For instance, the continental doctrine of *raison d'Etat* raises difficult issues, but their complexity would detain us unnecessarily here. My criticisms of doctrines of sovereignty in Chapter 7 should undermine the position of some of those who would exempt states from the constraints of justice.

and rational justification will be distinct. I think that internalism ought to be relaxed, so I find myself in this position.[64] I think as well that there may be an interesting conception of rational justification to be developed, different from the varieties of "realism" influential in international relations. But the issues are simply too complex to be taken up here.

6.6 EFFICIENCY

We should require of states that they respect the constraints of justice. A state is justified insofar as it is just. Further, we should also require of states that they provide justice (e.g., enforcement, adjudication, collective choice). A full rationale for this positive requirement of justice may not be provided until it is shown that securing justice is a public good and that states may provide public goods when they can do so more efficiently than feasible alternatives (see Chapter 9).

Justice may be a necessary condition for the legitimacy of a state, but it may be argued that it is not *sufficient*. The gross evils of states aside, the typical inefficiency with which they perform their tasks and their characteristic tendency to assume additional tasks amount to considerable costs. A state that satisfies the constraints of justice will not commit the evil acts that concern us, and that is to be said in its favor. However, its pursuit of justice and other activities may be very inefficient and costly. It is not clear that a just, albeit extremely inefficient, state may permissibly limit our liberties and call on our resources in the necessary manner. The requirement of justice does not, by itself, address the problem of the disadvantages of states just mentioned. Given these costs it is not clear that states are justified even if they are just.[65]

64. Some contemporary moral theorists reject or relax internalism. Some others do not think moral norms necessarily bind universally. For the former, see Foot, "Introduction," *Virtues and Vices,* and David O. Brink, *Moral Realism and the Foundations of Ethics* (Cambridge: Cambridge University Press, 1989), esp. chap. 3. For the latter, see Gauthier, *Morals by Agreement,* and Gilbert Harman, "Moral Relativism Defended," *Philosophical Review* 84, 1 (January 1975), 3–22, and "Relativistic Ethics: Morality as Politics," *Midwest Studies in Philosophy,* vol. 3 (1978), ed. P. French, T. Uehling, and H. Wettstein, pp. 109–128. I endorse relaxing the internalist condition in "Justice, Reasons, and Moral Standing," in *Rational Commitment and Justice: Essays for Gregory Kavka.*

65. The efficiency of government has been a central concern of the Public Choice school of political economy, founded by James Buchanan and Gordon Tullock. For a survey of recent work skeptical about government, see Peter H. Aranson and

The general criticism seems right, and it may be that the account must be supplemented by an efficiency condition. A state is justified insofar as it is just and it provides goods and services (e.g., collective goods) to inhabitants of its territory more efficiently than alternative providers. Or, if this is unworkable for various reasons, a threshold efficiency condition could be substituted: Minimal efficiency is required of justified states. Efficiency generally has to do with the accomplishment of tasks with the minimum use of resources. A standard interpretation of efficiency is the familiar Paretian concept: An outcome x is *Pareto-efficient* if and only if there is no other outcome y such that someone prefers y to x and no one prefers x to y.[66] The related, more practical notion of Kaldor-Hicks efficiency is commonly used: An outcome is *Kaldor-Hicks efficient* if and only if there is no other outcome such that those who would gain from moving to it could compensate those who lose. Under certain conditions (e.g., low transaction costs), a Kaldor-Hicks improvement *with* compensation is equivalent to a Pareto improvement.[67]

As noted, the Paretian concept of efficiency is not very practical. There can be a surfeit of Pareto-efficient outcomes, and the status quo, however seemingly inefficient in other ways, could be Pareto-efficient. But the Kaldor-Hicks criterion has problems of its own.[68] My concern is less with practicality than with conceptual issues. Insofar as one favors mutual benefit, one will be drawn to Paretian notions. Some of what many find appealing in utilitarianism may commend Kaldor-Hicks notions.[69] As the latter allows some to be made worse

Peter C. Ordeshook, "Public Interest, Private Interest, and the Democratic Polity," in *The Democratic State*, ed. R. Benjamin and S. Elkin (Lawrence: University of Kansas, 1985), pp. 87–263. But see Donald Wittman, *The Myth of Democratic Failure: Why Political Institutions Are Efficient* (Chicago: University of Chicago Press, 1995).

66. Pareto efficiency can also be formulated in terms of well-being or welfare, where these are not interpreted, as is common, in terms of preference satisfaction. (This Paretian notion often is called "Pareto-optimality," but this is very misleading given that 'optimal,' in ordinary English, means best or most favorable.)

67. The Kaldor-Hicks criterion is sometimes called "the hypothetical compensation principle," as it requires only that losers *could* be compensated by winners. It is also sometimes misleadingly called "the potential Pareto test".

68. Not the least of which is the "Scitovsky Paradox," according to which two outcomes could each be Kaldor-Hicks superior to each other. See Tibor Scitovsky, "A Note on Welfare Propositions in Economics," *Review of Economic Studies* 9, 1 (November 1941), 77–88.

69. One needs to be very careful about conflating Kaldor-Hicks with utilitarianism, as taking the former as a measure of utility (or welfare) would require applying it with interpersonal comparisons of utility, something rarely done. For an argument for distinguishing utilitarianism from both Paretian and Kaldor-Hicks notions of

off without being compensated, it is subject to many of the criticisms leveled against utilitarian theories. But, beyond expressing sympathies with Paretian notions, I shall not adjudicate these quarrels here. Some efficiency condition seems to be required for justification. A just but grossly inefficient state would not seem to be justified; certainly we might have little reason to obey and support it.

An efficiency condition may, however, be redundant. Many accounts build efficiency into justice. Contractarian and consequentialist theories do this most clearly. So considerations of efficiency may already be built into our account of justice. This would be to misunderstand the concern here. If a state, by respecting the constraints of justice, does not bring about a Pareto-superior state of affairs, it is not clear what positive reason there would be for its existence. Unless a state improves our situation from what it would otherwise be, it seems that an alternative form of political organization would be preferable. In addition, without improvements in efficiency, we have not yet provided a reason for ascribing to state positive duties with regard to justice (e.g., enforcement, adjudication, collective choice). So it may be important to consider questions of efficiency separately from justice.[70] Comparative advantage over other forms of social organization should figure prominently in our evaluation of states.

It may strike some that efficiency, however important, has nothing to do with legitimacy. The thought may be that this is one of the places where legitimacy and justification come apart. Or more likely, the concern may be that legitimacy entitles an institution to act even if it does not do as well as others might or if it does not know best. Compare the state's position with protected spheres of individual choice: We are allowed to make our own mistakes in various domains. Or compare it with the right of parents to make choices for their children even when these may be erroneous or when others could do better. Legitimacy may allow states to act even if they do not do so for the best or as well as others might.

The issues, as my examples show, are complex. It is, after all, not incoherent or absurd to say that it is, in fact, usually best for people to be allowed to make mistakes or for children to have caring but

efficiency, see Coleman, "The Economic Analysis of Law," *Ethics, Economics, and the Law, Nomos,* vol. 124, ed. R. Pennock and J. Chapman (New York: New York University Press, 1982), pp. 85–89.
70. Additionally, some accounts do not factor considerations of efficiency into justice – e.g., certain natural rights theories.

imperfect parents.[71] But I do not think comparisons with individual and parental choice will go far to settling the issue about states. The latter, after all, are *artifices*, which we collectively create and sustain. Do we want to accord them this status of legitimacy if they perform their assigned tasks poorly or much worse than others? I am inclined to some sort of efficiency condition for justification. But the matter is controversial and difficult to resolve quickly. It will turn out, I think, that assuming some such condition will not bias much of the rest of my inquiry. Starting with the next chapter, I investigate to what extent legitimate states have the properties or powers they claim. Assuming that legitimacy requires both justice and minimal efficiency may be permitted me, as I shall argue for skeptical conclusions all the more likely to be true of states that are not particularly efficient or just. So readers who resist the imposition of an efficiency condition on legitimacy may nevertheless provisionally grant it in order to consider what follows.

6.7 LEGITIMATE STATES

Let us return to the matter of the two sorts of requirements of justice on states. I claimed earlier that these requirements were mainly two: to respect the constraints of justice and to secure justice. The second requirement for states typically takes the form of enforcing the rights of subjects and citizens, ensuring distributive justice, adjudicating disputes, providing means for collective decisions (e.g., elections, parliaments). I have just discussed why the first requirement should be imposed on states. The second requirement, however, is more problematic. For no account has yet been offered for ascribing to the state any *positive* functions.

Suppose that the requirements of justice for individuals are not merely *negative* – that is, constraints on action, requiring forbearance. Justice presumably also imposes *positive* duties, for instance, to provide aid or services to some in need. Then individuals will be required so to act. Suppose, for instance, that there are duties of

---

71. Those inclined to such a view, as well as many of those more tempted by nonperfectionist defenses of the autonomy of individual or parental choice, will limit the sorts of errors permitted. See Raz's defense of the value of autonomy in *The Morality of Freedom*, chaps. 14 and 15. See also William A. Galston, *Liberal Purposes: Goods, Virtues, and Diversity in the Liberal State* (Cambridge: Cambridge University Press, 1991), and George Sher, *Beyond Neutrality: Perfectionism and Politics* (Cambridge: Cambridge University Press, 1997).

mutual aid that require us to assist someone in urgent need of help, even at some significant cost to ourselves. If there is such a duty, we are obligated to act accordingly. The duty itself implies the permissibility of the required act. But the matter is not so straightforward with states. For they act by preempting the actions of individuals and by redirecting the energies and resources of individuals. Even supposing there are positive duties of justice, what would *entitle* states to employ the energies and resources of their members in these ways? The challenge of the libertarian anarchist reappears, albeit this time in a stronger form, without the assumption of natural rights.

It is important to understand the problem clearly. We may, as individuals, have duties to aid the needy. Suppose our state takes some of our resources without our consent – as states do when they tax[72] – and give our resources to the needy. The justification cannot merely be that we, as individuals, have duties to provide aid. At most, such duties would be part of the justification that others (including government) might give for imposing sanctions on those who fail to give as required. The duties themselves are not sufficient to justify the state's employing our resources to give for us. An additional justification must be offered (Chapter 9). The argument essentially is that states may assume positive duties when they can carry them out efficiently. Because one condition for the state's fulfillment of some of its positive duties (e.g., ensuring justice) is that it forbid individuals to use force (e.g., to protect themselves), the efficiency constraint is important.

States, I am suggesting, are legitimate to the extent that they are just and minimally efficient. The first condition has two parts: respects for the constraints of justice, and provision of justice. The question I take up in the remaining chapters concerns the implications of these conditions of legitimacy. Suppose a state to be reasonably just and efficient. What are its attributes? For instance, is it sovereign? Does it have a claim to its territory (what sort of claim)? May it seek to monopolize the use of force? What sorts of tasks should government perform? I could discuss further the conditions of justice and efficiency, if only to make them more precise. But mostly, in the next two chapters at least, I argue skeptically against almost all the central characteristics of modern states. Even if such states are

---

72. I am assuming that (individual) consent and representation are not the same. Appeals to principles such as "no taxation without representation" do not solve the problem here.

reasonably just and efficient, their self-image is not credible. Critics of my conditions of legitimacy can take my argument as a conditional and not worry too much about the antecedent.

6.8 APPENDIX: NOZICK'S DERIVATION OF THE MINIMAL STATE

There are many problems with Nozick's derivation of the minimal state from libertarian anarchy. First, even supposing that we have natural rights to our lives, liberty, and possessions, and granting that Nozick's story is plausible, all we are justified in concluding is that a (minimal) state *can* emerge from the voluntary interactions of individuals without violating anyone's rights. We are *not*, however, justified in concluding that states that do not in fact so emerge are justified. In an early chapter Nozick claims:

A theory of a state of nature that begins with fundamental general descriptions of morally permissible and impermissible actions, and of deeply based reasons why some persons in any society would violate these moral constraints, and goes on to describe how a state would arise from that state of nature will serve our explanatory purposes, *even if no actual state ever arose that way.* (p. 7)[73]

While such "fundamental potential explanations" may *explain* (p. 8),[74] it is not clear how they can also *justify*, at least on Nozick's account of justice.

In Part II of *Anarchy, State, and Utopia*, Nozick argues that the conception of justice to which he is committed by his assumption of (natural) rights is *historical:* The justice of a distribution of goods is entirely a function of how it arose (pp. 150–160). It is hard to see how choice-protecting natural rights theorists could hold any other view of justice, just as it is difficult for them to demand anything less than genuine, explicit consent in order to justify restrictions on liberty. If justice is historical, however, fundamental potential explanations, because they are "fact-" or "process-defective" (pp. 7–8), cannot justify actual events or institutions.

---

73. In this appendix, page references in parentheses are to Nozick, *Anarchy, State, and Utopia.*
74. But see Alan Nelson, "Explanation and Justification in Political Philosophy," *Ethics* 97, 1 (October 1986), 154–176.

From the competition of private protective agencies, then, will emerge a *dominant protective agency*. This is because protection is a good that gives rise to natural monopolies. (See the discussion of this matter in Chapter 3.) As Nozick notes, the dominant agency is not (yet) a state since it does not protect all the residents of its territory. Since it is a profit-making institution, it protects only paying clients; those who do not or cannot pay go without protection. Nozick argues that nonetheless the dominant agency within a territory will end up providing protection for all. Since nonclients, or independents, have a right to defend themselves, they are owed compensation by anyone who forbids them from doing so. Thus the dominant agency must compensate the independents, and the easiest way for it to do this is to offer them free services.

The tricky part of Nozick's argument here – the part that has been most heavily criticized – is the argument for compensation. If it is held that each individual possesses a natural right to self-defense, in my sense, then it may be implausible to suggest that it is permissible to violate such rights if one adequately compensates the victim. Natural rights are stronger than this. Nozick, however, does not explicitly characterize the moral rights that are part of his account, so I cannot be sure that the natural rights I impute to his story are those he would accept.

Some libertarian anarchists claim that *any* state violates the moral rights of individuals and consequently is illegitimate (p. 6). Nozick and the libertarian anarchists share the same assumptions ("individuals have rights" [p. ix]) but reach different conclusions (a minimal state can be/is not justified) (p. xi). Since Nozick seeks, at the least, to refute the anarchists, he explicitly begins his inquiry with a statement of their assumptions: a "state of nature" with optimistic ("Lockean") characteristics.[75]

Although Nozick's aim appears to be to refute the libertarian anarchists (pp. 114, 119), he *also* appears to want to develop a general justification for the minimal state (pp. xi, 5, 53). It is unclear what the structure of that general justification would be. Some have argued that Nozick supposes that a state is justified insofar as it *could have*

---

75. It is important to note that Nozick defends his optimistic assumptions by the nature of his project in Part I – namely, the refutation of the libertarian anarchist. (See also pp. 114 and 119, where the refutation of the libertarian anarchist is said to be the goal of Part I.) Others may not grant him these assumptions so easily. Certainly, justifying the (minimal) state to the libertarian anarchist cannot be understood to be the same as justifying the state *tout court*. But see note 76.

developed in a certain manner, even if in fact it did not.[76] What exactly does Nozick's argument purport to show? Specifically, does a state have to have a particular history in order to be justified?

Let us carefully examine the argument. Nozick's argument for the Minimal State (MS) is in five stages and may be outlined as follows:

1. *State of Nature* (pp. 10–12): individuals with natural rights
2. *Protective Associations* (pp. 12–15): the formation of protection agencies
3. *Dominant Protective Association* (pp. 16–17): one agency becomes dominant
4. *Ultraminimal State* (p. 26): the dominant agency acquires a monopoly of force
5. *Minimal State:* "redistribution" from clients to independents

The first stage of the argument, the Lockean state of nature, assumes a set of laws of nature protecting life, health, liberty, and possessions. In addition, it is supposed that individuals possess rights of defense and of punishment. Note, in light of my account earlier of natural rights, that there is some ambiguity as to the exact nature of Nozick's moral assumptions or of Locke's theory. As I mentioned earlier, the latter may be better interpreted as holding a natural duty than a natural rights theory. And Nozick himself may hold some other account.[77] Certainly he does not wish to interpret the rights as absolute in my sense (pp. 29–30n). His argument requires that they be defeasible (e.g., permissible border crossings).

Private enforcement of rights and interests leads to feuds. The difficulty of some and the inability of others to defend themselves lead to Stage 2: the formation of Protective Associations. These are private protection associations or agencies that provide different services at a different price.

---

76. Robert Holmes interprets Nozick as claiming that a state is justified if it can be given a "fundamental potential explanation" and that explanation is or makes use of an "invisible hand explanation" involving no morally impermissible steps. See Holmes, "Nozick on Anarchism" [1977], in *Reading Nozick: Essays on "Anarchy, State, and Utopia,"* ed. J. Paul (Totowa, N.J.: Rowman & Littlefield, 1981), pp. 59 and 66 n. 2. See also Ellen Frankel Paul, "The Time-Frame Theory of Governmental Legitimacy" [1979], in *Reading Nozick,* pp. 270–285. It is hard to see how such accounts of justification could be compatible with Nozick's historical account of justice or with choice-protecting natural rights theory.
77. Cf. his discussions concerning permissible border crossings (chap. 4) and procedural rights (p. 107), as well as a long note (pp. 98–99).

Competition between different protective agencies, unlike competitive markets in other goods and services, gives rise to a Dominant Protective Association (Stage 3). Protection is a service unlike most others in that its value is relative, and the protection provided by the most powerful agency is necessarily the best protection available (p. 17). The dominant protective agency achieves a natural monopoly.

The dominant agency becomes an "ultraminimal state" (Stage 4). It monopolizes force in a territory. The transition from Stage 3 to Stage 4, if it is to have the moral importance Nozick seeks to attach to it, must be by morally permissible means (p. 52). The transition to Stage 5 is more complicated, albeit equally necessary. For the ultraminimal state is not a state (minimal or other): It does not provide protection for "independents" (who do not buy protection), and it does not consequently charge clients for the protection of those who do not pay for protection.

Nozick's argument for the transition from Stages 4 to 5 may be outlined as follows. (1) One may prohibit people from performing risky actions that might harm one if (a) they violate one's procedural rights, (b) purchasing their abstention is an unproductive exchange, and (c) one compensates them for resulting disadvantages. (2) The independents' unreliable and unfair enforcement of their rights constitutes the performance of a risky action that might harm one and (a) that violates one's procedural rights and (b) whose abstention if purchased would be unproductive. (3) Only the dominant protective association will have the power effectively to prohibit others from performing risky actions. (4) Offering them inexpensive or free protection may be the best way of so compensating them. (5) The result is a minimal state.

The argument for (1) consists of arguing first that crossings of moral borders is sometimes permissible. A system that permitted all such crossings, subject to the payment of compensation, would (a) be unfair, as it would favor buyers (p. 63). It would also (b) cause general apprehension and fear (pp. 66–7). Further, (c) such a system would use people as mere means to the ends of others. Knowing this and the consequent readjustment are costs; further, some injuries are not compensable, and some compensations are too much for an agent. A system that permitted no border crossings would seem to have distinct disadvantages when (a) obtaining the prior consent of the individual is not possible or (b) very costly. Nozick's conclusion is that given (a) fear, (b) the potential unfairness of the division of benefits from exchange, and (c) transaction costs, border crossings are permissible if compensation is paid (p. 73).

The argument for (2), the unreliable enforcement of the independents constituting a risk, is very complex and may be passed over here (see p. 107). The argument for (3), however, is simple. Any protective agency may judge procedures and forbid the use of those known to be unreliable and unfair; the dominant protective association, however, has a *de facto* monopoly, a unique position (pp. 108–9). It alone enforces prohibitions on others' procedures; it alone exercises its right to forbid risky actions. The argument for (4) is simply that the cheapest means of compensating independents is to offer them protective services (minus some charges) (p. 110). The dominant protective association is now a minimal state, though not an authorizer of violence (pp. 113–15, 117).

A number of criticisms may be, and have been, made of this argument. First, the assumption of "procedural rights" seems ad hoc. They are not natural rights, it may be argued, because they are not compossible[78] and because there is no reason to expect agreement, even among good-willed people, on a unique set of ideal procedures (p. 97).[79] In addition, they may be incompatible with the natural right to punish (p. 101). This assumption makes the argument too easy (p. 103).

Second, it is not the case that the dominant protective association may prohibit nonrisky procedures. All that it may do is publish a list of reliable and fair procedures (p. 103). If independents and other agencies merely use those on the list, there need be no natural monopoly.

Third, although this may be relatively unimportant, the minimal "state" is not a state of the sort with which we are familiar. It merely possesses a *de facto* monopoly; it has merely a liberty but no claim right to monopoly. It would seem to have no authority, much less sovereignty. And it is unclear what rights it might have to the state's

---

78. "Individual rights are co-possible" (p. 166); see also the important discussion on p. 238. See also Hillel Steiner, "The Structure of a Set of Compossible Rights," *Journal of Philosophy* 74, 12 (December 1977), 767–775.

79. As usual, Nozick recognizes the problems here: "The natural-rights tradition offers little guidance on precisely what one's procedural rights are in a state of nature. . . . Yet persons within this tradition do not hold that there are *no* procedural rights; that is, that one may not defend oneself against being handled by unreliable or unfair procedures" (p. 101).

territory.[80] Since the dominant protective association, even when transformed into an ultraminimal or minimal state, is a sort of firm, there presumably will be different classes of clients or "citizens". There will be clients and former independents (pp. 112–13). There will also be the shareholders of the dominant protective association, who may be privileged by virtue of their ownership rights.

80. I shall argue that many of these attributes of states are hard to justify. (See Chapters 7 and 8.) I noted earlier that Hobbes accords sovereigns only liberties and no claim rights.

Chapter 7

Sovereignty

There is and must be in all of [the several forms of government] a supreme, irresistible, absolute, uncontrolled authority, in which the *jura summi imperii,* or the rights of sovereignty, reside. – Blackstone

7.1 SOVEREIGN STATES

Sovereignty is a central attribute of modern states, as argued in Chapter 2. There I offered a preliminary and rough characterization of sovereignty as the ultimate source of political authority within a realm. It is common to distinguish internal and external aspects of sovereignty, and today these are often treated separately. Internal sovereignty pertains to the governance of the realm; external sovereignty, to independence of other states. The two aspects are related, as will be made clear when I examine what I call the classical account of sovereignty.

Sovereignty is not a simple idea. As one would expect of a notion with a long and controversial history, it is rather complex. Determining the relations among all its parts is no easy matter. To understand the ideas contained in the notion of sovereignty, it is important to keep in mind certain aspects of the history of the emergence of the modern state. Medieval rule was feudal, imperial, and/or theocratic. The early modern competitors of the state were city-states and leagues of cities, as well as empires, the Church, and various remnants of feudalism. Two features of modern governance were scarce in all these earlier forms of rule: territoriality and exclusivity of rule (a "closed" system of governance). A determinate realm, with relatively unambiguous geographic boundaries, is a prerequisite of the state and is largely missing from early forms of political organization. And the state only emerges when its claim (or that of its head, the monarch) to govern alone, exclusively, is recognized. A "sovereign" is the unique ruler of a realm, whose sphere of authority encompasses the whole realm without overlapping that of any other ruler. It – initially the monarch, later the state, then "the people" (of a state) – rules without superiors. As F. H. Hinsley claims, "At the beginning, the idea of sovereignty was the idea that there is a final and absolute political authority in the political community . . . *and no final and absolute authority exists elsewhere*". The last clause alone suggests that the notion is new.[1] With the development of the concept of sovereignty, we have the main elements of what is called the state system: independent states and "international relations".

The modern notion of sovereignty developed slowly with the interest shown in Roman law in the twelfth century and with the discovery of Aristotle's works in the thirteenth.[2] By the time Bodin formulated it, most of the elements needed for its emergence were to be found in Western Europe, or at least France.[3] I shall rely especially on Hobbes's account, as it is familiar and especially clear; it also combines the internal and external aspects of sovereignty neatly.[4] In addition, some of Hobbes's arguments for his conception of absolute sovereignty are worth studying.

My principal aim in this chapter is to consider the sovereignty claimed by states. I consider states that are legitimate – on my view, they are reasonably just and minimally efficient. The question will be

1. Hinsley, *Sovereignty*, pp. 25–26.
2. Government (*politeuma*), Aristotle noted, is "the supreme authority [*to kurion*] in states [the *polis*]", Politics III, 7, 1279a26–27. '*To kurion*' might be better translated as "authority" (or "that which has authority"), without adding 'supreme', since Aristotle could have used the superlative '*kuriotatos*' or the superlative substantive '*to kuriotaton*' to suggest possession of the greatest or most authority. (I am indebted to Fred Miller for discussions on these matters.)
3. See Spruyt, *The Sovereign State and Its Competitors*, pp. 79, 104. The thirteenth-century jurist Beaumanoir used the term '*souverain*' to express his view of the king's authority over his barons; see Ullmann, *Medieval Political Thought*, pp. 155–156, and Olivier Beaud, *La puissance de l'Etat* (Paris: Presses Universitaires de France, 1994), pp. 38–39. See also John B. Morrall, *Political Thought in Medieval Times* (Toronto: University of Toronto Press, 1980 [1958]), p. 61, and Mairet, *Le Dieu mortel*, chap. 2, esp. pp. 55–58. Bodin is normally regarded as the first theorist of the modern notion, but London Fell argues that he borrowed extensively from the jurist Johannes Corasius; see Fell, *Origins of Legislative Sovereignty and the Legislative State*, vol. 1: *Corasius and the Renaissance Systematization of Roman Law* (Boston: Oelgeschlager, Gunn & Hain, 1983).
4. A useful discussion of the intellectual context and sources of Hobbes's account of sovereignty is in Johann Somerville, *Thomas Hobbes: Political Ideas in Historical Context* (New York: St. Martin's Press, 1992), chap. 4.

to determine the nature of their sovereignty and authority. I shall be arguing that the sovereignty of (justified) states is problematic and their authority generally is not what it is claimed to be. I shall start with a "classical" account of sovereignty before considering more plausible and influential notions of limited and divisible sovereignty.

7.2 CLASSICAL SOVEREIGNTY

In early modern times, European monarchs fought the limits imposed on them by imperial and papal authorities and sought as well to overcome the powers of feudal lords, self-governing towns, and autonomous guilds. The struggles that ensued, as well as the ferocity of religious conflicts, suggested to many the need for unitary absolute power, and the modern notion of sovereignty was born.[5] Hobbes's preferred sovereign was a monarch. Rousseau and some of the founders of the American system attributed sovereignty to "the people", and the French *Déclaration des droits de l'homme et du citoyen* claims sovereignty for *la nation*. In Britain it is customary to attribute sovereignty to the trinity of the "Queen in Parliament". On the Continent sovereignty is usually understood to be a defining attribute of *states*, as opposed to governments.

Many, if not most, modern political thinkers have shared Blackstone's view that "there is and must be in all of [the several forms of government] a supreme, irresistible, absolute, uncontrolled authority, in which the *jura summi imperii*, or the rights of sovereignty, reside."[6] States have been widely understood to be forms of political organization with considerable authority over all internal persons and entities ("internal sovereignty") and independence from all external powers ("external sovereignty"). This authority is to be exerted over the residents of well-defined territories, the boundaries of which must be recognized and respected by all alike. This dual concern with internal and external authority reflects the historical context of classical conceptions of sovereignty.

---

5. Hinsley claims, "Sovereignty has been the 'constitutional' justification of absolute political power. Historically, it has been formulated only when the locus of supreme power was in dispute. . . . It is the justification of absolute authority that can arise and exist only when a final power is considered necessary in a body politic". *Sovereignty*, p. 277.
6. *The Sovereignty of the Law, Selections from Blackstone's "Commentaries on the Laws of England,"* ed. G. Jones (Toronto: University of Toronto Press, 1973), p. 36.

States are still thought by many to possess sovereignty, especially in their ("external") relations to other states. But it is also widely thought today that *peoples* are the rightful bearers of sovereignty. The doctrine of *popular sovereignty* is especially influential in the American and French political traditions and may be a central feature of conceptions of political power of Enlightenment political cultures. My concern here, however, is with the state's claim to sovereignty.[7]

To be sovereign is to be the ultimate source of political authority within a realm. This I take to be the core of the modern notion of sovereignty that is developed by Bodin, Hobbes, Rousseau, and other political thinkers. The notion will become clearer as I explicate my initial characterization.

Sovereignty pertains to authority *within a realm*. The notion of sovereignty is characteristically modern. The principal realms in question, then, are modern states, territorially defined. The jurisdiction of the rulers is a well-defined territory.[8]

Sovereigns are sources of political *authority*. Some speak of "political *power*" in these contexts, and sometimes they seem to refer to a species of causal power. But it is clear that the state's "power" here is first of all normative.[9] At the least, a political power aspires to be a justified or legitimate power – that is, an agent justified in using force. But, as I argued in Chapter 2, states aspire to more, namely, to authority.

Something is an authority, in the sense relevant here, only if its directives are (and are intended to be) action-guiding. The law, for instance, forbids us from doing certain things, and it intends these prohibitions to guide our behavior; specifically, these prohibitions are intended to be reason-providing (in a certain way). This is, for instance, Hobbes's view of the law: "Law in generall, is not Counsell, but Command . . . addressed to one formerly obliged to obey him [who commands]", whereas command is "where a man saith, *Doe*

---

7. I discuss popular sovereignty elsewhere.
8. While Christendom, with ambiguous boundaries, could be a suitable realm for a "sovereign" (i.e., a monarch), in modern times the notion of sovereignty is typically connected to territories with well-defined borders.
9. For Locke *political power* is "*a Right* of making Laws with Penalties . . . for the Regulating and Preserving of Property, and of employing the force of the Community, in the Execution of such Laws, and in the defense of the Common-wealth from Foreign Injury, and all this only for the Publick Good." *Second Treatise of Government*, chap. 1, para. 3, p. 268. For the most part, when I speak of political power *simpliciter* I shall refer to an ability or capacity to get one's way (*puissance* or *die Kraft*, rather than *pouvoir* or *die Herrschaft*).

this, or *Doe not this,* without expecting other reason than the Will of him that sayeth it."[10] Authorities, then, guide behavior by providing reasons for action to their subjects. On this view, political authority is not to be understood merely as justified force or coercion. Something is an authority only insofar as its directives are meant to be reasons for action.[11]

It is logically possible for something to have authority in this sense without possessing any power, that is, without being able to impose sanctions for disobedience. It is unlikely that we should need authoritative states were we able to get by with "powerless" authorities such as these. The point is merely the conceptual one that being an authority does not entail possession of force. But it may be that *political* authority cannot be *justified* if it is not, to some extent, effective, and effectiveness for most political regimes is likely to require some capacity for imposing sanctions. On this view, justified political authority requires political *power*, understood as a *de facto* ability to influence or control events (e.g., by imposing sanctions).[12] I understand the state's claimed authority, then, to include a claim to justified political power.

Sovereignty is the ultimate source of *political* authority and power within a realm. What is the scope of 'political' here? Clearly, the law is included. Sovereignty is the source of positive law within a realm. The law, presumably, does not exhaust the state's powers. Does 'political authority' also include morality? What might this mean? It might mean that sovereignty is a source of moral authority in that it could determine what is morally right or wrong; that is, its determi-

---

10. Hobbes, *Leviathan,* chap. 26, p. 183, and chap. 25, p. 176. Influenced by Raz's account of exclusionary reasons, H.L.A. Hart interprets Hobbes's account of a command to mean that "the commander characteristically intends his hearer to take the commander's will instead of his own as a guide to action and so to take it in place of any deliberation or reasoning of his own: the expression of a commander's will that an act be done is intended to preclude or cut off any independent deliberation by the hearer of the merits pro and con of doing the act." See Hart, "Commands and Authoritative Legal Reasons," in *Essays on Bentham* (Oxford: Clarendon Press, 1982), pp. 253, 244.
11. My analysis follows Raz, *The Authority of Law,* chaps. 1 and 2, and *The Morality of Freedom,* chaps. 2 and 3. See also Raz, *Practical Reason and Norms,* and Green, *The Authority of the State.*
12. This thesis, discussed in Section 6.6, is substantive, for it depends on the reasons for which political authorities are desirable (e.g., resolving assurance problems). Raz holds that effectiveness is a condition of something's being a legitimate political authority and makes the point that this is a substantive condition. See *The Authority of Law,* pp. 8–9, and *The Morality of Freedom,* pp. 75–76.

nations or decisions would constitute the right.[13] One might read Hobbes in this way, but it would not be a very plausible view of morality, even for moral conventionalists.[14] So I shall not understand sovereignty to be a source of moral authority in this way. Rather, one might instead understand political authority to preempt morals; accordingly, one's political obligations are supposed to have precedence over one's moral duties. A consequence of this view would be the possibility of being politically or legally obligated to do something that is morally wrong.

What is it for a source of authority to be *ultimate?* An authority may be ultimate if it is the *highest* authority. Sovereignty then requires a *hierarchy* of authorities, such that one or more can be at the summit. Recall that a distinguishing feature of modern governance is that it is *direct* (no intermediaries), by contrast with the indirect rule characteristic of medieval Europe. The highest authority in a chain of direct rule, then, has authority over all levels of the hierarchy. An ultimate authority in this sense is the highest element of a continuous chain of direct governance.[15] Second, an authority may also be ultimate if it is *final*. There is no further appeal after it has spoken; it has, as it were, "the last word". And last, an ultimate authority may be one that is *supreme*. Sometimes 'supreme' may be just a synonym for 'ultimate'. But I shall understand it to imply that the supreme authority can regulate all other sources of authority (e.g., conscience, kin, church, syndicate, corporation).[16] Hobbes and many

---

13. See W. J. Rees, "The Theory of Sovereignty Restated" [1950], in *In Defense of Sovereignty*, p. 212.
14. Rousseau understands sovereignty of the people to determine right and wrong. See *Du Contrat social*, II, chap. 3, p. 371. Even though references to natural law or right are found in his work, I understand Rousseau's account of sovereignty and of the general will to be incompatible with traditional natural law theory. His references to natural law, at least after the *Second Discourse*, should be understood in the context of his expressivist account of individual conscience and of natural right. Robert Derathé's judgment that Rousseau never was able to reconcile his account of the authority of conscience and of civil law (the general will) seems right. See Derathé, *Jean-Jacques Rousseau et la science politique de son temps*, 2nd ed. (Paris: Vrin, 1988 [1950]), p. 343.
15. As was clear to most at the time of ratification, the U.S. Constitution, although "federal", established a system of direct rule. William Findlay, an antifederalist from West Pennsylvania, attacked the proposed constitution as such: It was not, as it should be, "a CONFEDERATION of STATES, but a GOVERNMENT of INDIVIDUALS" (quoted by Pole, "The Politics of the Word 'State' and Its Relation to American Sovereignty," p. 8).
16. See Raz, *Practical Reason and Norms*, pp. 150–152.

classical theorists of the modern state understand the state's authority in this way: It overrides all competing sources of authority, even that of morality.[17]

Summarizing, then: Sovereignty is the highest, final, and supreme political and legal authority and power within the territorially defined domain of a system of direct rule. This is the core of the notion of sovereignty. What I shall call the classical conception of sovereignty adds three features to this account: absoluteness, inalienability, and indivisibility. Hobbes insists that sovereignty is "absolute", and by this he means unconstrained or unlimited.[18] Additionally, sovereignty is *inalienable* – it cannot be delegated or "represented" – and *indivisible* – it is unique and cannot be divided. This conception of sovereignty, which I attribute to Hobbes (and Rousseau), I refer to as "the classical view":[19] the sovereign is the ultimate source of absolute, inalienable, indivisible political authority within a realm. The doctrine that states are sovereign in the classical sense proved to be enormously influential. Blackstone's views are not unrepresentative. He thought that "there is and must be in all of [the several forms of government] a supreme, irresistible, absolute, uncontrolled authority, in which the *jura summi imperii*, or the

17. Supremacy in this sense does not mean that moral appeals are excluded. Modern legal systems can, and do, incorporate moral principles and rights.
   'Ultimate' may also mean something like "determining in special circumstances". For instance, Carl Schmitt famously attributes sovereignty to whomever decides in exceptional circumstances: "*Souverän ist, wer über den Ausnahmezustand entschneidet.*" Schmitt, *Politische Theologie: Vier Kapitel zur Lehre von der Souveränität* (Berlin: Duncker & Humblot, 1996 [1922]), p. 13. It is unclear, however, why the body with the greatest say in a particular circumstance has sovereignty. It should not be supposed that the body determining what happens when social order breaks down has to be the same one deciding matters in other circumstances. It is as if 'ultimate' here means something like "when all else fails", and this is thought to secure some reduction ("it all comes down to . . .").

18. "For Power Unlimited, is absolute Soveraignty." *Leviathan*, chap. 22, p. 155. Rousseau appears to agree; see *Du Contrat social*, IV, chap. 4, pp. 374–375, and chap. 5, p. 376. See also Derathé, *Jean-Jacques Rousseau et la science politique de son temps*, chap. 5, esp. pp. 332–341.
   If sovereignty is unlimited, then it is unconstrained legally (and morally?). This entails that it is *comprehensive* in Raz's sense: It claims authority to regulate any type of behavior. Raz, *Practical Reason and Norms*, pp. 150–151; see also *The Morality of Freedom*, pp. 76–77 (where most states are said to claim unlimited authority), and Green, *The Authority of the State*, pp. 83–84. As we shall see, a state may be limited (or nonabsolute) and yet retain the claim to comprehensive authority.

19. Even though Bodin's account antedates it. For Rousseau, sovereignty is also indivisible and inalienable (*Du Contrat social*, II, chap. 2, pp. 369–370; II, chap. 1, p. 368). Additionally, the sovereign cannot bind itself to itself or to others (I, chap. 7, pp. 362–363).

rights of sovereignty, reside." While recognizing that the sovereignty of Parliament is constrained by natural law, he held that

> it hath sovereign and uncontrollable authority in making, enlarging, restraining, abrogating, repealing, reviving and expounding of laws, concerning matters of all possible denominations, ecclesiastical, or temporal, civil, military, maritime or criminal; this being the place where that absolute despotic power, which must in all governments reside somewhere, is entrusted by the constitution of these kingdoms. All mischiefs and grievances, operations and remedies, that transcend the ordinary course of the laws, are within the reach of this extraordinary tribunal. It can regulate or new model the succession of the crown. . . . It can alter the established religion of the land. . . . It can change and create afresh even the constitution of the kingdom and of parliaments themselves. . . . It can, in short, do every thing that is not naturally impossible.[20]

Classical sovereignty no longer is as popular as it once was. It is now widely thought that sovereignty can and should be limited. It is often thought as well that one of the most effective institutional means of limiting the authority and power of states is to divide sovereignty among a plurality of agents or institutions; there need be no single authority. *Contra* Hobbes and others, republican and democratic theory has stressed the value and importance of divisions of power within states. So we dismiss the classical view. But we shall see that Hobbes has some arguments for unlimited sovereignty that have been influential and that are quite instructive, even though they may be wrong.

Are states sovereign in this sense? That is, suppose a state is reasonably just and minimally efficient, thus satisfying our two main conditions for the justification of states. Is such a state classically sovereign? An important motive for the classical account of sovereignty

---

20. William Blackstone, *The Sovereignty of the Law, Selections from Blackstone's "Commentaries on the Laws of England,"* pp. 36, 71. Gareth Jones notes that it is "impossible to reconcile Blackstone's ideas about natural (absolute) rights which no human law could contradict, with his conception of a sovereign" (p. xxxviii).

On the influence of Blackstone's views, Gordon Wood writes, "By the early 1770's, particularly with the introduction of Blackstone's *Commentaries* into the colonies, the doctrine that there must be in every form of government 'a supreme, irresistible, absolute, uncontrolled authority, in which the *jura summi imperii*, or rights of sovereignty, reside,' had gained such overwhelming currency that its 'truth,' many Americans were compelled to admit, could no longer 'be contested.'" Wood, *The Creation of the American Republic, 1776–1787* (New York: Norton, 1969), p. 350; see also p. 345.

is the conviction that there must be a single, overriding source of authority within a territory if there is to be social order. It is not that states need to use their enormous power at all times; rather, it is that it must be available.[21] This conviction is, and has been, widespread. It is, of course, clear in Hobbes's writings, and the fact that his work was generally looked upon with horror by most seventeenth- and eighteenth-century political writers should not lead us to underestimate his influence, much less to neglect his account. But Hobbes may be most instructive and, possibly, influential in his argument that the notion of a limited or constrained sovereign is not coherent. One of his most important defenses is a "regress argument" of considerable philosophical interest. He says, in effect, that establishment of an unlimited – indeed, illimitable – sovereign state is inevitable if we are to have any sort of state.

Hobbes states his thesis in terms of "powers". Any attempt to limit the sovereign power, Hobbes argues, requires creating a yet greater power, which will consequently itself be sovereign:

> It is therefore manifest, that in every city there is some one man, or council, or court, who by right hath as great a power over each single citizen, as each man hath over himself considered out of that civil state, that is, supreme and absolute, to be limited only by the strength and forces of the city itself, and by nothing else in the world. For if his power were limited, that limitation must necessarily proceed from some greater power. For he that prescribes limits, must have a greater power than he who is confined by them. Now that confining power is either without limit, or is again restrained by some other greater than itself, and so we shall at length arrive to a power, which hath no other limit but that which is the *terminus ultimus* of the forces of all the citizens together. That same is called the supreme command; and if it be committed to a council, a supreme council, but if to one man, the supreme lord of the city.[22]

Hobbes is claiming that if we wish to have a state, we cannot avoid (classical) sovereignty, for to limit a power entails establishing a greater power and the latter will be unlimited unless itself limited by a yet greater power, and so on. That is, "whosoever thinking

---

21. And if it is not available, then it will be too late to obtain it when needed. See Hobbes, *Leviathan*, chap. 29, p. 222.
22. Hobbes, *De Cive*, ed. S. Lamprecht (New York: Appleton-Century-Crofts, 1949 [1642]), chap. 6, para. 18.

Soveraign Power too great, will seek to make it lesse; must subject himselfe, to the Power, that can limit it; that is to say, a greater."[23]

Hobbes's complete case for the necessity of a classical sovereign is both conceptual and practical. The latter aspect was, in effect, addressed and rejected earlier (Chapter 3). The conceptual argument is very powerful, yet it seems influential no longer. In part this may be because few people take seriously attributing unlimited power to any human individual(s): "This is to think, that men are so foolish, that they take care to avoid what mischiefs may be done them by *pole-cats*, or *foxes;* but are content, nay, think it safety, to be devoured by *lions*."[24] But it is also because of recent arguments in legal theory according to which a legal or political system can be "closed", possessing a hierarchical structure within which decisions are in some sense final, without there being a final *human* decider or deciders. All that is necessary is that there be a set of rules (e.g., a "constitution") determining the finality of deciders in various domains.

Hans Kelsen's theory of the "basic norm" is an example of an account of a closed system in this sense. "A norm the validity of which cannot be derived from a superior norm we shall call a 'basic' norm. All norms whose validity may be traced back to one and the same basic norm form a system of norms, or an order."[25] M. M. Goldsmith has specifically argued that Hobbes has confused the idea that political systems must be "closed" in this sense with the claim that

---

23. Hobbes, *Leviathan*, chap. 20, p. 145; see also chap. 19, pp. 134–135, chap. 22, p. 155, and chap. 29, p. 224. John Austin argues similarly: "The power of a sovereign . . . is incapable of *legal* limitation. . . . Supreme power limited by positive law, is a flat contradiction in terms. . . . The power of the superior sovereign immediately imposing the restraints, or the power of some other sovereign superior to that superior, would still be absolutely free from the fetters of positive law. For unless the imagined restraints were ultimately imposed by a sovereign not in a state of subjection to a higher or superior sovereign, a series of sovereigns ascending to infinity would govern the imagined community. Which is impossible and absurd." Austin, *The Province of Jurisprudence Determined*, ed. W. Rumble (Cambridge: Cambridge University Press, 1995 [1832]), p. 212. And Kant: "Indeed, even the constitution cannot contain any article that would make it possible for there to be some authority in a state to resist the supreme commander in case he should violate the law of the constitution, and so to limit him. For, someone who is to limit the authority in a state must have more power [*Macht*] than he whom he limits. . . . In that case, however, the supreme commander in a state is not the supreme commander . . . and this is self-contradictory." Kant, *The Metaphysics of Morals*, trans. M. Gregor (Cambridge: Cambridge University Press, 1996 [1797]), p. 96.
24. Locke, *Second Treatise of Government*, chap. 7, para. 93, p. 328.
25. Kelsen, *General Theory of Law and State*, p. 111; see also pp. 110–116.

they must have a classical sovereign.[26] Hart's influential criticisms of Austin's conception of sovereignty have lessened the influence of the regress argument, and Goldsmith's argument may be a reflection of this.[27]

The need for a closed system, albeit one without final (human) deciders, is often established by a regress argument much like Hobbes's:

There must be found in every legal system certain ultimate principles, from which all others are derived, but which are themselves self-existent. . . . It seems clear that every political society involves the presence of supreme power. For otherwise all power would be subordinate, and this supposition involves the absurdity of a series of superiors and inferiors *ad infinitum*.[28]

[T]he logic of the concept of sovereignty involves two notions: (1) hierarchy and (2) closure. The first is the notion of a chain of norms or authorities, each subordinate to the next higher link and superior to those below it. The notion of closure ensures that the chain does not extend infinitely upward and that the system is independent, i.e., not subordinate to another system of authorities or norms. This implies that there is no appeal outside the system, or, to put it another way, other systems or authorities external to it.[29]

In other forms, then, Hobbes's regress argument is very much alive. And, in these forms, the argument appears to involve authorities or norms and not merely causal powers.

Jean Hampton has argued that responses such as Goldsmith's miss Hobbes's point. He recognizes, she points out, "the possibility of 'Hart-like' systems of government whose ultimate deciders are sets of rules" but he argues that such systems are unstable in practice.[30] Moral rules do not suffice to forestall conflict. "All Laws, written, and unwritten, have need of Interpretation", and so-called natural law

---

26. Goldsmith, "Hobbes's 'Mortal God': Is There a Fallacy in Hobbes's Theory of Sovereignty?" *History of Political Thought* 1, 1 (Spring 1980), 33–50.
27. See also Ivor Wilks, "A Note on Sovereignty" [1955], in *In Defense of Sovereignty*, pp. 197–205, where the analogies between Hobbes's and Kelsen's arguments are drawn. For Hart's account of what I am calling a closed system, see *The Concept of Law*, 2nd ed. (Oxford: Clarendon Press, 1994 [1961]), chap. 6.
28. John Salmond, *Jurisprudence*, 10th ed., ed. G. Williams (London: Sweet & Maxwell, 1947 [1902]), pp. 155, 490.
29. Goldsmith, "Hobbes's 'Mortal God': Is There a Fallacy in Hobbes's Theory of Sovereignty?" p. 38.
30. Hampton, *Hobbes and the Social Contract Tradition*, p. 99. See also Hampton, "Democracy and the Rule of Law", in *The Rule of Law, Nomos, vol. 36*, ed. I. Shapiro (New York and London: New York University Press, 1994), pp. 13–44.

"is now become of all Laws the most obscure; and has consequently the greatest need of able Interpreters."[31] Hampton convincingly argues that Hobbes's concern was the establishment of a system of final arbiters whose tasks would importantly include that of interpretation of law:

> To those theorists of his day who, like Hart, argue that we can have a state based on a constitution or set of laws that regulate and define the powers of government officials, Hobbes will reply that such a constitution is impossible. . . . Hobbes is assuming that human beings can never agree on one recognized interpretation of this constitution, so that a judge will need to be instituted to interpret and define it for them. But this means that the judge of the constitution will become the sovereign, because he has the final power of decision in the commonwealth.[32]

Hampton is right about Hobbes's concerns, and she is right to remind us about the problems that Hobbes found in constitutional systems. I wish, however, to make different criticisms of Hobbes's regress argument, so I need not determine the merits of systems of ultimate deciders versus Kelsen–Hart systems of basic norms or rules. In addition to attacking Hobbes's regress defense of sovereignty, we may wish to investigate the sense in which it is true, as Hampton says, that "an independent political regime must be a closed decision-making entity" – a claim Kelsen, Hart, and many endorse.[33] The regress argument is used in support of this thesis, as well as Hobbes's; it is possible that it fails to support either. I focus first on Hobbes's argument.

Does the argument establish that states (or something) must be the ultimate source of authority/power, lest we have a regress? I think not, for the argument assumes a particular hierarchical conception of power and authority relations, and it is one we need not accept. Let us first consider the case with causal powers. Hobbes understands power and authority relations to be such that if one power is greater than another, and the second is greater than the third, then the first must be greater than the third; certainly the third could not be greater than, or equal to, the first. That is, power relations are understood to be fully *transitive*.

Need they be so understood? Hobbes's conception of power – any present means to some future good – is often rightly criticized as a

---

31. Hobbes, *Leviathan*, chap. 26, p. 322.
32. Hampton, *Hobbes and the Social Contract Tradition*, pp. 101–102.
33. Ibid., p. 98.

crude or simplistic account of power. But two assumptions are built into his account and the regress argument that are rarely the focus of attention. Full transitivity is one of these assumptions; the other is that of full *comparability* (on connectedness): we should always be able to say of any two powers that one is greater than the other or that the two are equal. That is, to any pair of powers, we should be able to apply the relation 'more or equally powerful than'; all powers must be comparable in this way.

As a general assumption about human societies, this is to be rejected. Power is usually relative to some particular dimension and to some given domain; power relations are multidimensional or multiattributive. Something might be greater in power than something else in one regard but be lesser in another; something might possess greater power than another in one domain but less in another. For instance, the power of the three branches of the American government are multidimensional in this manner. The same is true of the power of the American president, that of the pope, or that of Aung San Suu Kyi. Someone might say that the latter is less powerful than the military rulers of Myanmar (or Burma), as they can have her killed (the so-called ultimate power). But were this so, it would be difficult to understand the difficulties of the regime, or why she was freed. Similarly, if John Paul II could stop Warsaw Pact tanks from moving into Poland (as the rumors had it), it is hard to say that the former Soviet regime was more powerful *simpliciter* than the pope.

Consider Hobbes's crude account of power: a person's "present means, to obtain some future apparent Good." Power thus includes strength, prudence, eloquence, wealth, reputation, friends, luck, knowledge, and so on.[34] Suppose – what I take to be false – that we could exhaustively compare all pairs of *particular* powers, for instance, all pairs of eloquence, wealth, friends. It would not follow that we could thereby exhaustively compare all pairs of *bundles* of powers – for instance, two people each endowed with a certain amount of wealth, eloquence, and the like. For we would still need a weighting principle to determine how much a certain number of friends count relative to a certain amount of eloquence. (And, of course, these would all have to be weighted by probabilities or some other means of taking into account uncertainty and context.)

Now Hobbes, in an oft noted remark that brutally reveals the anti-Christian (and, by implication, anti-Kantian and anti-Marxist) impli-

34. Hobbes, *Leviathan*, chap. 10.

cations of his instrumentalist view of reason and value, can be read as *assuming* that there is such a weighting principle. He says, famously:

The *Value*, or Worth of a man, is as of all other things, his Price; that is to say, so much as would be given for the use of his Power: and therefore is not absolute; but a thing dependant on the need and judgement of another . . . let a man (as most men do,) rate themselves as the highest Value they can; yet their true Value is no more than is esteemed by others.[35]

Price is a measure of the value of a person, and price is nothing more than what people will pay for the use of someone's power (in Hobbes's sense). Price, then, is the measure of someone's power, in the way that market prices may be understood to measure the value of commodities. My concern is with the assumptions required for a certain account of power to be used to support classical sovereignty. Hobbes's appeal to the notion of a person's "price", the amount others would give to avail themselves of his or her services, in effect assumes that there exists a weighting mechanism by which we can fully compare the different powers that different individuals possess; that is, there is a single (market) scale for powers, even though power relations are multiattributive.

It is important to note, however, that there is no argument for the existence of this scale; it is merely assumed.[36] More important, with the insights provided to us by the theory of perfect competition, we doubt that this scale needs to exist under conditions of imperfect competition (or, at the very least, that it would possess the features required for full comparability and transitivity). Indeed, we may be aware of how full comparability is obtained in market theory: It is a consequence of various assumptions about the nature of commodities, indifference curves, and agents' willingness to trade. Critics eager to convict Hobbes of developing "an economic conception of man" typically overlook this fact, that the full comparability he needs for his conception of power is simply assumed and that it is not a simple consequence of his conception of human relations.

35. Ibid., chap. 10, p. 63.
36. Even if my reading of this passage is plausible, I do not mean to suggest that Hobbes should have been aware of the conditions needed for market measures. Whatever we think of markets as measures of economic value, we should place Hobbes's remark in its historical context. He is writing long before Smith and Ricardo, and even longer before the development of the theory of perfect competition. We do not yet have a fully developed "market" or "economic view of man" here.

Suppose we grant that Hobbes's account is question-begging in this respect, can it not be defended? I am skeptical. As with most skeptical claims, however, I cannot do more than simply point to failures to develop a fully comparable account of power and to the reasons why we should expect such accounts not to succeed. There have been many attempts by political scientists and decision theorists to develop accounts of power, and there are reasons to be skeptical of their success. In any case, these measures do not provide a satisfactory measure of power that would give Hobbes what his argument needs, namely, a measure of power that will enable us to compare and rank powers in civil society and in states of nature. (Power indices that measure voting power in parliamentary institutions and committees are too narrow for Hobbes's purposes.)[37] This want of a general measure of power is crucial, for Hobbes intended his argument to have practical force.

There is, of course, an old trick we might use to construct a single scale by which we can compare and aggregate differences of power: namely, behaviorism. Suppose we understand power in behavioral terms: x is more powerful than y if it *beats* y, where 'to beat something' is characterized locally or "operationally" in terms of some contest. Then comparability may be satisfied, at least trivially. We set up elections and tournaments so that they terminate with a winner, and some are often tempted to characterize relations such as 'is more popular than' or 'is a better player than' in terms of these elections and tournaments. But as we all know, a worse player can defeat a better one.[38] (This is not to deny that defeat in certain contests is *evidence* of inferiority.) Philosophical skepticism of behaviorism may serve to reinforce suspicion of this trick. I shall not, however, pursue this line of discussion any further, for if the assumption of full comparability is problematic, the problems with the second assumption, that of transitivity, are greater.

Power relations, even characterized behaviorally, may still violate transitivity. Consider athletic tournaments where players (or teams)

---

37. They also may not measure what we think of as power. See Brian Barry, "Is It Better to be Powerful or Lucky?" [1980], in *Democracy and Power: Essays in Political Theory*, vol. 1 (Oxford: Clarendon Press, 1991), pp. 270–302. See as well Barry's other essays on power in this volume; Peter Morriss, *Power: A Philosophical Analysis* (Manchester, U.K.: Manchester University Press, 1987); and Steven Lukes, "Power," *Encyclopedia of Ethics*, vol. 2, ed. L. Becker and C. Becker (New York and London: Garland, 1992), pp. 995–996.
38. As David Schmidtz put it to me, people who say "may the best team win" are expressing a hope, not a tautology.

are paired with one another and where the loser in each contest is eliminated until only one player remains. Although it is true that in such contests some player wins, the winning player need not be better than (or would beat) *all* of the other contestants (a "Condorcet winner"). Indeed, with a sufficiently large number of contestants we should expect that not to be the case. That is, in a different contest where each of these players is paired with each other, we should instead expect a violation of transitivity – for instance, a *cycle:* For any contestant there is another that is better (that is, who would beat the former). Social choice theory, beginning with Kenneth Arrow's famous theorem, has led us to expect such violations of transitivity under a wide range of conditions.[39]

Power relations are subject to similar violations of transitivity. If that is so, then, problems of comparability aside, Hobbes's regress argument does not go through. For it would no longer be true that for any finite number of powers, there must be at least one, greater than which there is none. Hobbes argues that one cannot understand the sovereign to be subject to civil law, citing the regress under consideration: "because it setteth the Lawes above the Soveraign, setteth also a Judge above him, and a Power to punish him; which is to make a new Soveraign; and again for the same reason a third, to punish the second; and so continually without end".[40] Suppose, however, that we subject power A, nominally "the Sovereign", to the civil laws, enforceable by power B. As we shall also want to constrain the acts of B, we establish a third power, C. Must there be a regress? Yes, if power relations are representable by a (weak) ordering. But that is precisely what is being questioned. Suppose the relation conjoining {A, B, C, . . . , N} fails to be transitive (or violates acyclicity); suppose that while B is more powerful than A, and C is more powerful than

---

39. Arrow's famous theorem is presented in *Social Choice and Individual Values,* 2nd ed. (New Haven: Yale University Press, 1963). See, for instance, Amartya K. Sen, *Collective Choice and Social Welfare* (San Francisco: Holden-Day, 1970), and "Weights and Measures: Informational Constraints in Social Welfare Analysis" [1977], in *Choice, Welfare and Measurement* (Cambridge, Mass.: MIT Press, 1982), pp. 226–263; Peter C. Ordeshook, *Game Theory and Political Theory* (Cambridge: Cambridge University Press, 1986), and Schwartz, *The Logic of Collective Choice.* While standard proofs of Arrow's theorem involve producing a violation of the nondictatorship condition, the theorem states only that a set of conditions is inconsistent, without saying which condition should be dropped. Arrow's and related results, however, can be used as part of an argument to the effect that certain social choice systems (e.g., most electoral systems) will violate transitivity in the absence of various institutional arrangements.

40. Hobbes, *Leviathan,* chap. 29, p. 367.

B, it is not the case that C is more powerful than A. In such a case, there is no regress and consequently Hobbes's argument does not go through.

It might be objected that Hobbes's argument does not require *full* comparability or *full* transitivity; all he needs is comparability and transitivity over a small subset of powers.[41] Thus, when arguing against those who propose to limit the power of the apparent Sovereign A, Hobbes wishes to say that some power B, more powerful than A, will need to be established, and for this claim only A's and B's powers must be comparable. (Similarly, *mutatis mutandis*, with transitivity, for some A, B, and C.) Now the manner in which Hobbes expresses the regress argument suggests greater generality than this interpretation. But even if we concede for the moment the point about *full* comparability and transitivity, we should not expect it to be true that the proper subset of powers for which comparability and transitivity must hold will be small; indeed, Hobbes's argument requires that it be quite large. For unless it is in fact more powerful than every other actual (as opposed to potential) power in the realm, Hobbes thinks, the sovereign will not be able to secure the ends for which it is established, namely, peace and security. And if comparability, but not transitivity, holds for the set of all actual powers, then Hobbes thinks there will be civil war (e.g., A can be defeated by B, who can be defeated by C, who can be defeated by A). The hierarchical conception of power is essential to Hobbes, as well as to many other political theorists.

If certain social choice theorists and political scientists are right, we may expect failures of transitivity, indeed, cycles, to be both common and quite general. As William Riker has argued, "Disequilibrium, or the potential [of] the status quo to be upset, is the characteristic feature of politics".[42] Instability, the result of cycles, is a feature of any collective choice that depends in certain ways on vote trading, compromise, and the like. This general result, it has been argued, "shows that the instabilities whose possibility is demonstrated by Condorcet's Voting Paradox example and by various impossibility theorems constitute the rule rather than the exception: far from being peculiar to special institutions, preference profiles, or feasible sets, they afflict almost all political, economic, and other interpersonal

41. I owe an objection like this to G. A. Cohen and to Alon Harel.
42. Riker, "Implications from the Disequilibrium of Majority Rule for the Study of Institutions," *American Political Science Review* 74, 2 (June 1980), 443.

activity almost all the time".[43] This is not to say that the outcomes of electoral and parliamentary systems are in fact easily reversed. For these institutions to a significant degree serve to suppress cycles and to stabilize the outcomes of collective choice.[44] Certainly, in the absence of institutions – for instance, in the conditions that obtain before the establishment of a sovereign state (the context relevant to Hobbes's argument) – cycles are to be expected.

I have distinguished political power of a causal sort from normative "political power", namely, political authority. The notion of power in Hobbes's regress argument is ambiguous between the two. I interpret him as talking about both. If, however, one were to interpret him as concerned with causal power alone, it is possible to transform his argument into one concerning authority, giving us, in effect, the argument provided by Kelsen, Salmond, and others.[45] As Goldsmith puts it, "the systematic character of a set of rules or norms or authorities is its hierarchical order: each subordinate rule or authority owes its validity to, is derived from, a superior authority. But to 'close' the system, to prevent its being infinitely regressive, a highest or supreme norm or authority is required."[46]

The regress argument for authorities that are limited need not, perhaps, fail as easily as Hobbes's original argument. For limited authoritative systems, such as the law in constitutional systems, need not be made to govern between all acts of, and relations among, individuals or groups. Further, conventional systems of authority (e.g., legal systems) are *constructed*. So, in principle, they may be designed to satisfy comparability and transitivity. The "constitution" may simply stipulate an ordering of authorities. For such a system the condi-

---

43. Schwartz, *The Logic of Collective Choice*, p. 254.
44. These may be understood as "structure-induced equilibria". See Ordeshook, *A Political Theory Primer* (New York and London: Routledge, 1992), pp. 278–286. What these institutional constraints do, in Arrovian terms, is create local oligarchies. I am indebted to John Ferejohn for this point.
45. It might be thought that power is different from authority in one respect: that it may be diminished or exhausted by use. But this may be to think of power as an exhaustible resource, which is not always right. Russell Hardin usefully distinguishes between *exchange* and *coordination power*. The former is power based on resources that can be used to influence or coerce others; the latter, in collective coordination (e.g., behind a leader). The collective coordination sort of power can sometimes increase with use as additional individuals coordinate with the group. See Hardin, *One for All: The Logic of Group Conflict* (Princeton: Princeton University Press, 1995), chap. 2.
46. Goldsmith, "Hobbes's 'Mortal God': Is There a Fallacy in Hobbes's Theory of Sovereignty?" p. 38.

tions for a regress would obtain and the argument for a highest authority would not necessarily collapse.[47] But note that the system must be one of limited authority, governing a relatively small set of acts and interactions, for full comparability and transitivity to be assured. So the conditions for a regress in a system such as this do not help Hobbes's case for an *unlimited* highest authority. (But it is unlikely that an ordering of authorities or powers is available even for limited legal systems with fairly small domains.)

Note as well that the regress argument would still not have established that there *must* be a highest authority in such cases. There would, contingently, be a highest authority – the system would have been so constructed – and there consequently would be no regress. But the question then would be why *should* we so construct our legal systems? Hobbes's answer was that we had no choice, lest we have an endless regress. But this does not answer our query about authorities. If we construct a system in such a way that authorities constitute an ordering, then we shall have no regress. But the regress argument itself offers no reason to do this. For we can also construct a system where authorities do not constitute an ordering, as I shall demonstrate presently. And the regress argument does not show that this is either impossible or undesirable.

I have mentioned the general claim, endorsed by many contemporary theorists, that "an independent political regime must be a closed decision-making entity". Goldsmith's use of the regress argument for this claim assumes that authority relations constitute an ordering. Recall his distinction between "closure" and "hierarchy":

The logic of the concept of sovereignty involves two notions: (1) hierarchy and (2) closure. The first is the notion of a chain of norms or authorities, each subordinate to the next higher link and superior to those below it. The notion of closure ensures that the chain does not extend infinitely upward and that the system is independent, i.e., not subordinate to another system of authorities or norms. This implies that there is no appeal outside the system, or, to put it another way, other systems or authorities external to it.

Goldsmith appears to be thinking that given hierarchy, a highest (or "basic") norm is necessary to close a system of norms. Closure of an

47. Note that this would work only if the constitutional system were not comprehensive in the sense claimed earlier (possessing the authority to regulate any type of behavior), something Raz would deny (*The Morality of Freedom*, pp. 76–77). I return to this matter in Section 7.4.

authority system, then, requires a highest authority, given hierarchy. But why assume that hierarchy is necessary? Goldsmith's reason seems to be that this is a condition of being a system. He says that "the systematic character of a set of rules or norms or authorities is its hierarchical order: each subordinate rule or authority owes its validity to, is derived from, a superior authority. But to 'close' the system, to prevent its being infinitely regressive, a highest or supreme norm or authority is required."[48]

Goldsmith's claim is, however, mistaken. It is possible to have closure without hierarchy. Closure presumably is necessary for a set of norms to constitute a system, and it may be desirable to have a system in this sense. Hierarchy may also be useful for various purposes. But the necessity or desirability of closure need not establish the necessity or desirability of hierarchy.

Consider the following diagram of a hierarchical system of norms:

A, B, C, and D are norms in a set, extending upward, each norm more basic than the next in the following sense: A norm is a more basic norm than another if the validity of the first is required for the validity of the second (e.g., B is required for the validity of C). It follows that in such a system there is one norm the validity of which does not depend on a more basic norm – if the tree is not to continue downward infinitely. Following Kelsen, I could call this the "basic norm" – "A norm the validity of which cannot be derived from a

48. Goldsmith, "Hobbes's 'Mortal God': Is There a Fallacy in Hobbes's Theory of Sovereignty?" p. 38. See also Goldsmith, "Hobbes on Law," in *The Cambridge Companion to Hobbes*, ed. T. Sorell (Cambridge: Cambridge University Press, 1996), p. 278.

superior norm we shall call a 'basic' norm." The depicted hierarchy is singular: There is only one line extending upward. But this is not essential. We could have a tree with many branches:

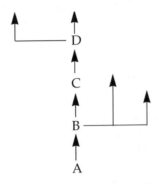

But such trees will remain hierarchies in the relevant sense: For any norm, except one, there are other norms that are more basic than it. By contrast, consider a representation of a different system of norms:

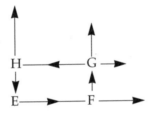

E, F, G, and H are norms that are related thus: The validity of H is derived from G, G's validity from F, F's validity from E, and E's validity from H. Such norms would, in Raz's words, "indirectly authorize their own creation". A system of such norms is conceivable. It is true, as Raz notes, that "the validity of each of these laws can be proved only if, in the last resort, the validity of one of the other laws is assumed and not proved, but this is also true of" E, F, G, and H. However, E, F, G, and H would not constitute a hierarchy in the relevant sense. The relation 'is more basic than' would violate acyclicity over the set {E, F, G, H}. Raz uses this hypothetical case to show that it need not be the case that every legal system presuppose a basic norm.[49] It also shows that one can have closure without hierarchy.

49. Raz, *The Concept of a Legal System*, pp. 138–140.

My conclusions so far are that the regress argument does not establish that there must be a greatest power or authority, much less an illimitable one, and it cannot be made to show that there must be a highest norm or authority. And it does not give us reasons to want such an authority. There are several lessons to be drawn from the failure of this argument. One important lesson is discussed in Section 7.6: The supposition that authority and power relations constitute an ordering offers a misleading understanding of politics.

Hobbes's regress argument for classical sovereignty is part of a larger argument for a sovereign state. He thought that sovereigns had to be all-powerful and that failure to understand this led in his time to social disorder. An important element in his overall argument is the belief that the ends of peace and security, for which states are constituted, require unlimited power and authority. Hobbes thought absolute power was necessary if states were to secure social order. I have, in effect, challenged this extreme claim in Chapter 3.

We have seen that it need not be the case that sovereign states are illimitable, or at least an influential argument to that effect has been shown to fail. Let us turn now to the question of the possible limits on the state's authority. We think, for the most part, that states are morally constrained[50] and ought to be limited. Indeed, for most of the dominant moral traditions today, it is hard not to be committed to this view. There are things no state or collectivity may do. But *can* the authority of states be constitutionally or otherwise legally limited? Hobbes and his followers think not. Sovereignty, according to the partisans of classical sovereignty, is not subject to law.[51] Some of the reasons given (other than the regress argument) are not original: One cannot bind oneself. Others turn on specific features of Hobbist social contract theory: The sovereign is not party to the original contract, so cannot be bound by it; and to revolt against the sovereign would be to act against oneself, as one is the "author" of the sovereign's acts.[52]

---

50. Even if Hobbes did not think there were moral limits on states, he believed there were some *rational* limitations, namely, the liberties that cannot be rationally alienated (by individuals whose main end is self-preservation). That these rationally inalienable liberties end up posing a problem for Hobbes's case for absolute sovereignty is a central claim of Hampton's *Hobbes and the Social Contract Tradition*.
51. "The power of a sovereign . . . is incapable of *legal* limitation. . . . Supreme power limited by positive law, is a flat contradiction in terms". Austin, *The Province of Jurisprudence Determined*, p. 212.
52. "For having power to make, and repeale Lawes, he may when he pleaseth, free himselfe from that subjection, by repealing those Lawes that trouble him. . . . Nor

Hobbists think that sovereigns could have no duties. This settles the matter if the only way juridically to limit their authority would be to impose duties on them. But it is possible to constrain an authority or institution by refraining from delegating certain juridical *powers* to it. The lack of such a power is not equivalent to possession of a duty. The Hohfeldian correlate to a juridical power is the absence not of duties but of *disabilities*.[53] The defender of Hobbes may reply that the fact that the sovereign lacks a legal power entails that it has no legal right to do something, but that this is of no relevance, for sovereigns have no (claim)rights in the first place, only Hohfeldian liberties (and a concentration of force). This reply is effective only if we wish to characterize the state's authority in terms of liberties and not powers or claim rights, which I do not. I suppose, *contra* Hobbists, that our rights limit the authority of states.

Part of the supposed problem with constitutional constraints on states has to do with the relation between law and its enforcement. Laws provide reasons by affixing sanctions to disobedience. Moral rights, without enforcement, it is sometimes thought, cannot legally constrain states. I discuss some of the issues raised here in the next three sections, but note for now that not all laws will typically be backed up by sanctions.[54] And moral constraints can be incorporated into law, for instance, through "bills of rights", now a common feature of modern constitutional states. In this way it certainly seems possible to constrain the state legally.[55]

is it possible for any person to be bound to himselfe; because he that can bind, can release" (*Leviathan*, chap. 26, p. 184). Rousseau does not differ from Hobbes on this point: "On voit qu'il n'y a ni ne peut y avoir nulle espèce de loi fondamentale obligatoire pour le corps du peuple, *pas même le contrat social*". (*Du Contrat social*, I, chap. 7, p. 362, emphasis added).
   The sovereign's not being a party to the original contract is central to Hobbes's account, but it is not a consideration relevant to noncontractarians. Rousseau argues that for the body politic or the sovereign to disobey the social contract would be to destroy itself. The sovereign for Rousseau, given his notion of the general will, cannot have interests against those of its members (*Du Contrat social*, I, chap. 7).
53. Hart, *The Concept of Law*, pp. 69–70.
54. For instance, certain laws addressed to officials (Raz, *Practical Reason and Norms*, p. 158). Note that the state is supposed to possess authority and so cannot claim that sanctions are the main reasons for obedience to law. Authoritative directives are reasons of a special sort (second-order reasons excluding certain first-order considerations); sanctions merely change the expected payoffs of actions, not how one is to reason about what to do. So the addition of sanctions is not even relevant to privileging legal constraints over moral ones.
55. As the history of American constitutional thought shows, these can include "unenumerated" rights. See also the Ninth Amendment to the U.S. Constitution:

Salmond claims Hobbes and Austin confuse limitations of power and authority with subordination. He argues generally that states of sovereign powers may be *de facto* limited, and that any such limitation in fact can be recognized by law and become *de jure*.

> The law is merely the theory of things as received and operative within courts of justice. It is the reflection and image of the outer world seen and accepted as authentic by the tribunals of the state. This being so, whatever is possible in fact is possible in law, and more also. Whatsoever limitations of sovereign power may exist in fact may be reflected in and recognized by the law.[56]

Salmond adds, "The contrary view is based on that unduly narrow view of the nature of the law which identifies it with the command of the sovereign issued to his subjects." The debate about illimitable sovereignty is, in large part, one about the nature of law, so it should not be surprising that inadequacies with command (or "gunman") theories of the law are involved with puzzles about ultimate authority. Rejecting such accounts in favor of more plausible ones may make legal limitations on states intelligible.

States are morally limited, and this is one of the main reasons for wanting them to be legally limited. Or so we believe. Hobbes and Rousseau, read as *moral* contractarians or conventionalists of a certain sort, could not claim this. For them (on these readings) the will of the sovereign *determines* what is morally right and wrong.[57] Virtually no contemporary moral theory could endorse this claim. Of the many varieties of moral conventionalism, none seems as statist or populist as Hobbes and Rousseau, respectively. Many could support what I called prior rights, even the seminatural kinds discussed in Chapter 6. So the claim that states are morally constrained by our rights (or by duties incumbent on them) should no longer be particularly controversial.

"The enumeration in the Constitution of certain rights shall not be construed to deny or disparage others retained by the people." See Morris, "Droits originaires et Etats limités: quelques leçons de la république américaine", *Science(s) politique(s)* 4 (December 1993), 105–115.

56. Salmond, *Jurisprudence*, pp. 493–494. Salmond refers to Bentham's argument that sovereigns are *de facto* limited by their subjects' habits and dispositions to obey. See Bentham, *A Fragment on Government*, ed. J. Burns and H. Hart (Cambridge: Cambridge University Press, 1988 [1776]), chap. 4, secs. 35–36. See Postema, *Bentham and the Common Law Tradition*, chap. 7.

57. For Hobbes, see esp. *Leviathan*, chap. 5, p. 33 ("for want of a right Reason constituted by Nature"). For Rousseau, see *Du Contrat social*, II, chap. 3, p. 371 ("la volonté générale est toujours droite et tend toujours à l'utilité publique").

The authority and power of states, then, is legally and morally limited. The partisans of classical sovereignty were then mistaken. But we should not move too quickly. For even if they are wrong about the illimitable nature of sovereign authority, they were on to something. States are not illimitable; there are too many limited states for this claim to be credible. But limited states claim to be limited only by constraints they recognize. When they are limited by external norms, it is because they acknowledge or incorporate these. There are limits to the authority of states but only those recognized by the state.[58]

That states are limited only by constraints they *recognize* or *acknowledge* does not necessarily mean that these constraints are *created* by them. Terms such as 'determine', 'recognize', 'decide', 'judge' are ambiguous in these contexts. They can imply that there is no independent fact of the matter and the "decision" or "judgment" create the thing decided or judged. Or it can be that the object of the enterprise is to ascertain or discover an independent fact of the matter and that a "decision" or "judgment" can be mistaken, even if it is authoritative. Some Hobbists, possibly the master himself, are radical moral conventionalists and statists and hold that all rights and duties are created by the state. This is implausible – all the more so if the state is taken to be a modern and Western creation – and few present-day theorists defend it. But the claim that states determine, recognize, or judge their own limits, interpreted to allow for an independent fact of the matter and for error, is not at all implausible. Indeed, it seems to be precisely the claim states make. They are limited, but only by constraints they acknowledge. Indeed, it is hard to see how it could be otherwise or how states could claim anything else.

There does seem to be something odd, possibly incoherent, about a legal or political order that claims the right to decide or settle certain matters and that also allows individuals, who are not officials of the system, to determine the merits of the case. That is, a system that would both claim the right to decide certain matters and permit individuals not to take its decisions as authoritative would be incoherent. What would it be saying about its judgments? Similarly, if we think of rebellion or revolution as necessarily anticonstitutional and

---

58. "On convient que tout ce que chacun aliéne par le pacte social de sa puissance, de ses biens, de sa liberté, c'est seulement la partie de tout cela dont l'usage importe à la communauté, mais il faut convenir aussi que *le Souverain seul est juge de cette importance.*" Rousseau, *Du Contrat social*, II, chap. 4, p. 373, emphasis added.

extralegal – for otherwise they would merely be forms of lawful dissent and petition – then there would be something similarly incoherent about a constitutional order that guaranteed a juridical right to revolution.[59] States claim to be sovereign within their realms, and even if this authority is limited, it remains *supreme* in the sense I explained earlier: It claims authority to regulate all other sources of authority.[60] A state cannot possess supremacy in this sense if subjects are permitted to determine for themselves the merits of the matters to be settled by the state. A state can, of course, exempt some from its determinations (e.g., conscientious exemption from military service), excuse others (e.g., duress), and so on. But these are limits recognized by the state.[61] I shall return to the issues raised here when I discuss the limited sovereignty and authority of states. Even if we reject classical sovereignty, we may still find the claimed authority of states incredible.

I consider only briefly now the question of the indivisibility of sovereignty. Hobbes, Rousseau, and many other theorists insisted sovereignty was indivisible. Hobbes's main argument is simple: "Powers divided mutually destroy each other."[62] The claim is not merely empirical, though one may consider the empirical evidence in Hobbes's time to have been quite powerful. Part of the claim is conceptual and is related to the regress argument considered above.[63]

---

59. Kant is well known for his view that "all resistance against the supreme legislative power . . . all defiance which breaks out into rebellion, is the greatest and most punishable crime in a commonwealth, for it destroys its very foundations." He uses the regress argument to establish the point ("On the Common Saying: 'This May be True in Theory, but It Does Not Apply in Practice'," p. 81). But he argues, as well, that the people's right to judge would be inconsistent with the authority of the state (p. 82).
60. I adopt Raz's account, that: "every legal system claims authority to regulate the setting up and application of other institutionalized systems by its subject community. In other words it claims authority to prohibit, permit or impose conditions on the institution and operation of all the normative organizations to which members of its subject-community belong." Raz, *Practical Reason and Norms*, p. 151.
61. See Green, *The Authority of the State*, p. 83.
62. Hobbes, *Leviathan*, ch. 29, p. 225; see also pp. 225–228 and ch. 18, pp. 127–128. Hobbes, of course, has scripture on his side; see Matthew 12:25 and 6:24.
63. The regress argument suggests that part of Hobbes's case for indivisibility is conceptual. If this is so, then the optimism of some neo-Hobbesians about divided government is unwarranted and it would be mistaken to say that "while Hobbes denied the possibility of dividing the governmental power, his grounds for this denial do not involve any propositions central to his political philosophy." Robert Landesman, "In Defense of a Hobbesian Conception of Law," *Philosophy and Public Affairs* 9, 2 (Winter 1980), p. 153 n. 25.

When the right or the power to decide is split among different parties, the possibility of conflict is present whenever there is disagreement.

It is especially this feature of classical sovereignty, its indivisibility, that makes it difficult to provide an account of the classical sovereignty of the American system or even the trinitarian British "Queen in Parliament". Some have said of the former, that it is the Supreme Court which is sovereign, as it is the ultimate interpreter of the American Constitution. Given that the Court has no enforcement powers, Hobbists could not endorse this claim. Austin finds himself forced to claim that sovereignty in the United States resides not in the executive and legislative branches of the federal government, but in the aggregate or collective body of the majorities of the (American) states needed to amend the constitution.[64]

The classical thesis of the indivisibility of sovereignty is really two: Sovereignty is *unique* and *united*. Sovereignty is *unique* if there is one and only one supreme source of authority within a realm. It is *united* if the supreme source of authority is in the hands of one person or one body of persons (or one institution).[65] The two theses are distinct. Consider a system where some body has supreme authority over religious matters, another has supreme authority over education, and a third has supreme authority over everything else; sovereignty in this case would be divided (not united) yet unique. Consider a different system where two bodies have supreme authority over all matters; sovereignty then would not be unique but it would be united. In the American system, one might argue, sovereignty – if it exists – is divided yet unique.

Must states have *unique* authority? Some do not. Consider the British system. The Parliament and the common law are sources of legislative authority, neither evidently derived from the other.[66] The laws of the British system have no single, common origin.[67] Federal systems are the counterexample to the second part of indivisibility (unity). In a federal system, the supreme source of authority is not in the hands of a single institution.

The authority of states is limited; that is, states are limited morally and rationally, and it is possible and presumably desirable to limit

---

64. Austin, *The Province of Jurisprudence Determined*, Lecture VI, pp. 209–210.
65. Adapted from Raz's analysis of Austin (*The Concept of a Legal System*, p. 8).
66. Notwithstanding the party line, which is that the Parliament tacitly authorizes common law.
67. See Raz, *Practical Reason and Norms*, pp. 130–131, citing an observation of Hume's about Rome.

them legally. Further, their authority is divisible (that is, neither unique nor united). There is little reason, then, to think of states, even when justified, as classically sovereign.[68] I take up the matter of the supreme and comprehensive nature of their authority later, after a discussion of certain issues pertaining to the state's monopolization of force.

7.3 JUST POWER AND MONOPOLIES OF FORCE

The influence of doctrines of classical sovereignty, and perhaps the sense of its inevitability or necessity, may be connected to influential confusions about the relations between political obligation and force. The idea that enforcement is conceptually necessary to law, coupled with a command conception, are closely associated with classical sovereignty. These have, of course, been the subject of devastating analysis and criticism by the great jurist Hart and by his followers. Many laws cannot be understood as commands, and the idea of coercive orders cannot account for law's claimed normativity. But even if these influential ideas about law have been effectively rebutted, the state's "power" remains closely associated with its alleged monopolization of legitimate force. And some of the considerations thought by many to support classical sovereignty have been invoked in favor of the state's monopoly on force. But much of my case against classical sovereignty has implications here as well.

States claim supreme authority – sovereignty, to be exact. They also claim a monopoly on the legitimate use of force. These are important and substantive claims. Whatever we think of states, we cannot avoid recognizing that they characteristically enforce their rules with sanctions and use force to secure order and the security of their realm. The history of virtually all states is a tale colored by much brutality and blood. The considerable power of modern states is, of course, one of the main reasons for our interest, both moral and philosophical, in them. So we need to consider the state's power and use of force.

However considerable the state's causal power (*puissance*), discussions, especially popular, often confuse a number of different things. They also tend to exaggerate the power of states. As I have suggested

68. Inalienability, the other attribute of classical sovereignty, I shall not discuss. It is not clear, in the absence of, say, an account of representation (e.g., Rousseau), that it is an interesting property.

(and shall argue later), underlying classical conceptions of sovereignty, as well as many of our misconceptions of the power of states, is a flawed understanding of political power and the nature of social order. The confusions about these powers and their exaggeration are related to this flawed understanding.

We should first of all distinguish sanctions from force. States affix sanctions to laws, but these rarely involve force directly. For the most part, sanctions imposed by states consist in the withdrawal of rights or the imposition of duties – for example, the duty to pay a fine or to remain in a certain place, the loss of the right to move about freely. Some sanctions do involve force, even violence (e.g., capital punishment). But, for the most part, force is merely an enforcement measure to ensure compliance with ordinary law and with sanction-imposing orders.[69]

We should expect that, in most societies, laws will be backed by the threat of sanctions and force. One reason, after all, for desiring a legal system is to ensure compliance on the part of those otherwise inclined or tempted to behave in the ways required by social order. But this does not mean that laws cannot provide reasons or motivate without such sanctions or that they must presuppose them. Unless one assumes that norms per se cannot be reasons, there should be no reason to insist that legal rules must necessarily be backed up with sanctions.[70] But we should expect them to be an important part of virtually all legal and political orders, at least given the way humans seem to be.[71] Were humans such that they could do well with sanctionless political systems, they would most likely not need much, if any, government in the first place.[72]

The reliance of states on force or sanctions is often exaggerated. It is worth remembering the resources states have other than force or

---

69. Raz is especially helpful on these points. See *Practical Reason and Norms,* p. 157.
70. It is an implication of the received theory of practical reason that all reasons for following a norm must be forward-looking. This need not, however, entail that sanctions are needed for reasons for obedience, as other forward-looking considerations could provide these.
71. We may agree with Raz that although sanctionless legal systems may be logically possible, they are "humanly impossible" (Raz, *Practical Reason and Norms,* pp. 158–159).
72. In such a world, "state interference in social relations becomes, in one domain after another, superfluous, and then dies out of itself; the government of persons is replaced by the administration of things. . . . The state is not 'abolished.' *It dies out."* Friedrich Engels, "Socialism: Utopian and Scientific" [1880], in *The Marx-Engels Reader,* p. 713.

authority. Attaching sanctions to disobedience is but one type of consequences that states or their governments can use to motivate compliance with law. Consider some of what they may do. States may prod by levying taxes or by imposing fees for various activities. They may as well impose various restrictions or requirements on anyone wishing to carry out certain activities – for example, licenses for those wishing to practice medicine, teaching, or plumbing, insurance for anyone wishing to drive a motor vehicle or run a business. These may modify behavior and motivate without force. States may also influence behavior by providing incentives, even paying people to act in ways desired – for example, salaries for government employment, tax exemptions for charitable deductions or business expenses, awards and honors for public service. They may also simply seek to persuade, educate, and advise, as J. S. Mill points out:

> Government may interdict all persons from doing certain things; or from doing them without its authorization; or may prescribe to them certain things to be done, or a certain manner of doing things which is left optional with them to do or to abstain from. This is the *authoritative* interference of government. There is another kind of intervention which is not authoritative: when a government, instead of issuing a command and enforcing it by penalties, adopts the course so seldom resorted to by governments, and of which such important use might be made, that of giving advice and promulgating information; or when, leaving individuals free to use their own means of pursuing any object of general interest, the government, not meddling with them, but not trusting the object solely to their care, establishes, side by side with their arrangements, an agency of its own for a like purpose . . .[73]

States may also influence behavior by simply recognizing or establishing standards for action.[74]

Insofar as subjects acknowledge the authority of their state or accept principles recommending conformity with the law, states may influence behavior just by determining and publicizing the law. Force need not, under these circumstances, be a significant motivator of compliance with law. Indeed, faced with a large population generally inclined to disregard or to disobey the law, force is not very

---

73. Mill, *Principles of Political Economy*, ed. J. Riley (New York: Oxford University Press, 1994 [1848/1871]), Book V, chap. 11, p. 325.
74. Raz, *The Concept of a Legal System*, pp. 232–234.

effective. Even popular regimes usually cannot legislate or effectively control certain domains, whatever they wish. (Consider the American experiment with "prohibition" of alcohol, or the difficulties most states have with many "victimless crimes".)[75] Regimes that depend on the massive use of force are often subject to swift disintegration, as they can govern only if most subjects do not resist at once, and collapse when many at the same time refuse to go along.[76] Note in any case that where compliance with most laws is thought to be conditional on the like compliance of others, enforcement may have as its main purpose the provision of assurance.

Last, not only is it important to keep in mind that not all of the state's acts are authoritative (in our sense), not all such acts fit well with Mill's description of "authoritative interference" ("issuing a command and enforcing it by penalties"). Much of the state's authoritative activity does not directly involve commands, much less sanctions. The state's authoritative capacities include, for instance, the right to adjudicate, to permit or exempt, to facilitate and support practices (e.g., certain business ventures, monogamous heterosexual relations). These and other capacities are not easily understood as commanding.

These uncontroversial facts about states need to be emphasized, as it is common to assume that state activity always involves force. Even Rawls seems to believe that "political power is always coercive power backed up by the government's use of sanctions".[77] This is simply false or an exaggeration. Not all state activities require the deployment of force, and many that involve the threatening of sanctions do not customarily involve force. Sometimes this may be acknowledged but it is claimed that the state's influence is "ultimately based on" or "comes down to" naked power or brute force.

---

75. Europeans are often surprised when they come to realize that the federal government could not, even if it wished to, disarm the American public. The American state may well claim a monopoly of legitimate force, but this may just be a face-saving response to a citizenry armed to the teeth.
76. For an interesting discussion of tyranny and force, see Kavka, *Hobbesian Moral and Political Theory*, sect. 6.2.
77. His full statement is: "Political power is always coercive power backed up by the government's use of sanctions, for government alone has the authority to use force in upholding its laws." Rawls, *Political Liberalism*, p. 136. Andrew Levine thinks that states "are 'grounded' in force in the sense that, by definition, they are coercive: they coordinate behavior through the use or threat of force." *The End of the State* (London: Verso, 1987), p. 176.

As I argue in Section 7.6, this is not convincing for the simple reason is that the state's power need not have a unique, "ultimate" explanation. Here, as elsewhere in our social and political lives, there need be no single factor or "bottom line". The hierarchical models of political power presupposed by proponents of classical sovereignty may be ubiquitous, but no less misleading for that.

This said, the state's use of force, actual or merely threatened, even if not as extensive as commonly thought, is considerable and raises questions of justification. I shall not, for now, address many of these. I assume that just as force may sometimes be justifiably used by individuals, so it may be by states, at least by legitimate ones (i.e., reasonably just and minimally efficient). I have been considering only the claims of justified states to sovereignty and a monopoly on legitimate force; I have assumed that, for the most part, virtually no illegitimate state has a credible claim to such authority or power. While the power of reasonably just states may be considerable and worrisome, it is especially that of tyrannical and despotic states that alarms. And their power is, by my account, illegitimate.

It may be that even if a just state's claims to authority are not justified, its use of causal power is often justified. So even if they lack the authority they claim, states may sometimes justly use force, attach legal (other) consequences to behavior, as well as bribe, persuade, educate, advise, recognize, and establish standards. I shall continue to focus on the state's central claims, those concerning authority (i.e., sovereignty), and leave consideration of justified force until the end of Section 7.5.

Let us return briefly to the Weberian thesis of the state as the monopolizer of legitimate force within its territory. I rejected this as a complete characterization, or "definition", of modern states, but accepted it as one of their attributes. Let us consider it now more carefully, in light of some of the conclusions just reached about the state's authority.

Some of the attributes of political authority are true as well for the Weberian monopoly. The Weberian thesis, as I shall interpret it, is not primarily an empirical thesis about the power of states, though it has empirical implications. It is a thesis about the state's *claimed normative powers:* states *claim a right* to monopolize *legitimate* force within their territories. Now, again, they must have some success with regard to this claim or they will not, we may suppose, be *de facto* states. But the state's claim is compatible with the existence of other wielders of force. Some of these the state will recognize (e.g., private security forces), others it may tolerate because it is unable to do anything about them (e.g., the Mafia).

What exactly is the state's claim? It is to monopolize the use of legitimate force within its territory. It claims it may legitimately use force and that no one else may unless authorized or permitted to do so by the state. All unauthorized uses of force are illegitimate according to the state. Such a monopoly of force is a *concentration* of legitimate force. But it is more than that; a mere concentration is compatible with many competitors, where a monopoly precludes any. Any unauthorized force is a challenge to the state's self-image and *"status"*.[78]

Some of the reasons for the failure of Hobbes's regress argument, even if it is interpreted as pertaining only to causal power, cast doubt as well on the Weberian thesis. A monopoly of force requires that forces constitute an ordering, or at least that there not be too many discontinuities. If there is too much incomparability of power, it becomes unclear in what its monopoly could consist. We saw that we should not expect this to be the case that political power generally constitute an ordering. Force being a species of power, we may expect that incomparabilities, and even cycles, of forces to be commonplace.

States, when just, may possess significant amounts, or influence significant concentrations of legitimate force. But we should not expect them to be able to monopolize it. As this may not be desirable in any case, our result may be fortunate. States, then, are neither sovereign in the classical sense nor Weberian monopolizers of legitimate force.

7.4 LIMITED SOVEREIGNTY

Contemporary fans of sovereignty usually understand it to be limited and divisible. Indivisibility has long been thought problematic. The possibility of federal states means sovereignty need not be *united* (i.e., in the hands of one person or body). More controversially, there may be separate sources of law for a realm (e.g., parliament and the common law), in which case sovereignty need not be *unique*. Most theorists today concede the former, and many concede the latter as

78. Michel Troper argues that "la thèse que l'Etat a le monopole de la contrainte n'est en définitive, comme Kelsen ne manque pas de le souligner, qu'un avatar de la vielle idée que l'Etat est souverain." "Le monopole de la contrainte légitime (Légitimité et légalité dans l'Etat moderne)," *lignes* 25 (May 1995), p. 40.

well. Most also take sovereignty to be limited. A popular view is to understand states to be *constitutionally* constrained by various principles and by individual rights. Limited states are ones that are constitutionally deprived of certain juridical *powers*. The American state, for instance, lacks the power to establish a religion or to dispense titles of nobility, and a variety of powers are denied it and are reserved to the individual "states". Let us suppose, then, that sovereignty is to be understood as limited and as divisible (or at least as not united). Sovereignty, I said, is the highest, final, and supreme political and legal authority and power within the territorially defined domain of a system of direct rule. We saw that it need not be absolute or indivisible. The question, then, is of whether legitimate states have limited, and divided, sovereignty.

A state's authority, even if limited, can nevertheless be "the highest, final, and supreme" in a domain. Recall that on my analysis supremacy means the capacity to regulate all other sources of authority. Hobbes, of course, so understands the state's authority; but so do Kant and others.[79] Raz, as I have noted, thinks that legal systems claim supremacy in this sense and that this claim is entailed by another, more general claim, the *comprehensive* nature of legal systems: the authority to regulate any type of behavior. Sovereignty as I have characterized it includes supremacy in the sense just explained. It may as well include comprehensiveness. It is worth being as clear as we can on this point.

If a state is sovereign in the classical sense, its authority is absolute (i.e., unlimited). It would therefore also be comprehensive in Raz's sense. There would be no limits to the range of actions it claims to regulate; it would claim authority to regulate any type of behavior. Now, "regulation" here need involve nothing more than permission.[80] And states may possess comprehensive authority without

---

79. Kant, "On the Common Saying: 'This May be True in Theory, but it does not Apply in Practice'," pp. 81–83, and *The Metaphysics of Morals*, pp. 95–98.
80. In *Practical Reason and Norms*, Raz claims the authority claimed is that "to regulate behaviour in some way but not necessarily in every way" (p. 151). In *The Morality of Freedom* his claim is stronger in this respect: (most) legal systems "provide ways of changing the law and of adopting any law whatsoever" and claiming authority for these (p. 77). In the earlier work he also allows for the possibility of legal systems with "constitutional provisions which cannot be changed by any legal means", something denied in the later book. *The Morality of Freedom* is an inquiry into the authority of states ("most contemporary societies"), so its characterizations are perhaps most relevant. In correspondence, Raz worries that his view in *The Morality of Freedom* "reflects a particular cultural conception of the state (secu-

actively exercising it. Classical states certainly are imperial in this way; their unlimited authority entails that it is comprehensive as well. It does not follow, however, that limited sovereignty is not also comprehensive. Limited states appear also to claim comprehensiveness. Consider, as mentioned earlier, that limited states claim to be limited by, and *only by*, the constraints they recognize – for example, those stated in (or implied by) the constitution or the founding practices. All complex legal systems have rules that allow exceptions – for example, excuses, conscientious objection – but the only ones allowed are those that are legally recognized.[81] As I have indicated, "recognition" does not mean that the constraints or rights have no independent status. And the set of constraints can be fairly open-ended. The U.S. Bill of Rights, as we have seen, recognizes "unenumerated rights" that are held to have a prior and independent existence: "The enumeration in the Constitution of certain rights shall not be construed to deny or disparage others retained by the people". The fact that the Ninth Amendment has generally been ignored in American judicial practice does not belie the theoretical points I am making. It specifies "rights retained by the people"; it does not, for instance, refer to other constraints or moral considerations (e.g., ideals or values that do not sustain rights). These, unless referred to elsewhere, are not recognized as constraints.[82] Are justified states, then, *limited* sovereigns?

My account of the state's authority is Razian in that authoritative directives are understood as providing reasons of a certain kind: "Authoritative reasons are pre-emptive: the fact that an authority requires performance of an action is a reason for its performance which is not to be added to all other relevant reasons when assessing what to do, but should exclude and take the place of some of them."[83]

---

lar and Hobbesian) . . . one [that] may be less firmly rooted in our culture, and possibly on its way out in any case."

81. "It is not that the law claims that one ought to obey the law come what may. There are many legal doctrines specifically designed to allow exceptions to legal requirements, doctrines such as self-defense, necessity, public policy, and the like. The point is that the law demands the right to define the permissible exceptions." Raz, *The Morality of Freedom*, p. 77; see also *The Authority of Law*, p. 31, and Green, *The Authority of the State*, p. 83.

82. Constraints recognized by constitutions can be considerable or substantial. The 1936 and 1977 constitutions of the Soviet Union guaranteed each of the fifteen recognized republics the right to secede (1936, chap. II, article 17; 1977, III, chap. 8, article 72).

83. "It will be remembered that the thesis is only about legitimate authority." *The*

The state *claims* authority, then, when it intends its directives to be authoritative, that is, to be pre-emptive reasons. They are meant to be binding and content-independent.[84] The state's authority is *recognized* by someone when that individual so treats its directives. And the authority of the state *exists* when its claim to authority is generally recognized; its authority is then *de facto*. To claim authority or to recognize authority (in these senses) is to regard it as legitimate. Something cannot be a *de facto* authority without being regarded as legitimate by a significant proportion of the relevant population.

To regard something as legitimate is not, of course, for it to be legitimate. A state has legitimate authority only insofar and to the extent that its is a *de facto* authority and its claim is justified.[85] In addition to adopting his analysis of authority, my account and general approach are consistent with Raz in other ways. States are to serve our needs to coordinate our actions, and their justification will be in terms of reasons that apply independently to individuals. "There is a strong case for holding that no political authority can be legitimate unless it is also a *de facto* authority. For the case for having any political authority rests to a large extent on its ability to solve co-ordination problems and extricate the population from Prisoner's Dilemma type situations."[86]

What considerations, then, *justify* authority? In particular, how would a state's limited sovereignty be justified? There is, Raz claims, "a normal" way of justifying authority. This he calls "the normal justification thesis":

Morality of Freedom, p. 46 (emphasis deleted). Such reasons were earlier called "protected": reasons to do the obligatory act and second-order reasons not to act on (otherwise valid) reasons to do something else (*The Authority of Law*, p. 18).

84. "A reason is content-independent if there is no direct connection between the reason and the action for which it is a reason." *The Morality of Freedom*, p. 35. See also Hart, "Commands and Authoritative Legal Reasons."

85. Raz, *The Morality of Freedom*, pp. 26, 46, 56, 75–76, and Green, *The Authority of the State*, pp. 59–60. The claim that a political authority cannot be legitimate unless it is a *de facto* authority I recognized earlier to be a substantive principle, one that follows from the ends for which political authorities are desirable.

86. Raz, *The Morality of Freedom*, p. 56. In earlier works Raz seems to think of PDs as species of coordination problems: "authority based on the need to co-ordinate the action of several people. All political authority rests on this foundation (though not only on it)" (*Practical Reason and Norms*, p. 64). Raz's understanding of coordination problems is not always clear. See "Facing Up: A Reply," *Southern California Law Review* 62, 3 and 4 (March–May 1989), 1189–1194. (For specific references to the PD, see *Practical Reason and Norms*, pp. 184, 193, and 198, and *The Morality of Freedom*, pp. 50–51.)

The normal way to establish that a person has authority over another person involves showing that the alleged subject is likely better to comply with reasons which apply to him (other than the alleged authoritative directives) if he accepts the directives of the alleged authority as authoritatively binding and tries to follow them, rather than the reasons which apply to him directly.

To be complete, a justification of authority must also "establish that there are no reasons against its acceptance which defeat the reasons for the authority."[87] This kind of justification of authority is an *indirect* one, similar to that involved in the revisionist accounts of practical reason discussed in Chapter 5. One has reasons to act, and the sources of these reasons may often be better served if one does not attempt to act on them directly but instead follows other reasons (e.g., protected or preemptory ones). Raz's "normal justification thesis" for the state's authority is similarly indirect.[88]

What are the implications of this kind of account for the authority of states and their limited sovereignty? Note first that justifying authority in terms of reasons that apply independently to individuals will not suggest an inquiry as to whether states have authority *simpliciter*. Rather, we are to determine how much authority a state has with regard to whom.[89] Raz's test is "does following the authority's instructions improve conformity with reason?" The scope of the state's authority will depend, then, "on the person over whom authority is supposed to be exercised: his knowledge, strength of will, his reliability in various aspects of life, and on the government in question." In most cases, a state's authority will undoubtedly vary from person to person. "An expert pharmacologist may not be subject to the authority of government in matters of the safety of drugs, an inhabitant of a little village by a river may not be subject to its authority in matters of navigation and conservation of the river by the banks of which he has spent all his life."[90] Whether one is likely to comply better with reasons that apply to one by accepting as authoritative a state's directive, rather than the reasons that apply directly to one, will depend considerably on circumstance. It is doubtful that

---

87. Raz, *The Morality of Freedom*, pp. 53 (emphasis deleted), 56, and "Facing Up: A Reply," p. 1188.
88. See also Green, *The Authority of the State*, pp. 56–59.
89. The reference to individual rationality does not mean we are presupposing a "subjective" account of reason. The argument ought to work even on realist accounts, even if many reasons are agent-neutral.
90. Raz, *The Morality of Freedom*, pp. 73–74.

the sweeping authority claimed even by states claiming limited sovereignty over all their subjects would ever be thus justified.

The state claims, I have said, *comprehensive* and *supreme* authority over all members and over all who find themselves in its jurisdiction.[91] Perhaps the best argument in favor of these claims is that the state "is in a better position to achieve (if its legitimacy is acknowledged) what the individual has reason to but is in no position to achieve."[92] This argument, however, will not grant states the comprehensive and supreme authority they claim. The reason is simply that "the normal justification thesis invites a piecemeal approach to the question of the authority of government, which yields the conclusion that the extent of governmental authority varies from individual to individual and is more limited than the authority governments claim for themselves in the case of most people."[93]

It is hard, then, to see how the limited – but nevertheless extensive – sovereignty claimed by states could be justified, even if we suppose them to be reasonably just and minimally efficient. Suppose that this authority is not, appearances to the contrary, comprehensive in Raz's sense. Still it will be *very* broad – consider the authority claimed by our constitutional democracies. It is difficult to imagine that this authority could be justified with regard to all persons in the state's jurisdiction. Too often people are better placed to comply with reasons that apply to them simply by following them rather than by taking the state's directives as authoritative. The matter of the state's authority, it is important to understand, is a normative one, concerning how we are to act for reasons. If one *conforms* with a directive – that is, acts as it says one should act – but does so for reasons other than its claimed authority, one has not treated it as authoritative. Regarding a directive as authoritative means taking it to be a reason to act as it directs but not for the reasons that normally directly apply

91. Some – for instance, diplomats – may appear to be exceptions. But their status may be best understood as a type of immunity, granted reciprocally by states. As such, diplomats are subject to a state's authority while residing in its jurisdiction. See Chapter 8.
92. This "has for a long time been the argument most favoured by political theorists." Raz lists four other common reasons capable of establishing the legitimacy of an authority: the authority's greater wisdom, its steadier will, the relative decision costs of deciding for oneself, and the self-defeating character of direct individual action. The last reason is central for PD situations and is, along with the reason just cited in the text, the sort of argument that contractarian theorists make. (See Raz, "Facing Up: A Reply," p. 1188, for remarks about the importance of relative decision costs.)
93. Raz, *The Morality of Freedom*, p. 80.

and that are preempted. It is hard to believe that we always, or even usually, will do best by taking our state's directives as authoritative, even if the state is just and efficient.

I have mentioned the view that many of the key concepts of the modern state are borrowed and adapted from Christian theology. The sovereignty, even classical, of an omnipotent and omniscient deity need not be feared if it is benevolent and cares for us. Its authority would be justified, presumably, by the Razian account I have adopted. On Hobbes's view, God's "irresistible power" is the source of his rule over us.[94] Rejecting "gunmen" accounts of law and obligation, we may be more inclined to recognize God's sovereignty by considering his competence and benevolence. Presuming a reliable way of recognizing divine directives – which may be a big presumption – God's command to us presumably always is a reason. Criticizing Hobbes, Leibniz concludes that "Hobbesian empires"

exist neither among civilized peoples nor among barbarians, and I consider them neither possible nor desirable, unless those who must have supreme power are gifted with angelic virtues. For men will choose to follow their own will, and will consult their own welfare as seems best to them, as long as they are not persuaded of the supreme wisdom and capability of their rulers, which things are necessary for perfect resignation of the will. So Hobbes' demonstrations have a place only in that state whose king is God, whom alone one can trust in all things.[95]

Leviathan, "that *Mortall God*", lacking God's competence and benevolence, will not possess authority over us. Classical sovereignty effectively demands "perfect resignation of the will", and Leibniz saw perfectly that Hobbes's story is credible "only in that state whose king is God, whom *alone* one can trust in all things" (emphasis added). Only a being with God's competence and benevolence could command that sort of authority.[96]

94. "The right of Nature, whereby God reigneth over men, and punisheth those that break his Lawes, is to be derived, not from his Creating them as if he required obedience, as of Gratitude for his benefits; but from his *Irresistible Power*." Hobbes, *Leviathan*, chap. 31, p. 246.
95. *Caesarinus Fürstenerius* (*De Suprematu Principum Germaniae*) [1677], in *Political Writings*, 2nd ed., ed. P. Riley (Cambridge: Cambridge University Press, 1988), p. 120.
96. On Robert Adams's revisionist account of divine command ethics, it remains logically possible that God could command cruelty for its own sake, but a believer must hold that "it is unthinkable that God should do so. To have *faith* in God is not just to believe that He exists, but also to trust in His love for mankind." Adams, "A Modified Divine Command Theory of Ethical Wrongness" [1973], in *Divine Commands and Morality*, ed. P. Helm (New York: Oxford University Press, 1981), p. 88.

Reflecting on indirect justifications of authority, Leslie Green notes that it is not so much authority's content-independence which makes it problematic as its preemptiveness. On the sort of account I have adopted, authoritative directives are preemptive: As Raz explains, "the fact that an authority requires performance of an action is a reason for its performance which is not to be added to all other relevant reasons when assessing what to do, but should exclude and take the place of some of them." Decisions and commitments, Green remarks, are both content-independent and preemptive: Promises "exclude in advance considerations of certain reasons for non-performance, and it is analytically true that one who is still deliberating has not yet decided." Justifying the preemptive authority of decisions and commitments "does not seem preposterous and has certain natural justifications". Green rightly notes:

> The case of authoritative commands is felt to be different simply because the power to cut off deliberation is in the hands of *another* person. This leaves one vulnerable to others; in the case of the modern state, to the requirements of a large and bureaucratic organization. How these can ever have the force they claim is indeed a pressing question, but not because of some obscure truth about the nature of practical reasoning. The authority of the state is problematic in large part because it is the state's.[97]

For contractarian theorists, as for some others, it is interesting to note, the *structure* of the justification of the authority of decisions, commitments, justice, and political arrangements is similarly indirect. Their authority is justified for a group of individuals, for a range of matters, whenever acceptance of and compliance with the practices is likely to be more beneficial than considering the matter on its independent merits. Other conditions will be relevant for practices that involve several parties – for instance, some assurances of compliance on the part of others must be forthcoming. Contractarian arguments for the *state's* authority are more problematic than the similar case for the authority of (a set of) *moral norms* for the very reasons Green mentions. But it is worth remarking that contractarian justifications also fail to account for the supreme and comprehensive authority claimed by *justice*, or so I argue elsewhere.[98]

97. Green, *The Authority of the State*, p. 59.
98. See especially "Reasons for Actions and The Scope of Justice" and "Well-Being, Reasons, and the Politics of Law." Nonuniversal, "popular" will-based accounts of right, such as Rousseau's account, do not easily generate duties of justice between

States, then, do not possess limited sovereignty. Their limited authority is more restricted than they recognize or admit. It is constrained by justice, whether or not states recognize this. And it is not rational for most people subject to a state to accord it the authority it claims, even if it is reasonably just and minimally efficient. The state's claim to limited sovereignty, then, is not credible. Its claims are too sweeping, and its demand to determine its own limits too imperious.

Sovereignty generally is the highest, final, and supreme political and legal authority and power within the territorially defined domain of a system of direct rule. I have argued that it is hard to see how most of the attributes of sovereignty, even if limited, could be justified even for reasonably just and minimally efficient states. I return to the matter of a "highest" authority later. For now, let me conclude this section with a few words about "finality". The state's authority is claimed to be "final": There is no further appeal after it has spoken. It has, as it were, "the last word". Is this not so? Are states not final in their decisions?

In a hierarchical chain of rule, with review and appeal procedures throughout, there is a point after which there is no further decision to be made and no further appeal available – within the hierarchical system. Many things are mistaken about this picture, some of which is taken up in Section 7.6 (e.g., the misleading understanding of political power and collective decision). But it is not certain whether this simple and familiar account is true or clear. In what sense is a final decision by a highest authority "final"? Surely, some decisions of a system's officials close off options for other officials; a "final" decision may require other officials to act in certain ways (e.g., refuse to entertain certain motions or appeals). But what wider significance does this "finality" have for the system's authority? It should be obvious that if the limited and partial authority of legitimate states is conditional in the ways I have suggested, some apparent final decisions will have little or no authority to many people and possibly to agents of the state. The authority of *any* particular decision may not be accepted. States and other final deciders do not concede this, but that is not relevant to its truth. But I need not belabor the point. Consider simply the fact that "ultimate" authorities can change their minds about "final" decisions; their decision need not be *their* last

peoples. Command or will-based accounts of *morality* seem credible only if theistic or if based in individual autonomy, as in Kantian ethics.

word.[99] "Final" decisions do change things, as do states. But their self-descriptions are misleading at best.

7.5 OBLIGATIONS TO OBEY

States, even when legitimate (i.e., just and efficient), do not possess the limited sovereignty they claim. It is usually thought that the state's authority, if justified, entails an obligation to obey. The question is now whether there still might be such an obligation. A legitimate state, even if lacking the sweeping authority it claims to possess, may nevertheless be permitted to make laws and to enforce them with sanctions – a right to rule. If the sanctions provide assurance that others will comply, one of the conditions of obligations conditional on the expected compliance of others will be satisfied. We may then have obligations to obey such states.

Clearly we often have sufficient reason to obey the directives of states, whether our own or simply those in whose jurisdiction we find ourselves. Disobedience usually makes the application of sanctions or some other bad consequence likely, and this often is a sufficient reason to obey. There often are sufficient moral reasons to do what the state asks of us. And many laws require us to refrain from doing things most people have little desire to do anyway (e.g., kill, take candy from babies). The more just and efficient the state, the more these sorts of considerations presumably will apply (especially the second).

Sanctions, it is important to realize, provide reasons essentially by altering the expected benefits of disobedience.[100] And the other considerations mentioned make reasons to comply parasitic on independent reasons. None of these considerations are what we seek when trying to account for obligations to obey. The latter are supposed to be reasons to obey simply because the state requires something. "The obligation to obey the law implies that the reason to do

---

99. In an important article on American statutory interpretation, John Ferejohn and Barry Weingast argue that "there is no 'last word' in politics. No person or individual ever gets to say what the law is finally; Congress can and often does react to court decisions, as can agencies and the president. Each actor in the political and legal setting – president, agency, Congress, litigants, court – can take new courses of action, devise new interpretations, or enact new statutes." "A Positive Theory of Statutory Interpretation," *International Review of Law and Economics* 12, 2 (June 1992), 263.
100. Sanctions may also communicate disapproval.

that which is required by law is the very fact that it is so required." In addition, the obligation is usually thought to be general, both in its object and in its scope: All those subject to the law are to obey, and they are to obey all the laws.[101]

The literature on this question is now considerable, and the general consensus appears to be that there are no such general obligations.[102] The problems with them replicate to a considerable extent those we found with authority and lie in the generality and particularity of these obligations. They are supposed to bind (1) *all* and (2) *only* those subject to the jurisdiction of a state to obey (3) *all* of its laws. These conditions are simply too demanding. Consider briefly the last requirement, that all the laws be obeyed. There are numerous laws that it seems reasonable not to obey on some occasions – for example, coming to a *full* stop at a stop sign on a deserted road, where there is good visibility. One could argue that the fact that traffic law requires one to stop at stop signs is a reason in favor of doing so, though a reason that can at certain times be outweighed. But the obligation to obey the law is not meant to be a mere additional consideration to be added to others; it is intended to be preemptive. Further, the manner in which laws are typically formulated makes it clear that the state does *not* give people discretion to determine whether they are to be obeyed or not; the law does not state, "when approaching a stop sign, come to a full stop unless in your judgment you think it not necessary."

Consider the first requirement of generality, that the obligation bind all those subject to the state's jurisdiction. We have seen that it rarely will be possible to justify the state's authority to *all* those over whom it claims jurisdiction. This is a simple consequence of the structure of the normal justification thesis and similar accounts. Now consider the particularity condition, that the obligation to obey is held *only* by those over whom the state has jurisdiction. The obliga-

---

101. "The obligation to obey the law is a general obligation applying to all the law's subjects and to all the laws on all occasions to which they apply." Raz, *The Authority of Law*, p. 234. Recall as well Hobbes's view of law as command, where "a man saith, *Doe this*, or *Doe not this*, without expecting other reason than the Will of him that sayes it."
102. In addition to works by Raz, Green, and Simmons already cited, see R. A. Wasserstrom, "The Obligation to Obey the Law," *UCLA Law Review* 10 (1963), 780–807, and M.B.E. Smith, "Is There a Prima Facie Obligation to Obey the Law?" *Yale Law Journal* 82 (1973), 950–976. Not everyone, of course, endorses the majority view. A brief but useful survey of the literature is found in Simmons, "Obedience to Law," *Encyclopedia of Ethics*, vol. 2, pp. 918–921.

tion to obey is meant to be some special relation binding people to *their* state. Many of the reasons we ordinarily have for respecting the law—its content—do not satisfy this condition. Our laws governing, say, criminal matters or pollution, may warrant our obedience not because they are *ours* but because they are good laws. In Chapter 8, I return to the matter of the relevance of something's being *ours*. But for now it is hard to see how this condition could be satisfied.[103]

It is often claimed that the obligation to obey, and the state's authority, are derived from "the consent of the governed". But as I argued in the preceding chapter, genuine consent is an engagement of the will, whether explicit or tacit, and most subjects of states have not consented in the ways needed to render their state legitimate, much less to support a general obligation to obey. This is not, of course, to challenge the imposition of consent as a sufficient condition of legitimacy or of obligations to obey. And it is not to challenge the idea that consent may be necessary or sufficient for something other than obligation or legitimacy – for instance, shared responsibility for the acts of one's state.[104]

"It is common to regard authority over persons as centrally involving a right to rule, where that is understood as correlated with an obligation to obey on the part of those subject to the authority."[105] If there is no general obligation, then can there be a right to rule? Claim rights entail obligations on the part of (some) others, so denial of the

---

103. I have not lingered over this issue in large part because the literature is well known and, in my view, convincing. Readers not persuaded are urged to turn to the works on this issue that have been referred to, especially those of Simmons and Green.

   The *principle of fairness* is sometimes invoked as a ground for obligations to obey. See C. D. Broad, "On the Function of False Hypotheses in Ethics" [1916], in *Broad's Critical Essays in Moral Philosophy*, ed. D. Cheney (London: George Allen & Unwin, 1971), pp. 43–62; Hart, "Are There Any Natural Rights?"; and Rawls, *A Theory of Justice*, pp. 111–114, 342–350. There are a number of problems with the principle. As usually formulated, it seems too demanding. See Nozick, *Anarchy, State, and Utopia*, pp. 90–95; Simmons, *Moral Principles and Political Obligations*, chap. 5; Richard J. Arneson, "The Principle of Fairness and Free-Rider Problems," *Ethics* 92, 4 (July 1982), 616–633; and Morris, "The Hart–Rawls Principle of Fairness Amended," *Journal of Social Philosophy* 15, 1 (January 1983), 18–20. Even if adequately amended, it is doubtful the principle could support obligations to obey on the part of all subjects of a state. The beneficiaries of practices and projects subject to the principle are not likely to be all and only those subject to the jurisdiction of a state. Again, the particularity requirement is not met. For a recent defense, see George Klosko, *The Principle of Fairness and Political Obligation* (Lanham, Md.: Rowman & Littlefield, 1992).
104. See Boxill, "On Some Criticisms of Consent Theory," p. 99.
105. Raz, *The Morality of Freedom*, p. 23.

obligation here would seem to entail denial of the right. We might be Hobbists in understanding the state's right as a mere Hohfeldian liberty; strictly, sovereigns have no claim rights on this view. But I should want to hold that states have powers. And if they can have powers, it is unclear that much is gained by refusing them claim rights.[106]

I should like to leave open the possibility, then, that states that are reasonably just and minimally efficient have a claim right to rule. So I must urge revision of our understanding of this right. Recall Locke's notion of "political power": "*a Right* of making Laws with Penalties ... for the Regulating and Preserving of Property, and of employing the force of the Community, in the Execution of such Laws, and in the defence of the Common-wealth from Foreign Injury, and all this only for the Publick Good."[107] We might read this somewhat literally and understand "political power" as merely a claim right to make rules for the public good and to enforce them. The right to rule, then, would merely be the right to issue directives (aspiring to be authoritative?), to attach sanctions to disobedience, to use force, and to do those other things that legitimate states may justly do. For a few people this right will correlate with an obligation to obey, for they may have consented (e.g, many officials) or may have other special grounds for an obligation. But for most people this right to rule will correlate with an obligation to refrain from interfering with the state's actions and possibly to contribute their fair share of the costs of the state's activities. The right to rule, then, will not be the same as the right to command.[108]

Earlier I stressed the distinction between justified authority and justified power or force. The facts that the state's authority fails to be as sweeping as it claims and that there is no general obligation to obey do not mean that states may not justly coerce those subject to its laws.[109] Those, if any, with no reason to obey the laws of a state may be *outlaws*, but they even may be justly coerced by a legitimate state.[110] Legitimate states may impose and enforce reasonable rules for the welfare of subjects. When these rules are reasonable, subjects may have content-dependent reasons to abide by them, in addition

---

106. See also Green, *The Authority of the State*, pp. 235, 239.
107. *Second Treatise of Government*, chap. 1, para. 3, p. 268.
108. See Simmons, *Moral Principles and Political Obligations*, p. 195.
109. Ibid., p. 37; Green, *The Authority of the State*, pp. 242–243.
110. See Morris, "Punishment and Loss of Moral Standing," *Canadian Journal of Philosophy* 21, 1 (March 1991), 53–79. Recall as well the discussion in Chapter 3 of the problem of "independents" in Nozick's account of the emergence of minimal "states" in conditions of anarchy.

to whatever consequential reasons they may have. What they will usually lack are reasons to obey the rules simply because the state issued them.

7.6 STATES WITHOUT SOVEREIGNTY

Hobbes is famous for his view that social order could not be secured in the absence of classical sovereignty. Part of his defense of this thesis rests on a particular view of humans in "states of nature" and in civil society that has been the object of considerable attention of political theorists. Hobbes may be interpreted as understanding social order to be a collective good and that its provision gives rise to a collective action problem. Some have argued that the problem people face in securing social order is an *n*-person Prisoners' Dilemma; others have offered alternative accounts. It would be a fair assessment of the contemporary literature to say that, whatever their disagreements, few theorists today believe that the problem of securing social order is as intractable as Hobbes made it appear. More to the point, there seems to be a fair amount of agreement that *some* social order can be secured independently of centralized political power or modern states.[111] I have argued that legitimate states will lack the authority they claim as sovereign. I shall assume that the state's sovereignty is not a condition for social order and consider what authority relations might be like in nonsovereign states.

I have said that the hierarchical conception of political power and authority presupposed by many defenses of sovereignty is misleading. We saw that power relations are not likely to constitute an ordering, and the same seems true of relations of authority, at least in most states. Our states claim sovereignty, if only the limited sort, but their claims are not credible. They and their friends assert that social order depends on the state's being the ultimate source of political authority and power within a territory, but this does not seem to be true. Our world in fact turns out to be one of states without sovereignty. In this world, social order is maintained, sometimes only precariously, by power, interest, justice, convention, compromise, benevolence, religious sentiments, ties of kin and nation, and the like. The sources

---

111. See Chapter 3. Social order may nevertheless be fragile in certain ways and subject to sudden and unpredictable changes (e.g., the French Revolution, the Great Depression, the collapse of the Soviet Union).

of political authority are multiple and none need be supreme.[112] A variety of things provides different people with reasons for action, and these often suffice to secure social order, even great prosperity and civilization.

The classical notion of sovereignty developed in early modern times when monarchs, freed from constraints imposed by popes and emperors, struggled to maintain and expand their power against internal and external rivals. The ferocity of civil and religious strife suggested the need to establish a single, strong "sovereign" who could maintain order in the face of extraordinary disagreement. Aside from Hobbes's regress argument, it is not clear what justification there was for requiring a *unique*, much less ultimate, source of political authority within a realm. We are now used to the liberal "art of separation" (to use Michael Walzer's phrase).[113] Peace is often secured by distinguishing and separating domains: "church and state", federal and provincial, various private and public realms, speech and action. These separations and divisions often are counterexamples to the claim of defenders of classical sovereignty that authority must be united. Some of the ways in which these distinct domains operate may as well suggest an alternative to the unitary vision of a social order implicit in classical as well as limited notions of sovereignty.

It is important for social order, and for many other social goods, that collective decisions be made and that conflicts be resolved in an efficient and predictable way. This fact does not require state sovereignty, however, and it may not even, under some conditions, require states. It is also important to understand that this fact does not entail that the exact manner of resolution for any particular decision be known beforehand, or even that it be known beforehand that there be a manner of resolving all issues. What is important is that manners of resolution be orderly, nonviolent, just, and reasonably efficient. And for this, there should be sufficient agreement about a number of matters – an "overlapping consensus", to adapt Rawls's phrase to a somewhat different end. Few determinations can be made *a priori* of the requisite agreement needed for social order.

---

112. Recall the effectiveness condition for *political* authority. None of these things can be a source of political authority unless it is widely recognized as such.
113. Michael Walzer, "Liberalism and the Art of Separation," *Political Theory* 12 (1984), 315–330.

In some societies in some circumstances, it can be very important that the exact manner in which certain specific controversies are to be resolved be clear and settled. But even then, it may even be useful – that is, conducive to peace and order – that the exact manner of resolutions of others not be settled beforehand. Consider the abortion issue(s) in our societies. Many Western European states have "resolved" some of the issues involving abortion essentially by fudging. In the United States this may not be possible, as this issue, as well as some involving the relation between religion and government, raises fundamental questions regarding "ultimate" sources of authority about which there is little agreement. The position that states (or "constitutions" or peoples) are sovereign, far from resolving the issue, is rightly understood by many to be merely one competing position. In this situation, better to fudge the issue and work out a compromise that permits people with significant disagreements to live with one another.

The American political system is in many respects a good example for the case I wish to build against sovereignty.[114] It is not merely the division among the executive, legislative, and judicial branches of government or the federal nature of the system that makes it a counterexample to many claims about classical sovereignty. It is also the political culture. In the United States, I suggest, there are several sources of political authority that, as a matter of fact, are widely but not universally recognized: the Constitution, the different branches of government, the "People", natural law, conscience, the Christian Bible, Anglo-American common law, and so on. What may be most distinctive about American political culture is the extraordinary authority of "the Constitution." But although the Constitution is widely regarded as the "supreme law of the land", what exactly this means is less than clear if one thinks of the various sources of authority just mentioned.[115] Further, and most important, I suggest there is

---

114. "It is interesting to note, therefore, that while the concept of sovereignty might still be thought to be useful in describing the workings of the UK constitution, its application to modern states such as the US (with true constitutional government) and the USSR (with a fiction of constitution) is in both cases problematic." Roger Scruton, *A Dictionary of Political Thought* (London: Pan Books, 1982), p. 442.
115. The apparent agreement about the supremacy of the Constitution, of course, is accompanied by great disagreement about how it is to be interpreted. And these disagreements, I would contend, often reveal disagreements about sources of authority. Quarrels about the Ninth Amendment, for instance, have to be deeper than disputes about literary meaning or original intention(s), as the latter seem

considerable uncertainty as to what, if any, priority these different sources of authority – the Constitution, natural law, religious scripture – have over one another for different people.

Now this is just as well, we may think. The issues that preoccupied seventeenth- and eighteenth-century political theorists have resurfaced in the last several decades of American life: the matter of civil disobedience, the (mislabeled) conflict between "church and state", the separation(s) of "private" and "public" spheres, the authority of conscience. But the questions Hobbes and Rousseau struggled with regarding competing authorities are not resolved in the American system; they are, in large part, fudged.[116] Certainly this is true of the British system, with its famous unwritten constitution. In practice, we usually get by without settling these issues "once and for all". In the absence of general agreement, it may be just as well that we do not resolve the issue of the "ultimate" authority to decide these matters. A moment's reflection about, say, constitutional systems, should make it clear that there is no way of resolving "once and for all" every or even most questions of political authority.[117] Consider only that for any existing or feasible constitutional system, it is possible to imagine all kinds of constitutional crises where no one would know what to do.[118] This suggests that an important part of the picture of a

not very difficult to determine in this case. See Morris, "Droits originaires et Etats limités".

116. This claim is not made with regard to the different branches of government and to the justly celebrated system of "checks and balances". The founders of the American system took a stand against Hobbes's critique of mixed constitutions and against the indivisibility of sovereignty. See, for instance, James Madison, *Letters and Other Writings*, vol. 4 (Philadelphia: J. B. Lippincott, 1865), pp. 61–62 [1830], 390–395 [1835].

117. See Ferejohn and Weingast, "A Positive Theory of Statutory Interpretation" ("there is no 'last word' in politics.").

118. There may not even be a way of ensuring that a constitutional order not degenerate into fascism, a fact Kurt Gödel may have noticed. See the amusing story of his interview for U.S. citizenship right after the war: "Even though the routine examination Gödel was to take was an easy matter, Gödel prepared seriously for it and studied the US Constitution carefully. On the day before the interview Gödel told [Oskar] Morgenstern that he had discovered a logical-legal possibility of transforming the United States into a dictatorship. Morgenstern saw that the hypothetical possibility and its likely remedy involved a complex chain of reasoning and was clearly not suitable for consideration at the interview. He urged Gödel to keep quiet about his discovery.

"The next morning Morgenstern drove [Albert] Einstein and Gödel from Princeton to Trenton. Einstein was informed; on the way he told one tale after another, to divert Gödel from his Constitution-theoretical explanations, apparently with success. At the office in Trenton, the official in charge was Judge Philip Forman, who had inducted Einstein in 1940 and [had] struck up a friendship

constitutional order that Hobbes, Blackstone, Kelsen, and many others present is mistaken – and that it doesn't matter.[119] Thomas Pogge also makes the point:

Law-governed coexistence is possible without a supreme and unconstrained agency. There is, it is true, the possibility of ultimate conflicts: of dispute in regard to which even the legally correct method of resolution is contested. To see this, one need only imagine how a constitutional democracy's three branches of government might engage in an all-out power struggle, each going to the very brink of what, on its understanding, it is constitutionally authorized to do. From a theoretical point of view, this possibility shows that we are not insured against, and thus live in permanent danger of, constitutional crises. But this no longer undermines our confidence in a genuine division of powers: we have learned that such crises need not be frequent or irresolvable. From a practical point of view, we know that constitutional democracies can endure and can ensure a robust juridical state.[120]

If I am right, determining ultimate political authorities is not feasible – in which case, it may be best not to try.

States, then, are not sovereign. Seldom does even a significant majority of the members of a particular state acknowledge one ultimate source of authority with the right to settle fundamental issues. Rather, there typically are a variety of sources of authority, many not recognized by the state in question. It is true, of course, that, given sufficient disagreement, a state or even other forms of social order cannot subsist. But this is not to say that the agreement required for a state to exist be of the sort that Hobbes, Rousseau, and others have sought. What is required is merely sufficient agreement on a sufficient number of significant issues to permit conflicts to be resolved in an orderly manner, without bloodshed.[121] In most situations, this agreement must include a conditional willingness to compromise

with him. He greeted them warmly and invited all three to attend the (normally) private examination of Gödel.

"The judge began, 'You have German citizenship up to now.' Gödel interrupted him, 'Excuse me sir, Austrian.' 'Anyhow, the wicked dictator! but fortunately that is not possible in America.' 'On the contrary,' Gödel interjected, 'I know how that can happen.' All three joined forces to restrain Gödel so as to turn to the routine examination." From Hao Wang, *Reflections on Kurt Gödel* (Cambridge, Mass.: MIT Press, 1987), pp. 115–116.

119. I are indebted to G. A. Cohen for helping me see this.

120. Pogge, "Cosmopolitanism and Sovereignty," *Ethics* 103, 1 (October 1992), 59.

121. I do not mean to say that a modus vivendi is the best we can do; rather, it may be all that is needed for basic social order, *contra* Hobbes and others. Rawls stresses the need for a normative political theory to do better.

and to accommodate oneself to the claims of others. Striving for "ultimate" sources of political authority is not only futile; it downplays and hides from view the cooperation and accommodation needed for social order. In a thoughtful discussion of these issues, Francis Sparshott claims that to "build one's political thinking around the concept of sovereignty is to encourage the strange and vicious notion that the truth of politics lies neither in joint action nor in mutual accommodation but in *command*."[122]

The agreement needed for social order is present in different ways in many places and is lacking in others. Hobbes thought that absolute sovereigns were needed to prevent the civil wars and strife characteristic of the Europe of his time. In our time, social order may be threatened less by religious wars and the problems associated with early "state-building" than by nationalist and secessionist movements. Perhaps the dangers we face are no less worrisome than those characteristic of Hobbes's time. But as absolute sovereigns did not turn out to be necessary for social order in early modern Europe, they should not be for us either.

States, then, are not and need not be sovereign. I conjecture, however, that the notion of sovereignty will continue to be employed in contemporary political discourse. It is too closely associated with the

122. Some of my skepticism about sovereignty is indebted to this essay. Sparshott's brief remarks are very suggestive: "In its original sixteenth-century formulations, the concept of sovereignty reflects and seeks to reverse the breakdown of empire. Deprived of the centre that authorized them and also limited them, heterogeneous devolved powers presumed autonomy, and, lacking demarcated spheres (Rome knew no *imperium* without its correlated *provincia*), conflicted anarchically. The 'sovereign' is invoked to restore order as a *de facto* mini-emperor within a territorial domain . . .

"That sovereignty be embodied in a single sovereign lord was never strictly necessary. What the ideal of sovereignty demanded was that the distribution of power be determinate and exhaustive, that within a given territory no class of decisions should lack a decider and none should have more than one. Even so, the necessity is not a practical one. The needs of common life are met by any reliable and expeditious way of settling disputes and defusing conflicts, and that does not require that every buck should have a definite place to stop at, only that every buck should stop somewhere. In practice, divisions of political powers tend to be incomplete and inconsistent, settled by political rather than constitutional means. No limit can be set a priori to what arrangements can prevail: confederations, cordial understandings, special relationships, customs unions, privileges, fudgings, and connivings are the rule . . . we are haunted by the ghost of empire." Sparshott, "Nation and Sovereignty – Reflections on the Two Concepts," in *Philosophers Look at Canadian Confederation/La Confédération canadienne: qu'en pensent les philosophes?*, ed. S. French (Montreal: Canadian Philosophical Association, 1979), pp. 107–108.

idea of a state, and neither of these is likely to pass away soon. And I may not have identified what it is that moves many political actors today – for example, secessionists eager for a state of their own. I suspect that many people are moved by mistaken conceptions of states as well as by illusory ideals of self-determination; others may merely be seeking forms of collective and national self-determination that they have been denied.[123] Whatever the merits of the claims of particular peoples or groups, I wish to stress the way in which concepts of sovereignty are distortive of politics. Political power is fluid and political life is – and to a considerable extent, ought to be – a result of compromise and accommodation. Relations of power, as well as of authority, are unconnected and replete with intransitivities. Conceptions and ideals of sovereignty, with their promise of hierarchy, decisiveness, and "finality", make us forget these simple truths about political life. Images of orderings of authority and power hide from view actual relations of authority and power.

Can there be *states* without sovereignty? Not if sovereignty is part of the *idea* of the state. I have challenged the sovereignty and authority even of legitimate states. "A state may exist even when some of its claims have no justification. A state cannot exist unless it claims authority with some success and general compliance."[124] If my skepticism is right, then the state may have "withered away"! Perhaps it would be better to suggest that we detach sovereignty from the idea of a state. Recommendations of conceptual change may be less exciting than the act of doing away with states, but my inquiry is first of all theoretical. There is nothing wrong with understanding the world before changing it.

7.7 RELATIONS BETWEEN STATES

The focus of this chapter is more on the state as a form of political organization of societies and less on the consequences for relations between societies – hence my emphasis on the "internal" aspects of sovereignty. But it has implications for "international relations". In

---

123. With regard to the latter, most arguments for the right of national or other groups to an independent state can be restated without any essential reference to sovereignty. See Chapter 8.
124. Green, *The Authority of the State*, p. 239.

premodern times, there was no such thing as "international relations" or, more accurately, relations between states.[125] For relations such as these presuppose particular relata – sovereign states. As I noted at the beginning of the chapter, medieval rule was feudal, imperial, or theocratic. Early modern Europe was composed of city-republics and leagues of cities, as well as empires, the Church, and various remnants of feudalism. Before the advent of two features of modern governance – territoriality and exclusivity of rule ("closed" systems) – relations between states as we understand them could not exist. A determinate realm, with relatively unambiguous geographic boundaries, is a prerequisite of the state and this was largely missing in early forms of political organization. States emerge only when their claim (or that of their rulers) to govern alone, exclusively, is established and recognized. A "sovereign" is the unique ruler of a realm, whose sphere of authority encompasses the whole realm, without overlapping that of another ruler. This "sovereign" – initially the monarch, later the state, then "the people" – rules without superiors. With the development of sovereign states, the central elements of the modern state system are present. "International relations" are the relations between independent states.

As I also mentioned earlier, it is common to distinguish internal and external aspects of sovereignty, and today these are often treated separately. Internal sovereignty pertains to the governance of the realm; external sovereignty, to independence of other states. The content of the latter is less clear, and it remains a matter of considerable controversy in the international relations literature. The core idea is that of the independence or autonomy of states. One interesting feature of classical sovereignty is that the internal-external distinction had a different significance than it has come to have; for the classical view, the one type of sovereignty is a simple consequence of the other. If "internal" sovereignty is unlimited in the way Hobbes and Rousseau thought, then states have no duties. Consequently, they also have no claim rights; no state can have a claim right against another state if the latter can have no duties. "External" sovereignty, then, simply amounts to the absence of any international claim rights or obligations, which is entailed by unlimited "internal" sovereignty.[126]

---

125. The confusing use of 'nation' and its cognates for 'state', 'society', or 'country' is noted in Chapter 8.
126. *Contra* Charles Beitz: "[E]xternal and internal sovereignty do not in any obvious way refer to the same thing. Considered as normative ideas, they pertain to different relationships and express different features of those relationships. . . . Nor

This feature of classical sovereignty is significant. It suggests that my criticisms of classical or unlimited sovereignty undermine some influential positions in the field of international relations. The most significant implication of the classical conception is that relations between states are, in effect, "states of nature." Hobbes, one of the patron saints of the "realist" tradition in international relations, is especially clear on this point: "Though there had never been any time, wherein particular men were in a condition of warre one against another; yet in all times, Kings, and Persons of Soveraigne authority, because of their Independency, are in continuall jealousies, and in the state and posture of Gladiators . . . a posture of War." It follows that there are no moral or legal constraints on states in this condition:

To this warre of every man against every man, this also is consequent; that nothing can be Unjust. The notions of Right and Wrong, Justice and Injustice have there no place. Where there is no common Power, there is no Law; where no Law, no Injustice.

So in States, and Common-wealths not dependent on one another, every Common-wealth, (not every man) has an absolute Libertie, to doe what it shall judge (that is to say, what that Man, or Assemblie that representeth it, shall judge) most conducing to their benefit. But withall, they live in the condition of a perpetuall war.[127]

does external sovereignty *derive* from internal sovereignty in any simple way." Beitz, "Sovereignty and Morality in International Affairs," in *Political Theory Today*, ed. D. Held (Stanford, Calif.: Stanford University Press, 1991), pp. 243–244. Beitz also claims dubiously that the "idea of internal sovereignty plays no substantial role in contemporary political theory" (p. 236). At best, this can be said to be true of the American philosophical literature; the continental literature, especially French, is filled with discussions of internal sovereignty.

127. Hobbes, *Leviathan*, chap. 13, p. 90; chap. 21, p. 149. 'Liberty', recall, is a technical term in these contexts for Hobbes, signifying "the absence of externall Impediments" (chap. 14, p. 91). The "laws of nature" for him are not true laws but mere "counsells" (chap. 15, p. 111; chap. 25, p. 176). So when Hobbes asserts that "the Law of Nations, and the Law of Nature, is the same thing" (chap. 30, p. 244), he is denying there are any claim rights or duties constraining states.

It may be important to note, as I have done in Chapter 6, that Hobbes's position is more complex than may at first appear. Covenants in the condition of nature are valid if there is no reasonable suspicion that the other party will defect. Supposing another to perform first, perhaps irrationally, one may be bound to do one's part consequently, even in the absence of a Sovereign enforcer. See *Leviathan*, chap. 14 XIV, esp. p. 96. Abstracting away from his pessimistic psychology, we can see that Hobbes's theory leaves some room for genuine obligations in the absence of the Sword. The texts are not clear, but we might hesitate before attributing to Hobbes the contemporary orthodoxy that counterpreferential action is never rational.

Let us call this position the "nothing-is-forbidden view" of international relations, one in which there are no moral or juridical constraints on the interactions of states. Sometimes it is interpreted as a normative position, and more commonly, at least in the international relations literature, as a descriptive view. I shall take no stance on the view as a descriptive account of the behavior of states, as my concerns here are normative. Note that the nothing-is-forbidden view is not a moral or normative position per se. It does not prescribe how states should act. It merely rules out all moral positions according to which there are moral constraints on the behavior of states, as well as individuals, in international contexts. It is a type of moral skepticism. As it has been noted in the recent literature, it is an extremely unstable type of skepticism. It is hard to defend it without sliding into more general forms of moral skepticism.[128]

If the classical view of unlimited sovereignty is not sustainable, an important support for the nothing-is-forbidden view has been removed. We would have no *a priori* reason to suppose that constraints on states are incompatible with their standing. The central piece in the picture that seems to have gripped so many theorists and statesmen does not survive my criticisms of classical sovereignty. They may undermine, as well, the influential view that states possess an immunity against international "intervention". But this is a more complicated matter, as the view that states possess such an immunity *cannot* be a skeptical position like the no constraints view. For the immunity amounts to a constraint, moral or legal, on "outside" intervention. The immunity position may also be undermined by the failure of the classical, as well as of the limited notions of sovereignty. But I shall leave a systematic treatment of these difficult issues to another time.[129]

Just as I think the notion of sovereignty of little use in understanding the nature and jurisdiction of modern states, so I believe that our discussions of "international" questions might be helped by abandoning it. Instead of talking about sovereignty, we might instead examine the sorts of independence that states and peoples currently

128. See Beitz, *Political Theory and International Relations*, Part 1 (Princeton: Princeton University Press, 1979).
129. For some recent discussions of some of the issues regarding intervention, see *Beyond Westphalia? State Sovereignty and International Intervention*, ed. Lyons and Mastanduno, and the special issue of *Social Research* 62, 1 (Spring 1995) on "Rescue."

possess[130] and determine which kinds are worth preserving and strengthening, and which should be weakened. For instance, the strengthening of international law, or the development of the European Union, may be (un)desirable for a variety of reasons, but none, I think, have anything much to do with sovereignty. The interesting question for Westminster is thus not whether the agreements of Maastricht are compatible with the sovereignty of the "Queen in Parliament", but whether the independence of British government is worth restricting in certain ways. The same, I suggest, might be true of the merits or demerits of military or humanitarian assistance to besieged and oppressed people residing in tyrannical states. But understanding the history and nature of the concept of sovereignty and the claims that have been made about the state's sovereignty are essential to abandoning the notion.[131]

130. "Belief in the necessary existence of the legally unlimited sovereign prejudges a question which we can only answer when we examine the actual rules." Hart, *The Concept of Law,* p. 218.
131. I recommend as well abandonment of most notions of "popular sovereignty", but that complicated story is for another time. See "Popular Sovereignty, the Very Idea" (manuscript).

Chapter 8

Boundaries

8.1 ISSUES AND PROBLEMS

States are *territorial* forms of political organization, which raises a number of difficult questions. What are the boundaries of a state's authority? Specifically, why should the jurisdiction of states be *territorial?* And who are the subjects of states? Are subjects to be understood as members? Who may form a state?

These are some of the most intractable questions that can be raised about states, and little I have said thus far provides any easy answers to them. Most of the time we simply assume that the residents of a territory are the proper subjects or members of the state that is coextensive with that territory, and that the interests of nonsubjects can be ignored.[1] But this assumption, tacit or explicit, requires defense. What is the rationale for the boundaries of that territory? There are many ways of dividing the set of residents into smaller subsets. Why privilege the set of the whole? In this chapter, I address some of the issues that are raised by questions about boundaries. I critically examine some of the influential answers to these questions, particularly the influential view that states are to be "nation-states".

The first European answer implicitly given to these questions of boundaries and membership was simple. The boundaries of a state are the boundaries of the kingdom – or, in later postcolonial times, the colony – from which it evolved. The subjects are simply the residents of the kingdom, and subjects are, for the most part, assumed to be

---

1. Recall Rawls's aim "to formulate a reasonable conception of justice for the basic structure of society conceived for the time being as a closed system isolated from other societies. The significance of this special case is obvious and needs no explanation." *A Theory of Justice,* p. 8 (see also p. 457). A quarter of a century later, the significance of the special case is perhaps less obvious.

members.[2] Of course, these boundaries and the associated manner of determining the state's subjects were never as clear as heads of states would have liked. For one thing, older notions of a realm are not the same as modern notions of territory – the borders were indeterminate and often temporary. For another, boundaries determined by domination and conquest were not always acknowledged by all parties, and not all assumed subjects obliged their rulers with the requisite loyalty. Nevertheless, the answer to the questions of boundaries and membership was reasonably clear and relatively efficacious.

This simple, early modern answer to these questions was not, of course, satisfactory for long. Two significant changes occurred in eighteenth- and nineteenth-century Europe. First, "the people" and their spokesmen became a significant political force and demanded increasingly that rulers rule in their interest – and in their name. And second, subjects demanded increasingly a different status, namely, that of membership – specifically, citizenship.

The term 'the people' remains ambiguous in contemporary European languages. It may designate all of the inhabitants of a geographical area or merely a proper subset of them. It used merely to designate the latter. The privileged used the term more or less interchangeably with 'the many' (*oi polloi*), 'the rabble', and other terms for those of lesser (or no) dignity. Gradually, the scope of the term expanded and came to include all inhabitants of a realm or citizens of a state. This expanded meaning is seen in Rousseau's *Social Contract*, for instance, where '*le peuple*' is clearly not meant to designate a proper subset of individuals.[3]

Implicit in the emerging concept of "the people" was an answer to the questions of boundaries: The state is the people's, and they determine its boundaries. For new states, the thought is that this may be done by allowing the people to decide the nature of their political association(s) ("We, the People . . ."). For old states, questions of boundaries can be settled by making them coextensive with the territory inhabited by the people. But both these answers may be question-begging, for they suppose that peoples come into existence clearly individuated. What constitutes a single people? Why do certain collections of individuals constitute one people and not many?

2. When subjecthood and membership are initially distinguished, it is only adults and, at first, propertied males that are accorded the latter status.
3. Still, ambiguities persist to this day: A "man of the people" is someone who comes from, or is identified with, the less advantaged majority of inhabitants. (Contrast 'popular' with 'populist'.)

In the French and American Revolutions, the peoples in question were roughly coextensive with the inhabitants, respectively, of the French kingdom and the British colony (forgetting, in the case of the latter, African slaves, aboriginal inhabitants, and British Loyalists). So the people, as a new source of legitimacy or authority, do not offer a radically new answer to the questions of boundaries. The voluntarism implicit in the people "deciding" how to associate is, of course, a challenge to some influential early modern conceptions of political authority. But the determination of the state's boundaries and membership by the people is continuous with older views. However, another sense of the term, however – namely, that of "*a* people" – is that of a group of individuals united by similarity or, to use an old term, by "race". To be a member of a people in this sense is to be a member of a group distinguished from other groups by certain attributes of members. Do peoples in this sense determine the boundaries and memberships of states?

8.2 PEOPLES AND NATIONS

One answer to the territorial nature of states is based on the entitlements of peoples. The Declaration of Independence starts not with an account of the rights of individuals but with a reference to "the separate and equal station to which the laws of nature and of nature's God entitle" *peoples*. The boundaries of a state, then, are determined by the extent of its people(s) and of their land. Peoples determine the territoriality of states. But there is an important ambiguity in the notion of people, that between "*a* people" and "*the* people". The latter, I said, is the unit of self-government referred to by Rousseau and by French and American proponents of popular sovereignty. The view of these "populists" is that *the* People,[4] as opposed, say, to the monarch (the "Sovereign"), is the ultimate source of political authority. This notion of "the People" presupposes that the problems of individuation have been resolved; it supposes that the relevant set of individuals is already individuated. But this is the question I am raising. It is the notion of "*a* people" that is relevant to my concerns here. What, then, is "*a* people"?

4. Hereafter, I capitalize 'people' whenever this notion, with the definite article, is used.

The idea expressed by Jefferson in the opening paragraph of the Declaration is suggestive. The laws of nature, he says, entitle each people to a separate and equal station. British Americans, Jefferson suggests, were not so entitled until they became a distinct people; but by the 1770s they had become a separate people, entitled to go their own way. Jefferson's claim about the rights of peoples seems linked to influential republican ideas of self-rule. The appropriate unit of self-rule he thought to be a people. This is one reason why British Americans would not necessarily think of including Indians or freed Africans in their schemes for self-rule, whatever was thought about their natural capacities.[5] What, then, are peoples in this sense, and why do they have a right to self-rule?

Classical Athenians felt affinities with other Greeks, in relation to *oi barbaroi*. But they did not think that units larger than the *polis* were appropriate for self-rule. And in classical times – indeed, until the late eighteenth century – the notion of a people seems not to have been central to most questions of political governance. The relevant notion here is of a collection of humans bound together by common attributes that distinguish them from others ("foreigners" or "aliens"). In premodern times, perhaps before the French Revolution, most of the distinctions relevant to political rule seem to cut across "peoples" in this sense. For questions of governance, the attributes common to members of the same *class* were more important than those shared by residents of the same realm.[6]

---

5. A deleted passage of Jefferson's draft of the Declaration accuses King George of waging "cruel war against human nature itself, violating its most sacred rights of life and liberty in the persons of a distant people who never offended him, captivating and carrying them into slavery in another hemisphere, or to incur miserable death in their transportation hither." After condemning "this execrable commerce" ("a market where *MEN* should be bought and sold"), Jefferson goes on to condemn the monarch for inciting rebellion among the slaves, "thus paying off former crimes committed against the *LIBERTIES* of one people, with crimes which he urges them to commit against the *LIVES* of another." Jefferson's outrage against his "British brethren" seems to be as much about broken bonds of kinship ("our common kindred") as about justice: "They too have been deaf to the voices of justice and of consanguinity". Jefferson, "The Declaration of Independence" (original draft), in *The Portable Thomas Jefferson,* ed. M. Peterson (Harmondsworth: Penguin, 1975), pp. 238–239. Rereading this American national document – especially the original draft – with a sensitivity to the distinctions between "the People" and "a people" can be revealing.
6. This said, class relations may have been experienced as a type of kinship. "Nobility in a sense constructed a new type of kinship, not based on tribal affiliation but on genealogical superiority and caste differentiation. Knights recognized members of this caste across the boundaries of duchies and counties." Spruyt, *The Sovereign State*

As Jefferson's words indicate, a mere collection of individuals can become a people, as he presumes British Americans had in the mid-eighteenth century. But the process is neither an act of will nor something in the control of single individuals. That one is a member of this or that people, we may presume, is something one discovers, as Jefferson discovered that British Americans had become a separate people. It is this seeming independence of the will that allows the notion of a people to function as it does in doctrines of self-rule. If one could choose what "people" one wished to join, there would be no principled end to claims to self-rule and independence.[7]

The notion of a people seems to be the precursor to that of a *nation*. The *Déclaration des Droits de l'Homme et du Citoyen*, decreed by "Les représentants du *peuple français*, constitués en Assemblé *nationale*" (italics added) does not distinguish sharply between 'people' and 'nation'. (Article 3 attributes sovereignty to "*la nation*".) Let us examine the idea of a nation and see whether the entitlements of nations help determine boundaries of states.

It is difficult to characterize the notion of a people with much precision, and it appears even harder to reach agreement about that of a nation. While both notions are relatively imprecise, the content of the second is much more contested than that of the former. In Chapter 2, I characterized nations vaguely as societies whose members are linked by sentiments of solidarity and self-conscious identity based on a number of other bonds (e.g., history, territory, culture, race, "ethnicity", language, religion, customs). But this characterization, like most, proves to be controversial. There is an interminable quarrel in the literature about what constitutes a nation, a quarrel that usually takes the form of disagreement about the "definition" of a nation or the necessary and sufficient conditions for nationhood. Renan's famous essay is representative. He considers and eliminates one after another various conditions as constitutive of nationhood – race, language, religion, common interests, geography – and concludes:

and Its Competitors, p. 72. Of course, European rulers were often kin in the normal sense as well.

7. This is, of course, not completely true. Consent theorists do have ways of imposing limits on the size of communities that may form states by secession. See, for instance, Harry Beran, "A Liberal Theory of Secession," *Political Studies* 32, 1 (1984), 21–31; "Self-Determination: A Philosophical Perspective," in *Self-Determination in the Commonwealth*, ed. W. Macartney (Aberdeen: Aberdeen University Press, 1988), pp. 23–35; and "Who Should Be Entitled to Vote in Self-Determination Referenda?" in *Terrorism, Protest and Power*, ed. M. Warner and R. Crisp (Aldershot: Edward Elgar, 1990), pp. 132–166.

Une nation est une âme, un principe spirituel. Deux choses . . . constituent cette âme . . . L'une est la possession en commun d'un riche legs de souvenirs; l'autre est le consentement actuel, le désir de vivre ensemble, la volonté de continuer à faire valoir l'héritage qu'on a reçu indivis. . . . Avoir des gloires communes dans le passé, une volonté commune dans le présent; avoir fait de grandes choses ensemble, vouloir en faire encore, voilà les conditions essentielles pour êitre un peuple.[8]

Renan's characterization is not mine, but I do not object to it as much as to the method of analysis, which is problematic and representative of the literature. Consider the manner in which language, for instance, is eliminated as a defining feature of nationality. Why is language not a condition according to Renan? Well, because the Swiss people have several languages, yet are not several peoples. And the English- or Spanish-speaking countries do not constitute single nations. The same method of counterexample is used for the other possible defining conditions.[9] The problem with this method is that it can be question-begging: One might have thought Switzerland to be a state composed of several nationalities (a multinational state). And language could be a necessary condition, even if it is not sufficient. Or maybe the relations different peoples have to their language are significantly different (consider French and English Canadians, Spaniards and Filipinos).

Attempts at "definition" often tacitly assume there should be a single sufficient condition for nationhood. Quarrels between rival characterizations then often take the following form. There are several relevant characteristics: language, culture, history, and so on. Partisans of one of these will show, usually by counterexample, that none of the others suffices to determine nationhood; ergo, the defining condition must be the remaining one on the list. (Then another counterexample is produced.) This method sometimes creates a certain amount of agreement around allegedly "subjective" conditions (e.g., consent, recognition, self-consciousness) rather than "objective"

8."A nation is a soul, a spiritual principle. . . . Two things . . . constitute this soul. . . . One is the possession in common of a rich legacy of memories; the other is actual consent, the desire to live together, the willingness to continue valuing this joint heritage. . . . To have past glories in common, a present common will; to have done great things together, to want to do more, here are the essential conditions of a people" (translation mine). Ernest Renan, *Qu'est-ce qu'une nation?* (Paris: Pierre Bordas, 1991 [1882]), p. 40.
9. E. J. Hobsbawm, *Nations and Nationalism Since 1780: Programme, Myth, Reality,* 2nd ed. (Cambridge: Cambridge University Press, 1992 [1990]), pp. 5–11, is representative of the genre.

ones (e.g., language, history and common descent, traditions and customs, religion). If it isn't language, etc., then it must be some will- or desire-based property. So some consensus emerges around the idea that it is people's desires or will that enable them to constitute a nation. In Renan's oft quoted phrase, "L'existence d'une nation est (pardonnez-moi cette métaphore) un plébiscite de tous les jours."[10] But it is a mistake to think that desire, will, much less consent, are sufficient.

Part of the problem with "definitions" of the concept of a nation is a difficulty familiar to philosophers. If a definition must consist of necessary and sufficient conditions, then definitions will not lack for terms in natural languages. (For instance, the notion of the modern state cannot so be defined, as I argued earlier.) The search for such definitions may be one of the illusion fostered by modeling knowledge on (classical) geometry. The distinctions of ordinary language are many, and it is difficult to capture them all in "definitions". Conceptual clarity is very important, but artificial "definitions" do not contribute much to that.[11]

There are other, more interesting difficulties in characterizing the notion of a nation. It is a term that has undergone many evolutions and that is used in a variety of ways, not all of them obviously consistent. Just as we saw the terms 'government' and 'state' sometimes being used more or less interchangeably, especially in cultures where the state (in my sense) is not very evident, so 'nation' and its cognates are used in various ways. We speak of the wealth of nations – even though Britain, for instance, is not a (single) nation. American newscasters talk about "the worst crisis/disaster/storm to hit the nation".

---

10. "The existence of a nation is (forgive me this metaphor) a daily plebiscite" (translation mine). Renan, *Qu'est-ce qu'une nation?*, p. 41. There is greater consensus on the necessary or sufficient "subjective" conditions, but that may reflect only that the analysts, not being philosophers, do not distinguish carefully among desire, belief, and the will. But even here analysts often go wrong. Mere desire or will cannot be sufficient; to be a member of a national group requires being recognized as a member by other members, and this recognition must be based on attributes of the individual. (See especially the discussion in Section 8.3.)
11. The obligatory opening "definitions" in social scientific and historical studies of nationalism are analogous to the introductory discussions of "methodology" in social science texts. Fortunately, in the best works, the definitions are usually ignored after the first chapter. See, for instance, Hobsbawm, *Nations and Nationalism Since 1780*, and Benedict Anderson, *Imagined Communities: Reflections on the Origins and Spread of Nationalism*, rev. ed. (London: Verso, 1991 [1983]). The latter's oft-quoted (and misunderstood) "definition" is uninteresting, especially alongside the brilliance of the rest of the book. See my review, *Journal of the History of European Ideas* 21, 5 (September 1995), 721–722.

And there is the United Nations – even though a nation needs to be a state to be admitted. Foreigners can acquire American "nationality", suggesting we mean something like "citizenship" when we talk thus of nationality. But, when immigrants do acquire American "nationality", they are for a time "hyphenated Americans" (e.g., "Irish-Americans"), suggesting something other than citizenship.[12] We often use 'national' as a substitute for 'federal' or 'state' – for instance, the national currency, national parks, national health, national debt, national interest.[13] The discipline of "international relations", as noted in Chapter 7, characteristically focuses on relations between states, not on those between nationals (e.g., the French and the Basques, the United States and its "domestic dependent nations" or "native peoples").[14]

The concept of a nation, like that of a state, changes with time. It is hard to attribute to seventeenth- or eighteenth-century usage of the term 'nation' much of the content that one finds in the word today. Hobbes and Smith spoke of nations when referring to commonwealths or societies; either term might be substituted in the title of Smith's major work.[15] By contrast, consider what terms might be substituted in 'One nation under God' or '*La nation reconnaissante*' today. 'Country' might work in the first ("For God and Country") and '*la patrie*' in the second; but 'state' could not be substituted in either. This is what we might expect when we reflect on the slow development of the notion.[16]

We should not fret too much, as students of the subject so often do, about "defining" nationhood. The concept is imprecise, complex,

---

12. Ordinary language may be suggestive here. One can speak of "American nationality" or of "U.S. citizenship", but "U.S. nationality" and "American citizenship" sound a little odd. Much depends on context, too. (For example, Catalans and Castilians may be tempted to give a different answer to the question "What is your nationality?")
13. "National assemblies" usually represent the citizens of a state. Quebec's parliament is an exception, but here another predicate cannot easily be substituted.
14. There are important differences between invoking the "national interest" and citing a *raison d'Etat*, but none turn on nationality. Still, it is interesting that the latter idea is invoked explicitly only in cultures with a strong statist tradition (e.g., France).
15. Hume may be different. See Donald C. Ainslie, "The Problem of the National Self in Hume's Theory of Justice," *Hume Studies* 22, 2 (November 1995), 289–313.
16. Of course, some of the imprecision or ambiguity in the notion may be intentional. Heads of state may wish to speak as well for a particular nation. (This is something, incidentally, that royal heads of state could not do before becoming members of the same nationality as the people they governed, a recent development in European history.)

and problematic. And it is widely contested, as many believe that so much rests on it. We do need a preliminary and general characterization in order to raise certain issues that interest me about boundaries and membership. And it is possible to offer a general characterization that is not question-begging and that serves to bring out some of the important features of a particular type of human grouping. For these purposes, I shall think of nations in terms of clusters of properties, related in various ways and allowing of degrees, and I shall characterize them accordingly. A group of humans will constitute a nation in this sense insofar as the members share certain properties and insofar as they are conscious of this shared condition and recognize one another by virtue of these common properties. Nations, then, will be collections of individuals with common histories, cultures, languages, and the like, members of which recognize other members by virtue of their possession of these attributes. This characterization may be incomplete; for instance, many nationalities seem based on "ethnic" attributes, and the common history may be thought to involve common ancestry (see note 19). But it will help in understanding and evaluating certain significant ways humans have of understanding themselves.[17] As I wish to investigate some of the normative relations between nations in this sense and states, the characterization makes no reference to states. We can make it more precise and revise it when necessary.

Different nationalities will attribute different significance to different attributes or to different ways of characterizing these attributes.[18] My general characterization allows for this, as it should. As I mentioned, some groups will stress common descent rather than culture, or they may understand descent in "racial" or "ethnic" terms rather than in terms of common history or common customs and traditions. Similarly, different nations may have different relations to their language(s) or religion(s).[19] This should not unduly worry us. The phenomena are complex, and they are also political.

17. Another reason not to worry too much about "definitions" is that it is not easy to characterize particular cultures or traditions without relying on some prior sense of their unity and distinctiveness. Contrast, for instance, the Japanese, French, and American cultures.
18. Anderson is especially good at distinguishing different types of nationalisms. See esp. *Imagined Communities*, chaps. 4–7.
19. Ancestry or ethnicity plays a more central role in Japanese and German nationalism than in French or (English) Canadian nationalism. Religion is central to many nationalisms but not to others. Language is a centerpiece of French Canadian but not Mexican or Filipino nationalism.

On my characterization, it will turn out that some groups are clearer cases of nations than others. In this century, the Japanese, the Germans, and the French presumably are reasonable candidates. By contrast, the nationality of French-Belgians, English-Canadians, and perhaps Austrians, as well as some second-generation immigrants in various countries, is problematic. But this implication of my characterization is as it should be. Being a nation is something that permits degrees, and the national status of some groups *is* problematic. One should be able to say, intelligibly, that, for example, France is more of a nation today than it was before World War I or that the United States is a nation today in a way it was not in the first half of the nineteenth century.[20] One wants to be able to say that it is unclear or indeterminate whether Italy is a single nation. And one should be allowed to say that Switzerland or Austria are not nations in the ways that France, Germany, and Japan are. To insist that these and other countries are equally single nations is either to close one's eyes to important differences or to misdescribe the phenomena.[21] In any case, my interest lies in evaluating certain claims made on behalf of peoples, concerning the relations between nations and states, and my characterization should serve for this.

Questions about nationality or nationhood arise in modern contexts where issues of *identity* are at stake. The characteristic question of modernity – "Who am I?" – asks for the sources of one's *identity,* for that with which one *identifies.* In other times, the doubts that are the source of this question, or this worry, were answered by locality, hierarchy, and deity. We do not worry about who we are, when our place in our (unchanging) local community is secure, when our (unchanging) social station and its duties are known, and when our (unchanging) relation to the deity is clear. Further, these things

20. Walker Connor argues that the fact that nationhood is a mass phenomenon – the bulk of the members must be conscious of their nationality – creates problems for dating the birth of nations. See his important essay, "When Is a Nation?" [1991], in *Ethnonationalism: The Quest for Understanding* (Princeton: Princeton University Press, 1994), pp. 210–226. Connor reflects on the significance of Eugen Weber's famous study of rural France: "Most rural and small-town dwellers within France did not consider themselves members of the French nation in 1870 and . . . retained this view until World War I" (p. 220) – remarkable in light of modern France's so often being taken as the paradigmatic "nation-state". See Weber, *Peasants into Frenchmen: The Modernization of Rural France, 1870–1914* (Stanford, Calif.: Stanford University Press, 1976).

21. One should also be able to say that some individuals do not have a nationality (e.g., Augustine, Elias Canneti), or have at most an ambiguous one (e.g., Franz Kafka, Joseph Conrad).

were once connected in premodern Europe: Our place of community and the hierarchy of the whole mirrored the structure of the cosmos. Modernity supposes all of this to be founded on false belief and superstition. "Emancipation" involves not only overthrowing the rule of tyrants, but overcoming the *ancien régime* in all of its other manifestations, especially the myths that functioned to keep people satisfied with their unhappy lot.[22]

Modern people are no longer *at home* in the world, at least in the manner permitted in stable premodern times. Nationality, as a source of identity, addresses this problematic feature of modernity. One feels "at home" when one dwells in a place that is one's own or that is filled with familiar things. Similarly, one feels at home in a community with familiar features, as in a place where one grew up. Fellow nationals are those with whom one shares a variety of attributes – language, culture, traditions – and whom one recognizes, and who recognize one, as sharing them. One feels at home with them. One recognizes oneself in them – the question of identity. One also finds there the comfort of home – what "emancipated" moderns have lost in the world, they find in their fellow nationals.[23]

Nationality, then, may offer us a solution to some of the woes of modernity. It may also provide an answer to my queries about the boundaries of states. In fact, nationality has been suggested as a basis – *the* basis – for the authority of states. A state, it is now often said, is justified only insofar as it serves the interests or articulates the aspirations of "the nation".[24] In nationality, then, we may find a con-

---

22. See Charles Taylor, "Why Do Nations Have to Become States?" in *Philosophers Look at Canadian Confederation/La Confédération canadienne: qu'en pensent les philosophes?*, pp. 19–35, and, more recently, "The Politics of Recognition," *Multiculturalism: Examining the Politics of Recognition*, ed. A. Gutmann (Princeton: Princeton University Press, 1994 [1992]), esp. pp. 26–37.

23. There are other, more practical, advantages to sharing a language and culture with others; one can understand members of one's linguistic and cultural group better, facilitating cooperation and protection. Brian Barry suggests that "cultural similarity is a good basis for association . . . the ability to interpret the behaviour of other people depends on a mass of shared understandings". "Self-Government Revisited" [1983], in *Democracy and Power: Essays in Political Theory*, vol. 1, p. 177. An interesting conjecture about ethnic discrimination is offered by Bradford Cornell, "A Hypothesis Regarding the Origins of Ethnic Discrimination," *Rationality and Society* 7, 1 (January 1995), 4–30. For a powerful explanatory account stressing more or less self-interested factors behind ethnic and national association (and conflict), see Hardin, *One for All*, especially the discussions of "the epistemological comforts of home".

24. Nationalism "determines the *norm* for the legitimacy of political units in the modern world" (Ernest Gellner, *Nations and Nationalism* [Ithaca and London: Cornell

dition for the legitimacy of states, a solution to some of the problems of modernity, and answers to my queries about boundaries. States perhaps are, or ought to be, *nation-states*. Claims such as this are sometimes identified with *nationalism*.

Many people now believe that "the political and national unit should be congruent."[25] There are a number of different claims that should be distinguished. Some have claimed that states should consist of single nations, for one reason or another. Becoming a state might be *a good* for the nation, even if other considerations could overrule statehood (e.g., political circumstances, economic development). More strongly, it is sometimes thought to be an essential part of their self-development that they become states, that statehood is the *telos* of nations. Just as a people's consciousness of its nationality may be understood to manifest its self-development, so the nation's development into a state may be seen as its fulfillment. Either of these claims – or something else – may be the basis for a principle entitling nations to become states, a principle of "national self-determination". Finally, there is the position just mentioned, that states are legitimate only insofar as they serve the interests or articulate the aspirations of the nation. We have several theses, then, which need to be distinguished: (1) States should consist of single nations, (2) statehood is the *telos* of nations, (3) nations are entitled to become states, and (4) a state is legitimate only insofar as it serves the interests or articulates the aspirations of the nation.

It is a mistake, albeit an understandable one, to characterize nationalism in terms of the third claim, or even the first and second. (The fourth, not surprisingly, I shall claim to be false.) Some nationalists do not seek statehood for their people, and characterizing nationalism in terms of statehood begs the question against "liberal" or anarchist nationalism and other moderate positions.[26] Of course,

University Press, 1983], p. 49). "Nationalism . . . holds that the only legitimate type of government is national self-determination" (Elie Kedourie, *Nationalism*, 4th ed. [Oxford and Cambridge, Mass.: Blackwell, 1993 (1960)], p. 1). "Modern states have, therefore, chosen to adopt national self-determination as their justifying principle, even when their members do not constitute a nation" (Yael Tamir, *Liberal Nationalism* [Princeton: Princeton University Press, 1993], p. 124).

25. Gellner characterizes nationalism as the political principle "which holds that the political and national unit should be congruent." *Nations and Nationalism*, p. 1. It is not unusual to include in the "definition" of a nation the desire or claim to become a state. See the extract from Weber, *From Max Weber: Essays in Sociology*, p. 179.

26. We usually take note only of nationalist movements demanding statehood. But the national sentiments – for instance, of the Welsh, Bretons, or French Catalans – can be understood without reference to an aspiration of a separate state. Many national

many, if not most, contemporary nationalist *movements* do claim a state for their nation. This is not unexpected given the dominance and status of statehood in our times.

Why, then, accept the claim that nations are entitled to become states? And what relation does one's acceptance of this claim have to the first, that nations should become states? I raise these questions principally for two reasons. I wish to determine in what ways nationality might be relevant for determining matters of boundaries, and I must consider as well whether a particular link between nation and state is a condition for the justification of the state.

As seen in my brief discussion of Jefferson, the idea that peoples or nations are entitled to become states is, or at least was, connected to that of *self-rule*.[27] The partisans of the French and American revolutions, it is worth recalling, were *patriots* and fought for their respective *"patries"*. The eighteenth-century conception of a nation was not as fully developed as ours. Nevertheless, the connections made then between self-rule and nationality appear to be similar to those made in this century. Let us distinguish two questions raised by these connections. First, we might ask whether self-rule need take the form of statehood. It has often been assumed, in this century and the last, that it must. Second, we should ask why nations are the appropriate unit of self-rule.

Regarding the first question, note that states are not the only form of political organization consistent with self-rule. Federalism, which was, after all, the intended form of union of the original thirteen American *states*, is consistent with self-rule. In certain circumstances, it may be a superior form of self-rule. Settling this matter, however,

---

groups in the former Soviet Union do not seem interested in statehood. Anarchists, presumably, could be nationalists. Others could have ideological or religious objections to statehood (e.g., the orthodox Jewish groups in Israel that do not recognize the legitimacy of the current state). For a theoretical case for separating the demand for statehood from nationalism, see Tamir, *Liberal Nationalism*: "The era of homogeneous and viable nation-states is over (or rather, the era of the illusion that homogenous and viable nation-states are possible is over, since such states never existed), and the national vision must be redefined" (p. 3).

27. "... to assume among the powers of the earth the separate and equal station to which the laws of nature and of nature's God entitle them [a people]". Jefferson, "Declaration," p. 235. "Where the sentiment of nationality exists in any force, there is a prima facie case for uniting all the members of the nationality under the same government, and a government to themselves apart. This is merely saying that the question of government ought to be decided by the governed." J. S. Mill, *Considerations on Representative Government* [1861], in *On Liberty and Other Essays*, ed. J. Gray (Oxford: Oxford University Press, 1991), p. 428.

as well as the second question, requires a better understanding of the ideal of self-rule.

There is an important ambiguity in the notion of self-rule in these contexts. We often say that a society has achieved self-rule when one of two things is true. Consider a country, once dependent on another in a manner incompatible with self-rule, which has broken away and become "independent". It was once ruled by "foreigners" and now no longer is. This is one sense of self-rule: being ruled by "one's own". A group is self-ruled in one sense, then, if its rulers are drawn from the same group. This notion of self-rule has no implications about the relevant form of government; autocratic or despotic rule by "one's own" is self-rule in this sense. Another, and older, sense of self-rule has to do with autonomy in the classical sense of creating one's own laws (*nomoi*). In this sense, a group is self-ruled if the members collectively rule themselves – that is, determine the laws, control the government, and the like. This ideal we may think of as republican self-rule; the former, as a postcolonial or "national liberation" conception.

The republican concern with self-rule is addressed first by *poleis* and city-states, then by federalism and democracy. The success of either of these forms of governance is not a topic for this essay. It is the postcolonial conception of self-rule that is at issue here. Why is it an ideal? Why is it preferable to be ruled by one's own than by foreigners? The question may seem absurd, so much do we take a particular answer for granted. (No one seems even to raise the question.) But it is worth recalling that this is a relatively recent development in history. Until this century the norm for most peoples, European included, was rule by foreigners. Great Britain, for instance, was ruled until 1917 by the House of Saxe-Coburg-Gotha, now the House of Windsor. It is true that one finds nationalist resentments against foreign rule in earlier times.[28] Still, until recently, just and efficient rule by foreigners seemed preferable to most people to unjust or inefficient rule by one's own.[29] Now virtually no one will put up with rule by foreigners. Why is that so?

One reason, it might be argued, has to do with trust. One might have greater trust in rulers drawn from one's own than in foreigners.

---

28. Marie-Antoinette was called "*l'Autri-chienne*" (the Austrian dog or bitch).
29. It needs to be remarked that some of the more unjust and cruel postcolonial regimes have been made up of members of one ethnic or tribal group who treated members of other groups barbarically. 'One's own' can have different extensions.

What sort of trust? That they might govern consistently with one's interests? This is the reason often given for the preference for "minority" representation in federal systems. Why might one expect that? It might be that people identify with their own, thus rulers drawn from a group might be better at serving the interests of members than others. This idea of *identification* is crucial. One's pride in the merits of those with whom one identifies is similar to pride in one's own merits. Both are satisfaction with one's own, as it were.[30] But why do people identify with others in this manner? And why is *identity* important to politics in the first place?

I have said that questions about nationality arise in modern contexts where issues of *identity* are at stake, and I noted that in earlier times people assumed their identities from locality, hierarchy, and deity. There is, however, something misleading about this way of putting the matter. For the modern notion of an identity or, rather, the context in which the modern notion of an identity is found is pluralistic in a significant way: There are a number of different identities that any single person *could* have. This was not conceivable for most people in earlier and more stable times. One's identity, as it were, was just who one was, which was determined by one's place in one's community, in relation to the social and cosmological hierarchies. The elements of contingency and plurality in the modern predicament seem to have been lacking in earlier times.

Language and culture assume a particular importance for identity. They determine who we are, it is often said.[31] There have always

---

30. The "feeling of nationality may have been generated by many causes.... [T]he strongest of all is identity of political antecedents; the possession of a national history, and consequent community of recollections; collective pride and humiliation, pleasure and regret, connected with the same incidents in the past." Mill, *Considerations on Representative Government*, p. 427. Possession of a "national history", presumably depends on identification. African immigrants to France must identify with "*nos ancêtres les Gaulois*" or Italian-Americans with "our Forefathers" before they can take pride in or share the humiliation of past exploits and defeats.

31. "Our mother tongue embodies the first universe we saw, the first sensations we felt, the first activities and pleasures we enjoyed.... The perpetuation of thoughts and feelings through language is the essence of tradition". Johann Gottfried Herder, *Essay on the Origin of Language* [1772], in *J. G. Herder on Social and Political Culture*, trans. and ed. F. Barnard (Cambridge: Cambridge University Press, 1969), p. 164. "[T]he first, original, and truly natural boundaries of states are beyond doubt their internal boundaries. Those who speak the same language are joined to each other by a multitude of invisible bonds by nature herself, long before any human art begins; they understand each other and have the power of continuing to make themselves understood more and more clearly; they belong together and are by nature one and an inseparable whole. Such a whole, if it wishes to absorb

---

been languages and cultures, and others have been as conscious of the multiplicity of them as we generally are today. But language and culture used to differentiate different social classes of the same country or realm. To a limited extent they still do, and expressions such as 'a cultured man' or even 'she speaks the Queen's English' may remind us of their differentiating functions. But language and culture are now, for the most part, what unites peoples and separates them from others. The ruling elites of Europe once conversed with each other in French; they certainly conversed more easily among themselves than with their respective subjects. Now this tongue serves both to unite the French and to differentiate them from other peoples.[32]

Language and culture, and not a universal human nature, serve now to determine our identity. For our identity is given by what distinguishes us from other humans.[33] Since they shape us, they are, or become, *ours*. Thus language and culture become as well means of fulfillment and realization. As our language and culture prosper, so do we. They are objects of pride (or shame). But the pride we can take in our culture is conditioned by the recognition of others. To the extent that its merits are not acknowledged by outsiders our pride is reduced. Here we have a connection with the state. The respect achieved by our nation is only enhanced by its becoming a state, given the exalted status of states in our time.

There are worries about this type of argument. It should be remembered that not all nationalities attribute to their language the significance European Romantics thought appropriate. This is especially true of "New World nationalism". Americans, for instance, are

and mingle with itself any other people of different descent and language, cannot do so without itself becoming confused, in the beginning at any rate, and violently disturbing the even progress of its culture." Johann Gottlieb Fichte, *Addresses to the German Nation* [1807–1808], ed. G. Kelly (New York: Harper & Row, 1968), 13th address, p. 190.

Isaiah Berlin's writings on nationalist thought are especially useful. See "Herder and the Enlightenment," in *Vico and Herder: Two Studies in the History of Ideas* (London: Hogarth Press, 1976), pp. 143–226; "Nationalism: Past Neglect and Present Power," in *Against the Current: Essays in the History of Ideas*, ed. H. Hardy (London: Hogarth Press, 1979), pp. 333–355; and "The Bent Twig: On the Rise of Nationalism," in *The Crooked Timber of Humanity: Chapters in the History of Ideas*, ed. H. Hardy (New York: Vintage Books, 1992), pp. 238–261. See also John Gray, *Isaiah Berlin* (Princeton: Princeton University Press, 1996), esp. chap. 4.

32. See Gellner, *Nations and Nationalism*, esp. chap. 2.
33. The contemporary individualist who would have every person determine his or her own individual identity merely adopts a variant of this modernist thesis.

relatively indifferent to their language, at least compared to the English, the French, or the Hungarians. And note the number of national groups outside of Europe that prosper in Spanish or Portuguese or French.[34]

The argument may, in certain ways, be question-begging. What language or culture is to count? As I mentioned, it is not easy to characterize particular cultures or traditions without relying on some prior sense of their unities and distinctiveness. The individuation of languages and cultures is, in part, a political matter.[35] There is a related problem. "L'oubli, et je dirai même l'erreur historique, sont un facteur essentiel de la création d'une nation".[36] Many, if not most, nations did not exist before the development of political structures or entities – in particular, states. The French and American nations are consequences, if not creations, of their respective states, and the same is largely true of Italy (insofar as it is a nation). This is not true of all nations, for instance, the nations of various former empires. But it is true of many, and this truth undermines the national myths of some of these nations.[37]

The fact that one's identity rests on false beliefs might be thought to undermine it. However, one must be careful here. Consider, for

34. Anderson's *Imagined Communities* is intended as a corrective to the European bias – indeed, Central European – of studies of nationalism.
35. What distinguishes a language from another, or a language from a dialect? What determines whether someone speaks a language correctly or whether the version of a language spoken by a particular group is proper? Linguists often quip that "a language is a dialect with an army". This is to say that all "languages" are also dialects (just as all speakers have an accent). But it is also to point to the *political* factors that determine what constitutes a language. Languages are distinguished from dialects by political considerations. The same is true of cultures.
36. "Forgetfulness, and I would even say, historical error, are an essential factor in the creation of a nation" (translation mine). Renan adds, "Et c'est ainsi que le progrès des études historiques est souvent pour la nationalité un danger. . . . Or l'essence d'une nation est que tous les individus aient beaucoup de choses en commun, et aussi que tous aient oublié bien de choses. Aucun citoyen français ne sait s'il est Burgonde, Alain, Taïfale, Visigoth; tout citoyen français doit avoir oublié la Saint-Bathélemy, les massacres du Midi au XIIIᵉ siècle." ("And it's thus that the progress of historical studies is often a danger to nationality. . . . Now the essence of a nation is that all individuals have many things in common, and also that all have forgotten many things. No French citizen knows if he is a Burgundian, an Alain, a Taïfal, a Visigoth; every French citizen must have forgotten the Saint Batholomew [massacre], the massacres of the thirteenth century in the South.") Renan, *Qu'est-ce qu'une nation?* p. 34 (translation mine). To understand these puzzling words, see Benedict Anderson's brilliant interpretation in the revised edition of *Imagined Communities*, pp. 199–203.
37. The fact that nationhood is a mass phenomenon means that the development of a nation is a slow and complicated process. See Connor, "When Is a Nation?"

instance, the case of religious beliefs. Atheists, as well as most believers, are committed to thinking that many of the religious beliefs of others are, in part at least, false; theists are similarly committed to understanding some of the central beliefs of atheists as mistaken. But would we want to say that the identity of others, when founded on false beliefs, is undermined? It is not clear.[38]

One thesis, at least, is falsified by these considerations. I mentioned the fourth thesis, that nationality is a basis – *the* basis – for the legitimacy of states. A state, on this view, is justified only insofar as it serves the interests or articulates the aspirations of a, or its, nation. This has to be false, at least as a general principle – and this independently of the correctness of my views about legitimacy. Many states existed before their respective nations (e.g., France, the United States, Italy).[39] Some of these, presumably, were or could have been legitimate. Insofar as they were illegitimate, this was not due to their not serving the interests of their respective nation (which did not yet exist). The view that the legitimacy of states is based on their serving the interests of the nation is relatively recent. Its putative plausibility derives, perhaps, from confusion with another view that justified states serve the interests or preferences of their members. In Chapter 9 I come back to this claim when I examine the legitimate functions of states and the tasks governments have in facilitating the production of collective goods.

If many nations come into existence only after their respective state, then the second thesis, of statehood as the *telos* of nations, is less plausible. If it is not an essential part of the self-development of nations that they become states, one possible support for the third thesis – nations are entitled to become states – disappears. But other reasons remain. It may be that becoming a state is the only way a particular group can protect itself against exploitation or annihilation.[40] Or there may be more general considerations supporting a right to statehood. Avishai Margalit and Joseph Raz have made a case for a right to national self-determination based on the importance of

---

38. The problem is related to that of respecting those with cultures and values incompatible with one's own. See Raz's remarks on the conflict endemic in multiculturalism in "Multiculturalism: A Liberal Perspective," in *Ethics in the Public Domain: Essays in the Morality of Law and Politics* (Oxford: Clarendon Press, 1994), pp. 163–165.

39. Many states, of course, are made up of more than one nation (e.g., Canada, the United Kingdom, Belgium, Spain, the former Soviet Union).

40. See Allen Buchanan, *Secession: The Morality of Political Divorce from Fort Sumter to Lithuania and Quebec* (Boulder, Colo.: Westview Press, 1991), chap. 2.

groups of certain sorts to individual well-being. Their argument is based on normative considerations congenial to some I have invoked in earlier chapters. It is also the best defense of the right of national groups to statehood that I know. So I shall examine it in some detail.

Margalit and Raz defend the thesis that there is a limited moral right to self-determination, and this right belongs to certain groups. The right is that to national self-determination: "the right to determine whether a certain territory shall become, or remain, a separate state (and possibly whether it should enjoy autonomy within a larger state)." This right of self-determination, they argue, is not ultimate but is "grounded in the wider value of self-government", which is itself only instrumentally justified.[41]

The structure of their argument is rather complex. They ask first what groups might have such a right. Their answer is "encompassing groups". What is the value of political independence for such groups? Basically, membership in such groups is important for individual well-being; the prosperity of the group is important to the well-being of members; and sometimes, being an independent sovereign state is helpful or even crucial to a group's prosperity. What is the case for attributing a *right* to such groups? Often it is best to give the individuals concerned the power (e.g., a right) to determine what to do.

The right is conditional. Its exercise should be by "overwhelming majority"; it must be exercised for right reasons, namely, "to secure conditions necessary for the prosperity and self-respect of the group"; the group must respect the basic rights of all inhabitants of its territory, and measures must be taken to prevent or minimize damage to the interests of others.[42]

The first step in Margalit and Raz's argument is the determination of the group who possesses this right. They agree that it "is far from clear that peoples or nations rather than tribes, ethnic groups, linguistic, religious, or geographical groups are the relevant reference groups." Their strategy in determining the relevant group is to rely on their understanding of the benefits of self-government; the relevant groups are those whose characteristics are such that they stand to benefit from self-government. These turn out to be "encompassing groups", with six defining characteristics:

---

41. Margalit and Raz, "National Self-Determination," *Journal of Philosophy* 87, 9 (September 1990), 440–441.
42. Ibid., pp. 458–460.

1. "The group has a common character and a common culture that encompass many, varied and important aspects of life. [The groups] have pervasive cultures, and their identity is determined at least in part by their culture."
2. "[P]eople growing up among members of the group will acquire the group culture, will be marked by its character."
3. "Membership in the group is, in part, a matter of mutual recognition. Typically, one belongs to such groups if, among the other conditions, one is recognized by other members of the group as belonging to it."
4. Membership is important "for one's self-identification." These are "groups, membership of which has a high social profile, that is, groups, membership of which is one of the primary facts by which people are identified, and which form expectations as to what they are like".
5. "Membership is a matter of belonging, not of achievement. . . . Qualification for membership is usually determined by non-voluntary criteria. One cannot choose to belong. One belongs because of who one is. One can come to belong to such groups, but only by changing, e.g., by adopting their culture, changing one's tastes and habits accordingly – a very slow process indeed."
6. "The groups concerned are not face-to-face groups. . . . They are anonymous groups where mutual recognition is secured by the possession of general characteristics."

Virtually everyone belongs to some such group, Margalit and Raz claim; they add that membership need not be exclusive.[43]

Encompassing groups are important in part because of how they shape the goals and relations of individuals. Given the relation between people and culture, the prosperity of the latter is important for the well-being of the individual. Specifically, "individual dignity and self-respect require that the groups, membership of which contributes to one's sense of identity, be generally respected and not be made a subject of ridicule, hatred, discrimination, or persecution."[44]

43. Ibid., pp. 443–447. Some of these groups "are rather like national groups, e.g., tribes or ethnic groups. Others are very different. Some religious groups meet our criteria, as do social classes, and some racial groups. Not all religious or racial groups did develop rich and pervasive cultures. But some did and those qualify" (p. 447).
44. Ibid., p. 449.

Margalit and Raz reject the thesis that self-government has ultimate or inherent value. "There is nothing wrong with multi-national
states, in which members of the different communities compete in
the political arena for public resources for their communities."[45] The
case for a right to self-determination, then, must be instrumental:
"Sometimes the prosperity of the group and its self-respect are aided
by, sometimes they may be impossible to secure without, the group's
enjoying political sovereignty over its own affairs. Sovereignty
enables the group to conduct its own affairs in a way conducive to its
own prosperity. . . . It depends on historical conditions."[46]

All these considerations, Margalit and Raz claim, amount to is a
case for self-government. They do not by themselves establish a *right*
to self-determination. This right, I noted earlier, is "the right to determine whether a certain territory shall become, or remain, a separate
state (and possibly whether it should enjoy autonomy within a larger
state)." That is, this right is a "right to determine that a territory be
self-governing, regardless of whether the case for self-government,
based on its benefits, is established or not."[47] The case for this right
derives from "the value of a collective good", "the value of membership in encompassing groups":

> It rests on an appreciation of the great importance that membership in and
> identification with encompassing groups has in the life of individuals, and
> the importance of the prosperity and self-respect of such groups to the well-
> being of their members. That importance makes it reasonable to let the
> encompassing group that forms a substantial majority in a territory have the
> right to determine whether that territory shall form an independent state in
> order to protect the culture and self-respect of the group, provided that the
> new state is likely to respect the fundamental interests of its inhabitants, and
> provided that measures are adopted to prevent its creation from gravely
> damaging the just interests of other countries.[48]

45. Ibid., p. 453. See also Raz, "Multiculturalism."
46. Margalit and Raz, "National Self-Determination," p. 450.
47. "In other words, the right to self-determination answers the question 'who is to
    decide?', not 'what is the best decision?' . . . [If a group] has the right to decide, its
    decision is binding even if it is wrong, even if the case for self-government is not
    made." Ibid., p. 454. Note that this feature of the right (or of rights in general) does
    not rule out its being "conditional on its being exercised for the right reasons, i.e.,
    to secure conditions necessary for the prosperity and self-respect of the group"
    (p. 459).
48. Ibid., pp. 456–457. "In our world, encompassing groups that do not enjoy self-
    government are not infrequently persecuted, despised, or neglected. Given the
    importance of their prosperity and self-respect to the well-being of their members,

The structure of the argument is one I cannot easily resist, given some of my normative commitments; in fact, the conclusion seems right. I mentioned earlier the qualifications of this right.[49] Given the conditions on the exercise of the right, it is not clear that it will justify statehood for many encompassing groups, at least in present conditions.[50] My main purpose in examining it is to determine the truth, if any, in the first three theses about the relation between nations and states, especially the third one about the entitlement of nations to statehood. I wish to see if this thesis enables us to determine the boundaries and memberships of states in nonarbitrary ways. I concluded that it need not be the case that nations should become states, as part of their self-development (thesis 2). I suggest later that it is not generally the case that states should consist of single nations (thesis 1), although I recognize that this will frequently happen over time. But I do accept a version of the first thesis: Under certain conditions, encompassing groups have a limited right to self-determination.

The question, then, is what implications does this right have for my question(s) about boundaries? It provides some rationale for fixing or maintaining the boundaries of states to accommodate the wishes of relevant encompassing groups, subject to the constraints already mentioned.[51] I claimed that some federal states can accommodate the self-determination goals of encompassing groups at least as well as unitary or nonfederal states can. Nevertheless, it may be

---

it seems reasonable to entrust their members with the right to determine whether the groups should be self-governing."

49. Many criticisms I have heard of the argument do not take into account these conditions; the right is highly constrained. It is important to study Margalit and Raz's defense of a group right to self-determination alongside Raz's piece on multiculturalism. Some have read his essay as a retreat from the unpopular conclusions of the self-determination paper, but it is not. Raz's view is that liberal multiculturalism is the best policy for our societies; separation and independence is only for those who fail to live together (personal correspondence).

50. "On any reasonable calculation, the . . . number of potential nations is probably much, *much* larger than that of possible viable states. . . . [N]ot all nationalisms can be satisfied, at any rate at the same time. . . . [V]ery many of the potential nations of this world live, or until recently have lived, not in compact territorial units but intermixed with each other in complex patterns. It follows that a territorial political unit can only become ethnically homogeneous, in such cases, if it either kills, or expels, or assimilates all non-nationals." Gellner, *Nations and Nationalism*, p. 2.

51. The argument "is in keeping with the view that, even though participation in politics may have intrinsic value to individuals, the shape and boundaries of political units are to be determined by their service to individual well-being, i.e., by their instrumental value." Margalit and Raz, "National Self-Determination," p. 457.

that the boundaries of states, federal or not, are to be determined by the wishes of the relevant encompassing groups.

Margalit and Raz's right of self-determination is territorial.[52] "The right [to self-determination] is over a territory. This simply reflects the territorial organization of our political world." Their argument for this claim also seems complex. Several considerations, they think, support attributing this to "substantial majorities": the value of membership, the irreversibility of decisions, the territorial nature of the right, and the importance of local environment.[53] The argument, as Margalit and Raz say, is meant to reflect the fact of "the territorial organization of our political world." They

assume that things are roughly as they are, especially that our world is a world of states and of a variety of ethnic, national, tribal, and other groups. We do not question the justification for this state of affairs. Rather, we ask whether, given that this is how things are and for as long as they remain the same, a moral case can be made in support of national self-determination.[54]

But note that this is not my project. I wish to determine the rationale for the territorial nature of the state. That the world is one of peoples and nations is certainly relevant to my inquiry, and it may be an assumption of some of my arguments. But that it is a world of states I cannot assume uncritically. For I wish to determine whether the way the world is has a rationale.[55] So I must determine whether there is a deeper rationale to the territorial nature of our fundamental forms of political organization. What can be said about that? (I return to the question in Section 8.4.)

Roger Scruton draws our attention to the different ways in which wandering peoples and settled ones conceive of the bases of their unity. Nomadic people, he claims, attach importance to ideas of "kind" – notions of "a continuity across generations, based in kinship and intermarriage, but supported also by a consciousness of common descent." Wandering peoples differ from settled ones. "Lacking territory, and lacking, after a time, even the common lan-

---

52. Ibid., pp. 440, 454, 458.
53. Ibid., pp. 457–459.
54. Ibid., p. 440.
55. The "natural fact about our world that it is a populated world with no unappropriated lands" (ibid., p. 440, note 1) is relevant. I made use of this fact in my discussion of anarchism, especially of secondary state formation, in Chapter 3.

guage that may have once united them, such people base their loyalty on ideas either of faith or of kinship, and usually on both. Kinship becomes, as for the Jews, a continuous and developing *story*, whose meaning is religious, and whose aspect is that of a homeless culture, based, however, in a consuming nostalgia for home."[56]

The unity of settled peoples, by contrast, develops an "idea of membership based in those relations between people which come from *occupying the same place*. People who are not, like the Jews (before 1948), 'strangers and sojourners' in the land, may have things in common sufficient to constitute a 'kind'. The most important of these is territory." Scruton argues that for land to be shared by a group of people it must first be *theirs*, that is, they must first have a collective claim to it: "Until territory is *ours*, there is no real 'mine' or 'thine'." The "we" which determines the terms of the occupation and division of the land, Scruton argues, is the group defined by, for instance, shared language, shared associations, shared history, and common culture – a nation.[57] "What holds together the features that I have identified as part of nationhood? Why is the emergence of this new kind of loyalty not just a passing accident?" Scruton asks that we appreciate "the importance of nationhood as I have described it. We need only reflect on the difference of predicament between a wandering and a settled people. What I have been defining is a special case of being *at home*, and of the attachment to home which is common to all people fortunate enough to have one."[58]

Suppose we accept Scruton's analysis and his thesis that "every political order depends, and ought to depend, upon a non-political idea of membership" and a nonpolitical form of loyalty.[59] The question, then, is why should that loyalty be *national?* Scruton's argument seems to depend on the desirability of the modern, liberal state:

The answer is contained in the nature of the modern state. All law requires jurisdiction: that is, a principle for determining who is, and who is not, subject to its edicts. . . .

56. Scruton, "In Defense of the Nation," in *The Philosopher on Dover Beach* (New York: St. Martin's Press, 1990), pp. 305, 312.
57. Ibid., pp. 314–315.
58. "National attachment defines a home; confessional attachment does not. Loyalty to the *polis* also defines a home, as is clear from the famous funeral oration of Pericles". Ibid., pp. 316–317.
59. Ibid., p. 303.

The safety, continuity and stability necessary to a rule of law are unobtainable until territory is secure. And only a territorial idea of jurisdiction will permit the final separation of law from confessional attachment. . . .

[T]he national idea . . . establishes a social loyalty suited to territorial jurisdiction; and without territorial jurisdiction, there is no possibility of a liberal state.[60]

The structure of Scruton's argument is not altogether clear. He seems to be defending "the 'national idea' as the foundation of political order" in the modern world by arguing that national loyalties alone can provide the unity that is a condition for the liberal state. He argues plausibly that the political unity of paradigmatic liberal states such as the United States depends in fact – *contra* the claims of many defenders – on a national identity.[61] He appears impressed (rightly) by the recent history of Lebanon. But it is still not clear why the non-political loyalty allegedly required by modern polities need be *national* (in my sense). Scruton may have a point if we understand him merely to be pointing to the relative success of the national basis of political unity, compared to alternatives. It is here that the comparison of the United States (or Japan) with Lebanon (or even Canada or Belgium) may be telling. A detailed comparative study is required to support this sort of thesis. Suppose Scruton is right and that strong sentiments of nationality are essential to the political unity of states. Again, like Margalit and Raz's argument, Scruton's case would not be one I can use easily, at least in a skeptical inquiry

60. Ibid., pp. 320–322. "It is a peculiar feature of wandering peoples that they tend to be governed by laws which are co-terminous with their religious confessions, and which derive their authority from the same divine source. When the people are 'strangers and sojourners' this gives rise to an enormous problem of law-enforcement. . . . In modern Lebanon, legal order rests on appeals to Rome, to the Sunnite Mufti, to the Shi'ite *'ulema* and the Druze *'aql*. This undermines the idea of political unity, while establishing in the minds of the people the idea that those who do not share their religious beliefs and customs are in some important sense outside the law. Such an idea of jurisdiction is incompatible with the emergence of a state in which rights are offered regardless of confession."

61. The United States "has all the characteristics of nationhood, and actively renews itself from its own national consciousness. America is first of all a territory, possessed through a 'union' of states. It has a common language, common habits of association, common customs and a common Judaeo-Christian culture. It is intensely patriotic. . . . There is also a strong religious dimension to the American idea. . . . And this loyalty has its own historical myths, its own 'dreams', its own sense of missions, its own powerful self-image, in which the American land is the last refuge of the dispossessed, and also the birthplace of a new and unfettered enterprise and will." Ibid., pp. 323–324.

into the justification of states. I cannot presuppose the desirability of states in order to ascertain what implications nationality has for determining the territorial nature (and membership) of states. In this section I ask whether nationality offers any independent support for some of the features of states, without presupposing that these very features are already justified. I may suppose that some state is legitimate – that is, reasonably just and efficient – but I ask then what is the basis for its territorial nature and how should it determine membership. The fact, if it is one, that nationality is essential to its unity may be of importance only insofar as we are convinced we have no serious alternative to states (as they conceive of themselves).[62]

Scruton's comparisons of wandering and settled peoples, and his account of the sense of identity of the latter as being tied to territory, are suggestive. Our attachment to place or land may explain, even if it does not justify, the territorial nature of most societies. But it is not clear that this will suffice to justify to territorial nature of the state. I return to these issues in Section 8.4.

Let us turn for a moment to the first thesis associated with nationalism: States should consist of single nations. Insofar as people accept the other theses, it may be best that states consist of single nations. For then no other basis of organizing a state will be successful. In his *Considerations on Representative Government,* J. S. Mill defends the thesis "that the boundaries of governments should coincide in the main with those of nationalities."[63] Mill was neither a political romantic nor a defender of collective rights, so we may be surprised by his defense of nationalism. His argument presupposes the existence of "free institutions" (i.e., electoral systems, basic liberties). Mill argues that when different nationalities coincide in single states, in the presence of strong national sentiments, the interests of government often lie in dividing, not in uniting. This is especially true when the differing nationalities are of similar strength. He notes that

when there are either free institutions or a desire for them, in any of the people artificially tied together, the interest of the government lies in an exactly

---

62. For some interesting reflections on the matter of social unity in the context of contemporary debates about multiculturalism, see Will Kymlicka, "Social Unity in a Liberal State," *Social Philosophy and Policy* 13, 1 (Winter 1996), 137–163.
63. Mill, *Considerations on Representative Government,* chap. 16, p. 430.

opposite direction. It is then interested in keeping up and envenoming their antipathies that they may be prevented from coalescing, and it may be enabled to use some of them as tools for the enslavement of others.

Mill's claim was based, in part, on his observations of the rule of the Hapsburgs.[64] It has, alas, surprising contemporary relevance. Mill's point is that electoral politics may, under certain conditions, exacerbate potent divisions. Certainly much that we have learned in the last several decades studying democratic systems would appear to support this hypothesis.[65]

Without taking the time to explore Mill's conjecture and to determine the extent of its truth, let me just concede the first thesis in some cases and recognize that sometimes it will be best for a nation to become a state. This would be consistent with Margalit and Raz's defense of a limited right to national self-determination, as well as with the claim of others that cultural ties facilitate cooperation.[66] Even admitting all this, it is hard to see how the boundaries of all or even most contemporary states – that is, their territorial nature and their membership – could be determined by nationality. Only a few encompassing groups will be in a position permissibly to exercise their limited right to national self-determination. And most of our societies are now irretrievably multinational or multicultural. This does not by itself entail that liberal, North American multicultural policies are best for all places. But it does suggest that nationality can no longer, if it ever could, determine boundaries in the manner sought by partisans of the so-called nation-state.

---

64. Ibid., p. 430. His observations on the unity of nineteenth-century France antedate recent historical scholarship: "The most united country in Europe, France, is far from being homogeneous: independently of the fragments of foreign nationalities at its remote extremities, it consists, as language and history prove, of two portions, one occupied almost exclusively by a Gallo-Roman population, while in the other the Frankish, Burgundian, and other Teutonic races form a considerable ingredient" (pp. 430–431). It should also be noted that Mill's defense of the thesis that nations should, under some circumstances, become states, does not depend on any idealization or romantic conception of the state – much less an idealization of state-building and war. This is not true of many other defenses of this or similar theses. See, for instance, Hegel, *Elements of the Philosophy of Right*, para. 324.
65. American political science stresses the manner in which electoral politics can be divisive. In the United States the divisions are multiple, but race is a particularly salient division. Just as electoral systems may worsen national divisions, so they exploit racial hatreds and fears.
66. See Barry, "Self-Government Revisited."

8.3 MEMBERSHIP

I have talked casually of the subjects and members of states, and of wandering peoples (who usually are not members of any state). The notions of a subject here is ambiguous. Someone may be a subject *of* a state or subject *to* its authority. Someone who is subject *to* the authority of a state is, in most cases, also a subject *of* that state. This latter notion is ancient and has, for the most part, been superseded by that of citizenship. We can still speak, as I have, of anyone who is subject to the state's authority as a subject of the state, but we should not forget an important aspect of the classical notion – namely, *submission* or *subjugation*. The king's subjects, in this older sense, were to submit or to be subjugated. Their status is clearly that of a dominated inferior.[67] The monarch's realm may thus be a "dominium".

The notion of "subject of" is natural when political authority or power is personified.[68] On this ancient view of governance, the ruler is the determinant of the unity of the realm and its inhabitants. What makes the inhabitants part of the realm is being subjects of the ruler's, and what makes the realm one is the monarch. Essentially, it is the king who makes the realm – *his* kingdom – one.[69] But modern governance is impersonal, and the unity of the modern state is not to be understood as dependent on the will of the ruler. In addition, the revival of Greek and Roman notions of citizenship, and their association with the principles of modern republican revolutions, make the notion of a "subject" no longer suitable for a characterization of our conceptions of membership. We remain subject of our states in one sense – we are subject to their authority – but we no longer are subjects of rulers in any ways that require our submission or subjugation. We take ourselves to be, in certain ways, the equals of our rulers and regard them as "public servants".[70]

---

67. American Indians and West Bank Palestinians are sometimes referred to as "subject peoples."
68. I believe I owe this point to someone, but I know not whom.
69. Recall the discussion of the claims of Louis XIV and Louis XV in Chapter 2. For a modern account of the crown's essential role in unifying the state, see Hegel, *Elements of the Philosophy of Right*, para. 275–286, esp. pp. 319 ("*Without* its monarch . . . *the* people is a formless mass.") and 323 ("the *majesty* of the monarch . . . the *actual unity* of the state . . .").
70. These remarks are most true of contemporary republics, less so of constitutional monarchies.

The general notion of citizenship is that of a kind of membership. I am not concerned with some of the more active or participatory conceptions of citizenship that have been the focus of much recent republican political theory.[71] Rather, I am interested in a more general notion of membership. Citizenship does not exhaust the relations I am interested in examining. In all states, citizens form only a proper subset of those subject *to* the state's authority. Visitors and temporary residents (e.g., foreign officials, foreign students, immigrants, refugees, illegal workers) are subject to the laws of the state. Such laws apply to all members and to all residents or visitors, with some exceptions.[72] Still, full membership today consists in the univocal status of citizenship.[73] It is now the characteristic and central relation individuals have to their states. In Chapter 2, I characterized the state's rule as direct and unmediated, in contrast to earlier forms of rule. This feature is built into the notion of citizenship. All citizens are equal, and their relation to the state is supposed to be direct and unmediated.[74]

How is citizenship or any other basic type of membership to be acquired? The question is only now being seriously studied by political philosophers. As I have noted, one often finds that theorists assume the matter to have been settled already: All (and primarily) residents of the territory in question are members. This may not be adequate, and, in any case, delimiting the state's territory is no simple matter.

Sometimes it is supposed that consent, often invoked as the basis for the state's legitimacy, can serve to determine membership. But the matter of membership is more complicated. Were membership to be determined thus, the consent must be mutual. To be a member of a group, both the candidate and the prior members must agree. Consent theorists presumably would be reluctant to accept an account of membership permitting current members to reject applicants on whatever grounds they chose. So it is not clear what a consensual account of membership should be. Nevertheless, there is an impor-

---

71. See the essays in *Theorizing Citizenship*, ed. R. Beiner (Albany: State University of New York Press, 1995), esp. Will Kymlicka and Wayne Norman, "Return of the Citizen: A Survey of Recent Work on Citizenship Theory," pp. 283–322.
72. For instance, diplomats. As I mention in Chapter 7, their status is best understood as a type of immunity, granted reciprocally by states; so, to this extent, they are subject to a state's authority while residing in its jurisdiction. See Section 8.4.
73. "Second-class citizenship" is normally understood not to be true citizenship.
74. Various corporate conceptions of membership might challenge this aspect of modern governance, insofar as they would prevent direct rule.

tant contrast to be made between what may be termed consensual and nonconsensual conceptions of membership.

Most people in the modern world acquire citizenship of a state at birth, either by being born in a territory (*jus soli*) or by virtue of their parentage (*jus sanguinis*). But citizenship usually may also be acquired by "naturalization", the process of acquiring a new citizenship. Those wishing to become members of another state may seek to do so, and if they satisfy various conditions, they may be accepted. There may be additional considerations – for instance, a limit to the number of new members a particular state can absorb at a time. But my interest for now lies in the conditions for membership. For many states these conditions include willingness to respect the laws of the state, elementary familiarity with the history and culture of the state, mastery of the relevant language(s), possession of certain skills, and the like. For others, the list may include parentage (i.e., ethnicity), national allegiances, or religion. Some states make naturalization conditional on satisfaction of the first sort of conditions – for example, Canada, the United States, France. Others grant citizenship only, or primarily, to those who belong to the relevant religious or national group – for example, Germany, Japan, Israel.[75]

Contrast the kinds of attributes required for membership. To the extent that the conditions a state requires for new members are attributes someone can willfully acquire, albeit with effort – for instance, elementary knowledge of the language – the state's policy is *consensual*. To the extent that these conditions are attributes whose acquisition is independent of a person's will – ethnicity or nationality – the policy is *nonconsensual*.[76] Policies such as the Canadian and

---

75. The immigration laws and policies of virtually all the countries I have mentioned are subjects of considerable controversy, and many are under review. My interest is not in the details of the policies but in a general contrast between two types of conceptions of membership. For helpful discussions of some of the moral, political, and economic aspects of current citizenship and immigration law, see *Justice in Immigration,* ed. W. Schwartz (Cambridge: Cambridge University Press, 1995). The first section of its chapter entitled "Citizenship, the Demands of Justice, and the Moral Relevance of Borders" (pp. 18–34), by Jules L. Coleman and Sarah K. Harding, offers a useful summary account of the immigration policies of the United States, Canada, the United Kingdom, Germany, France, Sweden, Israel, and Japan. See also *Free Movement: Ethical Issues in the Transnational Migration of People and of Money,* ed. B. Barry and R. Goodin (University Park, Pa.: Pennsylvania State University Press, 1992).

76. Although my analysis is not quite hers, I am indebted to Jean Hampton for this distinction (as well as for discussions of these issues and criticisms of this chapter). See Hampton, "Immigration, Identity, and Justice," in *Justice in Immigration,* pp. 66–93, and *Political Philosophy* (Boulder, Colo.: Westview Press, 1996), chap. 6.

American ones are consensual.[77] Policies such as the Japanese or German ones, which stress parentage and ethnicity, are nonconsensual.

Nonconsensual policies today usually are nationalist.[78] Such policies are often thought to be illiberal and wrong, and they are under attack in virtually all of the countries I have mentioned. That they may be illiberal is not in itself a determining consideration here. Rather, the question is whether they are impermissible. If nations have limited rights to self-determination, it may be that states, especially "nation-states", have limited rights to exclude on national or nonconsensual grounds. If the distinctiveness of a particular community is of value, then closure may be permissible. The issues here are fairly complex and are not exhausted by the matter of the special rights of encompassing groups. They raise difficult questions about justice – especially distributive justice, if we think of membership as a type of good. So we are likely to need an understanding of justice more detailed than any invoked in this essay, to resolve these issues. To complicate matters, some accounts relativize justice, in part or in whole, to communities.[79] It is likely that little progress can be made here without appeal to a developed theory of justice. My main concern, however, is not so much to address (and resolve) these difficult issues as to ascertain what can be said generally about the bases of membership in a particular sort of political community, namely, in a state.

Membership in national groups is important for determining people's identity, mainly because of the relatively nonconsensual nature of that membership. This, I think, is a central insight in Margalit and Raz's account of an encompassing group. "Membership is a matter of belonging, not of achievement", they say.

One does not have to prove oneself, or to excel in anything, in order to belong and to be accepted as a full member. To the extent that membership

---

77. Allowing for the fact that they give priority to family members.
78. In an extended sense, perhaps, in the case of Israel, insofar as being Jewish is not a nationality (or "ethnicity") like others.
79. Michael Walzer, in a pioneering essay on these issues, characterizes membership in some community as a primary good of a very special sort: "What we do with regard to membership structures all our other distributive choices: it determines with whom we make those choices, from whom we require obedience and collect taxes, to whom we allocate goods and services." Walzer, *Spheres of Justice: A Defense of Pluralism and Equality* (New York: Basic Books, 1983), p. 31. Walzer's view is, "The theory of distributive justice begins, then, with an account of membership rights. It must vindicate at one and the same time the (limited) right of closure, without which there could be no communities at all, and the political inclusiveness of the existing communities." Many contractarian theories face the same tasks.

normally involves recognition by others as a member, that recognition is not conditional on meeting qualifications that indicate any accomplishment. To be a good Irishman, it is true, is an achievement. But to be an Irishman is not. Qualification for membership is usually determined by nonvoluntary criteria. One cannot choose to belong. One belongs because of who one is. One can come to belong to such groups, but only by changing, e.g., by adopting their culture, by changing one's tastes and habits accordingly – a very slow process indeed.

Why is membership in such groups important to a person's identity or valuable as such?

The fact that these are groups, membership of which is a matter of belonging and not of accomplishment, makes them suitable for their role as primary foci of identification. Identification is more secure, less liable to be threatened, if it does not depend on accomplishment. Although accomplishments play their role in people's sense of their own identity, it would seem that at the most fundamental level our sense of our own identity depends on criteria of belonging rather than on those of accomplishment. Secure identification at that level is particularly important to one's well-being.[80]

The value of nonconsensual membership, then, turns on its relative independence of the will. This is, of course, what many object to.[81] But insofar as stable identification is important to well-being, it is hard to see what arguments could be made against this claim, other than various consequential considerations. I do not mean to disparage consequential values. Even mild and relatively nonethnic forms of nationalism often go bad.[82] These likely consequences may be sufficient to make us wary of virtually any nonconsensual policy. But the theoretical point is significant nevertheless.[83]

80. Margalit and Raz, "National Self-Determination," pp. 446–447.
81. See Hampton, "Immigration, Identity, and Justice," and *Political Philosophy*, chap. 6. Many thinkers contrast nonconsensual conceptions of membership with liberal, consensual ones. The latter, it may be thought, are supported by universalist or cosmopolitan conceptions of justice that accord all persons or all humans equal moral standing. *This* standing presumably is itself nonconsensual. If it is argued, in defense of the equal basic standing of all, that it is a status people have by virtue of their humanity or rationality, then the position turns out to be, at this level, nonconsensual. The only difference from the nonconsensual conceptions of membership that we are examining is that the attributes that support one's standing, while independent of one's will, are shared by all humans or persons. Only moral theories that allow moral standing to be forfeited would seem to be consensual in the relevant sense.
82. Cases are to be found daily in the press. A powerful general explanation for group conflict, in particular ethnic or national conflict, is offered in Hardin, *One for All*.
83. Some may deny that "membership [which] is a matter of belonging, not of achieve-

The nonconsequential case against nonconsensual conceptions of membership has not, I think, been made. To be certain, some nonconsensual policies are unjust or are enacted by unjust states, and they may be condemned as such. But that is true of virtually any policy. The question here is whether the permissibility of some nonconsensual policies has any general implications for the nature of acceptable membership policies. I do not think it does. Much depends on various conditions and on the implications of justice, especially "international" justice. It may well be that the justice of limited exclusions will turn considerably on considerations, for instance, of size or structure.[84] Similarly, much may depend on the history of the state in question and its past treatment of certain nonnationals (e.g., Koreans in Japan, Arab citizens and Palestinians in Israel, Russians in the newly independent Baltic states). Certain new developments complicate matters as well: Borders are difficult to seal, and increasing interdependence limits the liberties of states to choose policies.

Modern states make strong demands on their members' loyalty, much more than many other forms of political organization (e.g., empire, medieval kingdom). Typically, they insist on exclusive loyalty and take this to rule out multiple membership. Some states (e.g., the United States) no longer prohibit dual citizenship. But this is usually a recent development, and worries about dual allegiances remain. The concern is ancient: "No man can serve two masters: for either he will hate the one, and love the other; or else he will hold to the one, and despise the other."[85] The problem, of course, is most acute if the object of loyalty is very demanding – for example, Yahweh, Mammon, the state. One can have many friends, even though conflicts of loyalty can be expected and force difficult choices. But friendship does not usually require that one be ready to sacrifice all.

---

ment" is illusory, as any identification can be acquired or lost through acts of the agent, possibly over a long time. For instance, it is sometimes claimed that nationality (as opposed to citizenship) can be acquired late in life, albeit with great difficulty. (See Buchanan, *Secession,* pp. 54–55, and Tamir, *Liberal Nationalism,* pp. 26–27.) But the rarity of genuine "assimilation" after childhood suggests that this will be exceptional – and limited primarily to exceptional individuals (e.g., Julien Green). One can, of course, choose "to accept" the identity thrust on one by one's culture and community. But if nothing one can do will bring it about that one ceases to be Japanese or Jewish – because one's parents are Japanese or Jewish – then there are limits to the effect of one's possible "rejection" of one's nationality.

84. Nonconsensual policies might be more permissible for very small states, in a world of small states, than large ones. And certain unitary states may be more justified in enacting such policies than federal ones.

85. Matthew 6:24.

I have argued that the authority of states is much less than claimed. Insofar as that is so, the case for exclusive membership is weakened. We could then understand membership as permitting multiple allegiances. Multiple citizenship should not, then, seem problematic. There will be problems of conflict, but there are with the state's authority to begin with. There we saw that the claim to comprehensive and preemptive authority or sovereignty is not made more credible by pointing to potential conflicts of authority; these are inevitable and cannot all be resolved in advance.

The permissibility of multiple citizenship raises the possibility of differential membership. Citizenship consists in part in a bundle of rights and liberties (and duties and liabilities). Different packages could be made and allocated. In effect, they typically are. Immigrants with the right to reside and work are not thought of as possessing citizenship, even in countries that do not require them to take out citizenship after a number of years of residence. In the European Union, citizens of member states may soon, for instance, be permitted to vote in the local elections of the state in which they reside; in the Netherlands long-term foreign residents already can. We could bundle the rights and duties of citizenship differently and offer different types of membership. The major worry has to do with status distinctions and the development of class distinctions.[86] Some such distinctions may also enable states to separate ethnicity and nationality from citizenship. Assimilation into the dominant culture may not be required for citizenship, as it is in Canada.

States may tend to become, over time, nation-states of sorts, at least when they attain a common culture and their members develop sentiments of patriotic allegiance. But this does not affect my conclusion: National ideals do not offer a general answer to the question of the membership of states.

8.4 TERRITORY

States are territorial. But what exactly is the relation between the state and its territory? Monarchs once claimed dominium over their

---

86. In Israel, Arab citizens are not required to serve in the military. Like jury duty, the duty of military service can reinforce status distinctions. See Simmons, *On the Edge of Anarchy*, pp. 242–243, for a discussion of different "grades" of citizenship in the context of Locke's theory.

realms. Their kingdoms were *theirs* ("*l'Etat c'est à moi*"). Their relation to their realms we may think of as a species of ownership.[87] But
contemporary notions of property do not seem adequate for a characterization of the relation of modern states to their territories.

Recall the difficulties Nozick encounters in attempting to justify the
minimal state. The first steps of his argument, up to the establishment
of the "ultraminimal" state, are not difficult. But this is because the
ultraminimal state is not yet a state, as it does not claim jurisdiction
over "independents", those who refuse to buy the protective services
of the dominant protection agency. The next step in the argument is
problematic, and the one needed to generate something analogous to
a right over a territory. Nozick, given his natural rights starting point,
cannot accept Margalit and Raz's view that "the shape and boundaries of political units are to be determined by their service to individual well-being, that is, by their instrumental value."[88]

A lesson to draw from the failure of Nozick's argument has to do
with ownership and territoriality. What Nozick in effect shows is that
one cannot account for the authority of states solely in terms of individual rights to liberty and property. A reason for this failure is that
states claim rights that do not seem derivable in any simple way from
the rights of individuals and that seem, in fact, inconsistent with individual natural rights. But there is another reason for the failure. It is
the state's authority that is territorial, and it is not possible to understand this in terms of property rights. The problem is not so much the
individualism of accounts such as Nozick's. Rather it is that the
state's authority is not an ownership relation; it is jurisdictional.[89]

When Connecticut acquires property in land in Massachusetts, it
does not enlarge its territory or diminish that of its neighbor. The
land remains under the jurisdiction of Massachusetts, subject to its
laws. Similarly, if Canada acquired a large piece of land in Florida (or
a wealthy Canadian willed his Florida estate to the Canadian state),
it would not thereby come to be part of Canada. Property rights, as
legal systems currently understand them, do not include full juris-

---

87. "Already by the fourteenth century it was possible to argue that to have a right was
to be the lord or dominus of one's relevant moral world, to possess *dominium*, that
is to say, *property*." Richard Tuck, *Natural Rights Theory: Their Origins and Development* (Cambridge: Cambridge University Press, 1979), p. 3; see also pp. 61, 160, 171.
88. Margalit and Raz, "National Self-Determination," p. 457.
89. See especially Lea Brilmayer, "Consent, Contract, and Territory," *Minnesota Law
Review* 74, 1 (October 1989), 1–35, and "Secession and Self-Determination: A Territorial Interpretation," *Yale Journal of International Law* 16, 1 (1991), 177–202.

dictional powers. That is, in acquiring property in land, one is not ordinarily understood to acquire the sorts of powers over it that states claim over their territory.

Some cases may suggest a different analysis. The embassies and consulates of foreign states are the property of those states. Anyone who sets foot on the grounds of a foreign embassy may be regarded as being under that state's jurisdiction, or at least outside the reach of the host state. This exception to the separation of ownership and jurisdiction is more apparent than real. Article 22 of the Vienna Convention on Diplomatic Relations (1961) specifies that the premises of diplomatic missions are "inviolable" and may not be entered by agents of the host state without the consent of the mission.[90] But note first the basis for this arrangement in treaty law. Generally, however, the territorial rights of states are not determined by treaty.[91] Although embassies and consular properties may be "inviolable", there undoubtedly are implicit conditions for their privileged status; one need only consider how states would react to an embassy storing nuclear or chemical weapons on its premises.[92] The special status of embassies and consular properties are immunities granted by the host states to facilitate mutually beneficial diplomatic relations. As such, they do not challenge the territoriality of states.[93]

---

90. Shaw, *International Law,* p. 465. Note that "precisely what the legal position would be in the event of entry without express consent because, for example, of fire fighting requirements or of danger to persons within that area, is rather uncertain and justification might be pleaded by virtue of implied consent, but it is a highly controversial area."

91. "There is no right as such under international law to diplomatic relations, and they exist by virtue of mutual consent." Shaw, *International Law,* p. 464. Transfer of territory may be effected by treaty (e.g., the Louisiana Purchase, Alaska, Panama Canal, or, for a different sort of case, the Hudson's Bay Company). But the jurisdictional powers that states generally claim are not traceable to any prior agreement.

92. In 1973 the Iraqi embassy in Pakistan was subjected to an armed search, during which considerable quantities of arms were found; several diplomats were expelled as a consequence. In the 1984 incident, where shots fired from the Libyan embassy in London killed a policewoman, the British government took the position that after a break in diplomatic relations the mission ceased to be inviolable and could be searched, citing Article 45 (a) of the Vienna Convention. See Shaw, *International Law,* p. 466 ("and this [interpretation] would appear to be correct").

93. Similarly, the privileged status of diplomatic personnel is that of general immunity to the laws of the host country and consequently does not challenge the territorial jurisdiction of states. Diplomats accused of wrongdoing (of any sort) may be declared *personae non grata* and expelled from the country. This right of states to expel foreign diplomats is clearly territorial and extends to conduct in embassies and consulates.

The natural rights position is radically revisionist. The defender of Nozick's argument may, after all, concede that the minimal state to be justified does not resemble a state in many of the usual ways. For instance, such a "state" may permit groups of property owners to secede and join another "state" as long as all parties consent. The mere fact that actual states are not like this would not negate the normative thesis that only states that are like these could be justified. That states claim different rights over their territories than property owners could claim does not refute the property rights libertarian. That is not my purpose, for I am assuming that the latter fails to construct an argument for the state (see Chapter 6). Given this, a lesson to be drawn from the failure of this sort of case for the state is that the state's territoriality is not a species of ownership.[94]

Something cannot be a state without a territory, and the state's authority is essentially territorial. If the state's territoriality cannot be understood in terms of ownership, how is it to be understood? According to some, there cannot be territory without states: "Under traditional international law, until one has a state one cannot talk in terms of title to territory, because there does not exist any legal person capable of holding the legal title."[95] Leaving aside international law, this seems implausible as a general thesis about states (as I have understood them). On some of the views about peoples and nations that we have just examined, groups of certain kinds can have the requisite corporate standing to be entitled, in certain circumstances, to be states. If so, it is unclear why they could not, in principle, acquire territory without first becoming a state.[96] International law could be adjusted accordingly.[97]

---

94. The attempt to understand states in terms of individual rights, especially to property, may issue in a conception of states as a type of joint stock company. See Part III of *Anarchy, State, and Utopia*. Supposing the whole world to be privately owned thus may lead to some interesting consequences for natural rights theory. See Hillel Steiner, "The Natural Right to the Means of Production," *Philosophical Quarterly* 27 (1977), 41–49.
95. "So to discover the process of acquisition of title to territory, one has first to point to an established state." Shaw, *International Law*, p. 283.
96. Presumably, something like this would have to be the position of those orthodox Jews who refuse to recognize the legitimacy of the current state of Israel.
97. "One possibility that could be put forward here involves the abandonment of the classical rule that only states can acquire territorial sovereignty, and the substitution of a provision permitting a people to acquire sovereignty over the territory pending the establishment of the particular state. . . . However, the proposition is a controversial one and must remain tentative." Shaw, *International Law*, pp. 283–284.

Territoriality is essentially jurisdictional. So it might be useful to distinguish different types of jurisdiction, as international lawyers do. We might first distinguish *prescriptive jurisdiction*, the capacity to make law, from *enforcement jurisdiction*, the capacity to ensure compliance. We might distinguish further *legislative, executive*, and *judicial jurisdictions*.[98] The jurisdiction of a legislature to make laws, that of a judiciary to apply, interpret, and make laws, and that of an executive to enforce them and, generally, to act, are normally understood to be territorial. Many states hold their citizens to be liable to their laws even when outside their territorial limits, but for the most part these jurisdictions seem to be understood territorially.

It is hard to see how the justification for territoriality could be other than consequential, broadly speaking. There is a large literature on nonconsequential, especially "Lockean", accounts of private ownership of land and other resources. Whatever plausibility these accounts may have, they do not seem to carry over to the thesis of the territoriality of states. The main rationale for the latter would seem to be convenience and practicality. Understood thus, it would seem to be conditional and limited.[99]

It is not evident that there are any *general* solutions for the question of determining the boundaries of states. And it is no longer clear that our current conceptions of these boundaries, as territorial, national, and relatively determinate, are plausible. At the least, we should be open to the idea that different solutions can be advanced to different questions. The simplistic dichotomy between state and anarchy, revealed to be far from exhaustive in earlier chapters, can be as misleading here as elsewhere.[100]

---

98. Shaw, *International Law*, pp. 392, 397–399.
99. "The main justification for the appropriation of land to the exclusive use, either of individuals or of groups of human beings, is that its full advantages as an instrument of production cannot otherwise be utilised; the main justification for the appropriation of territory to governments is that the prevention of mutual mischief among the human beings using it cannot otherwise be adequately secured." Sidgwick, *The Elements of Politics*, p. 252 (see also p. 255).
100. "[U]nless anarchy is feasible, it may suffice for the moment to note that a world without boundaries implies a world government, and I am not in bad company when I warn that we should be wary of a world government." Boxill, "On some Criticisms of Consent Theory," p. 100. Anyone as skeptical as I am of the pretenses of states would find it hard to be enthusiastic about "world government". But fortunately, undermining the self-conceived boundaries of states need not lead to that (or to anarchy).

Chapter 9

The functions of governments

9.1 THE NATURE AND EXTENT OF LEGITIMATE STATE POWERS

What should governments do? Suppose a state to be legitimate – on my view, reasonably just and minimally efficient. What is it entitled to do? I have argued that states have much less authority than they claim. But legitimate states may nonetheless have considerable powers to govern, that is, to legislate and enforce rules.[1] Even if their claims to authority are too ambitious to be warranted, their powers may be legitimate. To what ends should they use these powers?

Answers to these queries depend to a great extent on the nature of justice and the account we invoke. I have tried to make a large part of this book independent of specific controversies about justice. But ascertaining the proper functions of states seems to require determinate norms of justice – or so one would have thought. But some have claimed that most moral traditions in fact will justify very few state functions. It may be that states are so inefficient that virtually no plausible account of justice would endorse most of their activities.[2]

---

1. They may also have considerable powers to influence behavior in the ways I have noted: by establishing standards, providing information, advising, persuasion, education, offering awards and honors, and so on. Even if legislation and enforcement of rules are the main activities of a particular government, it may need to employ little force in securing compliance. I argue in Chapter 7 that the state's use of force is often exaggerated. This would not make it, or any of the state's other activities, less problematic.
2. "The outlines of a consensus have emerged concerning the appropriateness of public-sector activities in representative' democracies. This consensus holds that most public-sector programs in these nations are inappropriate, or are carried on at an inappropriate level, or are executed in an inappropriate manner." Aranson and Ordeshook, "Public Interest, Private Interest, and the Democratic Polity," p. 87.

An investigation of the efficiency of particular states is beyond the scope of this essay, so I focus here on a recent account of the purposes of government.

Suppose we have negative, natural rights to our lives, liberty, and possessions and that these rights are (virtually) absolute or indefeasible.[3] Then, it is widely thought, at best only "minimal states" will be legitimate, where such are states that restrict their activities to the enforcement of the basic rights of individuals and the like. (It is more likely that no actual states, minimal or not, will be legitimate.) Such appears to be the consequence of (virtually) absolute natural rights.[4] When made aware of these implications of absolute natural rights, many philosophers deny their existence. In the absence of a convincing defense of (virtually) absolute natural rights, the moral case for restricting states to "minimal" functions may lose force.

Many contemporary philosophers appear to believe that the political implications of "Hobbesian" contractarianism are not all that different from those of "Lockean" natural rights theory.[5] The appeals I have made on occasion to considerations of mutual benefit, as well as to efficiency, are consonant with neo-Hobbesian contractarianism, so this conjecture is relevant to my concerns. I shall consider a Hobbesian defense of minimal states developed by Michael Levin. Without making any strong assumptions about people's moral rights in a "state of nature" – indeed, assuming that people have none in such a situation – Levin argues that no state more extensive than a minimal one would be chosen by rational individuals.

Hobbes himself, of course, defended what I have called classical sovereignty. Whatever the Sovereign judged to be necessary for the defense and well-being of the commonwealth, it could do. But Hobbes does not appear to have thought that sovereigns need have many tasks; he did not think the state needed to have all the functions we assign it today.[6] By 'Hobbesian contractarian theory', however, I

---

3. An absolute or indefeasible right, I have said, is one giving rise to a duty that may not be violated, *whatever the consequences*. Negative rights are those giving rise only to negative duties – roughly, duties to desist or refrain from action. The negative-positive distinction is notoriously problematic, but nothing will turn on that in my discussion.
4. See Chapter 6.
5. See Michael Levin, "A Hobbesian Minimal State," *Philosophy and Public Affairs* 11, 4 (Fall 1982), 338–353; Jan Narveson, *The Libertarian Idea* (Philadelphia: Temple University Press, 1988); and, to a lesser extent, Gauthier, *Morals by Agreement*.
6. I defend this reading in "Leviathan and the Minimal State: Hobbes' Theory of Government." This account of Hobbesian theory, as well as Levin's, are criticized by

do not mean Hobbes's actual conclusions. For one thing, as I have said, there is reason to think that his attachment to absolute sovereignty is incompatible with his theory of rationality.[7] Nor do I mean to endorse every element of Hobbes's theory. Rather, I take 'Hobbesian contractarianism' – better, "*neo*-Hobbesian" – to refer mainly to the rational choice theory and Paretian principles that many other political theorists use to discuss and evaluate institutions and forms of political organization. I wish to consider what sorts of states, if any, would be collectively preferred to alternative arrangements. Social contract theorists ask whether states would be the object of collective choice in hypothetical "states of nature", where these are whatever condition rational individuals would find themselves in, given their talents, resources, and the like, before the establishment of a state.[8] The project of neo-Hobbesian contractarianism is to determine (1) whether a state would be collectively agreed to in such a situation and (2) what sorts of institutions would constitute a state.[9]

Kavka in "Hobbes as a Modern Liberal," *Hobbes Studies* 1 (1988), 373–395. On issues of redistribution and of revolution, Kavka argues that Hobbes is on the side of contemporary "liberals" rather than "conservatives" (in the American sense). I want, however, to distinguish between Hobbesian theory and Hobbes's own writings. Although I do not disagree with Kavka concerning the logic of the former, I would claim that the latter are extremely minimalist, surprisingly so given Hobbes's enthusiasm for absolute sovereignty and given the pre-Smithian character of his thought. See my "A Hobbesian Welfare State?" *Dialogue* 26, 4 (Winter 1988), 653–673, from which much of this section draws.

7. This is one of the conclusions of Hampton's *Hobbes and the Social Contract Tradition*.
8. It is doubtful that the relevant state of nature can be identified with sufficient precision – or, more important, with the requisite uniqueness – necessary for this sort of comparison. Just as modern political philosophers have been led astray in understanding state and anarchy to be exhaustive forms of political organization, so social contract theorists have mistakenly tended to assume that the "state of nature" could be well defined and, moreover, that it is unique. But brief reflection on the multiple situations that could emerge, say, if a particular state disintegrated should suffice to caution one against making much use of this notion. In this section, I mostly ignore such difficulties with state of nature theories and construct my argument without taking them into account. In the end, I believe they threaten contractarian theory, at least of the "Hobbesian" variety, with indeterminacy.
9. Neo-Hobbesian political theory is sometimes thought to conceive of individuals as self-interested and amoral. This may be, but neither assumption is necessary. For the question of self-interestedness, see my "The Relation of Self-Interest and Justice in Contractarian Ethics." Assuming that agents are nonmoral is a necessary part of a neo-Hobbesian *moral* theory that hopes to show the rationality of morals. But it need be no part of a neo-Hobbesian *political* theory that seeks the rationale of states. The best developed version of the first project is Gauthier, *Morals by Agreement*, of the second, J. Buchanan, *Limits of Liberty*. For some of the distinctions between types of contractarian theories, see the first section of my "A Contractarian Account of Moral Justification."

Rational individuals may well agree to establish a state in order to secure the order and protection that otherwise eludes them in the absence of government. The standard tale is that they accomplish this by surrendering certain liberties to a power ("the Sovereign") in exchange for greater security. What do they surrender? In Hobbes's account, they surrender virtually all of their liberty to the Sovereign, who thereby becomes absolute. In Levin's account, rational individuals surrender only their liberty to use their "swords", and this is the heart of his argument.

Consider two possible Hobbesian "social contracts".[10] One is an agreement to give up one's sword in exchange for greater security of person and possessions. The other is an agreement to give up both one's sword and one's plow in exchange for greater security and food. The first agreement is called the "less extensive bargain"; the second, the "more extensive bargain".[11] Levin argues that there is a significant difference between the two. Each addresses a different need, but only one of them fully satisfies the need in question. The first bargain addresses the need for protection; the second, the need for food and protection. The first bargain fully satisfies the need for protection: Security is obtained when individuals turn in their arms. The more extensive bargain, however, does not similarly answer the need for sustenance: The need to eat remains intact after the plows have all been transferred to the Sovereign.

The difference is important as it suggests that rational individuals have no reason to give up their plows to the state. The difference between swords and plows, Levin argues, is that swords are needed *solely* to protect oneself against others. Plows, by contrast, are required to satisfy needs that exist independently of other people. Thus, turning in our weapons to the Sovereign will solve our security problem.[12] But the need for food is not in the slightest affected by surrendering farming equipment to the Sovereign. The difference between the two needs is thus crucial: one is created by mutual beliefs, the other is given by our biology.

---

10. The metaphor of a social contract need not be taken too literally or seriously, certainly not as representing any sort of promise or commitment, as Levin in fact supposes ("A Hobbesian Minimal State," pp. 340, 352). This misinterpretation of the Hobbesian original agreement as a pledge or a binding agreement does not, however, affect his argument.
11. Levin, "A Hobbesian Minimal State," pp. 343–345.
12. Provided, of course, we can solve the problem of controlling the Sovereign now that it has all of our swords. I shall ignore this important but seemingly intractable problem for now.

My need for my sword and my incentive for keeping it are constituted by my beliefs about your beliefs and intentions. If you did not think that you might need your sword against me, I would not need my sword against you. I thus have an incentive for surrendering my sword that I do not have for surrendering my plow: by surrendering my sword I alter those of your beliefs and intentions that make it necessary for me to possess a sword. I have no such incentive for surrendering my plow.[13]

Individuals in a Hobbesian state of nature thus have a reason to surrender only their arms to the Sovereign. This conclusion is reinforced if we suppose that such individuals have at hand information available to us about, for instance, the Soviet economy, the agricultural programs of the European Union, or U.S. farming policies. The inefficiencies of most, if not all, actual systems of state control of food production would not inspire our Hobbesian bargainers with enthusiasm for the more extensive bargain.[14] The state agreed to by Hobbesians will thus be minimal. Their goal in establishing it will be to secure protection against one another. Turning in their arms and asking the Sovereign to police their neighborhoods and to defend them against invaders will be all they require of the state.

The crux of Levin's neo-Hobbesian argument for the minimal state is his analysis of the need for security in the state of nature. The questionable nature of this analysis can be seen easily if we state explicitly the preference rankings that Levin is attributing to Hobbesian individuals. Simplifying, let us consider situations with only two people.[15] With regard to their swords, there are then four possible states of affairs they have to consider: They can both disarm (mutual disarmament), they can both remain armed (status quo), or one can remain armed while the other disarms. Levin claims that the *only* reason anyone wishes to be armed is the threat posed by the swords of others. Thus each person clearly prefers mutual disarmament to the status quo, mutual armament. What about the other two outcomes, one party disarming while the other remains armed? Assuming arms to be costly, each party should prefer mutual disarmament to remaining armed while the other disarms. And we may suppose that each individual least prefers disarming while the other retains possession of his or her sword. Thus we have the following preference ranking: (1) mutual disarmament, (2) status quo, (3) arm, disarm, and (4) dis-

13. Levin, "A Hobbesian Minimal State," p. 345.
14. Ibid., p. 351.
15. This simplifying assumption will not have any effect on my argument.

arm, arm (where 'disarm, arm' is short for 'I disarm, the other remains armed'). The problem, then, is one of information and belief. I believe that the other (Michelle) might attack me, thus my need for weapons. The status quo is better for me than my disarming while Michelle remains armed, there being no guarantee in such a situation that she will not attack me. Swords are unproductive resources, however, so we would both be better off not needing any. The Sovereign enables us to give up our swords and attain our first choice, mutual disarmament. The game theoretical structure of the Hobbesian state of nature, as Levin analyzes it, can be illustrated thus:

Matrix 9.1

Michelle

disarm   arm

	disarm	arm
disarm	4,4	1,2
arm	2,1	3,3

What is the rational strategy? In situations of this sort,[16] there is no dominant strategy. It is rational to disarm, provided the other also disarms; it is not rational to disarm if the other remains armed. Given the parties' preferences, however, it may not be difficult to have them disarm. Mutual disarmament is their first choice; it is merely lack of information concerning the other's preferences that keeps each from disarming unilaterally. There is no fundamental conflict of interest in this game.

Levin believes that the Hobbesian "state of nature" presents individuals with a situation like that of an Assurance Game. The *only* reason for having a sword, he claims, is fear of others. With their disarmament, there no longer is a reason to keep one's sword, "swords" presumably being costly investments.

As soon as you and I give our swords to Jones [the Sovereign], and assuming our confidence in Jones is well placed, neither of us *needs* his sword any longer. . . . The need to fight is, so to speak, in the eye of the beholder, and in the eye of the beholder of the beholder. . . . Remove the mutual perception of

---

16. Readers familiar with game theory will recognize this as similar to an Assurance Game.

the need to fight and you remove the need to fight, and hence any reason for retaining the liberty to fight.[17]

This is a most unusual analysis of a Hobbesian state of nature. Were it to hold, it is not clear why rational individuals would need government at all, even a minimal one. For if the problem confronting Hobbesian bargainers is similar to an Assurance Game, mutual disarmament could be achieved through the effective dissemination of information about people's preferences. As soon as they realize that they all prefer peace to any other outcome, they can rationally throw down their swords, all the while saving themselves the expense of maintaining a Sovereign.[18]

Why think that the Hobbesian "state of nature" is an Assurance Game? Hobbesian individuals have "swords" for two main reasons, one defensive, the other predatory. Swords are useful for defense. They are also useful for offense – for instance, helping oneself to the possessions of others; indeed, swords can sometimes be better investments than plows, when the fruits of others' labor are available for plunder. Normally this would be unjust, but neo-Hobbesian theorists suppose that many will be so inclined. Predation may be often imprudent, but one cannot assume it will never be rational.

The rationality of predatory activity in the state of nature suggests a different preference ranking for Hobbesian individuals: (1) arm, disarm, (2) mutual disarmament, (3) status quo, and (4) disarm, arm. These preferences give rise not to an Assurance Game but to the familiar PD. Each party has a dominant strategy, to remain armed whatever the other does.[19] On this more standard view, rational agents in a Hobbesian world prefer being armed while others are disarmed to all other outcomes. They know, however, that others also

---

17. Levin, "A Hobbesian Minimal State," pp. 344, 345. Levin's references to "Schelling effects" (p. 349) reinforce my suspicion that he has confused coordination and similar problems with games of partial conflict.
18. Adapting Engels's remark, quoted in Chapter 7, "the government of persons is replaced by the administration of things. . . . The [minimal] state is not 'abolished.' *It dies out.*"

    As Hillel Steiner once pointed out to me, Levin's analysis is similar to those of many supporters of unilateral disarmament in the 1970s and 1980s: If the *only* reason for the Soviets to possess nuclear arms was their fear of the West's nuclear arsenal, the West could have unilaterally disarmed without any fear.
19. For simplicity, I am ignoring repeated-play representations of the situation (see Chapter 3). These would be relevant in other contexts, but my primary aim in this section is merely to show how certain types of contractarian theories could support more than "minimal" functions of government.

have similar preferences. Given that their first choice is unlikely to be realized, and seeing that if they each act on their first choice, the outcome will be worse for each than if they acted differently, they may elect to establish a state to disarm all. Governments are thus understood as means of enabling individuals to cooperate.

What difference does this alternative analysis of the state of nature make to Levin's argument? I shall argue that it completely undermines his and similar defenses of the minimal state. The structure of the argument of a Hobbesian defense of the state turns out to justify more than minimal functions.

Let us say, for the moment, that a *minimal state* (or, rather, government) is one whose task is to assure the basic security of person and possessions that would otherwise elude people in its absence. I shall understand 'basic security of persons and possessions' mainly to involve security from bodily harm and protection of possessions. Whether "minimal states" are to enforce legitimate agreements is a matter that I discuss later in this section.[20]

Understanding the state of nature as (analogous to) an n-person PD, the Hobbesian argument for the minimal state is that it enables rational individuals to secure greater security of person and possessions – the mutually advantageous, cooperative outcome that is each individual's second choice among the possible outcomes we considered earlier. Why is such security not available to rational individuals as individuals? Because basic security of person and possessions is largely a collective good, albeit an "impure" one (see Chapter 3). Social order generally can be a collective good.

If the Hobbesian argument for government turns on security being a collective good, more than the minimal state can be justified thereby. One notable task of actual governments is the provision of other collective goods, such as pollution control, protection of the environment, public safety regulations, public health (or disease control). If the efficient provision of security is a rationale for a minimal state, it is also a rationale for a more-than-minimal state, one that provides additional collective goods.[21]

---

20. The "minimal state, limited to the narrow functions of protection against force, theft, fraud, enforcement of contracts, and so on . . ." Nozick, *Anarchy, State, and Utopia*, p. ix; see also p. 26.
21. This is one of the main theses of J. Buchanan, *The Limits of Liberty*. The provision of collective goods, as well as fiscal and distributive decisions regarding their provision, are the concern of what he calls "Productive State." And Buchanan contrasts

By failing to notice the indivisible and nonexcludable nature of security, neo-Hobbesian defenders of the minimal state like Levin fail to understand the logic of this sort of argument for states. If it justifies state provision of basic security of person and possessions, it also justifies state provision of other collective goods. The metaphors of swords and plows may be partly responsible for Levin's misunderstanding of the nature of neo-Hobbesian justifications for the state. It is especially the metaphor of the plow that is misleading. For only if agricultural production enjoys extraordinary economies of scale would there be an argument for collectivization of "plows". Levin, however, never mentions pollution control, protection of the environment, problems of soil erosion, public health, and the like. Yet, to pursue the agricultural metaphor, modern methods of farming (e.g., mechanized "plows", pesticides) may have spillover effects, the relief of which may be collective goods. In addition, public transportation, national parks, public health, a patent system, safety regulations, and the protection of cultural objects are examples of quasi-collective goods that are forgotten in discussions of swords and plows. If we let ourselves be distracted by colorful but simplistic images, we may forget about the many collective goods we may want government to assist in providing.[22]

The casual manner in which the "minimal state" is usually characterized ascribes to it a number of tasks that, I shall now argue, cannot be attributed to a *Hobbesian* minimal state. It is usually taken for granted that prevention of fraud and enforcement of contract are tasks of the minimal state. Historically, the concept of the minimal or the "nightwatchman" state developed alongside that of "the system of natural liberty" or laissez-faire capitalism. Necessary conditions for perfect competition and its benefits include the effective prohibition of force and fraud and the enforcement of voluntary contract. Without these, the impressive theorems of welfare economics cannot

this to the "Protective State," which has as its central concern the enforcement of law.

22. The move from state provision of one collective good, security of person and possessions, to its provision of others may be blocked by pointing to asymmetries between goods that consist in the absence of invasion or harm (e.g., defense, pollution control, prevention of fraud) and goods that involve the provision of some benefit or positive service (e.g., public transportation). I am skeptical of a general asymmetry; support for this line of objection might, however, be found in Gauthier, *Morals by Agreement*, chap. 7. It should, of course, be noted that efficient state provision of one collective good is *not* an argument for inefficient attempts to provide others.

be proved. It may be natural for theorists to assume that the state has this "minimal" role of prohibiting force and fraud and enforcing voluntary agreements, and insofar as one is impressed by the welfare theorems (or depressed by the activities of governments) it is equally natural to claim that the state ought not to assume tasks beyond these "minimal" ones.

The Hobbesian state, by disarming its subjects, assures basic security of person and some possessions.[23] It would, however, be stretching the metaphor of swords to claim that by disarming its citizens the state also prevents fraud, which does not require weapons of any sort. Further, there is no plausible way to construe general disarmament as involving the state in the enforcement of contract.[24] Such tasks are supplemental to that of collecting the subjects' swords. Thus a *Hobbesian* minimal state – one rationalized in the manner suggested by Levin – will be limited, insofar as it remains "minimal", to disarming people and prohibiting force. The minimal state of Lockean natural rights theory or of welfare economics is not the minimal state of Hobbesian theory.

This point is important for understanding contemporary debates about the proper role of government. Consider the enforcement of voluntary contract. Why is it that the state should enforce voluntary agreements among people? Natural rights theorists might argue, after Nozick, that this is a task for private protective agencies and, consequently, given Nozick's famous argument, one of the tasks for the minimal state. This argument, whatever its merits for adherents to natural rights theories, will not do for Hobbesians, who will justify state enforcement of contracts only insofar as it produces benefits for all. If enforcement of agreements – or, for that matter, preven-

23. A "Lockean" minimal state protects the considerable (and unequal) holdings individuals may amass, given the nature of Lockean natural property rights and the limited constraints on initial acquisition. However, in a Hobbesian "state of nature," given the absence of natural property rights, it is unlikely that individuals would amass many possessions. In Hobbes's own account, they could amass no *property*, given that there are no moral or legal rights before the establishment of a Sovereign. Gauthier's neo-Hobbesian moral theory is quite different; see *Morals by Agreement*, chap. 7.

24. J. Roland Pennock interprets Levin as conceding to the Hobbesian state the establishment of the right to make contracts and, he presumes, that of eliminating fraud. Although Levin does not challenge this interpretation in his reply to Pennock, I think that the original article is unclear on these matters. See Pennock, "Correspondence," esp. 256–257, and Levin, "Reply to Pennock," both in *Philosophy and Public Affairs* 13, 3 (Summer 1984), 255–262, 263–267.

tion of fraud – is a private matter, with few or no external benefits, there is no Hobbesian rationale for attributing such a task to the state.

It turns out that enforcement of contract, as well as prevention of fraud, have third-party effects and are (impure) collective goods. Thus, the Hobbesian rationale for attributing these tasks to the state. However, regulations concerning product safety, product standards, and the like may also be rationalized thereby, and so may be conditions on enforceable contract. Most states do not enforce *any* agreement, even if voluntary. States may be justified in imposing conditions on the agreements it is willing to enforce, for this task is additional to that of disarming its subjects and prohibiting force, and it is justified only insofar as it offers collective benefits. The point is nicely made by Raz:

> By providing facilities for private arrangements between individuals the law helps individuals in pursuing ends of their choice. It does not impose its will on individuals but serves them in realizing their own will. . . .
>
> While doing so the law makes use of the facilities provided depend on observing various conditions. It does not allow individuals to invoke the protection of the law for any arrangement they may like. It creates frameworks within which individuals must make their arrangements and pursue their objectives if they are to enjoy legal protection. These restrictions are necessary to protect one party to an arrangement from being exploited by the other party, and to protect third parties from unfair consequences affecting them resulting from arrangements in which they did not participate. Hence the various restrictions on the freedom of contract, the limitations on the ways in which companies can be established and operate, etc.[25]

If we think of a Hobbesian minimal state as one that disarms its subjects and prohibits force, then prevention of fraud and enforcement of voluntary contract makes the state more than minimal.

The important point is that a minimal state rationalized in a Hobbist manner will provide a variety of collective goods. A Hobbesian rationale for government activity, once invoked in defense of a minimal state, takes on a life of its own. *Welfare states* have tasks additional to those of minimal states, notably the *redistribution* of goods. I argue that insofar as Hobbesian arguments provide rationales for minimal states, they do the same for some welfare states.

25. Raz, *The Authority of Law*, pp. 170–171.

Redistribution I understand as politically mandated and typically nonvoluntary alteration of the distribution of wealth and resources. The intended beneficiaries of redistribution can be any class or income group; it should not be supposed that redistribution is necessarily directed to the least advantaged. The *redistributive* function of the state is simply to redistribute resources.[26] It is especially this task of states that is controversial today, some people arguing that the state should redistribute wealth downward, others arguing against.[27]

Let us distinguish between *cooperative* and *noncooperative* redistribution, where cooperative redistribution is politically mandated alteration of the distribution of wealth and resources beneficial[28] to all affected. How is that possible? After all, redistribution involves taking from some and giving to others, an activity that would seem to be Pareto-inefficient if anything is.[29] If we distinguish between people's wealth and their interests, we may readily think of instances where loss of income can render someone better off. Ordinary exchange is the most obvious case in point. In terms of people's interests, sometimes all parties to a redistributive program may benefit *ex ante* or even *ex post* from the transfer of resources. The literature contains many analyses and defenses of such redistribution. It has been argued that some redistribution may be a form of nonvoluntary collective insurance.[30] Other redistribution may be necessary to give

---

26. This is what the Musgraves have called the "distribution function", contrasting it with allocation and stabilization functions. See Richard A. Musgrave and Peggy B. Musgrave, *Public Finance in Theory and Practice*, 4th ed. (New York: McGraw-Hill, 1984), chap. 1.

27. It turns out to be very difficult to ascertain how much redistribution actually goes on in most democracies, and who, if anyone, is the net beneficiary. The incentives for disguised (and inefficient) means of redistribution are significant.

28. Here when I talk of "benefits", "interests", and their cognates I speak restrictively and do *not* mean "preferences". The latter can be other-regarding and do not range only over human interests.

29. Redistribution is possibly wasteful in other ways. One of these may be an unproductive use of resources to bring about the desired transfers – Arthur Okun's "leaky bucket". Another may be the expenditure of resources by parties interested in securing redistributed resources for themselves. The latter activity has been called "rent-seeking" by political economists. See *Toward a Theory of the Rent-Seeking Society*, ed. J. Buchanan, R. Tollison, and G. Tullock (College Station: Texas A and M University Press, 1980). I shall not discuss complications resulting from these important inefficiencies.

30. Buchanan and Tullock, *The Calculus of Consent*, chap. 13; Richard Zeckhauser, "Risk Spreading and Distribution," in *Redistribution Through Public Choice*, ed. H. Hochman and G. Peterson (New York: Columbia University Press, 1974),

everyone a stake in the social order.[31] When we take into account status and relative standing, yet other forms of redistribution may be understood as cooperative in the above sense.[32] Cooperative redistribution may be justified in some circumstances by the same considerations that justify the tasks of minimal states: Such redistribution is a collective good. Let us say that a *libertarian welfare state*[33] is one that redistributes in cooperative ways. Then Hobbesian arguments for states provide a rationale for libertarian welfare states.

We may now understand further what is misleading about Levin's metaphors of swords and plows. Plows represent property, specifically physical, nonhuman means of production, and it is initially difficult to see why rational individuals would wish to turn over their plows to a state, barring unlikely economies of scale from state-run agricultural production. But if there is a rationale for state redistribution, albeit cooperative, some state control over the assets (e.g., plows) of individuals is required. We may understand the metaphor of "turning over of the plows" to the state as expressing this idea. Thus, insofar as rational individuals in a state of nature find certain redistributive programs mutually beneficial *ex ante*, they will consent to give the state some control over their "plows".

Further, the metaphor of plows is misleading insofar as it suggests that property rights are determinate and fully specified independently of the form of political organization (e.g., state). I do not deny that some stability of possession and limited ownership are possible prior to and independently of states or other forms of political organization. However, it seems clear that the *nature* and *extent* of (just) ownership in contemporary societies is in part dependent on state determination, regulation, and enforcement of property.[34] One need only think of inheritance or of patents and copyrights to see the point. Property law ideally facilitates private arrangements between

---

pp. 206–228; and Robert Goodin, *The Politics of Rational Man* (London and New York: Wiley, 1976), p. 115.

31. See Morris, "A Non-Egalitarian Defense of Redistribution," in *Social Justice, Bowling Green Studies in Applied Philosophy IV*, ed. M. Bradie and D. Braybrooke (Bowling Green, Ohio: Bowling Green State University, 1982), 68–84, as well as the references therein.

32. See Robert H. Frank, *Choosing the Right Pond: Human Behavior and the Quest for Status* (New York: Oxford University Press, 1985), esp. chap. 6.

33. The term comes from ibid., chap. 12.

34. But *only* in part. I stress that I do not deny that some of the just norms of ownership can exist prior to and independently of states.

individuals in ways that provide considerable benefits for all. This surely is the Hobbesian rationale for property generally, as well as for particular forms of ownership (e.g., private or collective property in the means of production, limited liability). Insofar as this is a rationale for state-assured protection of possessions, it is also a rationale for state regulation of the nature and extent of ownership rights – what is also expressed by the metaphor of "turning over of the plows".

The redistributive tasks of the libertarian welfare state need not be limited to those just mentioned. For at least some goods are essentially "manna from heaven", to employ the metaphor Nozick so effectively uses against defenders of redistribution.[35] Land and other natural resources are both finite and not in themselves the product of human labor. There is no reason to suppose that ownership of these resources ought to be treated by neo-Hobbesian theorists in the same way as property in the fruits of one's labor.[36] Collective ownership of such assets may be perfectly compatible with Hobbesian defenses of private ownership of other goods.

Cooperative redistribution, I have said, is the politically mandated alteration of the distribution of wealth and resources in a manner beneficial to all affected. And a libertarian welfare state is one that redistributes cooperatively. Let us call a *liberal welfare state* one that, in addition, redistributes noncooperatively to the least advantaged. There may also be Hobbesian arguments for liberal welfare states. Suppose people are not completely self-interested and care about the least advantaged. Then there may be some nonegoistic rationales for noncooperative redistribution. Nonegoists may take an interest in the interest of the least advantaged. If the former are relatively well-off, they may wish to transfer some of their assets to the latter. The well-off, or at least some of them, may wish to do this, however, only if others follow suit. The well-off may have a collective action problem, a solution of which might be state redistribution.[37] Suppose

35. Nozick, *Anarchy, State, and Utopia*, p. 198.
36. I owe this thought originally to the late Alan Donagan. For relevant but different considerations, see also Hillel Steiner, "The Natural Right to the Means of Production," *Philosophical Quarterly* 27 (1977), 41–49.
37. This is the "collective charity" argument of Harold M. Hochman and John D. Rodgers. See their "Pareto Optimal Redistribution," *American Economic Review* 59 (1969), 542–547, as well as the extensive literature their idea provoked. See also Nozick, *Anarchy, State, and Utopia*, pp. 265–268, for some criticisms of this line of argument.

individuals care not so much about their relative share of the benefits of society or their relative status as about the pattern of distribution of goods. Then there may be a nonegoistic rationale for noncooperative redistribution.[38] Suppose we have good reason for establishing a *democratic* state, one with equal rights of citizenship. Some rationale would thereby be provided for the noncooperative redistribution that is consequent to citizens' exercising their rights to vote.[39] It is hard to see how neo-Hobbesian *theory* would rule out a libertarian or liberal welfare state.

State paternalism I characterize as state interference with the liberty of an individual for the sake of that individual's interests or well-being. An act of state or a law would be paternalistic, then, depending on its object or rationale. Seat belt legislation designed to get drivers to protect themselves would be paternalistic unless the real object were to save the public the expense of the greater medical costs incurred by imprudent drivers.[40] The *tutelary* function of the state is to ensure that individuals act prudently for their own sakes.[41]

Can Hobbesian defenses of the state provide a rationale for paternalistic laws? It is normally assumed that they cannot. But this depends in part on the characterization of individuals. Even if rationality is understood instrumentally, people can fail to be rational, for example, to take efficient means to their ends. Their ends may not be "coherent" (i.e., connected or transitive). The assumption that agents are rational must, in neo-Hobbesian theory, be normative. People

38. Lester Thurow, "The Income Distribution as a Pure Public Good," *Quarterly Journal of Economics* 85 (1971), 327–336.
39. See J. Buchanan, "The Political Economy of Franchise in the Welfare State," in *Capitalism and Freedom*, ed. R. Selden (Charlottesville: University of Virginia Press, 1975), pp. 52–77.
40. It can sometimes be difficult to determine what legislation actually is paternalistic. For instance, requiring hockey players to wear helmets may actually be nonpaternalistic. See Schelling, "Hockey Helmets, Daylight Saving, and Other Binary Choices," in his *Micromotives and Macrobehavior*, pp. 211–243.
41. It is important to distinguish clearly the ways in which paternalistic and nonpaternalistic practices affect people's interests. Prohibitions of theft are not paternalistic, even though our interests are secured thereby. For it is, at most, the *system* of rules forbidding theft that is in my interests. More precisely, it is the state's prohibition of theft by others that is in my interests, just as the state's prohibition of theft on my part is in the interests of others. It is not in my interest to refrain from taking the possessions of others; this, however, I must do if I am to secure my possessions against others. By contrast, the law requiring me to wear a helmet when I ride a motorcycle or to save part of my income for my retirement can be paternalistic if the state requires something of me for my interest. (Recall that interests, well-being, and prudence are not, in these contexts, to be understood in terms of desires or preferences.) The term 'tutelary function' I may owe to William Galston.

may suffer from weakness of will, or myopia, or simply intransitivity of preference.[42] Children certainly do, but adults may as well. If so, there may be a Hobbesian rationale for state paternalism. It depends on how rational we actually are.

The alternative analysis of the Hobbesian state of nature that I have given to Levin's account undermines his and similar defenses of minimal states. Neo-Hobbesian defenders of the minimal state may instead wish to argue that the inefficiency of state provision of collective goods, our apparent inability to control states, and their tendency to redistribute to the wrong groups (e.g., the powerful and wealthy) may suffice to condemn welfare states. This may be true.[43]

Suppose, however, that Levin's analysis is correct, that the Hobbesian state of nature is something like an Assurance Game. What then? This consequence would be pleasing to anarchists, who could then argue that no state, minimal or other, would be needed to provide security of person and possessions. Suppose the anarchist is mistaken, however, and that minimal states are necessary to collect all of the swords, even though no one wishes to use his or her sword for predatory purposes. Why would minimal states be *justified* in so doing? The argument would have to be that states are ideally suited (1) to inform people about the preferences of others – that no one most prefers unilateral predation – and (2) to gather all the weapons. Suppose this is true, that the state is uniquely suited to carry out these tasks. Why might this be so? It might be that gathering and distributing information about people's preferences is too costly for any individual or small group of individuals. Further, collecting all the swords might be an activity that benefits from important economies of scale; it would be much cheaper to let a central agency do this than to have individuals melt down their own swords. Why, then, would a state be justified in disseminating the information about preferences and in collecting the swords? Surely the justification would have to be that this is a collective good. But if that is the case, then the justification of this state function carries over to the other tasks I have

---

42. Admitting that people are not always fully rational is not inconsistent with rational choice theory. The literature, starting with Jon Elster, is now enormous. See the references in Chapter 3 to game-theoretic assumptions of irrationality (or "irrationality").

43. Questions of efficiency, as I have said, are quite complex. In the context of a debate about the "minimal" functions of government, we should be careful not to assume that governments are much more efficient at providing defense or police protection than they are for other services (e.g., education, "welfare" services, regulation of industry).

discussed. If states are thus justified in these minimal tasks, they will also be justified in the other activities discussed.

Natural rights accounts of the state appear to justify at most minimal states. (As I argued earlier, they may not even justify this much, depending on the nature and strength of the assumptions about moral rights.) Some have hoped to justify the minimal state on Hobbesian assumptions, but this attempt fails. Neo-Hobbesian political theory focuses on indivisible and nonexcludable benefits, and these may be provided by welfare states just as much as by minimal states.[44]

If the implications of these two sorts of theories are as different as I have argued, it is likely that the matter of the proper functions of government is more controversial than that of the attributes of states covered in Chapters 7 and 8. The claims of states to sovereignty seem to fail independently of controversies about justice, and nationality offers no independent support for the state's territoriality or for common ways of determining membership.[45] But the question of the proper functions of government seems to turn very much on the nature of justice. The extent of state redistribution of resources will depend, for example, on the nature of just ownership and the demands of justice regarding distribution. I probably need not belabor this point, given the focus on justice in recent Anglo-American political philosophy.

Much, then, turns on the nature of justice and its demands, and I have not said much about this matter in this volume. The claims of some states to rule independently of justice are not vindicated, in my judgment. Note, however, that my stress on efficiency does, to a considerable extent, moderate the centrality of justice. The justice of some objective or concern will not be sufficient to justify a govern-

---

44. Neo-Hobbesian *moral* theory does so as well. In "A Hobbesian Welfare State?" pp. 670–673, I also argue against minimalist understandings of the contractarian moral theory. Regarding Gauthier's theory, see Danielson, "The Visible Hand of Morality," *Canadian Journal of Philosophy* 18 (1988), 357–384.

45. Solutions to the problems of membership and territoriality may, of course, depend heavily on the nature of justice. But I am tempted to argue here that most of our present accounts of justice – whatever we think about their relative merits – do not have the resources to address these questions. Most theories of justice seem to ignore these issues or to assume that they are not problematic. As noted earlier, Rawls restricts his attentions to a society "conceived for the time being as a closed system isolated from other societies", and he assumes that "the boundaries of these schemes are given by the notion of a self-contained national community" (*A Theory of Justice*, pp. 8, 457; see other references in Chapter 2).

ment's pursuit of it. To give a simple example: Where the likely costs of apprehending minor criminals are exorbitant or simply beyond the resources of a state, there may be no sufficient justification to arrest them. One must, of course, be very careful with examples like these, as the likely costs of not pursuing wrongdoers, even minor ones, can be significant. One general point is that resources are finite, and no state is likely to be able to secure justice perfectly. But costs aside, governments suffer from institutional problems, and not all will be suited to all tasks we may want done. Further, cultural and contextual differences may be significant (compare the American, Canadian, French, and Italian bureaucracies).

My emphasis, in this chapter and elsewhere, on collective action problems and difficulties in individual provision of collective goods has implications for these issues. I have argued that states are justified to the extent that they are just and efficient. Governments' efficiency in addressing collective action problems and assisting in the provision of collective goods is likely to determine their capacity to satisfy the efficiency constraint. So there may be reason to conjecture that most, if not virtually all, of the proper tasks of legitimate states will involve collective goods of some sort. So tasks aimed at securing divisible and excludable goods for some, without benefit to others, may not be legitimate tasks of governments.[46]

Establishing this general conclusion, however, would require considerable work. Certainly, adjudicating the debates about the nature of value would become important (Chapter 5). If we are realists about value, it is easier to see how certain forms of state paternalism might be justified. If we are agent-neutral realists, and we believe the suffering of any person is a consideration favoring action, we are likely to endorse more redistribution of wealth than might be supported were value only agent-relative. I suggested that these issues about value were not likely to have significant implications for general issues concerning the legitimacy of states, their claims to authority, and the like. (All the positions I outlined in Section 5.2 appeared to be compatible with the general balance of reasons account of rationality, as well as with the revisionist accounts I considered in Section 5.4.) As I also conjectured, they do seem likely to affect matters concerning the proper tasks of government. So establishing the proper

---

46. The account is very simple and passes over many complexities (e.g., the provision of most collective goods by government involves providing divisible and excludable goods for some).

tasks of a particular government is a complex matter, and it is not to be expected that much more can be said here.

I have been discussing the proper tasks of government, issues of considerable controversy in the present day. I should mention that little I have said has implications for another contemporary debate, namely, that over "privatization" of state functions. It was often thought that government provision of some good meant government production or manufacture of that good. So if garbage collection or education are proper functions of government, they must be provided directly by government. But this conclusion does not follow.[47] Garbage and other "public" services can be "privatized", that is, assigned to nongovernment agencies, without their ceasing to be tasks or functions of government. Nothing I have said, beyond endorsement of abstract considerations of efficiency, has any specific implications for the question of privatization. It may be that, in particular circumstances, justice and efficiency are best served by government-provided schools and refuse collections, and in others, by private agencies contracted to do the job. It may even be that changes in liability laws prove to be efficient and fair ways of securing certain goods. Such issues are to be distinguished from the one we have been discussing. The point should be obvious, but some commentators seem to believe that privatization is the key to reducing the scope of state powers and activities. A government whose tasks have largely been privatized but whose budget and resources have not been diminished has not, in my sense, had its functions reduced.

9.2 PROBLEMS OF INSTITUTIONAL DESIGN

Determining the proper tasks of government is only one part of the general theory of political institutions. Another, not entirely separable, concerns their design. How are institutions to be structured so they do what we want them to do, all the while thwarting abuses of power? Designing institutions to do what we want involves enabling them to do so – giving them the means to accomplish their tasks. But minimizing abuses requires preventing institutions from pursuing other ends. These aims are, to a certain degree, opposing. Structuring institutions to do certain things invariably allows other ends to be

47. In the same way that the socialist doctrine of collective ownership of the means of production does not entail government-managed or -administered factories.

pursued. Enabling them to accomplish their assigned tasks makes it harder to prevent them from realizing others. There are inescapable and important trade-offs in the design of political institutions.

Part of the explanation for this is that the problems institutions are meant to address reappear at a higher level. Problems of cooperation that lead us to want government may often lead to problems in getting government to do what we want – for instance, we may find it difficult to cooperate against abuses by our governors. Recall that I suggested that one advantage of constrained government over "private protective agencies" is that such agencies may behave unjustly once they have accumulated sufficient power, whereas governments may be more easily controlled.[48] But some of the features of dominant protective agencies that allow them to exploit "clients" can permit governments to do the same. In addition, considerations of efficiency loom large, and government solutions may sometimes create new problems. Institutional solutions can sometimes be worse than the original problem. This is not an essay on the theory of institutional design, and I have little novel to suggest in any event. Much of our general wisdom on these questions is ancient, as notes the German sociologist Heinrich Popitz:

Only infrequently in the history of society has it been possible even to entertain in a purposeful and consequential manner the question of how to limit institutionalised violence. Basically, this has only happened in the Greek polis, in republican Rome, in a few other city states, and in the history of the modern constitutional state. And the answers to that question have been astonishingly similar: the postulate of the sovereignty of the law and of the equality of all before the law ("isonomia"); the notion of placing basic constraints upon the formation of norms ("fundamental right"); distinctive provinces of competence (division of powers, federalism); procedural norms (decisions by collective bodies, publicity, official avenues for redness); norms of occupancy (turn-taking, elections); and norms of the public sphere (freedom of opinion, freedom of assembly).[49]

I shall not address these issues of institutional design in any systematic way.[50] Some of my reflections on sovereignty and political power, however, have implications for these abstract questions. There

---

48. I also argue, in Chapter 2, that the historical counterparts of these protective agencies are typically much less respectful of people's rights and interests than the associations of libertarian anarchist lore.
49. Quoted and translated by Poggi, *The State*, pp. 78–79.
50. See the series inaugurated by Goodin, ed., *The Theory of Institutional Design* (Cambridge: Cambridge University Press, 1996).

is a practical problem of establishing and maintaining institutional structures that effectively constrain government. As noted by Popitz, the problem is not unique to modern states; although, given their relatively greater concentrations of powers, it may be a more difficult problem today than in earlier times. The suggestion is that the failure of relations of powers to constitute an ordering, which we saw when we examined Hobbes's regress argument, can in fact be of some use in understanding one way governments can be constrained.

The failure of power relations in large societies to be transitive parallels the intransitivity of aggregations of preferences or choices studied by social choice theorists.[51] Democratic government is set up to permit changes of policy, personnel, and even governmental structure in response to weighted shifts of public opinion. Given the existence of collective preference cycles, we can anticipate certain changes regularly occurring in the absence of stabilizing institutional arrangements. To counteract some of these, one might devise institutions that would tend to break various cycles.[52] However, one similarly might want to take advantage of, or even exacerbate, certain cyclical tendencies.

Consider one common way of constraining the powers of government, namely, division of powers. A problem with dividing government is, as Hobbes argued, that one part may become more powerful than the other(s), thus defeating the very purpose of division.[53] For any two divided parts of government, suppose (falsely) either one more powerful than the other, or they are equally powerful. If the latter, the purpose of establishing government is defeated; if the former, the purpose of dividing powers is lost, as the more powerful part can dominate the weaker. This argument, as we have seen, is part of Hobbes's defense of classical sovereignty, against all attempts to limit the power (or authority) of the sovereign. But as we have seen also, power relations are typically multiattributive, and we lack a decent cardinal, fully comparable measure of power. So cycles are to be anticipated, and we need not expect a single most powerful power to emerge from the competition of the divided powers of government.

Suppose we divide the powers of central government, concerned as we are that the accumulated powers of government can lead to

51. See the references in Chapter 7.
52. For the American constitutional system, see the interesting collection of paper in *"The Federalist Papers" and the New Institutionalism,* ed. B. Grofman and D. Wittman (New York: Agathon Press, 1989).
53. See Chapter 7.

tyranny. Then we can structure these powers so that each has incentives to resist the aggrandizement of the others. Divided powers thus can "check" the growth and tyrannical tendencies of government. If there are several separate powers, however, this may not work. For just as individuals can join together to form coalitions in order to dominate some other party, so can groups. So some of the divided powers may gang up on the others, defeating the purpose we had in mind. Here is where cycles can be exploited. We can structure things so that coalitions of divided powers are unstable, at least with regard to certain questions. Consider, for instance, the American separation of legislative and executive powers, both constrained by an independent judiciary. Each branch of government is such that a coalition with another, to restrict the powers of a third, will often be unstable in the manner that coalitions on problems of division frequently are unstable. This is not to say, of course, that the U.S. system of "checks and balances" works as the civic texts would have it. Still open is the question of the success of the Federalists' attempt at controlling American government by the judicious design of institutions. Many theorists, alarmed at the growth of democratic governments in this century, especially since World War II, are skeptical.[54] Others are worried by the inappropriateness of much of the output of governments. My point, however, is theoretical, and concerns the value of cyclical collective preferences. It is not that our understanding of government permits us to design and fine-tune institutions so that they do exactly what we wish; on the contrary, it is clear that we are not proficient at this art.[55] Rather, mine is the theoretical point that cycles can be used to our ends, especially that of controlling and constraining government.

54. For a survey of the literature on the growth of government, see Dennis C. Mueller, *Public Choice II* (Cambridge: Cambridge University Press, 1989), chap. 17.
55. Our lack of expertise and the possible limits of knowledge and capacities here can be reasons for investing more in institutional theory. Goodin argues that "the claim that the social world allows little scope for intentional change and direct design actually expands rather than contracts the scope of theories of indirect – that is, properly *institutional* – design." See his discussion in "Institutions and their Design," in *The Theory of Institutional Design*, esp. pp. 27–30.

Chapter 10

States: Pretenses, powers, prospects

This treatise, therefore, in so far as it deals with political science, shall be nothing other than an attempt *to comprehend and portray the state as an inherently rational entity.* – Hegel

States, I have said, are complex and distinctive territorial forms of political organization, characteristic of modernity, that claim sovereignty over their realms and independence from other states. My initial analysis was that they are to be understood in terms of a number of interrelated features:

1. *Continuity in time and space.* The institutions of the state endure over time, surviving changes in leadership, and governing a definite and distinct *territory.*
2. *Transcendence.* The state constitutes a unitary public order distinct from, and superior to, both ruled and rulers, one capable of agency.
3. *Political organization.* The institutions through which the state acts (e.g., the government, the judiciary, the bureaucracy, the police) are differentiated from other political organizations and associations, are formally coordinated one with another, and are relatively centralized. Relations of authority are hierarchical. Rule is *direct* and *territorial;* it is relatively pervasive and penetrates society legally and administratively.
4. *Authority.* The state is *sovereign,* that is, the ultimate source of political authority in its territory, and it claims a monopoly of the use of legitimate force within its territory. Its jurisdiction extends directly to all residents of that territory. In its relations to other public orders, the state is autonomous.
5. *Allegiance.* The state expects and receives the loyalty of its mem-

bers and of the permanent inhabitants of its territory, a loyalty that assumes precedence over that formerly owed to family, clan, commune, lord, bishop, pope, or emperor. Members of a state are the primary subjects of its laws and have a general obligation to obey by virtue of their membership.

It is customary, especially in Anglo-American political philosophy, to contrast the state with "anarchy" or "the state of nature", and to take these to exhaust all possibilities.[1] To justify the (or a) state then requires showing its superiority to "the state of nature".[2] This is a mistake, and things become more complicated when "anarchy or state" is seen to be a false dilemma, which becomes apparent as soon as one contrasts states with medieval forms of political organization. While states share some features with the classical *polis* and with Rome, they are strikingly different from the complex political arrangements of medieval Europe.[3] Once this is realized, states must be understood as modern and distinctive forms of political organization and contrasted with others (e.g., cities, city leagues, empires, Christendom). Matters are even more complicated when states are understood in terms of a number of interrelated and complex attributes. It is not surprising, then, that I have no simple, general conclusion. I cannot pronounce for or against states *simpliciter*. Even considered abstractly and generally, the state is too complex a form of political organization to permit simple conclusions. But I do reach some judgments.

Justification of forms of political organization, I have suggested, has to do with justice and efficiency. A state is legitimate to the extent that it is reasonably just and minimally efficient. This sort of account is not uncontroversial. Partisans of what I have called rational justification will reject it, as will consensualists, who will require consent of the governed for state legitimacy and will reject the sufficiency of

1. "Why the state? Why not anarchy?" as Keith Simmons once innocently asked me. See Nozick, *Anarchy, State, and Utopia,* p. 4, and Wolff, *An Introduction to Political Philosophy,* chap. 1.
2. In contemporary American political or economic theory "the market" sometimes is associated with states of nature or "anarchy". The justification of states then is thought to require "market failure".
3. Perhaps the education of philosophers encourages the neglect of medieval forms of political organization. We move from the works of Plato and Aristotle almost immediately to Hobbes, Locke, and Rousseau. The tendency to think they were all talking about the same thing is revealed, and reinforced, by the translations of *'polis'* by 'state' (or even *'Politeia'* by 'Republic').

justice and efficiency. I reject consensualism, but I have not pressed this matter here. For one thing, the issues in moral theory are very complex. For another, my account of legitimacy *could* be adapted by many consensualists: Justice, on their account, requires the consent of the governed.[4] Also, although I adopt an account of justification that may be easier to satisfy in some respects than consensualism, it turns out that my conclusions about the powers of legitimate states are not very different from those of many contemporary consensualists. States, on my view, turn out to have inflated conceptions of themselves, and many of their claimed powers will not be justified.

States claim sovereignty; that is, they claim to be the ultimate source of political authority in their territory. I have argued extensively against the credibility of this claim; even legitimate states, that is, reasonably just and efficient ones, will not be sovereign—or, if one prefers, the sovereignty they possess is very different from that claimed. They may have a variety of powers and immunities, but it seems misleading to appropriate traditional notions of sovereignty for these. The main difficulty is that the authority claimed by states is too extensive to be justified. (Also, the conditions for classical and limited sovereignty are not likely to obtain.) Similarly, our political obligations to states, even when legitimate, are not what they are claimed to be. It may well be said that we have a general obligation to do what the state commands, and to do it because so commanded, but this claim is not credible either. Here my judgment is likely to prove less controversial; many political and legal theorists now reject the general obligation to obey the law. We morally ought to obey legitimate states much of the time; the laws and policies of just and efficient states, presumably, will often ask us to do what we morally ought to do. Occasionally, we should obey simply because the state has so decided. But it is not likely that all subjects ought to obey all laws all of the time. This is to expect too much, even of legitimate states.

Political obligations are only part of the allegiance states expect of their members. Their additional demands, however, do not seem fully credible even to themselves. For states typically ask to be loved as embodiments or allies of a people or nation (the "nation-state"), suggesting that without these associations they could not expect this

---

4. If our rights are basic and protect choices, then consent may be required. Alternatively, if some of our interest-protecting rights protect autonomy, then consent may again be needed.

loyalty. It is hard to imagine people giving up their lives for "the state", even *their* state. Very often they may, in effect, do just that, but they usually think of themselves as fighting "for King and country" or *"la nation"*. "The state", by itself, is too cold and impersonal to die for. Perhaps, like many associations, it is also too contingent and optional a thing for such sacrifices.[5] The "nation-state", however, may elicit the requisite loyalties. The marked tendency to use terms like 'nation' to designate the state may facilitate this association (or confusion). But once we are clear about the differences between states and nations, we can ask about our loyalties to the former. These loyalties will then be found to be less than states should like. Certainly, they rarely are thought by most people to take precedence over loyalties to family, clan, community, country, nation, or, for some, pope. Occasionally a state manages to associate itself relatively successfully with a national group (or to construct one). But even then the emergence of the "nation-state" typically requires the assimilation or repression of national minorities and some falsification or dissimulation of the historical record.[6] The state's association with nation reveals its inability, by itself, to inspire us and win our hearts.

States govern *directly* and *territorially*. These aspects of their governance may prove more resilient than others. There is much convenience to both, but their bases and their necessity remain opaque. There are alternative ways of organizing political life, and it is not clear that we need remain limited to direct and territorial governance. As I shall suggest presently, there may be alternatives we should consider in the near future.

On my view, states, their pretenses exposed, may nevertheless be legitimate. It is possible to imagine reasonably just and efficient states, and some of ours may approximate this standard. Assessing the efficiency of state institutions – or of firms, for that matter – is very difficult, and we do not have a very complete picture of justice, especially for complex institutions. So this standard of legitimacy remains imprecise. Still, we can imagine some states could achieve it.

---

5. "Dying for one's country, which usually one does not choose, assumes a moral grandeur which dying for the Labour Party, the American Medical Association, or perhaps even Amnesty International can not rival, for these are all bodies one can join or leave at easy will." Anderson, *Imagined Communities*, p. 144. Anderson's analysis of the association of sacrifice with purity and fatality is characteristically insightful and bears reflection.
6. France and Japan, perhaps the best contemporary examples of nation-states, are cases in point.

I have argued against some powerful claims to the contrary. Legitimate states, even if they are not sovereign and cannot credibly demand our undivided loyalty and devotion, have powers, and they may use these for certain purposes. They may possess *political power* in Locke's sense: "*a Right* of making Laws with Penalties . . . for the Regulating and Preserving of Property, and of employing the force of the Community, in the Execution of such Laws, and in the defence of the Common-wealth from Foreign Injury, and all this only for the Publick Good."[7] We should add the power to adjudicate disputes and to provide mechanisms for collective decisions (e.g., contracts, corporate law, local governments, parliaments). States also have a variety of powers that enable them to facilitate and support practices (e.g., certain business ventures, churches, charities, educational institutions, familial relations). They may establish standards of various sorts. And as I emphasize in Chapter 7, they may also influence behavior simply by persuading, educating, and advising.

Legitimate states, then, may have a number of powers. And, while lacking all the authority they traditionally claim, states may nevertheless exercise these powers justly. Legitimate states may thus pursue, apprehend, and punish wrongdoers; they may requisition funds for their own defense and the interests of their members; they may protect members of groups who have been systematically exploited; they may issue rules and regulations for the protection of the environment; they may institute and support programs for the prevention of disease; they may counsel people to be moderate in their consumption of tobacco and drugs, or fattening fast foods; they may speak in favor of the rights of persons throughout the world. This list is illustrative; the details will depend on circumstance and the nature of justice. It may very well be that some legitimate states are permitted to support particular redistributive or paternalistic programs while others are not, the difference lying in context and history. The point is that legitimate states will have considerable powers even if their authority is much less than claimed.

A striking thing about this conclusion is that the powers of states are justified much in the way that the powers and public acts of other agents are justified. Nothing much turns on the fact that an act is an act of state. A state is justified in pursuing wrongdoers, helping the poor, or putting out fires in the same ways as other agents. Consid-

---

7. *Second Treatise of Government*, chap. 1, para. 3, p. 268. (Recall Locke's expansive understanding of 'property'.)

erations of justice and efficiency are determining. There is nothing special about the state's performance of these tasks. Two objections come immediately to mind. It will be said that the state is special as it puts out fires and helps the poor *with the resources of others*. And, second, others – "private" persons – are not *authorized* to do these sorts of tasks. There is some truth in both objections, which I now address in a somewhat circuitous manner.

One reason we should expect a legitimate state to be justified in carrying out some of the tasks mentioned has to do with our expectations. There are many tasks best carried out by a single agency or group of persons. Often, coping with disasters, prosecuting wars, and assisting the injured are best done by a single agent. We expect states to do these sorts of things; and when they do them, we facilitate their acts, at the least by not interfering. Suppose there were no such expectations; suppose instead that some other agent was, in each case, expected by most people to carry out these tasks. Then *these others*, when just and efficient, will be justified in doing so. That is an implication of my account, and one I willingly accept. The justification of state activity turns on its justice and efficiency, which depend to some extent on our expectations. In the absence of state institutions, individuals may often be justified in assuming certain tasks (e.g., organizing fire brigades, directing the defense of the community, assisting the indigent). Suppose this is done justly and efficiently, and that it is not expected that governmental agencies could do better; then there would be no justification in assuming these tasks.

It is said that states use the resources of others acquired, for instance, by taxation or conscription. This is largely true, although it is important to remember that many state activities require comparatively few resources (e.g., encouraging moderation in the consumption of drugs, regulating a system of weights and measures, allocating airwaves). There is also a difficult question as to the ownership of the resources in question. In olden times the monarch or Sovereign might have claimed the realm as his or her own (*"l'Etat c'est à moi"*). This claim may not be credible, but may not some of the natural resources of states be their property? It is certain that taxation involves appropriation of the *holdings* or *possessions* of others; but it is not necessarily their *property*. Determining who owns the wealth expropriated by legitimate states for just purposes is not a simple matter. Theories that would have everything "privately" owned by individuals, prior to and independently of states and law, must count taxation as theft, but I have challenged these sorts of accounts. The difficult questions cannot be resolved here. But part of the objection that states use resources belonging to others begs the question regarding ownership.

I have claimed there is nothing special about the state's powers and that others may often be justified in carrying out tasks associated traditionally with states, provided they satisfy the same standards I impose on states. States, it is said, command the resources of others to carry out their work; may individuals do the same? I do not see why not. If in some community – either part of a larger state or some other political system or in a stateless world – various groups or agencies carry out certain tasks justly and efficiently, then they may be equally justified in using the resources of others. The Church used to exact a tithe from persons or parishes, and in some places continues to. On my view, were this done justly, for just and efficient purposes, it would be as legitimate as the state's taxation.

It was said that states are *authorized* to do certain things and that others are not. So, on this view, even if other agencies could do as well or better, they could not legitimately do so. In effect, I deny this. It is an implication of the story I have told that the state's position here is not unique. It depends on how well it does, and this depends to a certain extent on our expectations. I have not, unfortunately, said much about "authorization", largely because I find myself still unclear about what this involves in these contexts, at least once consent has been removed as a necessary condition for legitimacy.[8] It may be that authorization in these contexts is to be understood largely in terms of consensus and expectations. General agreement – in the sense of consensus, not consent – may be all that need be involved, but I cannot explore these issues here. In the absence of a more systematic treatment of authorization, I merely conjecture that states, even when legitimate, are no more authorized to carry out their tasks than other agencies who act with equal justice and efficiency.

---

8. Hobbes's original account of political authority and of the unity of a multitude in terms of the individual or agency authorized is worth studying. But it is unclear how the notion of authorization should be interpreted once Hobbes's eliminativist account of the will is abandoned (as it should be). On authorization, see Gauthier, *The Logic of Leviathan: The Moral and Political Theory of Thomas Hobbes* (Oxford: Clarendon Press, 1969), chap. 4, and Hampton, *Hobbes and the Social Contract Tradition*, chap. 5.

Does not a state possess, or at least claim, a monopoly on legitimate force? I have agreed to consider this Weberian attribute a characteristic of states. This monopoly is now associated with the state by so many that it would be odd not to consider it part of our concept. I argued that although states typically rely on force, the degree to which they do, especially when they are widely believed to be legitimate, is exaggerated. Regimes that need rely principally on force are not always very stable. The state's claim to monopolize *legitimate* force is one with its claim to the sweeping authority we have examined at length. Such a claim is not credible. It is a claim that no force may justifiably be employed by someone if it is not accepted or authorized by the state. To begin to be plausible, partisans of this extreme thesis must count silence as implicit authorization.[9] But even then it does not seem plausible. Imagine some act of private force, where some agents restrained others, justly and efficiently, and suppose it is not permitted by the state. If the reasons for disallowing the private act are not sound – for instance, worries about inciting others, procedural concerns – it is not clear what reasons we could have for regarding the act as illegitimate. The conclusion is similar to that reached for the other normative powers of states. They claim too much, and most states – certainly all legitimate ones – can get by without everything they claim.

Is this thing still a *state*? I noted earlier that Nozick seemed able at most to justify something like a state, which, however, lacked a number of properties characteristic of states (see my appendix to Chapter 6). Are the "states" I think (can be) legitimate *states*? They are not sovereign and possess considerably less authority than they claim. States assert that their directives are reasons for their members; their decisions they understand, not as "Counsell, but Command".[10] But they are mistaken in this, even if we have a variety of good reasons to follow most of the rules of legitimate states. If the state is to be understood in terms of the characteristics I summarized at the beginning of this chapter, legitimate "states" lacking many of these will cease to be genuine states.

9. Just as fans of the sovereignty of the "Queen in Parliament" must count its silence as tacit authorization of common law.
10. ". . . addressed to one formerly obliged to obey him [who commands]", where command is "where a man saith, *Doe this*, or *Doe not this*, without expecting other reason than the Will of him that sayeth it." Hobbes, *Leviathan*, chap. 26, p. 183, and chap. 25, p. 176.

I have not sought to "define" the state, largely because of skeptics' doubts about definitions, so I shall not initiate a discussion of the essential and accidental properties of states. Once we are clear about the sorts of attributes this distinctive modern form of political organization has claimed for itself, it no longer matters much whether it continues to be called a "state" once it is seen without all its clothes and with all its pretenses exposed. Two centuries ago a collection of British colonies, self-described as commonwealths and states, formed a league or federation. Their treaty was the ill-fated Articles of Confederation of 1777, thought of by some as the first American constitution. Its second article stated: "Each state retains its sovereignty, freedom and independence, and every Power, Jurisdiction and right, which is not by this confederation expressly delegated to the United States, in Congress assembled." A decade later, the same states became "the United States of America" through an act of "We the People of the United States". The subunits of this new federal state – what would be provinces or departments elsewhere – are still called "states". Similarly, we may come to recognize the pretensions of our states but persist in calling them by their old name, just as New York and Massachusetts are deemed states or commonwealths.

More interesting than the evolving meaning of terms are the possible further transformations of our states. I have denied the state's claims to authority and have expressed skepticism about the sources of its territoriality and its characteristic ways of determining membership. Some of the changes that may be brought about by recent developments in the European Union, formerly the European Community, may transform Western European states radically. The development of European law has already instituted significant changes. Other possible changes are suggested, for instance, in a proposal for addressing the problems of Northern Ireland, discussed recently by the columnist William Pfaff:

> It is the condominium or shared-sovereignty solution. It has functioned satisfactorily in the past, in places divided by colonial history, or by dynastic or ethnic claims, most recently in the New Hebrides islands, now the Republic of Vanuatu which between 1887 and 1980 were under joint Anglo-French sovereignty.
>
> The condominium solution for Northern Ireland would make it legally part of both nations [i.e., states], permit its citizens to choose either Irish or British nationality [i.e., citizenship], to vote in the national elections of the chosen country, carry its passport, attend its universities and move freely throughout Britain, Ireland, and Northern Ireland.

Local affairs in Northern Ireland would be governed by local assemblies. Laws would be enforced by two systems of courts, British and Irish, each with jurisdiction over those who had claimed its nationality and guarantor of the rights of those persons. There could be parallel school systems, or a united Ulster system or all three.

Defense and external affairs would be provided jointly by London and Dublin. The new Northern Ireland would be the territory of both, its citizens the citizens of one or the other nation [i.e., state].[11]

I do not know whether this suggestion addresses the problems of Northern Ireland fairly.[12] But that it is proposed shows some of the transformations of states that may be to come. Whether they will continue to be states is less interesting than what they will look like. Hegel's skepticism about philosophy's capacity to transcend its time and designate the future is probably right, even if his skepticism of philosophical attempts "to construct *a state as it ought to be*" is to be questioned.[13] Our coming to see our states as they are, pretenses and all, may nevertheless have an effect on the shape of things to come.

I started with expressions of concern about the evils of states, puzzlement at the emergence of their normative properties, and alienation from their world. I am not entirely certain how my motivating concerns and worries have been addressed by my study. The evils of states have all been gross violations of justice, so this concern is addressed abstractly by my account of legitimacy.[14] The normative properties of states remain puzzling, but many I have argued are not justified. It is our alienation from the state that is the most intractable of my worries. The nation and the community offer answers to this concern, but their association with states is contingent and precarious.[15] Perhaps this alienation is with us and we should adjust. Adapting Benedict Anderson's remark, maybe we should come to think of states much as we think of "the Labour Party, the American

---

11. William Pfaff, "For Ulster, Shared Rule Might Be the Only Way," *International Herald Tribune,* 24 July 1996.
12. And I do not know whether it might work for Jerusalem. The joint suzerainty of Andorra, held by the President of France and the bishop of Urgel, Spain, is, admittedly, a special case.
13. Hegel's well-known views are expressed in the Preface to the *Elements of the Philosophy of Right.*
14. Some accounts of justice may not be able to condemn some of these evils. But I pass over this point. See my "Justice, Reasons, and Moral Standing."
15. In some parts of the world, cities offer an alternative object of affection and loyalty. But that is a story for another time. See A. K. Bierman, *The Philosophy of Urban Existence: a Prolegomenon* (Athens: Ohio University Press, 1973), esp. chap. 3.

Medical Association, or perhaps even Amnesty International". We will not have the same warm feelings we may have for our friends, kin, and nation, but when states are well structured and well behaved, we may come to feel somewhat more comfortable with them and to have greater appreciation for them. Perhaps by that time they will also look very different.

Index

Index

Index

folk theorem, 95–6
Foot, Philippa, 121n, 159n, 161n
force, 75, 176, 201–4, 266n; see also
    monopoly of legitimate force
Frank, Robert H., 97n, 278n
free rider, 66, 82
free rider problem, 90, 123–4, 131
Friedman, David, 62, 65, 66n, 98n
Friedman, Milton, 64n
Fudenberg, Drew, 96n

Galston, William A., 164n, 280n
game theory, 80–98, 116, 271, 281n
games
    Assurance, 271–2, 281, see also
        assurance, problem of
    Battle of the Sexes, 91
    Chicken, 88–9, 91, 92
    see also Prisoners' Dilemma
Gaus, Gerald F., 107n, 108n, 126n
Gauthier, David, 8, 120n, 126n, 127,
    130n, 133–4, 152, 161, 268n, 274n,
    275n, 282n, 294n
Gellner, Ernest, 30n, 238n, 243n, 249n
Gödel, Kurt, 220n
Goldman, Alan H., 159n
Goldsmith, M. M., 181–2, 189–91
Goodin, Robert E., 278n, 287n
goods
    collective (or public), 58–61, 64, 66, 73,
        80, 111, 273–4, 281, 283
    step, 84n, 86–90
government
    capstone, 30
    functions of, 9, 122, 158, 161, 266–87,
        292–4
    and paternalism, 280, 283, 292
    and "political failure," 11
    and privatization, 284
    world, 12, 26
    see also state(s)
Gray, John, 243n
Green, Leslie, 6n, 102n, 156n, 157n, 178n,
    197n, 206n, 207n, 208n, 211, 214n,
    215n, 216n, 223n

Hall, John A., 30n
Hampton, Jean, 61n, 86n, 90n, 127n,
    182–3, 193n, 257n, 259n, 268n, 294n
Hanseatic League, see city-leagues
Hardin, Russell, 83n, 84, 86n, 93n, 189n,
    238n, 259n
Harel, Alon, 188n
Hargreaves Heap, Shaun P., 96n, 97n

Harman, Gilbert, 161n
Hart, H. L. A., 155n, 176n, 182, 183, 194n,
    199, 207n, 215n, 227n
    and Hart–Rawls principle of fairness,
        72n, 215n
Hayek, Friedrich A., 63n
Hegel, G. W. F., 5, 41n, 47–8, 55, 116,
    141n, 254n, 255n, 288, 297
Held, Virginia, 107n
Herder, Johann Gottfried, 242n
Hinsley, F. H., 29, 40, 47n, 173, 174n
Hobbes, Thomas, 5–8, 10, 12, 24n, 25, 40,
    41n, 55, 57, 58n, 59, 67–8, 109, 111,
    114–15, 124n, 139, 141, 146, 149–50,
    153, 157n, 171n, 173, 174, 175, 176n,
    177–90, 193–5, 197–8, 205, 210, 214n,
    217, 220, 221, 222, 224–5, 235, 267–8,
    274–6, 286, 289n, 294n, 295n; see also
    contractarianism, Hobbesian
Hobsbaum, E. J., 233n, 234n
Hochman, Harold M., 279n
Hohfeldian juridical relations, 135, 141,
    194, 205n, 216
Holmes, Robert L., 168n
home (or homelessness), 18, 238, 251
Hume, David, 87n, 152, 198n, 235n
Hurka, Thomas, 142n

identity, 33, 35n, 42, 237, 242–3, 247, 252,
    258–9, 260n
instrumentalism, see rationality,
    practical; state(s)
internalism, moral, 159–60
international relations, 25, 41n, 173,
    223–7
    intervention in, 53, 226–7
    nothing-is-forbidden view of, 226
    and realism in international affairs,
        111, 114–15, 138, 160–1, 225–6

Jackson, Robert H, 52n, 99n
Jasay, Anthony de, 67n
Jefferson, Thomas, 143n, 146, 155n, 231–2
Jeffrey, Richard C., 132n
Jones, Gareth, 179n
jurisdiction, 17, 31, 33–5, 38–9, 41, 45, 53,
    262–5
justice, 106, 115, 135–71, 158–61, 164–5,
    212, 217, 258, 266, 282–14, 289–91,
    293, 294, 297
    distributive, 137–8, 148n
    and positive and negative duties,
        164–5
    see also rights